WORLD SINCE 1918

ABOUT THE AUTHOR

Stewart C. Easton, a native of England, spent two years at Oxford University, followed by a number of years devoted to business and to service in the Canadian army. He then received his B.A. degree from Ottawa University and his A.M. and Ph.D. degrees from Columbia University. He taught history at City College, New York, from 1947 to 1960, retiring with the rank of Associate Professor. He is the author of *Ancient, Medieval, and Modern History* (a Barnes & Noble College Outline), *A Brief History of the Western World* (a Barnes & Noble Everyday Handbook), *Roger Bacon and His Search for a Universal Science, The Heritage of the Ancient World, The Heritage of the Past to 1500, The Heritage of the Past to 1715, Twilight of European Colonialism, Western Heritage,* and *The Rise and Fall of Western Colonialism* and co-author of *The Era of Charlemagne.*

College Outline Series

WORLD SINCE 1918

Stewart C. Easton

Barnes & Noble, Inc.   New York

Publishers   Booksellers   Since 1873

This book is an original work (Number 51) in the original College Outline Series. It was written by a distinguished educator, carefully edited, and produced in accordance with the highest standards of publishing. The text was set on the linotype in Times Roman by Hamilton Printing Company (Rensselaer, N.Y.). The paper for this edition was manufactured by S. D. Warren Company (Boston, Mass.) and supplied by Canfield Paper Company (New York, N.Y.). This edition was printed by Hamilton Printing Company and bound by Sendor Bindery (New York, N.Y.). The cover was designed by Rod Lopez-Fabrega.

TABLE OF CONTENTS

MAPS

1 THE MAKING OF PEACE

World War I, which originally involved only the German and Austro-Hungarian empires, tsarist Russia, Great Britain and her dominions, France, Belgium, and Serbia, had expanded by the beginning of 1918 to take in numerous smaller powers and the major powers of Italy, Japan, and the United States. The United States, who was by far the most powerful of the newcomers and in a position to commit millions of fresh troops to the struggle, naturally exercised an unequaled influence in the concluding period. American troops played an active part on the Western Front during 1918 and contributed greatly to the sudden end of the four-and-a-half-year war, although when hostilities ceased, they still constituted only a small proportion of the Allied armies.

Despite the general European recognition of the magnitude of this American contribution, United States President Woodrow Wilson was unable to make all, or even most, of his views prevail at the Peace Conference, although without his presence the terms would surely have been far different. His most cherished aim, to achieve which he was willing to sacrifice much, was the establishment of a League of Nations. He did win acceptance of the League at the cost of many concessions, and the League in due course came into existence. But he was unable to persuade the United States Senate to agree to American membership in the League, with the result that for many years it was dominated by the European war victors.

THE END OF THE WAR

Prior to American entry into the war in April, 1917, President Wilson had attempted to bring it to an end on the basis

1

of "peace without victory." He did not thereafter cease his efforts to persuade the enemy to lay down their arms, but he naturally now looked forward to an Allied military victory, even though this, in his view, ought to be followed by a "just" peace. To this end in January, 1918, he proposed Fourteen Points for the consideration of his cobelligerents. First was the abolition of secret treaties (which Wilson believed to have been a major cause of the war). He proposed "open covenants, openly arrived at" (so that in the event of future wars every nation would presumably know exactly what would be the line-up). Other general proposals were: freedom of the seas in peace and war; a general reduction of armaments; adjustment of colonial claims in the interests of the peoples concerned as well as of the colonial powers; and the removal, so far as possible, of economic barriers to trade. Specific proposals included the following terms: that Belgium and Russia should be cleared of foreign troops; that Alsace-Lorraine should be restored to France; that the Balkan states should be granted their independence on the basis of self-determination; and that Poland should become an independent nation with secure access to the sea. Lastly Wilson proposed that a general association of nations should be formed to guarantee political independence and territorial integrity for big and small states alike.

Conditions at the time were far from favorable for the acceptance of these points. The Central Powers (Germany, Austria-Hungary, Bulgaria, and Turkey), who would have been required to make the territorial concessions, were preparing for an all-out offensive in the West, using troops made available by the collapse of Russia. On March 3, the Bolshevik government had signed the Treaty of Brest-Litovsk, under which Russia abandoned her western territories, including Finland, the Baltic provinces, the Ukraine, and Transcaucasia. The Germans, thus freed from any necessity for immediate negotiations, ignored the Fourteen Points.

On March 21, 1918, the Germans began their last great offensive in the West. Marshal Foch was named commander in chief of the Allied forces with full responsibility for planning the combined defense. But it was not until July that the Germans were halted and forced to retreat, mainly as a result of having to meet fresh American troops.

By this time the German commanders had lost all hope of victory. A new chancellor, Prince Max of Baden, therefore belatedly declared himself willing to accept the Fourteen Points as the basis for discussion of an armistice. Early in November the German fleet mutinied, and a revolution broke out in Munich. Kaiser Wilhelm II fled to Holland on November 10. Meanwhile an armistice commission met with Marshal Foch, who laid down terms—which, not unnaturally in view of the changed military situation, went much further than the Fourteen Points. The Germans were left with no choice but to accept. Turkey, Bulgaria, and Austria-Hungary had already signed their own armistices, and hostilities were coming to an end everywhere. On November 11 the armistice with Germany came into effect, and organized fighting ceased. But it was hardly to be expected that the defeated nations would simply settle down and accept the peace terms from the victors under the same governments that had led them to the debacle. It was therefore perhaps surprising that there should have been so few attempts at serious revolution, although all the monarchs except the tsar of Bulgaria at once lost their thrones.

THE ERA OF REVOLUTION

By the time of the armistice the Bolshevik Revolution was just one year old. But, as will be discussed in the next chapter, it was far from consolidated, and a civil war was still raging in Russia. Various Allied powers had also sent their expeditionary forces to the country, without adequate co-ordination and with no clear idea of their aims. The Bolshevik Revolution was the first one to be carried out by self-proclaimed Marxists, and it was widely believed that the war would lead to others. Indeed so great was the fear among the possessing classes in Europe that they were willing even to prolong the war in order to put an end to the Bolshevik attempt. But in fact the Bolsheviks were in such difficulties in Russia that they could not give any military support to their fellow revolutionaries abroad. In no other country was there a sufficient body of Communists to establish a Communist government; and the Socialists were too seriously divided among themselves to take revolutionary action, especially since in most countries they seemed to be on the verge of coming to power through democratic means without revolution. Thus military power everywhere remained in the hands of the conservative, or at least anti-Communist, elements. The result was that, unlike the situation after World War II when the Soviet Union possessed the preponderance of military power in eastern Europe, all the revolutions soon collapsed.

Bavaria. The first revolutionary attempt took place in Bavaria, which had been a state of imperial Germany ruled by its own king. This king abdicated a day before Kaiser Wilhelm, and a republic was at once proclaimed by the Socialist Kurt Eisner, who was head of the government until his murder three months later. Another Social Democratic government was formed under Johannes Hoffman, but in April, 1919, this was in turn overthrown by a Communist coup. Following the Russian example, a Soviet republic was proclaimed. It lasted for a bare month. In May the remnants of the regular army, whose numbers were swelled by Free Corps volunteers, easily restored the Hoffman government. The volunteers, mostly ex-soldiers who refused to accept the forced reduction of the German army, engaged in much terrorism, and the Hoffman government was never able to function effectively. In March, 1920, it was overthrown by a right-wing group quite out of sympathy with the moderate left-wing government which was now in power in Berlin. It was in Munich, capital of Bavaria, that the returned soldier Adolf Hitler first observed the overthrow of a democratic government—whose successor put him to work as an "instruction officer," inoculating his fellow citizens, as his biographer Alan Bullock puts it, "against contagion by socialist, pacifist, or democratic ideas."

Berlin. In Berlin, the national capital of Germany, the revolution that followed the war was led by Communists who called themselves Spartacists (after Spartacus, the leader of a slave revolt in Republican Rome). The Social Democratic government of Philipp Scheidemann, which had assumed office the day before the Armistice on the basis of a majority in the existing Reichstag, planned to hold a constituent assembly to write a new republican constitution. The Spartacists however demanded that a dictatorship of the proletariat be set up at once. The government, aided by the regular army, suppressed the Spartacists, and its leaders William Liebknecht and Rosa Luxemburg were killed while under arrest. The elected national assembly met, chose Friedrich Ebert president, and wrote the Weimar Constitution which was adopted at the end of July, 1919 (see p. 60).

Austria. When the former Dual Monarchy of Austria-Hungary was broken up into its component parts, German-speaking Austria was left as a separate small country. Her oft-expressed desire to become a part of Germany was forbidden by the Allies, and she had to settle down as best she could as an independent republic.

(The last emperor, Charles I, had abdicated on November 11, 1918.) There were many Communist-inspired disorders in 1919, but elections for a constituent assembly resulted in a large majority for two Socialist parties; and in spite of financial difficulties the new state survived without revolution.

Hungary. Hungary had declared herself separated from the dying Dual Monarchy in mid-October, 1918. Count Karolyi, a liberal former prime minister, became president of the new state and attempted to put into effect a much-needed and long-overdue land reform. But he resigned when the unfavorable peace terms for Hungary became known. His regime was replaced by a coalition government dominated by Bela Kun, who had recently returned from Russia, where he had been converted to Communism. With the moral support of the Bolsheviks, but, unfortunately for him, without any military support, Kun set up a "dictatorship of the proletariat" and promulgated a constitution modeled on the recent Russian Bolshevik one. But he soon involved his country in war with the new state of Czechoslovakia and with Rumania (which had been greatly enlarged by the peace treaties at the expense of Hungary). With the aid of anti-Communist Hungarian leaders, the Rumanians took the Hungarian capital of Budapest and forced Bela Kun to flee the country. They occupied the city for several months and looted it unmercifully when they left. In March, 1920, the Hungarian monarchy was nominally restored. But since neither the Allies nor Hungary's neighbors would permit the return of the Hapsburg King Charles (former emperor of Austria-Hungary), Admiral Miklas Horthy became "regent," a title he retained for the duration of the interwar period.

THE NEW STATES OF EUROPE

Seven new states were created after the war out of the former Austro-Hungarian and Russian empires. Of these only Poland had ever been an independent state before, although in the later Middle Ages a much larger duchy of Lithuania had also existed. Finland had been a personal possession of the tsars, administered separately from the rest of Russia. Estonia, Latvia, Czechoslovakia, and Yugoslavia were totally new states, although Serbia and Montenegro, which became part of the new Yugoslavia, had been independent as separate nations before the war. Here we shall deal briefly only with the comparatively peaceful establishment of Czechoslovakia, Poland, and Yugoslavia, leaving a discussion of the Baltic states, which Bolshevik Russia attempted to retain, to subsequent chapters.

Czechoslovakia. Czechoslovakia, carved from the Austro-Hungarian Empire and containing much of its most valuable land, was largely the creation of the Czechs, who for decades before the war had struggled for autonomy within the Empire. During the war Czech units fought on the Allied side, and several Czech National Councils were organized, the most important of which was in Paris. On the collapse of the Central Powers, the Allies recognized the National Council in Paris, led by Thomas Masaryk, as the *de facto* government of the new nation of Czechoslovakia (October 18, 1918). A few days later Karel Kramar, leader of the independence movement in Prague, overthrew the remnants of Hapsburg rule in a bloodless coup. Kramar became prime minister of the new state, while Masaryk became president. Masaryk's most faithful follower, Eduard Benes, the first foreign minister, succeeded Kramer as prime minister in 1921, and Masaryk as president in 1935.

Yugoslavia. Yugoslavia (officially called the Kingdom of the Serbs, Croats, and Slovenes until 1929) was made up of the former kingdoms of Serbia and Montenegro, together with the Croat and Slovene minorities of the Austro-Hungarian Empire. In July, 1917, representatives of these peoples signed the Pact of Corfu, under which they agreed to unite in a single state under the Serbian crown, as soon as the war was over. In December, 1918, the new kingdom was proclaimed. Her main territorial dispute was with Italy over the Adriatic seaport of Fiume, which was seized by the Italian poet-adventurer Gabriele d'Annunzio soon after the war. He remained in possession for many months in spite of all diplomatic efforts to dislodge him. Yugoslavia never did receive the city, which would have been her only substantial Adriatic port. It first became a free city by treaty, but was again seized by Italy in 1922.

Poland. In addition to having been an independent state prior to the partitions of the late eighteenth century, Poland had a distinctive language and nationality, and was thus in all major respects qualified for nationhood. But at the beginning of the war most of what the Poles thought of as their country was in Russian hands, with other valuable sectors in Germany and Austria-Hungary. During the war their territory was fought over and became dominated by the Central Powers rather than by Russia.

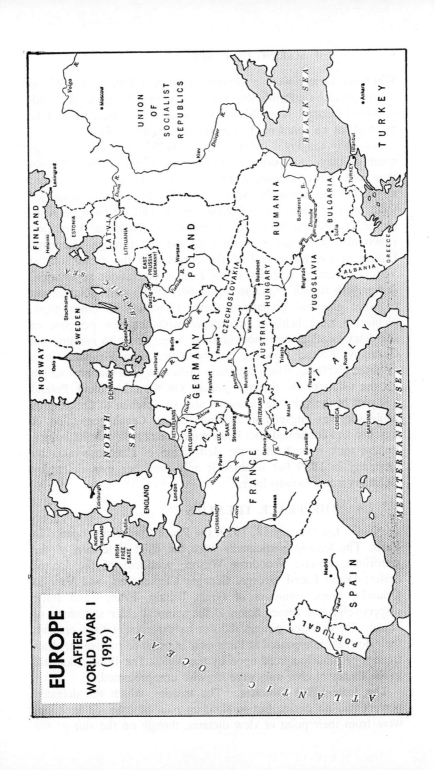

EUROPE
AFTER
WORLD WAR I
(1919)

When the former were collapsing in 1918 it became possible at last to proclaim a Polish Republic (November 3), under the leadership of General Josef Pilsudski, who at once proceeded to take as much as he could of the territory claimed for his state.

Naturally the Poles coveted their pre-1772 boundaries—or as much as they could persuade the victors to grant, and whatever they were powerful enough to secure through their own armed might. On the whole the Allies, especially the French, supported them in their aims. Part of West Prussia and Posen were relinquished to Poland by the Germans by the Treaty of Versailles, which also gave her a corridor to the sea through Germany. Danzig at the Baltic end of the corridor at the mouth of the Vistula became a free city under League of Nations supervision. A war with Russia (April to November, 1920) gave Poland most of what she had demanded there. However, in other areas, plebiscites were held, in accordance with the new principle of self-determination; and most of these areas chose to remain with Germany. Poland won the city of Vilna from Lithuania in a disputed plebiscite, which embittered relations with that new nation for the whole of the interwar period. On the other hand, Poland lost part of the valuable industrial area of Teschen to Czech arms while she was engaged in fighting Russia. Czech possession of Teschen was confirmed later in a conference of Allied ambassadors. Poland took it back after the destruction of Czechoslovakia by Germany in 1939 but retained it only until her own defeat by Germany a few months later.

THE PEACE TREATIES

On January 18, 1919, the Peace Conference opened in Paris. The leading participants were the chief statesmen of the victorious powers: Woodrow Wilson, president of the United States; David Lloyd George, Georges Clemenceau, and Vittorio Orlando, prime ministers of Great Britain, France and Italy, respectively; and Prince Saioniji, the samurai elder statesman of Japan. The defeated powers did not have representatives present; their delegation appeared at Paris only in order to receive the draft treaties previously agreed upon by the Allies. The Bolsheviks, still in the throes of civil war, were likewise unrepresented.

The Inter-Allied Disputes. The treaties, which the defeated powers had no option but to sign, on pain of renewed invasion, were from their point of view dictates, though on the side of the victors there was much often acrimonious discussion before agreement was reached. President Wilson, while regarded as a hero in most of Europe, especially by the common people, was on the whole looked upon by the other Great Power delegates as an interfering nuisance who, though ignorant of Europe, presumed to dictate to it. Wilson himself regarded his colleagues at the Conference as men out of step with the times, grasping and revengeful. But he was not deeply interested in the specific European problems which had to be settled by the treaties. His major interest was in expanding self-government and democracy through "self-determination" and in ensuring that serious differences among nations should be brought within the purview of a new international organization, the League of Nations.

Although many European representatives had serious reservations about this proposed League, they were aware that their own peoples in general backed it. Recognizing that it was the most cherished dream of the American President, they were willing to give the League priority in the discussions and accepted the largely American first draft. Armed with this draft, Wilson left for home, only to find opposition to it from his own people, especially Senators who would have to consent to an eventual treaty. When he returned to Paris to engage in discussions about the other clauses in the peace treaties and wished to make changes in the draft for the League, the other negotiators sold their support dearly, and Wilson had to make many concessions in exchange for their agreement to the final draft for the Covenant of the League. The actual treaties were not, in many respects, wholly to the liking of the President. But they all contained the provisions for the League. Thus, when the United States Senate eventually refused to ratify the treaties (March 19, 1920), the League was rejected at the same time; and in the administration of President Harding the United States had to negotiate separate treaties which belatedly declared hostilities at an end.

A number of secret treaties and agreements had been made among the Allies in some instances for the purpose of bringing one country or another into the war on the Allied side. For example, conflicting promises had been made to various Arab rulers and Jewish leaders regarding the disposition of Turkish possessions. These later gave rise to difficulties which have not yet been settled. The Russians had been promised Constantinople, a permanent objective of tsarist policy. Most fortunately for the Allies, this particular chicken never came home to roost, since the Bolsheviks repudiated the treaty and made no demands on Turkey at the Peace Conference. However, to the considerable embarrassment of the Allies, they published details of all the secret treaties to which Russia was a party. Most notorious of these was the Treaty of London (1915), on the strength of which the hitherto neutral Italians (who had in fact been yoked with the Central Powers in the Triple Alliance since 1882) entered the war on the side of Britain and France. The Treaty of London granted Italy South Tyrol, the Trentino, and several other territories at the expense of Austria and the island of Rhodes and some minor territories at the expense of Turkey. It made vague promises on the matter of increased colonial areas, presumably at the expense of Germany, or perhaps of Turkey. The South Tyrol, inhabited almost entirely by German-speaking people, might well have been refused to Italy on the grounds of self-determination. But President Wilson made no serious protest at the inclusion of South Tyrol in an expanded Italy. However, he did balk at letting Italy have Fiume, an Adriatic seaport which had been specifically reserved for the new Yugoslavia in the Treaty of London. In spite of continued Allied opposition, the Italians eventually won Fiume by the Treaty of Rome in 1924 (see p. 263), signed directly with Yugoslavia. On the other hand the Italians never did receive any of the colonies taken from Germany. They gained only a few unimportant sections of desert to add to their existing colonies in North Africa. Consequently, they continued to nurse a grievance against their allies in the late war, and Mussolini used to complain bitterly that Italy had been cheated in the peace negotiations.

Lastly, the Japanese had been promised by the British and French the former German settlement of Kiaochow in the Chinese province of Shantung, which had been leased from the Chinese by the Germans. President Wilson, under the impression that the Japanese were demanding the whole Shantung Peninsula, objected strongly, backed by American public opinion, in those days favorable to the Chinese. But when it was realized that the Japanese merely desired the transfer of the leasehold, together with the northern Pacific German islands, and that these were the sum total of Japanese demands on them, the Allies gave way.*

---

* For Japanese demands on China in 1915, see p. 185.

The Treaty of Versailles. The treaty with the Germans was approved by the victors at the Peace Conference on May 6, 1919, and it was at once presented to the German delegation. The delegates protested vociferously, claiming that the terms were quite different from those accepted when Germany laid down her arms and would be impossible to fulfill. The Allies, who had had enough difficulty in arriving at the terms, accepted no changes of substance. The Germans were thus faced with two apparent choices, outright refusal or acceptance. These in effect amounted to the same thing. Their country was still under blockade, and there was very serious hardship within it. Moreover the Allies were threatening to invade if the terms were not accepted. The result could only have been complete defeat, and an unconditional surrender—which would have meant a similar treaty or a worse one. To reject the treaty would therefore be a meaningless gesture. Rather than sign it the Scheidemann government resigned, but a new government under Gustav Bauer patriotically decided to bear the onus. German delegates therefore signed the treaty on June 28, 1919, in the Hall of Mirrors at Versailles. Two weeks later the Allies lifted the blockade.

The terms of the treaty, though severe, could have been much worse. Germany was required to cede to France Alsace-Lorraine, which she had possessed only since 1871, and the border industrial area of the Saar. The Saar, however, was to be administered under League of Nations supervision, and it was agreed that a plebiscite would eventually determine its final status. (The plebiscite was held in 1935, and the Saar was then restored to Germany.) All the German colonies were lost, but they were not taken outright by the Allied colonial powers. As will be discussed later (see p. 15), they became mandates of the League and were administered by the colonial powers. It was the military, "war-guilt," and reparations clauses and the physical separation of East Prussia from the rest of Germany that most offended the Germans. A large area of Germany on the left bank of the Rhine, which France had demanded but which had been refused by her allies, was subjected to an Allied occupation for fifteen years. The right bank, or German side, of the Rhine was demilitarized for a distance of thirty miles. The German army was reduced to 100,000 men. Germany was to have neither submarines nor aircraft carriers, and she had to hand over to the Allies as part of her reparations all merchant ships of more than 1,600 tons and half of her ships between 800 and 1,600 tons. Moreover, she was to build for her late enemies 200,000 tons of new shipping every year.

Article 231 of the treaty, which was very greatly resented by the Germans, attempted to lay the moral basis for reparations. This article, known as the "war-guilt" clause, in effect made Germany accept the responsibility for causing "all the loss and damage" suffered by the "Allied and Associated governments and their nationals as a consequence of the war imposed upon them by the aggression of Germany and her allies." There had been numerous arguments among the conferees as to the extent to which Germany should be made to pay—for example, whether she should pay for pensions to the surviving relatives and indemnities for the dead and wounded, whether she should pay for all the physical damage inflicted. It was generally agreed that she must bear the costs of the Allied occupation for as long as it lasted. In the end, the total sum was not agreed to at the Peace Conference but left to a commission to decide on the basis of a thorough inquiry as to how much Germany could in fact pay, irrespective of how much she *ought* to pay for the damage she had done. Lastly a clause provided for the trial of the Kaiser by an international tribunal for "a supreme offense against international morality and the sanctity of treaties." The treaty also made provision for the handing over of Germans guilty of violation of the laws of war. Since the Dutch refused to do more than intern their royal refugee, the Kaiser remained unharmed for the rest of his long natural life.

Treaties of St. Germain, Trianon, and Neuilly. The Treaty of St. Germain (September 10, 1918) with Austria compelled the Austrians to pay reparations, to hand over war criminals—not, however, including the Emperor—for trial, and to keep an army of no more than 30,000 men. She was forbidden to unite with Germany except by permission of the Council of the League of Nations. The most important clauses of this treaty were those in which Austria recognized the independence of the states carved out of her former empire. One territory (Klagenfurt) was restored to her by plebiscite. By the Treaty of Trianon (signed June 4, 1920) Hungary, who by this time had compelled the Rumanians to withdraw, was required to accept the loss of Transylvania to an enlarged Rumania and the loss of Slovakia to the new composite state of Czechoslovakia. Croatia went to Yugoslavia, as did most of Slovenia. Hungary too had to pay reparations, and her army was limited to 35,000 men. Under the Treaty of Neuilly, signed on November 27, 1919, Bulgaria lost her opening on to the Aegean through the cession of Thrace to Greece. She also agreed to pay specified reparations and to keep an army of no more than 20,000 men.

Treaties of Sèvres and Lausanne.   The Allied powers attempted to impose their severest terms on Turkey. But, though they were successful in extracting a signature to the Treaty of Sèvres (August 10, 1920) from the hapless government of the Sultan, the treaty could not be enforced. The nationalists under Mustapha Kemal, in part because of the harsh provisions of the treaty, overthrew the government which had accepted it. As a result a new, more realistic treaty was negotiated (Treaty of Lausanne, July 24, 1923), which was accepted by the nationalists after the Sultan had fled the country.

Before the Treaty of Sèvres was even signed, the Greeks, led by Eleutherios Venizelos, persuaded the Allies to help them take over some of the territories to which it would entitle them. The Allied governments, including the United States, supported with their warships a Greek expedition to Smyrna, a predominantly Greek city set in an almost wholly Turkish hinterland in Asia Minor. The city and its surroundings were to be placed under Greek administration for a period, and a plebiscite was to be held later. The coup was temporarily successful, since at the time the Turks were incapable of extended resistance. But the incident led eventually to a Greco-Turkish war, which lasted intermittently from 1921 to 1923, with the loss of many thousands of lives and a prolonged embitterment between the two peoples. After the war an exchange of populations between Greeks and Turks took place, with very great hardship for the peoples involved (see p. 126).

Under both treaties Turkey recognized the independence of her former provinces outside Asia Minor (Anatolia). The Treaty of Sèvres required her to pay reparations which were waived by Lausanne. At Sèvres Turkey lost virtually all administrative autonomy and had to submit to what amounted to an Allied protectorate. Most of her European territories were ceded to Greece; the straits of the Dardanelles became international waters; and Armenia was granted her independence. At Lausanne Turkey recovered her full administrative autonomy, including control of the Dardanelles, though they were demilitarized. She recovered Armenia (which she had prevented from seceding) and retained the territories ceded by the former treaty. An Allied army of occupation took possession of Constantinople in March, 1920, in order to enforce the conditions imposed by the Treaty of Sèvres. This army withdrew on August 23, 1923, after the Treaty of Lausanne was signed. However, by this time the nationalists had made Ankara (Angora) their capital, which it has remained to this day. The name of Constantinople was changed to Istanbul in 1930 as part of Kemal's nationalist program. Thus the connection with the Roman Empire was finally broken.

THE LEAGUE OF NATIONS

The League of Nations, whose "Covenant," incorporated in all the peace treaties, was intended, according to its preamble, "to promote international co-operation and to achieve international peace and security, by the acceptance of obligations not to resort to war, by the prescription of open, just, and honorable relations between nations, by the firm establishment of the understandings of international law as to actual rule of conduct among governments, and by the maintenance of justice and a scrupulous respect for all treaty obligations in the dealings of organized peoples with one another." It provided for an Assembly, a Council, a permanent Secretariat, various Commissions, and a Permanent Court of International Justice.

Constitution and Component Bodies. The Assembly was made up of all member states, each with one vote and not more than three delegates. Its primary task was to deal with all matters "affecting the peace of the world"; it was permitted to investigate disputes referred to it; it admitted new members to the League (by a two-thirds majority); and it elected the nonpermanent members of the Council. The Council was composed of permanent and nonpermanent members. The original permanent members were Britain, France, Italy, and Japan. To these were added Germany in 1926 and the Soviet Union in 1934 after the withdrawal of Germany and Japan from the League. Originally there were four nonpermanent members; they were increased to ten in 1933. Decisions in the Council had to be unanimous, including the affirmative votes of the nonpermanent members. But, unlike procedure in the United Nations Security Council, parties to a dispute were not permitted to vote on it. The Council could refer a dispute to the Assembly (which it very seldom did), and the latter's report had the same force as a report of the Council provided that all Council members (except parties to the dispute) and the majority of non-Council members concurred. All disputes were to be submitted to arbitration either authorized by the Council or carried on directly by the Council itself. No state was permitted to go to war until three months after the handing down of the award. If any member resorted to war in disregard of the Covenant, it was regarded as having committed an act of war against all other members of the League, and all members undertook automatically to impose economic sanctions, including the severance of all trade and financial relations and the "prohibition of all intercourse between their nations and the nationals of the Covenant-breaking states." If the offending state was not a member of the League the sanctions were still applicable. The Council, however, had the sole right to recommend military sanctions, though it could not compel any nation to take part in them.

The Secretariat, whose head could summon a meeting of the Council upon the request of any member, was located at Geneva, Switzerland. Also maintained at Geneva was the International Labor Organization, a permanent organization established by the League to promote the improvement of labor conditions in all countries, since universal peace, in the opinion of the signatories, "could be established only if it was based on social justice." Conferences on labor were to be held annually.

Numerous commissions were set up in the fields of health, economics, narcotic and white slavery control, and similar matters, in which the League did much excellent work; and it performed yeoman service in the settlement of refugees and persons displaced by the peace treaties. However, probably its most important commission was the Permanent Mandates Commission. After the war, the colonial possessions of Germany and several of the outlying provinces of Turkey had to be disposed of. Britain and her dominions, France, and Belgium, if left to themselves, would doubtless have parceled out among themselves these possessions (with the possible exception of some of the Turkish provinces which were ready for independence under their native rulers). But President Wilson was strongly opposed to this procedure, and through his influence a compromise was accepted under which the former colonies and provinces became "mandated territories" of three different kinds. Class A mandates were territories which were to remain under the tutelage of the various powers for a limited period until they were ready for independence. The Class A man-

dates were made up exclusively of territories formerly in the Ottoman Empire. Class B and C mandates were not expected to become
independent states in the foreseeable future, but were to be "a
sacred trust of civilization." C mandates were distinguished from
B mandates in that the mandatory power was permitted to administer its mandates as an integral part of its own territories. B and
C mandates had all been formerly colonies of Germany, either in
Africa or in the Far East and Pacific.

The Permanent Mandates Commission of the League of Nations was made up of experts in colonial administration, chosen
as individuals and not as nominees of their respective governments.
The Commission made recommendations to the Council and questioned the representatives of the mandatory powers on both the
reports and the written petitions occasionally received from inhabitants of the territories. Neither the Council nor the Commission, however, was authorized to interfere in any way with the
actual administration of the territories. Although the influence of
the League and its Commission was therefore exclusively a moral
one, there can be little doubt that this influence was none the less
real, since few powers relished questioning by experts on their
administration, and most greatly preferred to be able to present
reports showing that progress was being made. On a few occasions comments by the Commission members are known to have
been successful in changing unsatisfactory conditions. The Permanent Mandates Commission in the late 1930's refused to accept
the British White Paper on Palestine (see p. 199) and did not
hesitate to say that it was not in the spirit of the mandate.

League Actions in the Early Postwar Years. The major criticism that must be leveled against the League of Nations is that it
was too closely connected from the beginning with the peace
treaties. The Covenant of the League, in effect, sanctified the
status of the nations as they emerged after the war. By guaranteeing the territorial integrity of the member nations, many of
which had new frontiers and contained embittered minorities
within their borders, the system made evolutionary change difficult and modifications extremely unlikely. Few nations, new or
old, were willing to yield any part of their territories, however
recently acquired, unless compelled to do so—and it was too
much to expect the League to be able indefinitely to hold back the
tide of change. As might have been, and indeed was, predicted, the
League became the stronghold for those powers who had gained

most from the peace treaties, whereas the disgruntled "have-not" powers defied it when they felt strong enough to do so, especially when the Great Powers disagreed among themselves. In short, the burden of enforcing both a dictated peace settlement and the 1919 international boundaries proved too heavy for the League to bear.

Nevertheless, especially in its early years, the League had a number of successes to its credit—though it cannot be said with certainty that the Concert of Great Powers which would have policed the peace if there had been no League would have done any less well. Indeed, the League itself frequently had to refer disputes to an official Conference (or Council) of Ambassadors, comprising merely the ambassadors of the Great Powers resident in Paris.

A dispute between Sweden and Finland (1920–1921) over the Aaland Islands, which lie between the two countries, was settled by the League Council. It awarded the islands to Finland, but to satisfy the Swedish majority of inhabitants, provided that they were to remain unfortified and to enjoy a large measure of autonomy. The small Balkan country of Albania, who had achieved independence from Turkey in 1912, was coveted by Yugoslavia, whose troops occupied it after the war. Threats by the League Council to impose an economic blockade were effective in persuading the Yugoslavs to withdraw (1921), in exchange for an Albanian agreement not to militarize the frontier. Memel, a territory ceded by Germany at the end of the war, was administered by France pending final agreement on its disposition. A commission sponsored by the League proposed that the territory should be given to Lithuania. But there was to be some international supervision over the port; and the inhabitants, mostly Germans, were promised a large degree of autonomy (1924). A border quarrel in 1925 between Greece and Bulgaria in which several guards were killed resulted in a peremptory demand by the League Council for a cease fire. Both sides complied, and the Greeks paid an indemnity ordered by the Council.

Against these early successes must be placed the relative failures. The dispute between Poland and Lithuania over Vilna was settled by military means, contrary to the decision originally handed down by the League that the city should belong to Lithuania. All the League could do was to acquiesce in the Polish capture and retention of the city. The League was unable to compel Italy to withdraw from Corfu in 1923, when Mussolini ordered that island attacked in reprisal for the murder of some Italian officials who had been engaged in delimiting the boundary between Greece and Albania. The matter was eventually solved by the Conference of Ambassadors of the Great Powers. The League gave its general approval to the settlement, although the attack on Corfu, however great the provocation, was obviously an act of aggression within the meaning of the League Covenant; it was out of proportion to the offense committed by Greek nationals, not by the Greek government. But nothing untoward happened to Italy, not even a reprimand, and she was handsomely compensated in money for the murder of the two officials (1923).

In the 1930's, after the League's failure to discipline Japan when she invaded Manchuria (see p. 181), the League enjoyed two minor successes before its major failure in the case of the invasion of Ethiopia by Italy (1935) and minor failure to solve the Chaco War between Paraguay and Bolivia (1932–1935) (see p. 304). When Alexander I of Yugoslavia was murdered in Marseilles on October 9, 1934, by a Macedonian connected with a Croatian revolutionary society, recriminations arose between Yugoslavia and Hungary, who had evidently been too lenient toward the terrorist organizations sheltered in her territory. This time the League issued a relatively mild rebuke to Hungary, which put an end to the danger of war between the two countries. (A similar murder in Sarajevo, in June, 1914, it will be recalled, had led to demands on Serbia which in turn led directly to World War I.) In 1932 a dispute broke out between Peru and Colombia over the city of Leticia which had hitherto been under Colombian control. Peruvian troops suddenly seized the city, and United States Secretary of State Stimson came to an agreement with other Latin American states under which a League of Nations Commission, headed by an American and including a Spaniard as well as Latin Americans, was to administer the disputed area until such time as the states involved reached an agreement. In 1934 the Peruvians tired of the quarrel and left Leticia to Colombia, whereupon the League Commission withdrew, its mission accomplished. This, incidentally, is the only instance in which the United States has permitted an international organization (as distinct from a hemispheric one) to handle a dispute in her own hemisphere.

In addition to attempting to settle disputes, the League of Nations was entrusted with the task of implementing "self-determination," when this was the issue. It called for plebiscites and supervised them, especially in the immediate postwar years. Only an international body could have compelled the holding of a plebiscite, or been trusted by the disputing parties to supervise it fairly.

The World Court. Lastly mention should be made of the Permanent Court of International Justice (or World Court), whose seat was at The Hague in Holland. The League Covenant provided for this Court, but it was set up by a separate protocol, which in effect meant that nations not belonging to the League could join the Court. The United States did not take advantage of the opportunity, although Americans served on the tribunal. The task of the Court was to adjudicate quarrels between nations voluntarily submitted to it and to give advisory opinions when requested to do so by the League Council. In addition some sixty nations eventually signed agreements accepting the jurisdiction of the Court in disputes to which they were parties.

The Permanent Court (now known simply as the International Court of Justice) continued throughout the war years, and is still operating. The United States became a member automatically when she signed the United Nations Charter, but with the reservation that she herself must determine whether or not a case submitted to the Court fell within her domestic jurisdiction. The difficulties inherent in the structure of the Court remain as before. Advisory opinions may be colored by politics—especially by Cold War politics in the period since World War II. Too often the protagonists of one side or the other take a different stand on a legal question submitted to it (as, for example, whether the General Assembly has the right to make compulsory assessments for peace-keeping operations). Clearly the World Court's authority and influence will be limited as long as no nation truly wishes to allow foreign nations to play any part in affairs hitherto considered as under its own jurisdiction. The same, of course, may be said of the League of Nations itself, and the United Nations which succeeded it. But the League was the first major effort at the organization of what came to be called "collective security," the sharing of responsibilities for peace-keeping among the various nations of the world. It could hardly be expected that such an effort to reverse practices sanctified by millennia of history would succeed at the first—or even the second—attempt. But the League of Nations was, at least, a beginning.

THE AFTERMATH OF THE WAR— INTERNATIONAL RELATIONS TO THE RISE OF THE THIRD REICH

2

The early postwar years were marked by efforts to solve the numerous problems deriving from the war itself and from the peace treaties. The new nations were gradually establishing themselves, and the rest of Europe was growing accustomed to their presence. Germany, after a stubborn resistance to paying reparations decided at last to accept the inevitable, but not before a runaway inflation had almost ruined her middle class. Once she had agreed to a plan involving payments within her ability to make, her statesmen decided to make the best of things and entered into reasonably friendly relations with her former enemies. The Russians, after the death of Lenin and the exile of Trotsky, abandoned their hopes for an immediate world revolution and, under the leadership of Josef Stalin, decided to try to establish "Socialism in one country." Though her relation with the capitalistic powers continued to be one of mutual suspicion, the Soviet Union gradually edged back into the European community, beginning with a treaty with the equally outcast Germans and the recognition of the boundaries of the new nations, so many of which had been carved from the former Russian empire. Italy, oppressed by economic difficulties, accepted rule by a dictator, which for a time won her more respect from the other European nations than had been accorded her since her unification in 1870. Although her prestige rested on an insecure base, no one now questioned that she was a Great Power.

REPARATIONS AND WAR DEBTS

Of all the European countries, France and Belgium were most in need of money and materials for reconstruction and could use actual raw materials and labor from Germany. Britain, in spite of her casualties, had no postwar labor shortage, but she had been compelled to liquidate a large proportion of her foreign investments to pay for the war. Although she had lent money to her European allies, she and her allies had borrowed extensively from the United States. Britain therefore needed reparations in the form of money, which could be converted into dollars and used to repay this debt. But she was not in the least anxious to receive goods from Germany unless they could at once be resold abroad for dollars and did not compete with the products of her own industry. Britain remained, on balance, a creditor nation since she was owed by her allies more than she herself owed to the United States. However, she was willing at all times to waive repayment on these inter-Allied debts except insofar as the debtors were able to repay her from reparations they themselves received from Germany. The British therefore soon proposed that their war debt to the United States should be scaled down to the sum that they received as reparations from all sources.

The United States, not unnaturally, held a totally different view of the matter. War debts, about 30 per cent of which had been contracted for reconstruction after the Armistice, were, in her view a quite separate transaction, and she refused to tie them in any way to reparations, which she had herself waived. Although willing to scale down the debts to what she regarded as a reasonable figure, she adamantly insisted on receiving payment in the form of scarce dollars, which American tariff policy made even scarcer. In the end Britain repaid about two billion dollars, and France five hundred million, but both countries defaulted during the depression.

Early Negotiations on Reparations. By Article 231 of the Treaty of Versailles, Germany was made to acknowledge her responsibility for the war, thereby laying the groundwork for the payment of reparations. The Peace Conference, while handing over to a Reparations Commission the task of deciding upon the total, demanded an immediate payment of approximately five billion dollars, which, among other things, was to pay for the Rhineland army of occupation. Germany made an attempt to pay this sum, but the value of the materials supplied became an immediate subject of dispute. Although Germany claimed that she had paid the entire amount by 1921—which, at her valuation, she had—the Allies did not accept this figure, and claimed that she was in default. At the Spa Conference (July, 1920) the Germans submitted a plan for payment. Though the Allies did not find this plan acceptable, they did agree among themselves what proportion of German payments each should receive (France 52 per cent, British Empire 22 per cent, Italy 10 per cent, Belgium 8 per cent, the remainder being divided among the minor powers).

More conferences followed early in 1921, and the Allies disagreed as to whether Germany was simply stalling or was engaged in a genuine attempt to determine how much she could pay. The French believed she was stalling and issued an ultimatum, demanding that she should pay up the remainder of the five billion dollars or face invasion of the Rhineland. When the Germans made an unsatisfactory reply, France occupied an area on the right bank of the Rhine, which included the important industrial city of Dusseldorf (March 8, 1921). On March 24, 1921, the Reparations Commission as a whole agreed that Germany was in default, and a month later came to a final decision on the amount she should pay. This was 132 billion gold marks, or about thirty-three billion dollars. Annual payments were to be made of about five hundred million dollars, plus a varying amount dependent upon the quantity of her exports.

At a conference held in London in May, 1921, the Allies demanded the immediate payment of the first billion gold marks, in default of which they would take direct action and invade the Ruhr, the most important remaining industrial area in western Germany. The Germans settled this crisis by floating a loan in London and making the required payment.

It soon became clear that the sum of money demanded by the Allies was too high, or at all events was regarded by the Germans as so high that its payment would make their economic recovery impossible. The mark began to fall in value, and a full-scale economic conference was called in Genoa to which both Germans and Russians were invited (April–May, 1922). The major result of the conference was the negotiation by the Germans and Russians of the surprise Treaty of Rapallo (see p. 53), which contributed nothing to the solution of the economic problems except that both countries formally agreed not to demand reparations from each other! At the news of the treaty, the conference broke up in consternation, but a few days later the Reparations Commission recommended that Germany be granted a moratorium on payments for the remainder of 1922 in view of the imminent collapse of the mark. Great Britain then made a formal proposal to cancel all debts owed to her and all reparations as a contribution to the economic recovery of Europe. But since the offer was dependent on American acceptance of her suggestion that war debts also be canceled, it had no effect.

As events moved toward a crisis, the British and French positions on reparations diverged even more widely, while the United States, not directly concerned since she had waived the payment of reparations, could contribute little to a solution. Raymond Poincaré, the French premier, believed that Germany could and should pay, and he was prepared to exact payment by force if necessary. The French felt able to take this position because they thought it feasible to extract payments in kind which could be used for the extremely expensive reconstruction of northern France on which they were engaged.

In December, 1922, Britain offered to cancel inter-Allied debts (whether or not the United States agreed to do the same) on condition that Poincaré accept the proposed moratorium on reparations. But the amount Poincaré hoped for from reparations exceeded the amount owed to Brtiain, and in any event he needed the immediate income from reparations to aid in French reconstruction. He therefore continued his refusal to agree to the moratorium, and the Reparations Commission, over British dissent, declared, as was its duty, that Germany was in default. The immediate occasion was a failure to deliver supplies of timber. The following month she was again declared to be in default for not delivering promised supplies of coal. French and Belgian troops therefore invaded the Ruhr, which contained about 80 per cent of Germany's remaining coal, iron, and steel production (January 11, 1923).

The Ruhr Invasion and the Dawes Plan. The British government, thus faced with an accomplished fact, contented itself with declaring that the Franco-Belgian action was not a sanction permitted by the Treaty of Versailles. The German workers reacted to the occupation by passive resistance, strikes, and sabotage of the mines. They were abetted by their government, which provided strike pay and compensated their employers for their losses. But it was possible to do this only by using the printing presses to make money. Consequently, inflation escaped altogether from control, and the value of the German mark sank almost to zero, thus wiping out all German savings that were not banked abroad.

By September, 1923, both France and Germany were willing to come to terms. The value of the French franc had also dropped, by about a quarter, and it was clear that the purposes of the occupation were not being fulfilled. Nevertheless, only palliatives were forthcoming for some months while a committee headed by the American General Charles Dawes considered measures of a more permanent nature.

The Dawes Plan was promulgated on April 9, 1924, and a week later was accepted by the Germans. The Allies also gave their consent at a conference held in July and August of the same year. This plan did not change the ultimate total that the Germans would have to pay. But it did offer a practicable, if not necessarily very wise, plan by which the reparations payments could be made without bankrupting the precarious German economy. The central bank of Germany was to be reorganized under Allied supervision, and a foreign loan of eight hundred million gold marks was to be provided to enable Germany to stabilize her currency. For the first year the reparation payment was to be one billion gold marks, but the annual payments would thereafter rise until they reached 2½ billion after five years—though the sum might vary in proportion to German economic recovery. Certain German revenues, including bonds secured on income from the national railways, were earmarked for reparation payments.

As it happened, the loan specified in the Dawes Plan was only the first of many. In fact reparations were paid almost exclusively from foreign loans, most of them floated in the United States, whose citizens alone now had much money available for foreign investment. By 1930 over five billion American dollars (20 billion gold marks) had been invested privately in Europe, and of this sum the Germans had received a disproportionate share. For some years therefore they could pay their reparations out of the proceeds of loans and use the remainder for the modernization of their industries. But in the tariff-ridden Europe of the interwar period Germany's foreign markets were held precariously, and when at the end of the 1920's, American investments began to decrease she declared herself unable to meet the increased annual payments under the Dawes Plan. She asked for a reconsideration of the whole question of reparations and the fixing of a total sum to be paid. Another committee under the chairmanship of Owen D. Young of the United States was therefore organized, and in

June, 1929, it issued its proposals, which were quickly accepted (just two months before the stock-market crash).

The Young Plan and the End of Reparations.   Under the Young settlement Germany was required to pay a total of some $26,300,-000,000 including principal and interest of 5½ per cent, over a period of fifty-nine years. The provision for annual payments of under half a billion dollars seemed reasonable enough, and it was agreed that payment of about two-thirds of this could be postponed in years of serious economic difficulties. Moreover, there were also provisions under which if the United States reduced the sum of money she required on account of war debts, German reparations would be proportionately reduced. The irreducible one-third of the annual payments was secured upon railway revenues, and a new bank with German representatives on its board was to be organized at Basel, Switzerland (Bank of International Settlements) and given the responsibility of receiving German payments in marks and converting them to the required foreign currencies. As a result of German acceptance of this final settlement, the Rhineland was to be evacuated by Allied troops five years early, that is, not later than June, 1930. The evacuation took place on schedule. In 1930 new reparation agreements were also negotiated with the other former enemy powers.

But meanwhile the United States stock-market crash had occurred, and no more investment money was entering Germany. The Great Depression that followed hit Germany harder than it hit any other country. The transfer of funds had at all times been difficult since every country but Britain had high tariff walls, making difficult the earning of foreign currency through exports. It was especially difficult to transfer money to the United States, who by this time had the highest tariffs of all, so that dollars were an extremely scarce currency and reached Europe mostly in the form of American investments, not in payment for European goods. When Germany stated that she could no longer pay, President Hoover proposed a one-year moratorium on all debts, whether owed to the United States in the form of war debts or to the Allies in the form of reparations—with the single exception of the irreducible one-third of Germany's annual reparation payment. Even this would be immediately returned to Germany for investment in her economic recovery.

The moratorium, which was soon accepted by all parties, did

not, however, greatly help Germany. Her economic problems were not in the main caused by reparation payments but by the aftermath of the ruinous inflation of the early 1920's, by the economic nationalism of all the industrial and would-be industrial nations which made ordinary commercial exports extremely difficult, and by the domestic unrest engendered by the growth of National Socialism and Communism. A conference held in Lausanne in June and July, 1932, decided that Germany's reparations bill should be reduced by approximately 90 per cent, but made this reduction conditional on the waiving of the war debts owed to the United States. When President Hoover refused to agree, the Germans defaulted and paid no more reparations, while the French and Belgians defaulted on their war debts. The British paid one more installment on their debt to the United States in 1932, but in 1933 they made only the token payment of 8 per cent of the due sum. With it they sent a remarkable note to the United States government, explaining the impossibility of making payments in the existing world-wide economic situation and over the high American tariff wall. The United States Congress, however, furious at the defaults and token payments, in 1934 passed the Johnson Act, cutting off the American money market from all European nations who were in default, thus making European (and perhaps American) recovery more difficult. Only Finland of all the war debtors continued to pay her small annual installment and retained her right to borrow in the United States.

THE SEARCH FOR SECURITY—THE LEAGUE OF NATIONS AND DISARMAMENT

The problem of reparations was probably the most thorny of any in the early postwar period. But the peace treaties, as already noted, called for the reduction of the ex-enemy armies to a low figure, the maximum permitted to any of these nations being the 100,000 allowed Germany. But these reductions of former enemy forces presupposed the equivalent disarmament both of the victors and of the new nations. This in turn presupposed the establishment of an international security system which would make armies superfluous.

The League of Nations might prove to be an instrument for the enforcing of what came to be called "collective security"; but the League was so untried that none of the Great Powers was willing to trust it with the task hitherto performed by individual nations, united by treaties and with national armies at their disposal. The French from the beginning were in a position unlike that of the other nations. Their birth rate was declining and they had experienced very heavy losses both in men and in property during this last war, which had followed by a bare fifty years another war with Germany. Though Germany had just been defeated, it was feared that she might yet make a third attempt and next time conquer France altogether. It was therefore impossible for France to feel fully secure against Germany without strong and durable alliances, whether these were in the form of an enforceable League Covenant which called for binding economic and military sanctions or of old-fashioned alliances based on a balance of power. Alternatively Germany could be kept without an army capable of offense, and be prevented by superior French or Allied force from bringing such an army into being.

French Efforts toward "Collective Security." The French attempted all these alternatives, sometimes all at the same time. In the Peace Conference they tried to win the Rhine as their frontier with Germany, which would have given them a buffer territory beyond the boundaries of existing France. They had to settle for an Allied army of occupation for a limited period, though France was legally permitted to extend this period of occupation if she felt that her security was still threatened. She also tried to have the proposed League of Nations provided with an international army. But President Wilson's strong opposition defeated this proposal. Wilson hoped that wars were now done with forever and that his League would mediate and arbitrate without the need for national or international armies. But, most important of her early efforts, France signed a Security Treaty (June 28, 1919) with Britain and the United States, which had been suggested by British Prime Minister Lloyd George as an alternative to French occupation of the Rhineland. Under this treaty both Britain and the United States would guarantee her frontiers. But when Wilson submitted the treaty to the United States Senate for ratification, it was never even reported out of committee. The British, not wishing to be in a position where they alone would have to guarantee French frontiers, withdrew their consent, as permitted by the terms of the treaty. France thereafter felt she had no option but to try to win her security by formal alliances with those other powers who, like herself, feared German military recovery.

Treaty System of the 1920's. The first French treaty, signed on September 7, 1920, was with Belgium. This was followed by a mutual assistance treaty with Poland (February 19, 1921). Further similar treaties were concluded with Czechoslovakia (January 25, 1924), Rumania (June 10, 1926), and Yugoslavia (November 11, 1927). These nations also arranged alliances among themselves, as the "have" powers among the minor nations, and together they became known as the Little Entente, which was backed by France as a major power. The process of what Germany regarded as encirclement culminated in a non-aggression treaty between France and Russia, signed on November 29, 1932, which was converted into a full-fledged defensive alliance signed on May 2, 1935.

Meanwhile France was the leading proponent of two efforts to put teeth into the League of Nations. In 1923 the French sponsored a Treaty of Mutual Assistance, which gave the League Council the task of declaring when a member state was guilty of aggression and requiring all League members to come to the assistance of the victim. But, then as now, the definition of aggression gave rise to difficulties, and in the end no nation was willing to accept the treaty on which so much labor had been expended. The following year a Geneva Protocol came much closer to success. Initially this protocol had the backing of the first British Labour prime minister, Ramsay MacDonald. But when his government fell from office in 1924, his successor Stanley Baldwin did not view the project so favorably. Baldwin and the Conservative party were not willing to brave the opposition of the British Dominions to an arrangement by which they, who were so far away from any likely danger zone, would nevertheless be compelled to go to war if the League Council decreed it. The protocol, as it was accepted by the other powers, called for the submission of all international disputes to arbitration either by the League Council or by the World Court. Failure to do so would be taken as evidence of aggression, thus bringing into play the coercive provisions of the League Covenant.

After this failure, the British, who had refused to sign the protocol, in part because of their lack of interest in eastern Europe, welcomed an initiative of German Chancellor Gustav Stresemann and made an energetic effort to bring Germany, France, and Belgium together under a new treaty which they themselves would be prepared to guarantee. The Locarno Conference of October

5–16, 1925, was the first really successful postwar conference. It gave rise to a feeling of euphoria in Europe that came to be known as the "Spirit of Locarno." The major treaty resulting from the conference was a new Rhineland treaty, under which France, Germany, and Belgium accepted the new postwar frontiers. This treaty was guaranteed by Britain and Italy. Germany signed separate arbitration treaties with Poland, Czecholovakia, France, and Belgium, under which all parties agreed to arbitrate disputes among themselves; the French also signed treaties with Poland and Czechoslovakia, in which the signers bound themselves to mutual aid in case of attack by Germany. Germany herself agreed to enter the League of Nations and took her permanent seat on the League Council on September 8, 1926.

Lastly a universal peace pact outlawing war was sponsored by United States Secretary of State Kellogg and French Premier Aristide Briand. However, this Kellogg-Briand Peace Pact (1928), as it was called, contained no provisions for enforcement. Almost all the sovereign nations of the world signed it, but it had no noticeable influence in preventing aggression during the next decade.

The Spirit of Locarno appeared to favor other initiatives, and the League began to set in motion the machinery to put into execution those articles in its Covenant which called for disarmament. It was now widely believed that the European security system had become a reality and the war belonged to the past, as something to be forgiven and forgotten. As a consequence disarmament at last appeared feasible.

Conferences on Naval Disarmament.   Hitherto the only disarmament conferences had been concerned with the size of the world's navies which were obviously too large for peace time. But naturally no nation wished to be put at a disadvantage relative to the others. The agreement arrived at in the Washington Conference of November, 1921 to February, 1922, therefore decided to consider the ratio of ships that each nation should have, rather than to spend much energy in trying to arrive at total tonnage. It was decided that there should be a ten-year "holiday" in the building of capital ships (ships over 10,000 tons) and the ratios were agreed upon for the signatory powers (Britain and the United States 5, Japan 3, France and Italy 1.67 each). But it was not found possible to agree upon the tonnage for lesser ships, and a conference held at Geneva from June to August,

1927, between the United States, Britain, and Japan made no further progress.

The last effort to obtain naval agreement before the Japanese attacks on China was at a conference held in London from January to April, 1930. Although partly successful in that ratios were now established not only for capital but also for lesser ships, it was not effectively binding on the signatories. Moreover France and Italy did not join the conference—in part because of their own naval rivalry in the Mediterranean, and in part because France regarded the European security system of 1930 as sadly inadequate for her needs and did not propose to disarm further in a dangerous world. Japan was now granted parity in submarines with the United States and Britain, though all agreed to some regulations on the use of submarine warfare. Britain was permitted more light cruisers than was the United States, but the latter was given a slight superiority in heavy cruisers. Japan's ratio of ships in all categories other than submarines was slightly increased relative to the other two powers. However, an "escalator clause" permitted any of the three signatories to exercise her own judgment in increasing her navy if she felt that her security was endangered by the increase in tonnage of any nonsignatory power. In this case her only obligation was to inform the other powers of her intentions.

League of Nations Disarmament Conference (1932–1937).   As early as 1926 a preparatory commission sponsored by the League of Nations met to draw up a draft plan for disarmament, which would then be discussed by all the powers, including non-League members such as the United States and the Soviet Union. This commission worked intermittently for almost six years before the actual Disarmament Conference was convened in 1932, and during all this time the Spirit of Locarno had been evaporating. Germany in the last years was being ruled largely by decrees of President Hindenburg, and the Nazis were increasing their votes. Stresemann had died in 1929, and his policy of co-operation with the war victors virtually died with him. The paramilitary Nazi Storm Troopers (see p. 63) were being organized and armed, possibly to form the nucleus of a new and enlarged German army. There was certainly no greater security in Europe in 1932 than there had been in 1925, and thus little chance of being able to achieve any real measure of disarmament. As late as 1927 the German (and Turkish) members of the disarmament commission accepted a plan put forward by the Soviet delegate, Maxim Litvinov, calling for universal disarmament. But the other powers regarded this as a Bolshevik stratagem (as they have regarded Russian proposals to the same effect since World War II), and they would have nothing to do with it. In 1932 the other powers accepted in principle the German claims for equality of armaments, partly, no doubt, in the hopes of preventing the dangerous Hitler, with his avowed policy of putting an end to the Versailles system, from coming to power in Germany.

At last the formal Disarmament Conference opened in Geneva in February, 1932, under the chairmanship of Arthur Henderson, British foreign secretary in the second Labour Government until he was defeated for re-election to Parliament in 1931. The conference carried on its deliberations until July, 1932, when it adjourned until February of the following year. It met again for two weeks in 1934. But as time went on, and especially after Adolf Hitler became German chancellor in January, 1933, it clearly had ever less chance of success, though it maintained a shadowy existence until 1937. Hitler took Germany out of it in October, 1933, and left the League of Nations at the same time. Though the Soviet Union joined the League in 1934, this was no compensation for the departure of the nation whose proposed rearmament was the main issue of the conference.

Various proposals were put before the conference, but none was found acceptable by all the delegates. On the whole, Britain and the United States were agreed that there ought to be a budgetary limitation on arms and a reduction of national armies. President Hoover presented the suggestion that "police forces" should be distinguished from "defense forces," and the latter should be reduced by one-third. Prime Minister Ramsay MacDonald suggested that European armies should be reduced by about half a million men, and Germany be given parity with France. But Hoover wanted also to abolish tanks, bombing planes, and mobile guns. Britain and Japan in particular objected to this proposal, the British because their outlying imperial possessions could be maintained only by the threat of force. Bombing planes were by far the most economical instruments for demonstrating the British presence and putting down rebellions by unarmed or lightly armed natives. Before Germany left the conference she insisted that her Storm Troopers should not be considered effective troops to be taken into consideration if she were to be granted parity with

France. When the United States and the European Great Powers at last agreed to a four-year armament "holiday," in the hope that during this period agreement could be obtained on the armies permitted Germany, the latter insisted that she be permitted "defensive" forces at once—which brought the whole series of difficulties into the open again, as Hitler no doubt intended.

The conference, however, had the greatest difficulty with the points of view held by France and her closest allies—as indeed had been the case in all such conferences since the war. Nothing could alter the fundamental fact that Germany was far larger than France; and France had no reason to trust Germany after having so recently been invaded in two wars, in both of which much of her territory had been overrun and from the second of which she had been extricated only by the help of allies. No security system so far proposed seemed likely to afford her the guarantee that she needed against attack, least of all paper pacts without sanctions such as the Briand-Kellogg Pact. She could not but remember what Germany had said about the "scrap of paper," the tearing up of which enabled Germany to invade Belgium in 1914. She had in the interwar period no guarantee from the United States and Britain such as she had after World War II. The security treaty of 1919, which provided her with this guarantee, had fallen by the wayside. If she now accepted parity of armies with Germany, the latter could overwhelm her by virtue of the superiority of her reserves. Even though she had already begun the system of fortifications collectively known as the Maginot Line, there was no certainty that it could not be turned by the Germans if they invaded Holland and Belgium in an eventual war.

What France therefore fought for at the Disarmament Conference was an international police force which could be used at once against any aggressor and under the control of the League which she hoped to be able, as hitherto, to dominate. She would be willing to entrust her security to this force, if it came into existence and showed its effectiveness. Then both she and Germany would need relatively small national armies. Thus for France security had to come before disarmament, since otherwise disarmament of any kind would, as she thought, have played into the hands of Germany. The other powers, especially the United States and Britain, were totally unsympathetic to these demands, and France was therefore allotted most of the blame for the failure of the conference—though it is clear enough now to hindsight that the

Germany of the 1930's, especially under Hitler, would never have agreed to any system that France could have found acceptable. So there was no disarmament of any consequence, and Hitler eventually rearmed as he liked, and used his new armies to conquer most of Europe—including France, who was, as she expected, overwhelmed by the strength of the German reserves.

CONCLUSION

Thus the era of hope in which it was believed that Germany could be brought back into the family of nations and that the world could settle down into a peaceful future, came to an end, with three dictatorships of varying aggressiveness bestriding Europe and the democracies fearful and on the defensive. France had by far the greatest armies and armaments and encircled Germany with her alliances. But the 1930's were to show how feeble these were as a defense against Hitler's superbly effective diplomacy and ruthlessness, as will be discussed in detail in Chapter 11.

(CONCLUSION)

3 SOVIET RUSSIA BETWEEN THE TWO WARS

The Bolshevik Revolution, which began in November, 1917,* put power in the hands of a small group of professional revolutionaries who, contrary to most expectations, survived to organize a government in Russia which has persisted to this day under the title of the Union of Soviet Socialist Republics (USSR), commonly called the Soviet Union. Following World War II, the Soviet Union, who after initial heavy losses had beaten back the German attack of 1941 and driven the Germans out by mid-1944, became the greatest power in Europe and second only to the United States as a world power. The cost in Russian lives of the revolutionary government's consolidation between the wars can never be fully known. A further twenty million Russians are estimated to have died during World War II. Nevertheless, the nation had enough reserve strength to recover, and in the last two decades even to present a challenge to American supremacy.

THE ESTABLISHMENT OF THE SOVIET UNION

The Bolsheviks came to power as a result of the failure of the tsarist armies in World War I. It is unthinkable that a revo-

---

* Prior to the Revolution Russia had used the Julian calendar abandoned by the rest of Europe in the sixteenth century. According to this calendar the Revolution occurred on October 25, and it is therefore still often known as the October Revolution. Similarly the revolution which resulted in the establishment of the Provisional Government earlier in the same year is sometimes called the February Revolution. In this book the Gregorian dates will be used, even though the reformed calendar did not come into official use until February 14, 1918.

lution of this scope could have succeeded if they had been victorious. Even when the Tsar abdicated early in 1917 a moderate republic or a restored constitutional monarchy would have been a more natural outcome and would surely have won the voluntary support of most Russians provided that it had instituted a thoroughgoing land reform. But Lenin managed to establish his ascendancy over his Bolshevik colleagues, and through his mastery of tactics and skillful opportunism he divided his political opponents in the other left-wing parties until these parties fell apart. Thereafter the Red Army, organized by Lenin's principal aide Leon Trotsky, was able to defeat counterrevolutionary "White" armies, in spite of help given to the latter by the Allies. During the first few years of Bolshevik rule, terror was systematically used to demoralize or liquidate all enemies and potential enemies of the regime. Many times in the next two decades the terror was rekindled, especially by Lenin's successor, Josef Stalin, and it was never wholly absent. While the threat persisted, it was not possible to determine the degree of popular consent on which the Soviet government rested, and even today this cannot be known. Thus the Soviet Union must still be regarded as in essence a police state, although controls have been greatly relaxed since the death of Stalin in 1953.

The Bolshevik Revolution. The authoritarian government of the tsars, backed by a secret police which became adept at infiltrating revolutionary organizations, had prevented any diminution in the powers of the absolute monarchy until as late as 1905, when the Russians were defeated by the Japanese in the Far East. A series of disturbances followed, as a result of which Tsar Nicholas II granted a constitution which included an elected Duma, or Parliament. But the liberal franchise originally granted by the Tsar brought into office a large majority of deputies who were opposed to his policies. He therefore twice modified the constitution until he obtained a Duma more to his liking. It was this Duma, which the Tsar had vainly tried to dissolve, that forced him to abdicate on March 14, 1917 (the March Revolution), and offered his brother Michael the throne. When Michael declined, the Duma chose an all-party executive (the Provisional Government), pending the election of a Constituent Assembly which should decide on the future constitution of the country.

The Duma, however, contained relatively few members elected by the peasants and urban workers, who therefore did not, insofar as they were aware of political matters, regard themselves as represented. The most liberal party in the Duma, the *Kadet,* was composed of middle-class intellectuals and landowners. But it was willing to entrust at least one important deputy of the left, Alexander Kerensky, with a position in the Cabinet. Beginning as minister of justice, Kerensky later became minister of war, and finally prime minister in July, 1917. His success was not due so much to his executive talents, which were rather meager, as to the fact that he was a Socialist, a member of the Social Revolutionary party (even though this party did not regard his presence in the government as in its interests), and therefore might be expected to command necessary support for the government among leftists.

To the left of the Provisional Government were the revolutionary parties which had been persistently persecuted by the tsarist secret police and for many years had operated mostly underground. Almost all the leaders had spent time in tsarist prisons or in exile in Siberia, and many of them had left the country for the purpose of continuing their agitation abroad. The two major left-wing revolutionary parties were the Social Revolutionary party and the Social Democratic party. The former claimed most of its adherents among the peasantry, whereas the latter, which based its theories on those of Marx and Engels, appealed more to the urban proletariat and middle-class intellectuals. The Social Revolutionaries had a long history of political murder and terrorism, and many of its members were anarchists or former anarchists. The Social Democrats, on the other hand, did not believe in casual political murders. They were, on the whole, more serious and dedicated revolutionaries who thought that careful preparation was needed, so that one day they could take over power in the state. As Marxists they considered themselves part of a world-wide revolutionary movement which would eventually bring the workers to power everywhere. Since 1903 the Social Democratic party had been divided into left and right wings, known as the Bolsheviks (*majority,* because they were in a majority in a congress held that year) and the Mensheviks (*minority*).

The leading theoretician and tactician of the Bolshevik faction was Vladimir Ilich Ulianov, who came to be known by his revolutionary name of "Nicolai" Lenin. He was in Switzerland at the time of the March Revolution. Lev Bronstein, known as Leon Trotsky, had for a long time been a Menshevik and opposed to Lenin. He was in the United States at the time of the March

Revolution, but returned as soon as he could and joined the Bolsheviks. There was an important difference between the Mensheviks and Bolsheviks, although changing events came to blur the distinction. There was no universally accepted opinion on the question of what stage of development, according to Marxist canons, had been reached in Russia and whether or not it would be necessary to have a transitional stage of "bourgeois" government before it would be possible to establish a "proletarian government" (dictatorship of the proletariat). The latter might be attainable simply by having the workers overthrow the existing autocracy, replacing it by rule by themselves. On the whole the Mensheviks took the first position, while a significant number of the Bolsheviks, including Lenin and Trotsky, came to believe after the March Revolution that it was possible to establish at once a dictatorship of the proletariat.

Few except the tsarist police took the revolutionaries very seriously before the March Revolution—in which in fact they played no part except for their defeatist propaganda in the armed forces and among the peasantry during the war. But when the Kerensky government decided to attempt another military offensive it played into the hands of the revolutionaries with their slogan of "Land, Bread, Peace," which represented the true aspirations of the vast majority of the Russian people. The revolutionaries made every effort to discredit the government and their policy, especially after Lenin arrived in the capital of Petrograd (formerly St. Petersburg) in April, 1917. He had been permitted to return from Switzerland by the Germans, who provided him with a sealed train, in the well-founded belief that his presence would tend to increase the defeatism of the Russian troops.

Nevertheless Lenin found that there was much opposition to him even among his own Bolsheviks, who were divided over whether or not to co-operate with the Provisional Government to obtain needed reforms; not all the Bolsheviks even desired immediate peace, which they knew would mean the loss of much western territory to the Germans. In short their patriotism was at war with their revolutionary goals. However, Lenin and Trotsky, who soon joined him, did not look upon Russia as their homeland; their constituency was the international proletariat. By the force of his personality, his masterly abilities in political in-fighting, and his divisory tactics Lenin was always able to win a majority for his policies when he really needed it—though the final decision to accept the Treaty of Brest-Litovsk was won by a majority of one.

Ever since the March Revolution the revolutionaries had been busy organizing soviets (councils) of workers, peasants, and soldiers, especially in the major cities, including Petrograd. These were supposed to be the nucleus of the revolutionary forces, and they acted as pressure groups, often compelling the leaders to go further than they intended at any given moment. Control of these soviets did not fall fully into Bolshevik hands until late in 1917; until then they were usually led by Mensheviks. The soviets met regularly in congresses, either the Petrograd soviets by themselves or the All-Russian Congress of Soviets, which under the leadership of Trotsky finally authorized the Revolution. In July, 1917, the mutinous soldiers in Petrograd virtually compelled the more cautious Bolshevik leadership to take part in a premature attempt to overthrow the Provisional Government, which was easily suppressed. Trotsky was imprisoned, and Lenin escaped to Finland, whence he returned only a few days before the Revolution.

The soldiers and sailors had been mutinous because of the planned offensive on the Austrian front, which had been organized by Kerensky as minister of war and was now launched by him as prime minister. The offensive after a short advance was disastrously defeated. The new commander in chief, General Lavr Kornilov, holding Kerensky and the Provisional Government responsible, on the grounds that they had contributed to the relaxing of discipline, proposed that he should take over the government, presumably as a military dictator. At this point Kerensky had only one recourse. He did not have enough troops to stop Kornilov's threatened march on Petrograd. So he appealed to the workers and their leaders for their support in suppressing the Kornilov coup. When Trotsky from his prison urged them to take care of Kornilov and the counterrevolution now, leaving Kerensky himself for later, the workers obeyed him. They refused to transport Kornilov, whose followers in many instances fraternized with the revolutionaries and the rebellious soldiers. Kornilov's coup therefore failed. But the price had been high. In the pinch Kerensky, who was, after all, a Socialist, preferred the support of other Socialists, even extremists, to the right-wing government which would have resulted from either subordinating the revolution to the needs of the military or allowing the military to rule in his place.

The prestige of the Provisional Government sank catastrophically, and that of the revolutionaries soared proportionately. But there was still no consensus among the later as to what had now to be done. Lenin sent letters from Finland urging the preparation of an armed coup. Trotsky, who had been released from prison by Kerensky, spent the time organizing the military details and concerting measures with the soldiers and sailors who obeyed him in Petrograd. At last the Central Committee of the Bolshevik party agreed to the coup, and it was carried out with exemplary efficiency on November 7. The government offered little resistance, the one exception being in the Winter Palace, which was lightly defended but submitted quickly after being bombarded by a Russian ship under the control of mutineers.

Kerensky, who escaped from the city, tried to raise troops for its recapture but failed, whereupon he went into exile, eventually reaching the United States. During the next few days Bolshevik revolutionaries took over the other major cities; Moscow came under their control on November 13.

Though executive power in the cities was in Bolshevik hands, and a cabinet (called the Council of People's Commissars) was formed on November 8, with Lenin as chairman, the Bolsheviks controlled little else in the country. Peasants were seizing property from the landlords; soldiers were streaming home ("voting with their feet," as Lenin called it) to take advantage of the seizures; and there was virtual anarchy except where the Bolsheviks had been able to establish some semblance of order. Moreover the Constituent Assembly, which had been summoned by the Provisional Government, was scheduled to meet, following elections, due shortly. Lenin decided that the elections should be held as scheduled. Possibly he believed that the Bolsheviks would win now that they had assumed power. If so, he was sadly mistaken, for the Social Revolutionaries won easily, gaining 370 seats as against 175 for the Bolsheviks. Even with the aid of a splinter group of 40 who had separated from the Social Revolutionary party and were prepared to support the Bolsheviks, Lenin could command only 215 votes. When the Assembly met on January 18, 1918, it was still determined to take over the government from the Bolsheviks in accordance with the popular vote. For the first day Lenin, after addressing the Assembly, let it talk and pass resolutions. The following day he dissolved it by force. Unable to function without effective military power, which was in Bolshevik hands, the Assembly accepted its dismissal, leaving Lenin and the Bolsheviks to complete their revolution. Their principal instrument was the newly organized Extraordinary Commission for the Suppression of the Counterrevolution, a special police force under the control of Feliz Dzierzynsky, which came to be known, from its initials in Russian, as the *Cheka*. The Cheka instituted a systematic campaign of terror against all elements regarded as "counterrevolutionary." Many thousands lost their lives or were forced into exile, and gradually the home front became somewhat more stable, and the Bolsheviks succeeded in consolidating their power.

The Treaty of Brest-Litovsk.   But the crucial problem faced by the Bolsheviks was how to fulfill their promise to end the war. Obviously this could be achieved only by making a separate peace with the Central Powers, to which the Allies objected very strongly. But the Allies made the mistake of underestimating the Bolsheviks and, to some degree, underestimating the nationalistic feelings of the Russian people, who did not desert the government as widely as had been expected. The Allied leaders assumed that the Bolshevik seizure of the government was an ordinary coup d'état which could be reversed, probably as soon as the temporarily demoralized tsarist officers could organize their armies and restore discipline. It was of course clear that the Bolsheviks were a small minority, and the fiasco of the Constituent Assembly showed how little popular support they enjoyed. But Lenin was prepared to negotiate a separate peace, however great the cost, and the Allies determined to do their best to prevent this.

The Germans, on the other hand, felt that there was no particular hurry. They were convinced that the Bolsheviks could never defend themselves against a new German attack. In spite of the fact that the United States had entered the war, they had no thought at the end of 1917 that they were in any danger of losing. Some Germans even believed that the correct policy was to make a drive against Petrograd and overthrow the Bolshevik government. Nevertheless, they opened negotiations with the Bolsheviks late in November, 1917, realizing that success would mean the freeing of considerable armies for an attack on the West planned for 1918, which, it was hoped, would end in complete German victory.

The Provisional Government had conceded autonomy to both Finland and Poland, expecting that the former at least would voluntarily form part of a new Russian federal state. The Bolsheviks confirmed this concession on December 31, 1917. The provinces of Estonia and Lithuania had declared their independence soon after the Bolshevik coup, but Russian armies were attempting to suppress the rebellions in these areas. Latvia, the other Baltic state, was under the control of the Germans. Several leading Bolsheviks favored the independence of all these states, which they realized they were not strong enough to defend. But the Ukraine was a different matter. This province declared its independence immediately after the Bolshevik Revolution and was recognized as independent by the Allies. But the Bolsheviks were not prepared to let it go without a struggle. It had long been integrated into the Russian state, and was the most important grain-growing area in the whole country. The Ukrainians at first attempted to win Allied military support, but the price demanded, that they continue the war against Germany, was impossible for them in view of the proximity of the German armies. They therefore turned to the Germans, who then proceeded to insist in their negotiations with the Bolsheviks that this territory be ceded.

The German demands were so high that many leading Bolsheviks opposed Lenin's desire to make peace even at this cost. Lenin, however, argued that the cession would be temporary, since there would soon be revolutions on the Bolshevik model everywhere, not excluding Germany. When the Bolsheviks, nevertheless, delayed accepting the German terms, the Germans decided to teach them a lesson, and drove into Russian territories, meeting little organized resistance. By a vote of 7 to 6, the closest in the Central Committee of the Bolshevik party (now called Communist party, out of deference to the famous work of Karl Marx, the *Communist Manifesto* of 1848), a German ultimatum was accepted and peace was signed at Brest-Litovsk on March 3, 1918. A few days later the capital was moved to Moscow, since Petrograd was far too close to the Germans to be comfortable; Allied interventions in the north were to be expected; and Moscow (the traditional capital before the time of Peter the Great) was a better center for the organization of defense against counterrevolutionary armies.

The Treaty of Brest-Litovsk committed Russia to the evacuation of her troops from all her western territories. Poland, Courland, and Lithuania were ceded to the Central Powers, who would settle their future. Finland, Estonia, and Livonia were to be freed of Russian troops. Ukraine was to become independent in accordance with a treaty already signed by the new state and the Central Powers. Lastly a few territories were ceded to Turkey.

The Allies naturally regarded the treaty as a gross betrayal, and looked upon the Bolsheviks as little better than tools of the Germans. They therefore took whatever measures were available to them to keep the supplies they had sent to Russia out of German hands. In June, 1918, the British sent an expedition to the northern port of Murmansk; in August an Anglo-French force took the other main port of the north, Archangel. American contingents joined them the following month. The Allies also sponsored an anti-Bolshevik government in the north, led by a Social Revolutionary, which commanded little support from the local population.

Even though the treaty was signed, opposition to it continued within the ranks of the revolutionaries. The Council of People's Commissars still contained members of the splinter left-wing group of the Social Revolutionaries which had supported Lenin at the time of the Constituent Assembly. But rather than ratify the treaty they resigned from the Council, thus leaving it an all-Bolshevik body. For several months both the left and the right Social Revolutionaries continued their opposition to the treaty, and during the course of 1918 when the Germans began to occupy the Ukaine, they staged a number of rebellions, all of which were put down, though not without difficulty. Other Social Revolutionaries returned to their prewar practice of political murder, one of them (Dora Kaplan) wounding Lenin in an attempt at assassination. Although the Cheka executed many of the conspirators, it was by late 1918 still unable to put an end to the opposition to the Bolshevik government; nor were the Bolsheviks able to make much headway in the countryside, where the Social Revolutionaries had long been powerful. The Bolshevik requisitioning of supplies for the Red Army encountered sabotage, against which the Bolsheviks took many reprisals. Indeed by the time of the 1918 Armistice, it was still doubtful whether the Bolsheviks would be able to survive, so numerous were their domestic and external enemies. The so-called "White" armies organized for the purpose of counterrevolution and the Allied interventionists between them held more than half the country.

Foreign Intervention and Civil War.   One of the strangest anti-Bolshevik operations was carried out by Czech deserters and prisoners of war in Siberia, more than 40,000 in number, who had formed part of the Austro-Hungarian armies. It was their desire to join the Allies after the Treaty of Brest-Litovsk, but the Bolsheviks, possibly at the instigation of the Germans, ordered that they be disarmed. The Czechs refused to give up their arms and decided to march westward through Bolshevik-controlled territories to reach central Europe. Against relatively light resistance in that confused time, they took full control of the Trans-Siberian Railroad and drove into European Russia, reaching the river Volga. The murder of Tsar Nicholas and his family took place at a time when it was believed that the Czechs would capture them, an eventuality which would have created untold complications for the Bolshevik government. Indeed the Czechs did capture Ekaterinburg, where the Tsar had been imprisoned, just ten days after his murder (July 26, 1918). Thus the whole of Russia and Siberia east of the Volga was lost to the Bolsheviks, and two anti-Bolshevik governments were formed, one at Samara on the Volga, and the other at Omsk in Siberia. The latter, under Admiral Alexander Kolchak, the most substantial of the anti-Bolshevik "White" governments, was recognized by most of the Allies as the government of Russia. The Japanese seized Vladivostok, the eastern terminal of the Trans-Siberian Railroad in December, 1917.

At the time of the Armistice, the Ukraine was in German hands. The Germans had formed a government made up of local conservatives, led by General Skoropadsky. This was overthrown a few days after the German departure by a group of Socialists who refused to acknowledge the Bolshevik government and tried to retain the "independence" that the Ukrainians had enjoyed since the Bolshevik Revolution. The Germans in 1918 had attempted to exercise control in the area of the southern Russia inhabited by the Don Cossacks. Here General Kornilov, who had escaped from prison at the time of the Revolution, took command, but he had many difficulties with the local Cossack leaders and was killed in action. His successor, General Denikin, worked better with a new Cossack leader, General Krasnov, who had some initial successes against the Bolshevik armies. However, a counteroffensive by the latter recovered the Don region by the time of the Armistice, and Denikin was compelled to move into the Caucasus, where three republics, not under Bolshevik rule, were proclaimed: Georgia, Azerbaijan, and Armenia.

Lastly, in the north there were the Allied interventionists, and by the time of the Armistice the Germans remained in control of the Baltic states. As noted previously, it was in part because of these hostile forces in the north and northwest that the Russian capital had been removed from Petrograd, which was always in danger from a drive by the Germans and their Baltic allies.

The Bolsheviks were able to turn back all these threats for two major reasons. The Red Armies, ultimately as many as sixteen different ones, made up of volunteers, were organized largely by Trotsky as commissar for war. He himself directed their movements and general strategy, moving around Russia in a special armored train. Considerable numbers of former tsarist officers joined him when the country was threatened not only by anti-Bolshevik "White" elements but also by foreigners. Trotsky was remarkably successful in enlisting patriotic aid, even though his government was often detested. But, perhaps more important, the "White" armies never co-ordinated their offensives, and the leaders constantly quarreled among themselves. Once the Armistice had been signed, the Czechs in Siberia were more anxious to reach home and their newly independent country than to overthrow the Bolshevik government. They seldom co-operated with Admiral Kolchak and more usually opposed him. So the Red Armies, having the inestimable advantage of interior lines of communication, could pick off their enemies one by one. Lastly, the Allies were far from being of one mind about their objectives. If Admiral Kolchak had been able to establish his government and overthrow the Bolsheviks, all would have been happy. But the war-weary troops of the Allies were not willing to give unstinted support to the Whites, and early in 1919 most of these troops were withdrawn, including the quite considerable French armies which had intervened in southern Russia. Thereafter all the Allies provided some indirect support to the Whites, but this was by then far from sufficient for their victory.

In the second half of 1919, General Denikin captured Odessa in the Crimea, and drove into the Ukraine, capturing the capital of Kiev (September 2, 1919). But a Bolshevik counteroffensive forced him back into the Caucasus, where he resigned his command to General Wrangel. In May, 1920, the Poles invaded the Ukraine, which they had always coveted and which had at one time been a part of Poland. After initial Polish successes, the Bolsheviks turned the tide and drove into Poland itself up to the outskirts of Warsaw. Here the Poles received substantial aid from the French and drove back the Russians, who abandoned their conquests in Poland but retained the Ukraine.

General Wrangel meanwhile took advantage of Russian preoccupation with Poland to move into southern Russia and wrested much of it from the Bolsheviks. But the Red Army, once peace had been made with the Poles, concentrated its forces against Wrangel and drove him and his army out of the country. They were evacuated to Turkey, leaving the Bolsheviks in control of the Caucasus (November, 1920). Georgia and Azerbaijan were restored to the Bolshevik government, though Armenia had to be divided with Turkey. They became in due course one of the Soviet Union's component republics (Transcaucasian Socialist Soviet Republic).

Late in 1919 the Red Army drove into Siberia against Admiral Kolchak's regime. Omsk was captured on November 14, 1919. In February, 1920, Kolchak was captured and executed by the Bolsheviks, and all resistance soon afterward ceased. Driving further into Siberia, the Bolsheviks set up a Far Eastern Republic and negotiated for the departure of the Japanese from Vladivostok, since they were not strong enough to expel them. This settlement was not achieved until November, 1922.

In the Baltic area the Bolsheviks, after several attempts to restore the newly independent countries to their control, recognized their independence in 1920. In October, 1919, they had to resist a strong effort by a "White" army, led by General Yudenich, to capture Petrograd. He succeeded in reaching the gates of the city, and the Bolsheviks had even made preparations to evacuate their leaders if necessary. But Trotsky succeeded in inspiring the inhabitants with the will to resist, while Yudenich, who had hoped for support from British warships in the area and from Estonian and Finnish troops, received no aid of consequence. A Bolshevik counterattack, pressed with fanatical vigor, drove him from the city and back into Estonia.

"WAR COMMUNISM" AND THE NEW ECONOMIC POLICY

By 1921 there was no longer any chance that the Bolshevik government would be overthrown. But the civil war had been ruinous to the economy, and in spite of the army's victories it was clear to the leaders that the system by which the government had hitherto ruled could not be maintained.

When the Bolsheviks seized the government they were not simply power seekers but were motivated by certain definite ideas and ideals, in large measure derived from their understanding of the works of Karl Marx. For them the dictatorship of the proletariat meant that only workers and poor peasants should be permitted to vote and have a share in the government. Since the means of production must belong to the people, all land, industry, and trade should cease to be in private hands, though the peasants would naturally work the land confiscated from their former landlords. Industry would be run by the workers themselves, and the managing class would be replaced by committees of workers. This system was "Communism," as the revolutionaries envisaged it before they had experienced power and been compelled to face economic realities, and as soon as they won power they attempted to put it into operation.

But in the circumstances of the time, with civil wars to fight and inexperienced management in the production industries, the system of "War Communism" failed dismally to achieve its ends. The peasants now in possession of their land believed they had the full rights to its fruits. But with the city population as well as the armies in desperate need of supplies, the government could not allow them to keep their surplus. The factories could supply as yet little that the peasants needed; hence they had no incentive to produce and could not exchange their surplus for manufactured goods as would have been possible in a free market. The only method available to the government to obtain supplies needed for the army and for the urban proletariat was to use compulsion and terror. The result was a catastrophic drop in agricultural and industrial production, which forced Lenin and his colleagues to the conclusion that some modification would have to be made. These modifications, which lasted for several years, constitute what is known as the New Economic Policy (NEP).

In effect NEP restored incentives to agriculture by taxing the peasants a fixed amount, to be paid in produce, and permitting them to consume or spend their surplus. This was made possible in turn by the restoration of a stable currency and the removal of restrictions on small-scale industry and trade. The government still maintained its numerous controls over the economy, over means of communication, and over education. But with the aid of some good harvests the policy worked for a time, and agricultural production again reached prewar levels. As far as the revolutionaries were concerned, however, the prospect of Communism was receding, and capitalism was reappearing both in the cities and in the countryside. The more efficient farmers were becoming richer. They could rent land from the less efficient and even hire laborers, who no longer worked their own land. The same process was beginning to operate as in the evil past. The richer peasants (*kulaks*) were beginning to resemble the landlords who had been dispossessed by the state. A similar process was taking place in industry. The small businesses that became bigger were ever more frequently dispossessed by government action. But the peasants, who formed such a large percentage of the population, could not be dealt with so easily, and it took the tremendous upheaval of the first Five-Year Plan to alter the structure of Russian agriculture (see p. 50).

GOVERNMENTAL STRUCTURE OF THE SOVIET UNION

The fundamental unit of the Russian revolutionary government was the local soviet, organized on a village level in the countryside and by occupations in the cities. These soviets elected deputies to district congresses, which in turn elected deputies to regional congresses. At the top was the All-Russian Soviet Congress. In order to offset the peasants' immense superiority in numbers, urban voters received one deputy for each 25,000 people, whereas the peasants received only one for each 125,000.

The main task of the All-Russian Soviet Congress was to choose a Central Committee of 400, which in turn appointed a Praesidium of 40, and the Council of People's Commissars, which was the executive body of the state. Parallel with this official government was the Communist party, an elite body whose membership has always been kept under strict control and from which members who do not conform to and obey the ruling hierarchy may be expelled. The party had its committees in every area of the country. At the head of the party was the Central Committee, with its three organs: the Orgburo responsible in the main for organization, but with somewhat indefinite functions; the Politburo, responsible for the formulation of policy; and the Secretariat, led by its first secretary. Both Stalin and later on Khrushchev ruled the country as autocrats largely by virtue of holding the position of first secretary, which enabled them to choose their colleagues almost at will and to hold concurrently other offices carrying more responsibilities.

Initially the Russian Soviet Federated Socialist Republic (RSFSR) was the only body of its kind, and it is still by far the most important of the various republics which compose the Soviet

Union. During the civil wars similar autonomous republics were formed, as various parts of the country fell under Bolshevik control. These other republics, now fifteen in number, all had and still have some measure of autonomy and both the governmental and the party structures are duplicated in them. Khrushchev, for example, was First Secretary of the Communist party in the Ukrainian Republic before he moved to Moscow, where not many years afterward he held the same position for the whole Union. In 1922 the autonomous republics were federated into a tighter political structure, and the state thereafter was known as the Union of Soviet Socialist Republics. This change necessitated the change of the supreme governmental body into the All-Union Congress of Soviets, with its Union Central Committee, Council of Commissars, and Praesidium.

When a new constitution was promulgated in 1936 there were few changes of substance. All citizens were now permitted to vote by secret ballot, but there were still only official lists of candidates, all of whom had to be approved by the Communist party, even though not all belonged to it. Peasant voters now had the same representation as urban voters. A Supreme Soviet Council replaced the Union Congress of Soviets. This was composed of two houses, the Council of the Union and the Council of Nationalities, the latter representing several governmental units that did not yet belong to the Union but retained, in particular, cultural autonomy. The two councils chose the Council of Ministers (the equivalent of a cabinet under a parliamentary system, headed by a prime minister). The chairman of the Praesidium of the Supreme Council (Supreme Soviet) is the president (largely an honorary position) of the state. When Khrushchev fell from office late in 1964, it was the Praesidium of the Supreme Council which officially deposed him. The action was ratified at the next meeting of the Supreme Council, which cannot be regarded as in any way equivalent to Western democratic parliaments, since it still acts largely as a rubber stamp for decisions taken at a higher level.

THE DICTATORSHIP OF STALIN

Lenin had never been a dictator in the sense in which Stalin was for the long period of his rule which ended only with his death in 1953. Stalin, through his absolute control of the Communist party machinery and his elimination of all opponents, never had to submit to any serious challenge to his power, whereas Lenin made his will prevail largely through the prestige he had acquired as revolutionary leader and through his theoretical works, which were regarded as equal in importance to those of Marx. Lenin's fellow Bolsheviks could still in his lifetime make their views heard and might hope to influence policy. But once Stalin had triumphed over his opposition in the years immediately following Lenin's death he was no longer "first among equals," but absolute dictator, and it was in the highest degree dangerous to oppose him. Only those among the old Bolsheviks who, like Molotov, obeyed him in everything could hope to survive, and none of them, as far as is known, ever exercised any substantial influence over him.

The Struggle for Succession. Early in 1922 Lenin suffered a stroke. He was unable thereafter to take any really active part in affairs, contenting himself with sending letters and written instructions to his colleagues. During this time Stalin was building up for himself a strong, almost unassailable, position through the control of the party apparatus. It is now known that in his last year of life Lenin had come to distrust Stalin and would have preferred as his successor Trotsky, who, however, in part because of his brilliance, arrogance, and reputation as commissar for war and architect of victory, had many enemies and detractors. Stalin, who knew of Lenin's views, had nevertheless to be very careful not to make an open break with him and spent his energies in increasing his power and authority within the party, ready to take open steps only when Lenin died. When this happened, in January, 1924, he was in an extremely strong position. Two apparently like-minded colleagues, Zinoviev and Kamenev, shared authority with him in the party Politburo (of which Trotsky was also a member, though without political support in it). Stalin had acquired almost absolute control of the Central Committee of the party, whose members had been so largely chosen by him in his position as party secretary.

In the next three years before his final fall Trotsky showed little talent for political maneuvering; and though he opposed Stalin courageously enough, he won no victories. Although it may be contended with much justice that the main issue between Stalin and Trotsky, and then between Stalin and Zinoviev and Kamenev and later almost all the other old Bolsheviks, was simply who should hold power, there was also a difference in policy, in particular between Stalin and Trotsky. Stalin was moving toward the notion that "Socialism" could be achieved in one country alone; and that a world revolution would follow when the Russian experiment had succeeded. This idea was anathema to the old revolutionaries, who had been brought up on the teachings of Marx and Engels and the idea of the world solidarity of the working class. Zinoviev had been the leading figure in the Third International, founded in Russia in 1919, to be the instrument of the world revolution. But since Stalin was unsurpassed as a political infighter, and was able in due course to discredit Trotsky and the others, it was his policies that were adopted, and his theoretical justifications for these policies that had to be accepted. By 1928 he was supreme in the state, and his political enemies were routed. It was therefore now possible to put into effect his plans for establishing "Socialism in one country," through the medium of his first Five-Year Plan.

The Five-Year Plans.   As the result of the work of a State Planning Commission (*Gosplan*), which had been in operation for several years, Stalin was ready on October 1, 1928, to launch a huge plan for the establishment of full "Socialism" in Russia, which would put an end to the compromises of NEP. It had two major purposes, to industrialize the country and to collectivize agriculture; to achieve these aims Stalin was willing to make uninhibited use of state power. The industrialization program consisted primarily of the attempt to establish a heavy industry, with the aid of foreign technicians when necessary. This heavy industry, consisting of huge iron and steel plants, hydroelectric works, new railroads, and factories producing tractors and other machinery for the proposed collectivized agriculture, would be entirely under state control. Obviously the program would be immensely expensive, and in view of the Soviet repudiation of tsarist debts there could be no question of foreign credits. This meant that such foreign exchange as was necessary would have to be gained by selling abroad traditional Russian agricultural products for whatever price could be obtained in a world that was soon to enter a serious economic depression. For the rest, the Russians would simply have to tighten their belts and make do without consumer products, at least until the first phase of the program had been achieved. All the resources of propaganda that the state had at its disposal, including the hope of "surpassing America," would be used to stimulate production. In agriculture the emphasis was to be on the development of state and collective farms. The state farms were mostly new agricultural enterprises in areas where there was relatively little, especially large-scale, agriculture and where new land could be brought under the plow. Collective farms were to be co-operatives under strict state control, which could take in the existing peasant holdings. This of course meant that state power would have to be used against the Russian farmers who persisted in remaining attached to their own land, and particularly against the kulaks who had grown rich under NEP.

This extraordinarily ambitious program naturally met with tremendous obstacles. Even before the five years came to an end the Bolshevik leaders, especially Stalin, who had staked his reputation on the plan, were proclaiming loudly that the targets had already been reached. Only in later years did the true figures leak out showing serious underfulfillment of industrial goals, widespread dislocation in agriculture, and an almost catastrophe drop in production over the earlier NEP period. Not only the kulaks but even the smaller peasants bitterly resisted the efforts to force them into collective farms. They sabotaged crops, slaughtered their animals, and did everything in their power to halt the program. Local Communist party members had to aid the OGPU, the hated successor of the ill-famed Cheka, in compelling their obedience. In the process certainly millions of peasants lost their lives, and a serious famine occurred in 1932. In industry there was probably more damage done through inexperience than by deliberate sabotage. Yet many thousands of managers and workers were also liquidated by the government for the crime of sabotaging the Plan. Nevertheless, in view of the backward condition of Russian industry prior to the Plan, its achievements were indeed impressive and laid the basis for all later Russian industrialization. Whether it could have been carried out under other goads than the terror is a question that cannot be answered. Peter the Great had, in his time, with similar aims in view, used similar methods.

At the height of the terror there was serious division within the party leadership. Many old Bolsheviks attempted to restrain Stalin and persuade him to slow down the program—for which temerity they were later to pay with their lives. But in fact Stalin himself, now that 75 per cent of the peasants had been forced into the collectives, was ready to modify the pace of the drive. In the second Five-Year Plan (1933–1937) the goals were more moderate; collective farmers were permitted to work private lots of land for their own benefit, including selling their surplus produce;

and more attention was paid to the production of consumer goods. To offset the widespread starvation resulting from the 1932 famine, grain was imported by the state. But the major innovation for the improvement of industrial production was the return to a system hated by workers and largely abandoned long before in the capitalist countries—incentive payments on the basis of piecework. So the best Russian workers were now enabled to earn much more than their fellows, and their example was held up to the others to imitate ("Stakhanovism," after the name of the best piecework laborer in Russia). The result was indeed a greatly improved production, but the system took yet one more step away from Communism. It is from the 1930's and the second Five-Year Plan that significant variations in income date between the low-paid unskilled workers and the more efficient skilled workers. Also party functionaries, scientists, professors, engineers, and others were now able to enjoy a higher standard of living; and the Russian Communist system became gradually thought of abroad as simply state capitalism. This negation of the original revolutionary ideas was greatly resented by many of those who had remained true to these aims and had tolerated the terror because of the hoped-for future. To them the Soviet Union seemed to have become nothing but a police state, with all the worst features of nineteenth-century capitalism. For it they blamed above all Stalin, and he knew it.

The Great Purges of the 1930's.   The purges of the 1930's can be explained only in terms of a real opposition to Stalin, which, however, probably never reached the stage of actual conspiracy —perhaps only because he struck first. The Soviet government had not been designed as a dictatorship of an individual, but as an oligarchy of trained Communists who would have arisen from the ranks of the Communist party, which itself was organized throughout the whole country and open to talent. But Stalin managed to seize indisputable control of the government through political manipulation within the party and the Secretariat, which he dominated, and through the agency of the secret police (the OGPU, later called the NKVD). Beginning in 1934, Stalin moved against his enemies, mostly within the party itself, thus fulfilling the adage that all revolutions devour their children. One after the other, men who had opposed him were put on trial and either executed or sentenced to long prison terms from which they seldom emerged alive. Sometimes the trials were secret, particularly in the case of the military, and sometimes they were public show trials in which the accused men paraded their guilt and demanded punishment. Leading Communists confessed to every kind of counter-revolutionary crime, including conspiracy with foreigners, usually alleged to be under the direction of the exiled Trotsky, who was at last murdered in Mexico in 1940. In 1936, when many of the leading party men had been sentenced, Stalin turned to the army and begun to purge the army leaders in the same manner, usually on the charge that they had collaborated with foreign powers.

Much of this situation was not understood at the time, and foreigners were unable to make any sense of the purge, in part because nothing was known of opposition to Stalin within his own party. But posterity will probably believe Secretary Khrushchev's revelation to the Twentieth Party Congress in 1956 that Stalin himself had been personally responsible for the purges and for the execution of innocent men. Although he himself supported Stalin during these years, Khrushchev implied—as was probably true—that he had had no alternative but to join in the purging or be purged himself. The result of the purge was a very serious demoralization in the ranks both of the party and of the army, and it may well be that the decisions taken in foreign policy during these years, culminating in the nonaggression pact with Germany in August, 1939, were in part due to Stalin's own recognition of this fact.

FOREIGN POLICY OF SOVIET RUSSIA

Soviet foreign policy during the interwar period was always somewhat ambivalent. On the one hand the Bolshevik leaders were slow to modify their purpose of fomenting a world revolution and were on the lookout for favorable opportunities. However, on the other hand they were aware of their isolation in Europe and the *cordon sanitaire* that the Allies tried to fasten around them in the early years after the war. To improve their position they did not hesitate to make alliances with the bourgeois nations, whenever opportunity presented itself.

Role of the Comintern. Reference has already been made (p. 22) to the 1922 Treaty of Rapallo with Germany, which brought Soviet Russia for the first time after the war into an alliance with a Western power. Throughout the rest of the period between the wars Soviet relations with Germany were almost always fairly friendly, and the Treaty of Rapallo was renewed when it expired. The Russian and German general staffs co-operated with one another until Hitler had by his unilateral actions put an end to the military provisions of the Treaty of Versailles. Nevertheless, when the opportunity presented itself during the Ruhr invasion (see p. 23), Communists made a number of minor efforts to take over various state governments in Germany. During the Great Depression the Soviet Union believed that the capitalist states would collapse from their own contradictions and failures, but at the time Russia herself was undergoing the domestic upheavals described above and made no overt revolutionary efforts of any importance.

The Third International (Comintern) was active under Soviet direction from the time of its founding in 1919, preparing for its task of controlling the world revolution when it came, or of fomenting it when possible. Its main instruments were the Communist parties abroad, which were subsidized by the Soviet Union. The Comintern, being entirely under party control, changed its policy directives and tactics in accordance with Russian needs. The Communist parties abroad were therefore correctly looked upon as agents for the implementation of Soviet foreign policy—even though many of their adherents were won over to Communism during the Great Depression when it seemed to many that the capitalistic system had failed and that only some form of collectivism would rescue the Western world from its economic doldrums.

In 1935 Stalin at last came to the conclusion that the Soviet Union was in real danger from Nazism and that Hitler's government was not likely to collapse. He therefore through the Comintern switched world Communist policy over to the notion of the Popular Front. Instead of having to fight the bourgeoisie or at least refuse them all co-operation, foreign Communists were now directed to join with all left-wing parties everywhere that were willing to co-operate for the purpose of defeating fascism (Seventh Comintern Congress, July–August, 1935). The foreign Communists for the most part accepted this change with enthusiasm since at last they could enjoy some of the sweets of office. But only in France and Spain were Popular Front governments formed. The effort itself was significant in that it showed the patience and tactical flexibility of the Russians, and their willingness to postpone, perhaps for a long time to come, their ultimate revolutionary goals. Stalin was even bold enough to deny that it had ever been a Soviet goal to overthrow bourgeois governments—but the record is against him. It is, however, true that he at least was always willing to use every method to promote Soviet interests and security. Even in the 1930's when Hitler was executing German Communists and attacking the Soviet Union in unmeasured terms, Stalin was attempting to negotiate with him and made many overtures for better relations. Trade between Germany and Russia even increased during the period, with the aid of German credits.

Relations with Western Powers. The Soviet Union was at times feared and at other times, especially during the purges, despised by the Western European nations and the United States. But Russia was such a huge potential market that few nations wished to shut themselves out from it. Britain under the first Labour government, led by Ramsay MacDonald, entered into diplomatic relations with the Soviet Union in February, 1924, and was quickly followed by Italy, France, and most other European states. But British-Soviet relations were broken off in 1927 by the Conservative government of Stanley Baldwin, after a police raid on Arcos, an Anglo-Soviet trading association in London. The raid convinced the government that the Soviet Union was engaged in subversion and espionage in Britain. Nevertheless, when Ramsay MacDonald returned to power, relations were renewed, in exchange for a Soviet promise not to interfere in British domestic affairs. During the 1920's American trade with the Soviet Union was quite considerable, in spite of the refusal of the United States government to recognize the Soviet government (in this differing markedly from American policy toward Communist China in recent years). Indeed, trade between the two countries was much higher than it had been during the tsarist regime. The United States under President Roosevelt recognized the Soviet government in 1933. The Soviet Union signed the Kellogg-Briand Pact of 1928, in spite of the American intention not to invite her to do so. During the next few years the Soviet Union signed nonaggression pacts with Poland, Finland, and the Baltic states. All these were merely a prelude to the entry of the Soviet Union into the French security system (see p. 209).

Foreign Policy in Europe during the 1930's. The 1930's were of course dominated by the rise of Hitler to power in Germany and his subsequent aggressive policy, which at first alarmed the Soviet Union even more than it alarmed the Western European democracies. Hitler's nonaggression pact with Poland in 1934 (see p. 111) was regarded by Stalin as extremely dangerous to the Soviet Union; and though Poland renewed her 1932 nonaggression pact with the Soviet Union, Stalin was still not satisfied, and felt it best to try to escape his isolation by improving relations with the West, thinking that this might give him a better chance of defending his country against a possible drive by Germany through Poland.

This changed policy met with considerable apparent success. Maxim Litvinov, the Soviet foreign minister from 1930, was a talented diplomat, with an English wife, whom as a Jew no one could suspect of being in any respect pro-German and pro-Nazi. As long as he held office the Western powers had reason to believe that the Soviet Union was reliably anti-Nazi; when eventually he was replaced by the "hard-liner" Molotov, the change did indeed signal the approaching Soviet attempt to patch up differences with Hitler. It was Litvinov who was mainly responsible for the American recognition of the Soviet Union in 1933. In 1934 he led the Soviet Union into the League of Nations, from which Germany had so recently withdrawn. The Soviet alliances with France and Czechoslovakia (see p. 209) were his work. In 1936 a Popular Front government came to power in France under Léon Blum, a success for the new policy. But the organization of a similar Popular Front government in Spain in the same year proved damaging to Soviet interests. The right-wing rebellion led by General Francisco Franco against this government presented Stalin with a serious dilemma which he never really solved.

The Communist party line of the period called for the support of Popular Front governments, in which Communists would pay a constructive part. They were expected not to take active steps to overthrow the governments of which they formed part, but to see that they adopted an antifascist stance and honored their defense agreements with the Soviet Union. A Communist revolution in Spain would clearly be frightening to Stalin's Western collaborators and would probably spell the end of the Popular Front policy. Stalin therefore instructed the Spanish Communists not to try to overthrow the Popular Front government there, but only to work for victory in the Civil War. Thus for a time the Communists in Spain, who were heavily outnumbered by other left-wing parties, notably Trotskyites and anarchists, supported the right wing of the Popular Front government. When Soviet aid began to arrive, as well as volunteers from many countries, the NKVD arrived also, and busied itself in trying to purge the Trotskyites and the anarchists and syndicalists from positions of control in the republican regime. The total result was that the Soviet intervention was of little value to the government, and the Communists, Spanish and foreign, though ready to fight to the bitter end, sowed dissension in the Republican ranks. In the process they made themselves cordially hated, without being able to ensure a victory, which in any case could not have been won by such Soviet arms and troops as they had available to send to Spain. The whole episode tended to convince Soviet allies in Europe that Stalin was far from a reliable ally; that he would probably play his own game in the event of a showdown with Germany; and, since Russian military prowess was very little in evidence, that Soviet armies and war material might well be of no greater value than the recent purges had led them to believe.

The attitude of the Western powers during the Czechoslovakian crisis of 1938 (see p. 215) demonstrated their estimate of the Franco-Russian and Russian-Czechoslovakian alliances. Under the latter the Soviet Union was bound to assist Czechoslovakia only if the French did likewise. But France did not even consult with the Soviet Union, and Stalin was excluded from the Munich Conference. Stalin therefore drew the obvious conclusion, that neither the French nor the British would fight Hitler, and at a pinch both might even try to save themselves by encouraging Hitler to move eastward against Russia. The obvious retort was therefore to try to come to an accommodation with Hitler. Since the Popular Front policy of Litvinov was now in ruins, Stalin replaced him with Molotov in 1939.

When Hitler took over the rest of Czechoslovakia in March, 1939, in spite of the guarantees given by Britain and France, Stalin was confirmed in his suspicions. He did not take seriously the new Western policy of guaranteeing Poland, Hitler's next probable victim. Nor did he probably take very seriously their decision to enter into conversations with himself, especially when they sent only a second-rank official to conduct them. These negotiations were desultory, and the British and French made such difficulties about Soviet demands to be allowed to take the Baltic countries within the Russian sphere of influence that Stalin evidently lost patience. He was well aware that Germany would be likely to accept his terms since she was in greater need of Soviet assistance, and even Soviet neutrality would be of great help to him. Thus when Foreign Minister Ribbentrop proposed a nonaggression pact, with secret clauses calling for a partition of eastern Europe, including

Poland, who had shown herself quite unwilling to come to any kind of agreement permitting Soviet troops on her soil, Stalin quickly accepted. To the stupefaction of the world, which recognized at once that this meant war, the nonaggression pact was signed on August 23, 1939. Little more than a week later Germany invaded Poland, thus beginning World War II.

Policy in the Far East. Lastly, mention should be made of Soviet policy in the Far East. Immediately after the Revolution in 1917, the Bolsheviks renounced all tsarist claims to Chinese territory and entered into amicable relations with the Chinese president Sun Yat-sen and his revolutionary government. This policy involved the despatch at Sun's request of Russian military advisers. For many years the Russian Mikhail Borodin advised the Chinese government, while the famous Russian general Bluecher provided military advice. The Russians operated a military academy in Canton, of which Chiang Kai-shek, who had received his military education in Japan, was the first head. The Chinese army was patterned after that of the Soviet Union, and Communist commissars were active in it.

However, in the confusion and struggle for power that followed the death of Sun Yat-sen in 1925, the Chinese Communists attempted to foment a revolution, mostly based on the peasantry but with some worker support. This premature effort was suppressed by Chiang Kai-shek, who soon afterward established himself as head of the Chinese (Kuomintang) government. Borodin was forced to return to Russia, and thereafter the Chinese Communist movement was never under the control of, and scarcely even much influenced by, Moscow. When the Japanese attacked Manchuria in the 1930's (see p. 181), the Russians sold them their interests in the Chinese Eastern Railway. But, realizing that Japan was a greater danger in the Far East than was China, the Soviet Union aided Chang Kai-shek, who from 1936 onward was also supported against Japan by the native Chinese Communists. In 1939 Japanese and Russian forces clashed on the Mongolian frontier, and for some months there was a quite serious undeclared war between the Soviet Union and Japan in the Far East, little though this was realized at the time. It is probable that the strong Russian resistance to Japanese encroachments in this area led the Japanese to sign a nonaggression pact with the Soviet Union on April 13, 1941, which was of inestimable value to the Soviet Union, and saved her from having to fight a two-front war two months later. At the same time it freed Japan from a similar danger, and was perhaps the decisive factor in persuading her to drive southward at the end of that year.

CONCLUSION

By the end of the interwar period Stalin was firmly in control as dictator of the Soviet Union. Collaboration with the Western powers, such as it was, had apparently failed, and there was nothing left for him but to "appease" Germany in his own turn and in his own manner, meanwhile taking advantage of Germany's expansion to restore as far as possible the Russian frontiers as they had been in 1914. As will be discussed in Chapter 12, this policy brought him less than two years of peace, and the small countries taken in 1939 as a result of German victories could be held at first only during that period. But with the Russian victory in the war, all were restored, and the Soviet Union became the most formidable power, militarily and even industrially, on the European continent. This she remains today.

4 DEMOCRACY AND TOTALITARIANISM IN GERMANY AND ITALY

The immediate consequences for Germany of defeat in World War I have been described in Chapter 2. Not until the Treaty of Locarno in 1925 did Germany agree to accept the consequences of her defeat, pay reparations, and resume amicable relations with her former enemies. Meanwhile her government had become a parliamentary democracy, with a written constitution which in some respects served as the basis for the most advanced democratic system in Europe. Italy remained democratic for only three years after the war, thereafter falling victim to a legal coup which brought Benito Mussolini to power as prime minister, a position he used to become the first dictator of postwar Europe.

THE WEIMAR REPUBLIC

On January 19, 1919, a constituent assembly, elected by broad proportional representation, met in Weimar to write a republican constitution. By far the largest group (163) was made up of the Majority Socialists, the right wing of the Social Democratic party, which, though moderately Marxist, was nonrevolutionary. These Socialists entered a coalition, not with their left-wing associates, who refused to join them, but with the Christian Democratic Center party (88) and the Democratic party (75). The Communists (Spartacists) did not take part in the election to the constituent assembly but attempted a coup, which was quickly suppressed by the Free Corps and units of the regular army (see p. 4).

The constitution agreed upon by the coalition came into effect on July 31, 1919, a month after the Treaty of Versailles, which had caused so many disputes within Germany (see p. 11). It provided for: (1) a president, chosen by free, secret, and universal suffrage for a seven-year term; * (2) a chancellor, chosen by the president, but expected to command a majority of votes in the lower house; (3) a lower house, the Reichstag, elected by proportional representation, and by far the more important of the two legislative bodies; (4) an upper house, the Reichsrat, composed of delegates chosen by the eighteen state governments, which could delay, but not veto, legislation. In addition to the formal structure of government, the constitution guaranteed to all Germans equality before the law, freedom of speech and association, and freedom of belief.

Unfortunately for the Weimar Republic, the system of proportional representation, democratic though it was, made for weak governments and too many parties. Virtually every government had to be a coalition since small minority groups, even those which wished to destroy the republic, could always manage to elect at least a few representatives. (Under a system of voting for individual candidates in territorial constituencies, such as that used in England, the tendency is for the parties to coalesce.) Moreover, the voter voted for a list of candidates put up by the party of his choice and chosen by the party executive. Thus the executive could discipline party members even after they had been elected to the Reichstag. Many governments fell from office because one or other of the parties withdrew all its deputies from a particular coalition.

The central government possessed effective powers, and federal laws had priority over laws passed by states or municipalities. Although the states were required to adopt proportional representation, they retained extensive powers over local affairs. The president of the republic was granted the right to suspend all constitutional guarantees in the event of a serious emergency. During this period he could rule by decree if no majority was obtainable in the Reichstag, and he was permitted to use the armed forces at his discretion. No doubt such powers had to be granted in the disturbed conditions following the war, but as events were to show they could be misused. President von Hindenburg attempted to rule almost entirely by decree in the later years of the depres-

---

* The first president, Friedrich Ebert, had been chosen by the constituent assembly.

sion, when no majority could be found for the deflationary measures considered necessary by his advisers.

Opposition to the Republic.   Unhappily for the Republic, the government never succeeded in winning the full support of large numbers of Germans. On the left the Communists and left-wing Socialists hoped and planned for a revolution which would lead to a "dictatorship of the proletariat," as in Russia. On the right were an assorted group of monarchists and numerous reactionaries who preferred an authoritarian state of the kind later set up by Hitler. The army remained extremely powerful. Its officer class was composed mostly of aristocrats who had little use for the plebeians that ruled in Berlin, and its loyalty to the government could never be fully counted on. Imperial traditions died slowly, and there can be little doubt that these men would have preferred the kind of state provided for Germany by Bismarck. Although few of the influential industrialists and military men would have favored the Nazi government that eventually took over if they could have foreseen it, their failure to give full support to the republic was largely instrumental in securing Hitler's eventual victory.

The first two efforts to change the government by force were engineered by army elements in March, 1920, one in Berlin and one in Bavaria. The army leaders strongly objected to the reduction of the army to 100,000 men, a provision of the Treaty of Versailles that had been accepted under duress. The reduction meant, for example, that the Free Corps (see p. 4) and the German army that had been operating in the Baltic countries since the Armistice (see p. 105) had to be disbanded. The military commandant in Berlin and the recently returned Baltic army commander engineered a coup on March 13, 1920, which was to put Dr. Wolfgang Kapp in charge of the government (hence the attempt is known as the Kapp *Putsch*). General von Seeckt, the chief of staff of the regular army (*Reichswehr*) refused to defend the government on the ground that he would not order German soldiers to fire on other German soldiers. President Ebert and the Cabinet were therefore forced to flee Berlin. But the Berlin workers, at the urging of the leaders of the Social Democratic party, organized a general strike which was so effective that the putschists fled in their turn.

However, the army, instead of being disciplined for this failure in its duty, was almost at once called upon to suppress Communist-inspired uprisings in the Ruhr, which it was far more willing to do. The rebels were very severely treated, and their leaders were killed, executed, or sentenced to long prison terms. Meanwhile in Bavaria a similar coup had succeeded. The local army chief compelled the Social Democratic government to resign and installed Gustav von Kahr, an impeccably right-wing monarchist, as Bavarian premier. Though he had held office for little over a year, Kahr was invited in 1923 to become state commissioner, with virtually dictatorial powers, during the Ruhr crisis and the inflation. It was from this position that he hoped, with the help of the army on the one side, and the gifted agitator, Adolf Hitler, on the other, to overthrow the Berlin government. However, this time General von Seeckt, now commander in chief of the Reichswehr, agreed to support the government. On September 23 President Ebert, acting under Article 48 of the Weimar Constitution, proclaimed a state of emergency and conferred upon von Seeckt full powers to defend the state.

The Beer-Hall Putsch (November 8–11, 1923). Adolf Hitler, who had risen to the rank of corporal during the war and earned the decoration, unusual for his rank, of Iron Cross, First Class, had settled in Munich, though he remained an Austrian citizen. In 1920 he founded the National Socialist German Workers' party. Postwar Munich was an ideal city for right-wing agitation. It contained former Free Corps men, who were often unemployed and almost always underemployed; dissidents of all kinds, including monarchists; and army detachments which were hardly more loyal to the Republic. Hitler and his party were generally looked upon with favor, and often subsidized by the army leaders, who thought that the "Storm Troopers," a private army of brown-shirted young men who acknowledged Hitler as their Fuehrer, or Leader, might some day be useful to them. One of the regular army officers, Captain Ernst Roehm, indeed took a leading part in organizing the private Nazi army.

When Gustav Stresemann formed a government in Berlin on August 12, 1923, backed by the members of the first Weimar Coalition (Social Democratic, Center, and Democratic parties), he decided to put an end to the passive resistance in the Ruhr, which was ruining the country (see p. 23). This decision was unpopular with the right wing, which was against making any concessions whatever to the invading French. Moreover, just at this moment the Communists made their attempt to take over

the Saxon and Thuringian governments (see p. 62). All therefore seemed perfect for the putsch being planned from Bavaria
by Gustav von Kahr; General von Lossow, head of the local army
detachments; and Adolf Hitler and Ernst Roehm, who were quite
willing to use their Storm Troopers to suppress Communists, Jews,
and other alleged enemies of Germany and the party. Unfortunately
for Hitler, the Communist governments were quickly turned out
by regular army units acting under orders from the central government. This had the result of persuading the Bavarian putschists
other than the Nazis that they should hold back for a future more
propitious occasion.

Hitler, bitterly disappointed, therefore attempted the putsch on
his own, beginning with a meeting in a beer hall in Munich. He
was helped by his Storm Troopers and by the war hero General
Erich Ludendorff, who had aided in the Kapp Putsch and was
now close to insanity. This, however, did not prevent him from
distinguishing himself by his military bearing when the forces of
law and order fired a volley on Hitler and his band. Hitler himself
fled from the scene. Both Hitler and Ludendorff were arrested
and brought to trial. By this time Hitler had recovered his aplomb,
and he turned the trial into something of a propaganda victory for
himself and his party. He was sentenced to five years in jail but
served only one, during which he wrote his major work, a blue-
print for his party entitled *Mein Kampf* ("My Struggle").

The Stresemann Era of "Fulfillment." Meanwhile, Stresemann's government, like so many of its predecessors, lasted only
a few months (August 12 to November 23, 1923), but he himself
remained as foreign minister in all the governments that followed
until his death in October, 1929. Even while he was still chancellor the first steps were taken to stabilize the mark, and it was
the new policy of fulfillment (payment of reparations, adherence
to the provisions of the Treaty of Versailles, collaboration in the
League of Nations with Germany's former enemies) that became
the policy of the subsequent governments (Wilhelm Marx, Center
party, November, 1923 to January, 1925; Hans Luther, January,
1925 to May, 1926; Wilhelm Marx, May, 1926 to June, 1928).
Reichstag elections were held in May, 1928, in which the Social
Democrats greatly increased their vote, enabling Hermann Müller,
a Social Democrat, to take over the government. Meanwhile President Ebert had died in February 1925. He was replaced by the
aged Field Marshal Paul von Hindenburg, who defeated Wilhelm

Marx by a relatively small plurality. (The Communist Ernst Thaelmann gained in this election over two million votes, which would have elected the more moderate Wilhelm Marx if they had been cast for him in the run-off.)

During the later 1920's Germany made what appeared to be a spectacular economic recovery. But it was based on the constant influx of American capital, which made possible the modernization of German industry and the payment of reparations, under both the Dawes and the Young Plans (see pp. 23–25). The modernization of industry enabled the country to improve its export position, but its exports were extremely vulnerable, since every country except Britain had high tariffs, and it was only a matter of time before Britain would be compelled to follow the other countries into economic nationalism. As it happened, Germany at once felt the pinch following the stock-market crash of late 1929, when American capital ceased to be available for Europe.

The Last Years of the Weimar Republic and the Rise of Hitler to Power. During the years of prosperity the Nazi party experienced relatively little growth. Even so it presented a list for the 1928 Reichstag elections and won twelve seats, one of which was filled by Hermann Goering, a former air force officer and early member of the party, who after taking part in the Beer-Hall Putsch, had escaped imprisonment by going into exile. It was the onset of the depression, with the consequent increase in unemployment that provided Hitler with his chance. Hitler's appeal was primarily to the lower middle class rather than the workers. This class, which had seen its savings wiped out in the inflation, now felt it had little to lose. When the febrile prosperity came to an end, it was inclined to blame everyone connected with the Republic, especially the Jews, who were constant targets of Hitler and his leading propagandist, Joseph Goebbels. Hitler's promises, which were never very specific, likewise appealed to members of this class. Some German industrialists also began to back him with money, in part because they approved of his rabid nationalism and anti-Semitism, and in part because they feared the Communists among their employees.

The Müller government fell in March, 1930, mainly over the question of increased insurance payments to the unemployed, which the more financially orthodox members of the government coalition would not accept. But it did not seem possible for any alternative coalition to be put together which would be capable of winning a Reichstag majority. However, President Hindenburg, acting on the advice of General Kurt von Schleicher, who was one of his intimates, chose Dr. Heinrich Bruening of the Center party as chancellor, with the intention of using his emergency powers in case Bruening found it impossible to gain a majority in the Reichstag. Bruening and the presidential coterie proposed to master the depression by means of a rigid deflationary policy, including severe governmental economy and no concessions to the unemployed. In due course the Reichstag rejected Bruening's budget, whereupon the President put it into effect by decree. When the Reichstag objected, it was dissolved and new elections held.

This time the National Socialist (Nazi) party gained 6,500,000 votes and 107 seats in the Reichstag, thus becoming the second largest party. This victory was achieved with the aid of two private armies, the brown-shirted Storm Troopers (SA) and the black-shirted Schutzstaffel (SS), and a party organization that had been thoroughly overhauled in the last few years. Although the Social Democratic party was still the largest in the Reichstag, the Communist party also increased its vote, winning 77 seats.

After the 1930 elections, the Bruening government was faced with strong opposition from both the extreme right and the extreme left. As a result of the increasing disorderliness of Hitler's private armies and the Communist gangs, the Social Democrats for the first time recognized that the republican government was in danger. They joined the more moderate parties to provide Bruening with his needed majorities for most of his period of rule, though the President had to come to his aid also, with his decrees. But the Bruening policy for dealing with the depression was unsuccessful. By 1932 unemployment had risen to six million, not including the underemployed and those who did not register for work. A customs union with Austria arranged by Bruening was vetoed by France (it was in fact forbidden by the peace treaties). In 1931 the Credit Anstalt, the largest bank in Austria, failed, bringing down with it several important German banks. In early 1932 a presidential election was necessary. Hitler and the Communist leader Thaelmann stood against Hindenburg, who won by a relatively small plurality, Hitler gaining over eleven million votes. In April, 1932, Bruening at last suppressed Hitler's two private armies, but at the end of the following month Hindenburg refused to support him any longer. Bruening had also lost the confidence of the army, in part because of a plan he had put forward to divide some of the East Prussian Junker estates and settle some of the unemployed on them.

Another idea had been put into the President's mind by General von Schleicher. Since not even Bruening could command a majority in the Reichstag, President Hindenburg might as well have a cabinet to his liking and simply rule by decree until the emergency was over. Schleicher suggested a professional diplomat, Franz von Papen, to the President, who duly appointed him chancellor although he was not known to have any support in the Reichstag and was only nominally a member of the Center party.

Schleicher had obtained Hitler's promise not to oppose the new chancellor. Hitler, however, had calculated, quite correctly, that the Reichstag, feeling insulted by having a chancellor thrust upon it in this way, would make life difficult for Papen. When this result occurred, Papen requested the dissolution of the Reichstag, and new elections were held. This time the Nazi party became far the largest in the Reichstag, winning 230 seats to the Social Democrats' 133, and the Communists' 89. Papen now lifted the ban on the SA, and the smaller elite bodyguard, the SS and attempted to come to terms with Hitler, while the SA fomented disorders at will and consistently picked street fights with the Communists, who retorted in kind. The Nazis were particularly violent in the large state of Prussia, whose Social Democratic government was ousted by presidential decree on the ground that it could not maintain law and order. Papen took over the position of Reich Commissioner in Prussia himself (July 20, 1932).

Hitler of course desired to become chancellor, but on his own terms. For the last year before he became chancellor, he could have entered into deals with Papen or Schleicher and won the vice-chancellorship for himself and cabinet posts for his followers. But though he had now the largest number of seats held by any party during the entire Weimar Republic, he was still far from having an over-all majority, and at most the small Nationalist party led by an industrialist named Hugenberg, might consent to join him. If therefore he had been made chancellor, he might well have needed presidential decrees also to enable him to rule. It should be emphasized that Hitler, unlike many of his followers, wished to take power only by legal means. He continued to respect the army, and knew that his SA would be no match for the Reichswehr, in spite of the fact that the latter included numerous Nazi sympathizers, especially among the junior officers.

After the elections Hermann Goering became president of the Reichstag (Hitler as an Austrian could not sit in it). At its first meeting Papen was ready to try his luck again in new elections, which cost him nothing but were extremely expensive for the Nazis, whose treasury was by this time almost empty. A Communist deputy, however, was recognized by Goering and allowed to put his motion of no confidence in the government. The motion was passed by 512 to 42. Only when it had been counted was the Chancellor recognized and the President's decree of dissolution accepted. Nevertheless, it was no victory for the Nazis, who recognized how unprepared they were to fight another election. In fact they lost two million votes, and though they still formed the largest party, they had now only 196 seats. But it was quite clear that Papen could never win over enough deputies to rule through the Reichstag. He was totally dependent on the President.

At this point General von Schleicher came to the conclusion that he himself might be able to succeed where Papen had failed. As minister of defense in Papen's cabinet he informed the President that if he kept Papen in power through decrees, there would probably be civil war and he could not guarantee the army's loyalty. Faced with this threat, President Hindenburg accepted Papen's resignation and invested Schleicher with the chancellorship.

But the General was unable to persuade Hitler to agree to reasonable terms. In spite of considerable opposition within his own party, Hitler demanded the chancellorship, several leading ministries, and an assurance that the President would issue decrees to enable him to rule if he lacked the necessary majority. Papen, however, felt that he had been double-crossed by his minister of defense and thought that he himself could make arrangements with Hitler just as well as Schleicher could. He therefore began negotiations. He was in a position to use his influence with the aged President; he had influence with industrialists who could pay off the Nazi debts; and it was not essential for him to have the chancellorship. Although the negotiations were long and intricate, the result was that Hitler agreed to content himself with the chancellorship and two minor ministries for his party, leaving Papen as vice-chancellor and the ministers of defense and foreign affairs, in which Hitler was less interested, as nominees of the President. At the last minute Hugenberg agreed to join the coalition in exchange for two ministries for himself and his party. Hindenburg was finally satisfied; Schleicher gave up his efforts and resigned; and Hitler became chancellor of Germany on January 30, 1933, thus beginning the age of the Third Reich.

THE THIRD REICH

When Hitler became chancellor he did not appear to be in a very strong position. It was Papen, not he, who was head of the Prussian government; he did not control the army; his defense minister had been chosen for him by the President. Only two Nazis beside Hitler were in the Cabinet, one of them Goering, who was a minister without portfolio. The other was Wilhelm Frick, who held the position, hitherto not very important, of minister of the interior; he did not control the German police forces, which were under the various states. Nevertheless, Hitler used such forces as he had with efficiency and complete ruthlessness to establish himself as an undisputed dictator within a few months.

Establishment of the Dictatorship. The key to Hitler's rise to absolute power was the Prussian ministry of the interior, which Goering now headed. Goering, though nominally subject to the authority of the minister-president of Prussia, Franz von Papen, paid no attention to his superior. He succeeded in enforcing his absolute control over the Prussian police, and moreover he enrolled as many of the SA as he needed as auxiliary police. Soon afterward he founded the Prussian secret police, the notorious Gestapo. Armed with his police powers, Goering began to raid the offices of the Communist party, using appropriated documents to support his charge that the Communists intended to overthrow the government. On February 27, 1933, the Reichstag building in Berlin was set on fire, almost certainly with Goering's connivance, and a conveniently planted Communist arsonist was found at the site. President Hindenburg was then prevailed upon to sign a decree declaring a national emergency, which gave Hitler the police powers he needed in the rest of Germany.

Meanwhile Hitler had been performing the solemn farce of negotiating with his opponents in the Reichstag for the purpose of winning over a majority for his policies, as he had promised Hindenburg. He made sure that the negotiations would fail and then went to the President to request a dissolution of the Reichstag and new elections—which this time he proposed to win with all the force of the state behind his campaign. He also used some not very subtle blackmail to win contributions to the campaign from a number of leading industrialists. The election was marked by violence, as expected, but the police conveniently looked the other way when the SA toughs beat up their opponents. Even so the Nazis increased their vote by only 5,500,000 in much the largest poll held in Germany up to this time. Thus, at least in theory, the Nazis still needed the support of Hugenberg's Nationalist party.

However, Hitler was waiting for the right moment to exclude all the Communist deputies, whom he had permitted to take part in the election in order to keep the left-wing vote divided. Without the Communists he would not need Hugenberg's support, since the 288 Nazi deputies would then be a majority of the whole membership. But, true to his policy of acting within the law, he proposed to rule by means of an Enabling Act, permitting him to rule by decree for four years, which would make unnecessary further use of the Reichstag. This was a constitutional change, however, and would require a two-thirds majority of the Reichstag. So, for the moment, Hitler showed himself conciliatory. To President Hindenburg, he promised that he would not use the powers without consulting him, and to members of the other parties remaining in the Reichstag, he made many more promises, which he had no inteniton of keeping. When the Reichstag met in the Kroll Opera House, the SA toughs were naturally outside demanding passage of the bill. The result was the passage of the Enabling Bill by 441 votes to 94, the latter all Social Democrats, since most of the Communist leaders were already in jail and the remainder were excluded from the assembly. Hitler was now a legally appointed dictator, and only the President had the reserve powers to overthrow him. But Hindenburg was now eighty-six years old and a sick man—and the only alternative to Nazi rule even if he had used his reserve powers would have been rule by the army which would have meant a civil war.

The Policy of "Co-ordination" (*Gleichschaltung*).   The policy now put into effect by Hitler was the subordination of everything in the German state to his will and the will of the party he controlled. This required the conversion of the federal state into a unified national state with an all-powerful central government; the suppression of alternative centers of power and loyalty; the subversion of the independent law courts; the subjection of the churches; and, lastly, the exclusion of Jews from participation in national life and the enthronement of racism as a substitute religion.

Little difficulty was experienced with the states. Hitler, by virtue of his authority under the Enabling Act, merely sent party members into the various states to take over their governments. When the local governments appealed to the military to protect them, the military requested instructions from Berlin and were told by the defense minister that they were not to interfere in domestic politics. Hitler then sent in Reich governors with power to promulgate state laws as necessary. He himself assumed the title of Reichgovernor for Prussia and delegated his powers to Goering.

The political parties gave Hitler no more trouble. The Social Democratic party was declared to be a subversive organization, "an enemy of state and people"; its leaders were arrested and the party dissolved. Most of the other parties dissolved themselves in preference to waiting for the axe to fall. Even Hugenberg, Hitler's former ally, was forced to dissolve his party, after a futile appeal to President Hindenburg. On July 14, 1933, the National Socialist German Workers' Party was proclaimed the only party permitted.

The Labor Unions were "co-ordinated" into a German Labor Front, and a number of "Labor Trustees" were appointed with instructions to settle working conditions throughout the country. Collective bargaining was abolished and strikes forbidden. The Nazi dictatorship was hence more favorable, at least for a period, to employers than to workers. Hitler proposed to use the industrialists for his programs, especially for rearmament, and therefore to control rather than dispossess them. But he did fulfill some of his promises to the workers, in that he greatly reduced the number of unemployed, at first through public works programs, and later through rearmament. However, he performed no economic miracle, since the surplus workers were often to be found in labor camps earning bare subsistence wages. Moreover the ill-famed concentration camps for political opponents and Jews were already in existence before the end of 1933, and their inmates were not counted among the "unemployed." Nor were Jews outside the camps, who were systematically excluded from national life, and their jobs given whenever possible to "Aryans." The famed Prussian civil service was purged until its remnants could be regarded as totally subservient to the regime.

Hitler attempted to form a national church, under a "national bishop." This German Evangelical Church, directed by Bishop

Ludwig Müller, was never noticeably successful. Numerous Protestant pastors refused to take part in it, preferring to set up a German Confessional Church, which led a difficult existence for a few years. In September, 1935, the Protestant Church was placed fully under state control with a minister for church affairs. On July 20, 1933, Hitler signed a concordat with the papacy, in which it was agreed that the Catholic clergy should keep out of politics. Although Catholic schools continued, the Nazi youth groups and the state schools which recruited them had the full support of Hitler and the party, with which it was difficult for Catholics to compete. Pope Pius XI in 1937 bitterly denounced the Nazi religious policies, but this attack had little effect except to fortify those Catholics who tried to resist. The all-pervasive paganism of the National Socialist order was so inimical to all religious life that many leaders, both Catholic and Protestant, had little option but to oppose it, and a number, including the famous Protestant pastor Martin Niemöller, suffered imprisonment or worse as a result.

The German legal system was quickly subverted by the Nazis, especially after the trial of several Communists for their supposed part in the Reichstag fire. Three of four defendants were acquitted by the judges, thereby infuriating Hitler. According to the Nazis, National Socialist justice was now to take the place of traditional justice. A People's Court was set up to try persons accused of treason, and recalcitrant judges were replaced. Defense attorneys had to be approved by the Nazis, and Nazi leaders were permitted both to take further action if the courts handed down decisions of which they did not approve and to dismiss cases on their own initiative. However, by far the greatest perversion of justice was the arrest, torture, and punishment of opponents directly by the security services of the state, the SS and the Gestapo. These two secret police forces, co-ordinated under the command of Heinrich Himmler in April, 1934, played the leading part in the liquidation of dissidents within the Nazi party itself.

The Roehm Purge and the End of the SA.   By the time he had been a year in power, Hitler had succeeded in subjecting the state to his own will. But the army remained powerful, and was still under the command of the President. Both the President and the army disapproved of the continued presence and activity of the SA, which had been so valuable in bringing Hitler to power, but had no longer any real reason for existence. Moreover the SA was not at all happy with the right-wing tendencies of the Nazi government. Many of its leaders, indeed, were revolutionary socialists, and took seriously the word "Socialist" in the name of the party. Its head, Ernst Roehm, was a man of dissolute character, with many enemies. Notable among these were Goering and Himmler, the latter because his SS was still officially a part of the SA, and he wished to have undisputed command of the SS. The SA by mid-1934 was far larger than the Reichswehr, though it lacked the specialized training of the regular forces. Roehm was of the opinion that it should supersede the Reichswehr and continue the revolution that had been barely begun. He had little use for the conservative Reichswehr leaders or for Hindenburg.

The problem of the SA was a serious one for Hitler. He still needed the support of the Reichswehr, in particular if he wished to succeed Hindenburg, who could not live much longer. But if he dissolved the SA, he might well put himself at the mercy of the army leaders, including his own minister of defense. He decided to take the risk, and win the support of the army, in the expectation, which proved well founded, that after Hindenburg's death he could mold it to his liking. Goering and Himmler were therefore given their head, and they planned a purge with great care. The SS under Himmler suddenly struck at the SA leaders and, for good measure, other political figures, such as General von Schleicher, who might be dangerous, and who were accused of planning a conspiracy to overthrow the government. Roehm, Strasser (a former Hitler lieutenant in the party), Schleicher and his wife, and a few dozen others were murdered on June 30, 1934. The bargain between Hitler and the Reichswehr was faithfully kept. A part of the SA was enrolled in the army, and the remainder disbanded. Hindenburg died on August 2, and the army made no objection when Hitler assumed the title of Reichsfuehrer and commander in chief, an assumption of supreme power soon afterward confirmed in a plebiscite. The office of president was therefore abolished.

Hitler's Foreign Policy. In the next years Hitler turned his attention to foreign policy, and the fulfilling of his promise to tear up the Treaty of Versailles. This policy and the relations of Germany with the rest of the world will be dealt with in Chapter 11, which is devoted to the coming of World War II, primarily as the result of Hitler's actions. For the building of the new German army it was necessary to subordinate the German economy exclusively to the needs of the state. The economic policy of Dr. Hjalmar Schacht by which the Germans purchased the surplus goods of the other depression-ridden countries of Europe in exchange for marks, which could be cashed only by the purchase of German-produced goods, was brilliantly successful. These countries, which formally became creditors of Germany, were nevertheless unable to free themselves from German economic domination. If they refused to sell more goods, Germany would withhold payment for the goods sold to her previously. The blocked marks accepted in payment were worthless unless Germany unblocked them. Later in the 1930's a Four-Year Plan was proclaimed to make Germany self-sufficient and enable the rearmament program ("guns instead of butter") to be carried out. This involved the extensive use of *ersatz* (substitute) materials produced by the German chemical industry from materials available in Germany that could not be purchased abroad for lack of foreign currency. Schacht, who deeply disapproved of the rearmament policy, protested to Hitler, and was thereupon dismissed from his position as head of the German Reichsbank (January, 1939).

Although the cost was immense, Hitler was able to rearm Germany and to introduce conscription forbidden by the Treaty of Versailles; and by threat of its use he won a string of diplomatic victories in Europe. The cheap victories, however, came to an end in 1938 with the Munich Pact. In September, 1939, Hitler used the army to make his first conquests. But this was the beginning of the road that led to defeat in 1945 and his own suicide. The Third Reich that he had prophesied would last for a thousand years endured for a little over twelve.

MUSSOLINI'S ITALY

Like Hitler, Benito Mussolini rose to power by legal means with the aid of conservatives who preferred a strong-man government to the weakness of the multiparty democratic system. The Italian king, Victor Emmanuel III, however, unlike Hindenburg, was not unfavorably disposed toward his prime minister, whom he appointed long before he had converted any sizeable number of Italians to his viewpoint. It was, indeed, partly the support of the King that enabled Mussolini to triumph over his opponents and become a full-fledged dictator. Hitler always acknowledged Mussolini as his own model, and until 1938 was inclined to defer to him as his mentor, publicly stating that he was the greatest living world leader. Only in 1938 did he allocate that position to himself.

Weakness of Italian Democracy in the Postwar Years. The Italians had fought bravely, if without success, during the war, and incurred casualties of over half a million men. Since Italy could have remained neutral and perhaps won hardly less in the peace treaties than she did by fighting, there was a widespread sense of grievance in the country when she was given neither Fiume (see p. 6) nor any former German colonies—even though she did receive the Trentino and South Tyrol from her old nineteenth-century enemy Austria. Many Italian statesmen who were in office at the end of the war had opposed the Italian entry, and they were not particularly sympathetic to the returning Italian servicemen, most of whom found themselves unemployed and many without means of subsistence. Such men attached themselves to adventurers like D'Annunzio, or to Mussolini and his *Fasci,* groups of militant ex-soldiers who wore black shirts and engaged in various acts of violence and intimidation, sometimes paid by the industrialists to break up unions and prevent strikes. Others became sheer brigands.

Obviously it was necessary for any government to take strong action to solve these problems. But no government so inclined was found in the immediate postwar years, and the old Liberal party which held office for much of the time believed solely in laissez faire. Proportional representation, introduced in 1919, meant that there were many parties (as was the case in Germany), and all governments had to be coalitions. As in Germany, the Socialists were the most numerous, but the party divided several times, and the extreme left wing became the Italian Communist party early in 1921. The right wing and other splinter groups still calling themselves Socialists refused to collaborate with non-Socialist parties, thus compelling the latter to form all the governments, even though they seldom commanded secure majorities in the Chamber of Deputies.

In elections held in November, 1919, the Socialists won 160 seats, against the Catholic Popular party's 103, the Liberal party's 93, and the Radical party's 58. A Socialist-Popular party coalition would have brought some stability, but the Socialists refused to join. None of the other parties were cohesive and disciplined bodies, and the resulting coalitions could and did fall apart in the face of any emergency. Moreover, no government believed in taking any strong action to support the economy, to fight the growing inflation, or to establish a program for the unemployed. The governments did not even take consistent action to deal with brigandage, or act against disturbers of the peace, including Fascists and Communists; nor was there for more than a year any serious effort to discipline D'Annunzio, who had captured Fiume with his army of volunteers. It was not surprising therefore that many employers and other influential persons began to favor the substitution of a strong-man government. Though Mussolini himself was not the kind of man who would ordinarily have inspired their confidence, he and his *Fasci* had often proved useful in putting down Communist-inspired labor disputes. There can be little doubt that many of these men contributed financially to Mussolini, not expecting that he would ever be in a position to take over the government.

Rise of Mussolini to Power—The "March on Rome." Benito Mussolini was the son of a blacksmith, a convinced Marxian socialist who had suffered for his opinions. Mussolini, himself, however, was never a convinced socialist, though he edited the Socialist paper *Avanti!* successfully for some years. He was throughout his life an opportunist, and the Fascist movement that he founded lacked even the political philosophy of the Nazi movement in Germany, such as it was. During the war Mussolini, like other Socialists, at first opposed Italian participation. When he suddenly changed his mind, he was dismissed from his editorship and expelled from the Socialist party. He then founded *Il Popolo d'Italia,* which was to become the house organ of the Fascist party. Soon afterwards he enlisted, and he served throughout the rest of the war, rising to the rank of corporal.

On March 23, 1919, Mussolini founded his *Fasci di combattimento,* which he insisted did not constitute a party (the National Fascist party was formally organized in November, 1921), though they had a generally agreed program. The separate groups were more or less autonomous, though owing a vague allegiance to Mussolini. The Fasci (usually called Fascists) were stridently nationalistic, and took every opportunity to exalt the use of force. For the rest, their stated program was vaguely socialistic and syndicalistic. The Fascists fought the elections of November, 1919, but failed to win more than five thousand votes even in Mussolini's headquarters of Milan, and did not gain a single seat in the Chamber of Deputies. Nevertheless, the movement survived, in spite of ridicule, since the Fasci throughout the country were found useful by their paymasters in industry. They also managed to acquire arms for their armed bands, known as *squadristi,* through the connivance of sympathetic army officers.

In May, 1921, new elections were held, for the first time under universal suffrage, and this time the aged Liberal leader, Giovanni Giolitti, offered to make a deal with the Fascists for their electoral support. Mussolini accepted, and with thirty-four other Fascists was duly elected to the Chamber of Deputies. He at once began to use his new position (and his parliamentary immunity) to propagandize for his party and to demand that he be entrusted with absolute power in the state, though he was no clearer than before on what he proposed to do with it. During the following year, Fascists bands became steadily more aggressive and even seized control by force of the city governments of Milan and Bologna. A general strike called by the Socialists was broken with the aid of the *squadristi,* thus giving Mussolini and his propagandists the excuse for claiming that they had prevented the "Communists" from taking over the state.

In part the intention of the Fascists may well have been to provoke the government, now led by Luigi Facta, into taking action against them. It was a matter of common knowledge that King Victor Emmanuel III had lost confidence in the democratic politicians, even though economic conditions by 1922 were slowly improving. The Fascists formed their loosely organized bands into an official armed militia early in October, 1922, confident that the King would never give Facta power to suppress them.

The next step planned by a ruling group of four within the party (Mussolini, Dino Grandi, General de Bono, and Michele Bianchi) was a "march on Rome." This was carried out late in October, 1922, by a number of Fascists—using conventional transportation —not including Mussolini himself, who waited in Milan until he received the news that the King would receive him. King Victor Emmanuel refused Facta's belated request for martial law, probably in the belief that the army could not be relied upon to suppress the Fascists; then after first attempting to persuade Mussolini to join a coalition government of the right wing, the King invited him to form a government on the understanding that it would be a coalition. Mussolini accepted and formed a true coalition government, retaining for himself the ministry of foreign affairs and the ministry of the interior. Only three other Fascist members formed part of the cabinet, the remaining nine being drawn from all parties.

The Establishment of the Dictatorship.   At this time Mussolini was still not very well known in Italy. Even his *squadristi* were active only in a relatively few areas of the country, and he himself as editor of *Il Popolo d'Italia* was known mainly to its readers. Without any apparent administrative talent—his major talents were his oratory, florid but effective, and his acting ability—he always relied on others for both his ideas and his governmental policies. At this stage, when (at 39), he was the youngest prime minister in Italian history, he decided to go slowly, and as a result he won much support even in the most unlikely quarters. Though granted full powers for a year to legislate by decree, he used them, on the whole, with moderation to restore law and order and, symbolically, to "make the trains run on time." He received useful advice from a Fascist Grand Council under his domination, which met in secret and generally bypassed his official cabinet. He gradually subordinated other elements in the state to the rule of the Grand Council. Throughout Italy local leaders came to be appointed by him, and over the next years municipal elected councils were replaced by Fascist *podestas* (mayors) who carried out policies determined by the Fascist leaders. The young people were organized into Fascist youth groups. The Fascist militia was legalized by authorization of the King and became thus a private army paid by the state but altogether at the disposal of Mussolini.

When the one-year Enabling Act was about to expire, a Fascist deputy, in the supposed interests of stable government, proposed that in the next elections the party receiving the greatest number of votes should be granted two-thirds of the seats. Opposition deputies refused to take part in the vote in the Chamber on this bill, with the result that it passed without difficulty. As it turned out, the arrangement was unnecessary. With all the prestige of the government at their disposal, and with the aid of widespread intimidation which the police could not or would not suppress, the Fascists won over 65 per cent of the votes on their own account. A courageous Socialist deputy, Giacomo Matteotti, who had written a book exposing Fascist methods, severely criticized the government for permitting the violence in the elections and challenged their legality. Such insolence infuriated Mussolini. Soon afterward the deputy was found murdered in mysterious circumstances.

The murder, and the revelations that followed, caused a revulsion of feeling in the country, and Mussolini, who in spite of the bold front he presented to the world was in reality a timid man, was for a time shaken and even thought of resigning. The press openly blamed the murder on Mussolini's provocative speeches, and it was obvious that several leading Fascists, if not II Duce ("The Leader") himself, as he liked to be called, were implicated. To quiet the clamor Mussolini sacrificed his police chief, and himself gave up his post as minister of the interior. However, when the outcry began to die down he recovered his fortitude; and soon afterward he began to convert his hitherto constitutional, if violent, rule into a dictatorship. A secret police (OVRA) was organized, and special courts were set up to deal with political offenders; the press, which had played such a prominent part in exposing the Matteotti affair, was now effectively muzzled. The non-Fascist members of the Cabinet were dismissed, while conditions in the Chamber were made so intolerable for opposition members that they ceased to attend. Soon afterward strikes and lockouts in industry were forbidden and the working day was lengthened. In 1928 universal suffrage was abolished and a propertied franchise introduced. But even this was unimportant, since the candidates were put forward by the workers' and employers' syndicates, and from these the Fascist Grand Council chose four hundred, whose names were then submitted to the reduced electorate for its approval. Since the Fascist Grand Council was at all times controlled by Mussolini until his final fall in 1943, Italy became a dictatorship and remained one for the remainder of Mussolini's rule.

Domestic Policy.   During the next years the Fascists had one major success. This was a treaty (Lateran Treaty) between Italy and the Papacy, and a concordat regulating relations between Church and State. These documents, signed on February 11, 1929, put an end to the virtual state of war that had existed between the Italian government and the Papacy since 1870, when Pope Pius IX had declared himself the "prisoner of the Vatican." Rome, as the capital of a united Italy, could obviously not be ruled by the pope as it had been in former centuries. Pius XI now accepted his actual position but became at the same time sovereign of a small state of just over 100 acres, thereafter known as Vatican City. The Italian government under the treaty agreed to pay the pope an indemnity of 750 million lire and a further billion lire in the form of government bonds as compensation to the Church for the loss of its property in 1870. Under the concordat Catholicism was recognized as the religion of the state, and the state agreed to pay the salaries of the clergy in exchange for the right to approve the papal choices. Monasteries were again permitted to function, and the state recognized the provisions of canon law regarding marriage. Thus divorce was forbidden in Italy except through a dispensation of the Church. Priests were permitted to give religious instruction in the schools.

There is no doubt that this long-overdue settlement redounded to the credit of the state, even though it was favorable also for the Church. On the whole the disputes between the Church and the Fascist state were minor. The arrangement worked well and is still in force in republican Italy. The treaties were ratified by enormous majorities in Parliament against only token opposition.

Other domestic achievements of the regime were few, and none were of lasting value. There were attempts to make Italy into a "corporative state," in line with Catholic social ideas. But in fact the corporative institutions, though magnified in Fascist propaganda to such an extent that they were regarded as genuine by foreigners, were little more than façades to conceal Fascist domination of Italian social and economic life. Workers and employers were organized into syndicates, which, in addition to putting forward their lists of candidates for the elections, were expected to negotiate wages for their respective industries. Since strikes and lockouts were forbidden, if agreement could not be achieved, the dispute was submitted to arbitration by a court appointed by the Fascist Grand Council. In 1929 a National Council of Corporation was created, with Mussolini himself at its head as minister of corporations. However, all that the Council and the other corporations did could have been accomplished without the façade. But the system created a number of jobs, mostly sinecures filled by the party faithful. In 1938 the old Chamber of Deputies was abolished, to be replaced by a Chamber of Fasces and Corporations. But the same people were chosen for the same not very useful positions, and the country continued to be dominated by the dictator and by his consultative Fascist Grand Council. Nevertheless, it is true that the disorder of pre-Mussolini days was in general replaced by a more orderly form of government and a far better disciplined industry. But it was the discipline of a police state, though never as oppressive as the dictatorship of Hitler in

Germany—in part because of the corruptibility of most Italian officials and in part because of their lack of zest for repression.

When the Great Depression struck Italy, the government had no original ideas for overcoming it. Mussolini had always had a taste for the grandiose, and a number of very visible, if not always useful, public works were carried out during his regime. These provided employment for a few. Like Hitler's, Mussolini's main contribution to the solution of the unemployment problem was the increasing of armaments, many of which were expended during the Abyssinian War of 1935–1936. Colonial development was encouraged by Fascist Italy, and many peasants settled in the colony of Libya, taken from Turkey just before World War I. Even the most usable parts of the arid Italian colonies in the Horn of Africa were to some degree settled by Italians. But the main reason that Italy weathered the depression better than Germany was that she was largely an agricultural country, not so dependent on exports. Also, Italian overseas emigrants, especially in America, sent back a constant stream of remittances to their families, which, however individually small, made a respectable total to offset the unfavorable visible balance of trade. During the years of the depression the Italian government, through the control of foreign transactions, assumed a virtual control of all large-scale finance and industry in the country.

Foreign Policy.   Mussolini always had an exaggerated notion of Italy's power in the world, and Fascist propaganda attempted to depict the Italians as heirs of the long-defunct Roman Empire. In the 1920's when Germany was still disarmed and the United States was playing little part in European affairs, Italy did indeed play a role disproportionate to her real power. But in the 1930's, when she became increasingly tied to German chariot wheels— as will be discussed in Chapter 11—her weaknesses became more evident. After attempting to protect Austria from German interference, she was forced to abandon her efforts because of her need for German support; and in the end she had to content herself with picking up what Germany left to her and expanding the Italian empire in East Africa. But this very effort made her all the more dependent on German friendship. Italian foreign policy in the 1930's led straight to involvement in the war on the German side and a share in her defeat.

Against these failures her immediate successes after World War I, her occupation of the Dodecanese Islands (including

Rhodes) until 1947, when she ceded them to Greece, and her virtual protectorate of the independent kingdom of Albania on the eastern Adriatic coast, were small compensations. It is possible that Italy hoped to be allowed to keep Corfu, occupied in July, 1923 (see p. 18). If so, she was disappointed, and the withdrawal from the island at the insistence of the British, in exchange for a monetary indemnity, was widely regarded as a diplomatic defeat for the new Fascist regime, since Mussolini had proclaimed his intention of keeping it.

CONCLUSION

By the time of Hitler's assumption of power in Germany, Italy had been a Fascist state for more than a decade. Although the country was never completely totalitarian, and some elements of freedom survived throughout the period of Mussolini's dictatorship, Italy was third after Soviet Russia and Hitler's Germany in the control exercised over political and economic life by the government. In the next chapters the lesser authoritarian states of Europe will be considered, including those that like Germany became totalitarian after a brief attempt at working a democratic system.

5

DICTATORSHIP, DEMOCRACY, AND CIVIL WAR IN THE IBERIAN PENINSULA

Both Spain and Portugal are today ruled by dictators who are now in their seventies, who survived World War II, and who have been in no danger of being overthrown since their first access to power. The Spanish dictator, General Francisco Franco, however, came to power only through a savage civil war; and his safe tenure of office since has been due at least in part to the prevailing desire in Spain never to undergo again a similar experience. On the other hand, Prime Minister Salazar of Portugal has probably ruled for much of his period of office with the general consent of his people.

THE END OF THE SPANISH MONARCHY

The Spanish Bourbons ruled from the beginning of the eighteenth century until 1931, with two breaks—a period of French rule during the Napoleonic era and a short-lived republic from 1868 to 1874. In 1876 Alphonso XII granted a constitution under which Spain was supposedly governed until 1923. In fact all governments were corrupt; the elections were invariably rigged; and power rested mostly in the hands of local landowners and military leaders. Much of the wealth of the country still remained in the hands of the Church despite state sequestration of Church lands in the nineteenth century.

Postwar Disorders. Since long before World War I (in which Spain remained neutral), there had been constant unrest in the country. In the northeast there was a strong Catalan separatist movement, looking toward, at a minimum, a federal structure with substantial autonomy for Catalonia. In this area, which had its own language and possessed the largest industrial center in

Spain, Barcelona, there were strong and violent workers' organizations, mostly syndicalist with a dominant tendency toward anarchism. Similar movements existed in all the Spanish urban centers, especially in the mining cities of the northwest. Throughout Spain, but particularly in Barcelona, the employers also organized into syndicates, with the main purpose of resisting all demands from the workers. Frequently they hired bands of armed ruffians (*pistoleros*) to assassinate workers' leaders, while the workers themselves, likewise armed, took reprisals. All that the governments could do was to send military men as "civil governors" armed with superior force, who invariably sided with the employers. Sometimes they proclaimed martial law; more often they simply arrested and shot the workers' leaders when they could find them. Most notorious of these governors was General Martínez Añido, who "legally" terrorized Barcelona for almost two years soon after the war. Needless to say, during these years, in spite of protests from Catalan deputies sitting in Madrid, there was little chance that the grievances of the Catalan separatists would receive any serious attention.

Elsewhere in the country the ancient social system prevailed. The peasants were mostly hired laborers, tenant farmers, or sharecroppers, all at the mercy of their employers or aristocratic landlords. Some 50,000 landlords owned over half the land in the country; neither they nor the Church paid any significant taxes. But the demands for agrarian reform fell on deaf ears. Although the war years had brought high prices and a considerable growth of industry, especially in Catalonia, almost none of these benefits filtered down to the urban workers or to the peasants. It is therefore not surprising that the Bolshevik Revolution of 1917 had a profound impression on members of both classes and awakened in them the hope that a similar revolution in Spain might some day dispossess the employers and landlords. Nevertheless, there was at this time no Communist movement in the country. The revolutionaries turned more toward anarcho-syndicalism, which was better suited to the marked individualism of the Spanish character. The anarcho-syndicalist labor union CNT was very fond of the general strike as a weapon, which it used with great frequency, though rarely with much success. This union was strong in Barcelona and in the countryside. Its rival union UGT was stronger in Castile. It was run by the Socialist party, which was

Marxist, but which until 1934 believed in a slow progression toward Socialism, without a revolution.

Dictatorship of General Primo de Rivera (1923–1930). In spite of the general distress at home, the royal government, and especially King Alphonso XIII himself, was deeply interested in Spanish colonial adventures in Morocco. Part of Morocco had fallen to Spain during the French expansion in North Africa. In 1921 Alphonso ordered an expedition against Abdel Krim, a Moroccan chief. Largely due to the feebleness and general lack of discipline of the army the expedition was a ghastly failure. A relatively small force of Moorish tribesmen ambushed a Spanish army of over 20,000 men and utterly destroyed it at the Battle of Anual (July 21, 1921). All the enlisted men were massacred and the officers held for ransom. The Cortes (parliament) established a commission of inquiry, and it was widely known that the King himself was at least as much responsible as anyone else. A week before the report was to be published, the new captain-general of Catalonia, General Primo de Rivera, proclaimed himself dictator, with the obvious connivance of the King, though the latter was diplomatically absent abroad at the time. Since Primo de Rivera had the support of the army, and few Spaniards had any use for the current civilian government, the coup was bloodless, and the General remained in power until his resignation on January 28, 1930.

After the anarchy of preceding years the dictator's rule was for some time acceptable to the various classes of Spain, and he was aided by the general economic improvement in Europe. With the help of the French, he quickly pacified Morocco, while never revealing the report on the Anual defeat, which would have proved embarrassing to the King. The long series of strikes was brought to an end by the introduction of compulsory arbitration of disputes. The General favored the Socialist UGT over the anarchist CNT and formally prohibited the latter. However, he could not in fact dissolve it, and it merely went underground. But his dependence on conservative elements—the army, the Church, and the landowners—prevented him from carrying out the greatly needed land reform, which would have blunted the appeal to the peasants of the anarcho-syndicalists. On the other side his censorship was severe, earning him the persistent opposition of the intellectuals, and he was vehemently opposed to Catalan aspirations, even going so far as to abolish the small amount of local government that existed in Catalonia. Once his major work had been accomplished in the early years of his dictatorship, he found he could rely on no one, and he proved quite unable to organize any party of his own which would have given him political support. So when he became seriously ill—he was always a diabetic —he just gave up and retired to France, where he died soon afterward.

By this time few important Spaniards had any use for the King himself. Nevertheless the King tried to rule through another general, Damaso Berenguer, a man without conspicious political talents. Although Alphonso continued to promise a return to constitutional government and the constitution of 1876, this was no longer acceptable to most Spanish intellectuals and workers. They would settle for nothing less than a republic. When the King finally did permit municipal elections, the few parties supporting the monarchy were overwhelmed by republican votes in all areas except where the landowners managed the elections. The army and civil guard were unwilling to support a new military dictatorship even if a leader had been available. So Alphonso, like Primo de Rivera, gave up and went into exile (April 14, 1931), though without formally abdicating, in case times should change and he should be invited back.

THE DEMOCRATIC REPUBLIC

In the five years before the outbreak of the Civil War it proved impossible for the republicans to unite sufficiently to administer the government effectively. In the first period (1931– 1933), a new republican constitution was written, but its opponents (though defeated in the Cortes) were not willing to abide by it or by the fundamental laws then passed. When they won the elections of 1933, they either refused to carry out or repealed the laws of their predecessors, thus making the subsequent revolution almost inevitable. When they in turn were repudiated by the electorate in 1936, they planned a military take-over, in the hope of creating a Spanish replica of the contemporary German and Italian governments. Left and right wings in the Cortes and in the country became polarized during the few months after the 1936 election, and neither side would support the feeble government that tried to mediate between them. In short, as early as 1931 the situation was a revolutionary one, and it was not possible for a moderate democratic republican government, however well intentioned, to legislate changes regarded as revolutionary by the most powerful classes, which had been accustomed for generations to having all governments rule with due attention to their needs, positions, and prejudices.

The Constitution of 1931. Immediately after the departure of Alphonso XIII, Alcala Zamora, a moderate Catholic republican, became president, and in June, 1931, elections were held for a constituent assembly. These elections were won overwhelmingly by the republican parties, leaving only a tiny minority of members who favored the return of the King. A very distinguished body of men, including many of the country's leading intellectuals, sat in the assembly. Although Spain is nominally Catholic, relatively few people were regular churchgoers; and as a consequence of the Spanish Church's history and its attitude toward the republic, a considerable majority of the deputies (and their constituents) were anticlerical. In spite of the nineteenth-century sequestration of Church lands by the state, many of the higher clergy were still extremely rich, as were the monasteries and convents. The salaries of the clergy were paid by the state in compensation for the lands that had been taken from them, but there was nothing to prevent donations from the faithful, which seldom trickled down to the poorer clergy.

The subject which fascinated the deputies was unfortunately the question of religion and the relation between Church and State. The lawyers and intellectuals who formed the bulk of the assembly had little knowledge of agriculture and did not recognize the urgency of agrarian reform. A great deal of time was therefore spent in discussing and voting on the religious provisions in the constitution, and the conservatives, including Zamora, fought almost all of them. Indeed Zamora resigned before the constitution writing had been completed, in protest against the clause separating Church and State. The same Article 26 provided for the secularization of education and the nationalization of the remaining Church property. Later laws decreed the dissolution of the Jesuit Order and the abolition of Church schools. The attempt to abolish state salaries for the clergy, though strongly pushed by the anticlericals, failed in 1931. (The bill was passed later by the Azaña government.)

For the rest, the constitution was a liberal one, but with a peculiar electoral law intended to avoid the difficulties of a multiparty system. The law, in effect, favored those parties which entered into an electoral combination, giving them as a rule more seats than those which fought the election as separate parties. This law was to prove of great importance in the first elections held under the constitution (in 1933). The Socialist and Republican parties did not form an alliance, whereas the right-wing parties did. Although the former actually won more votes, the latter won more seats and were able to prevent any Socialist-Republican coalition from holding office.

The constituent assembly (which after all had been chosen in a free election only six months previously) continued in office after the adoption of the constitution in December, 1931. Zamora was persuaded to accept the new constitution, and was elected president of the republic. The Left Republican Manuel Azaña became prime minister.

The Azaña Administration, 1931–1933.   The Cortes continued to debate the measures to be taken in the direction of agrarian reform, on which no two parties were in accord. The Socialists, who had agreed to take part in the government, desired to establish collective farms, which might have been a solution to the agricultural problem in the large estates of Castile and Andalusia, where the Socialists had much of their strength. Republicans preferred to expropriate the land and give it to the peasants, irrespective of whether or not they were in a position to work it. The anarcho-syndicalists did not wholly approve of either plan, and in any case objected on principle to a bourgeois government and criticized the Socialists severely for co-operating with it. Indeed the anarcho-syndicalists, freed from the restraints imposed under the dictatorship, continued to foment strikes and attacked the new republican government at least as violently as it had the immediate postwar governments. By such actions they compelled the Azaña government to engage in severe repressions which were supported by the right wing but opposed by the Socialists. In 1932 a compromise statute was passed, which applied only in the center and south of the country. Regional committees were to decide on how the expropriated land was to be used—thus in effect continuing the dispute that had split the government parties since the founding of the republic. Little land was actually distributed before the fall of the government in 1933.

In these circumstances the revolutionary sentiments of the peasants were aroused, and they lost all confidence in the bourgeois government. When a group of Andalusian peasants seized their landlord's territories early in 1933, they were severely treated by the police, even though the land in question had been earmarked for expropriation. The incident, news of which was spread by the right-wing press in order to discredit the government, was probably an important factor in the loss of votes by the government parties in the next election. But the government did satisfy the Catalans by granting them virtually complete self-government, with the right to elect their own president. It promised a similar statute to the conservative and Catholic Basques but did not have time to implement the promise. The government resigned in September, 1933. By this time it was unpopular on all sides. Only four months before it had alienated the lower clergy by the Law of Associations, which abolished Church schools and state-paid clerical salaries. By concentrating on the controversial and not very urgent problem of the relation between Church and State and delaying interminably over agrarian reform, the government had lost most of its support on the left and had antagonized the right. Thus it was no great surprise when the right won the elections of November, 1933, even though—as noted earlier—it still did not command a majority of the popular vote.

Conservative Reaction, 1933–1936. The leading figure on the right was now José Maria Gil Robles, head of the largely Catholic CEDA. During the following years he incorporated into his speeches ever more Fascist and Nazi ideas and slogans. (There was a small, more definitely Fascist party already in Spain, which had been founded by the son of General Primo de Rivera.) Gil Robles made it clear enough from the beginning that he had no use for a democratic republic; but, being still young, he was willing to wait and try to gain power through elections. President Zamora, who could constitutionally choose his prime minister, always passed over Gil Robles, whom he distrusted. He preferred Alejandro Lerroux, a corrupt right-wing politician who headed the so-called Radical party. Lerroux governed with the aid of Gil Robles and his CEDA, as long as they would support him. His weak government, and the short-lived weak governments of his successors, passed no more social legislation. Moreover, they repealed or allowed to fall into disuse all the anticlerical and agrarian laws of their predecessors. Even so, Lerroux had great difficulty in weathering the depression, and his government fell late in 1935 when he proposed to increase the estate taxes from 1 per cent to

3½ per cent—a measure which lost him the support of CEDA.

In these circumstances it was not surprising that the left-wing parties became more revolutionary, especially when some peasants were made to restore the lands that had been expropriated and given to them by the Azaña government, while wages were cut and expenditures on education curtailed. In October, 1934, a series of revolutionary uprisings occurred. In Catalonia the autonomous government declared itself independent, but the movement quickly collapsed and the Catalonian president was arrested and condemned to a long term of imprisonment. (Later Gil Robles was to boast that he himself had provoked the rebellion at a time when the government was strong enough to repress it.) Catalonia then lost most of its autonomy. Another rising in Madrid at the same time collapsed almost as quickly. But a third rebellion in the Asturias was much more serious. Here the unions for once all united, and the Socialists, who had been reformist for fifty years, concluded that the time had come to take revolutionary action. The miners stormed a police barracks and took possession of Oviedo, the capital of the region. A committee of government was formed, made up of two Communists (who for the first time took part in such a movement), two anarcho-syndicalists, and four Socialists. Against these men the government sent both Foreign Legionaries from Morocco and actual Moorish troops in Spanish employ. They were despatched to the Asturias by General Francisco Franco, the military leader at the war office (against the vehement opposition of his brother Major Ramón Franco, a distinguished aviator).

The miners resisted for a few days before surrendering to superior force, losing over 3,000 dead and 7,000 wounded. The Foreign Legion butchered all the prisoners it took, and the Moors behaved with the utmost savagery. The reprisals, which went on for weeks, included tortures devised to obtain knowledge of the whereabouts of hidden arms. The Socialist leader Largo Caballero and the former prime minister Manuel Azaña were arrested and tried, but since no evidence could be found against them personally, they were acquitted.

The result of the repression, as might have been predicted in Spain, was an enormous increase in the popularity of the left-wing cause and loss of support for the right wing, which had brought Muslim mercenaries into the one part of Spain that had always remained Christian. The Basques, who saw their promised autonomy disappearing, became uncompromising enemies of the right wing, and later in the Civil War fought for the Republican side. But for the moment Gil Robles was triumphant. He was minister of war, from which position he was able to make preparations for a possible civil war in case he lost the next election. Numerous commands were shifted, and the less reliable republicans moved to where they could do little harm, while the more reliable right-wing military men were placed in key positions. When the Lerroux government finally fell late in 1935, no government could be found capable of obtaining a majority in the Cortes. After a few efforts the President, still refusing to appoint Gil Robles, dissolved it and called for new elections.

THE CIVIL WAR

When the elections were won by the left-wing parties, which this time organized into a Popular Front, the republic was doomed unless it could win the Civil War, for which it is now known the right wing had long been preparing. There is evidence also that Largo Caballero had come to the conclusion that the antirepublicans would not permit a Popular Front government to function, still less to carry out the reforms that had now become imperative to avoid revolution. The last months of the democratic republic were therefore filled with turmoil, and no effective government was possible. Until the outbreak of the Civil War, the government was headed by shadowy politicians who could not assert their authority against the militant right and left.

The Last Days of the Democratic Republic. Immediately after the election results were known, the caretaker government resigned, and President Zamora called upon Azaña to form a government. Although he did so, and ruled long enough to have an amnesty granted to the 15,000-odd political prisoners in the jails of the republic, he did not stay in power. The President was deposed by the Cortes on the grounds that he had exceeded his powers in calling for the recent election. This was clearly a pretext, since he had in fact had little option in the circumstances prevailing at the end of 1935. Azaña submitted his own name as Zamora's successor, presumably in the belief that as prime minister he was too moderate to be acceptable as a Popular Front leader and would find himself unable to control the parties to his left. These now included sixteen Communist deputies although the official strength of the entire party was only about three thousand. At all events

Azaña was elected president without opposition, and thereafter he attempted to keep the Socialists from power by choosing as prime ministers nonentities from the center. The Socialists themselves had meanwhile fissioned into two groups, the more important left-wing Marxists led by Largo Caballero, who refused to let his followers join any government except one under his control. The Communists supported this position, since they were primarily interested in increasing their membership and were not at all anxious to accept governmental responsibilities.

On the right, José Antonio de Rivera's Falange party, though represented in the Cortes only by himself, was extremely active in the streets, where Falange gangs fought with Socialists and Communists as Nazis had done in the last days of the Weimar Republic. The army officers formed a junta for the defense of the state, and were already conspiring with the Germans and Italians. Monarchist groups were in touch with Mussolini. The anarcho-syndicalists began to call strikes and burn churches, as was their wont, and fought their fellow leftists. The most important leader on the right was now no longer Gil Robles but Calvo Sotelo, a former finance minister returned from exile, who had some success in organizing all the antirepublican groups into a single whole, pledged to destroy the republic. It was the murder of Sotelo by some Socialists on July 13, 1936, that provided the spark for the long-prepared uprising by the army, which began in Morocco three days later. Immediately afterward the army garrisons in the cities joined in, and on July 18 Azaña authorized the distribution of arms to the people. The Civil War had begun.

Foreign Intervention and Nonintervention. The war, which lasted until the surrender of Madrid on March 28, 1939, cost about three-quarters of a million lives. Like so many civil wars it was fought with the utmost ferocity on both sides—though the Loyalists after the first few months made many attempts to temper it, and legal executions by the Loyalist government were few compared to those by Insurgents. The government forces (Loyalists) headed off the first attacks, in spite of the fact that by far the greater part of the regular army was on the side of the Insurgents, who were aided also by Moorish contingents and by the Foreign Legion. Important elements of the air force, small as it was, and the navy remained loyal to the government. But it was the mass uprising of the workers to defend the republic that enabled it to carry on the war as long as it did.

From the beginning Germany and Italy aided the Insurgents both with war material and with "volunteers." They could not possibly have won without this support since they never had a majority of the people on their side and did not control the major industrial centers. They set up their government under General Franco (General Sansurjo, the first Insurgent leader, was soon killed in an air crash) at Burgos, an old cathedral city in the north. Until the end they never controlled Barcelona or Madrid, though they captured Seville in Andalusia. The Germans aided most by sending planes and pilots, who thus gained invaluable experience. Their destruction of the defenseless Basque city of Guernica, an atrocity commemorated in Picasso's famous mural, was no doubt an example for the bombing of Rotterdam and numerous other cities in World War II.

Late in 1936 the Russians began to aid the Loyalists with arms and by organizing the International Brigades, which played the decisive role in the defense of Madrid. This support was maintained sporadically for two years, though never on the scale of the German and Italian aid. It was channeled not to the Loyalist government but to the Spanish Communists, who were thus enabled to play a part in the war far greater than their numbers would otherwise have warranted. Technical aid also came from Russia, especially in the technique of how to organize mass revolutionary armies—though curiously enough the Russian and Spanish Communists were not at all interested in making a revolution in Spain while the war was on. The Russians' avowed aim was to prevent a Fascist and Nazi take-over of Spain, and when they found this was likely to be beyond their means they withdrew their support. The Communists used Russian aid to control war strategy and to infiltrate and recruit members from all the revolutionary parties. The political commissars who arrived from Russia to help organize the defense, were able to overthrow the Socialist government of Largo Caballero and replace it with a more pliable regime under Juan Negrín, even though the latter was far from being a Communist himself. They infiltrated the government at all levels, and they persecuted political left-wing opponents such as the Trotskyite party (POUM), the anarcho-syndicalists, and the Socialists.

All this was made possible by the policy adopted by the Western democracies of "nonintervention," to which all the powers agreed. But neither the Germans, the Italians, nor the Russians made any attempt to abide by the agreement. They intervened as much as they wished, whereas Britain and France most of whose peoples were sympathetic to the Loyalists, refused to sell any war material to them. The Russians did not supply arms manufactured in the Soviet Union, of which there were, indeed, few to spare. The Spanish government sent the greater part of the Bank of Spain's gold reserve to Russia, who then proceeded to buy arms all over Europe (even from Britain and France) which they then sent to their own followers in Spain. Without the farce of nonintervention, therefore, the Communists would never have been able to win the control they did over the Loyalist government.

Victory of Franco. At no time during the war did it appear likely that the Loyalists would win. The initiative from beginning to end rested with the well-supplied Insurgents. When they were unable to take Madrid and they and their Italian allies were badly defeated by the International Brigades, they changed their strategy and began to mop up the rest of the country. First they attacked the Basques in the northwest, who had been granted substantial autonomy under their own president by the government and fought on the government side to preserve it. In June, 1937, the Insurgents captured the main Basque stronghold, the industrial city of Bilbao. Later in the same year they took the remainder of the northwest coast. The following year, the Insurgents were able to split Spain in two and at the end of it began the drive to Barcelona, which was captured on January 26, 1939.

It was now clear to all that there was no longer any hope of a Loyalist victory, and the British and French recognized the Franco government. In Madrid the Negrín government was deposed by the regular army, which hoped to obtain reasonable terms from Franco. However, the Spanish Communists in the city, who even after they had been deserted by Stalin continued to lead the fighting, refused to allow negotiations; and a brief struggle ensued with the remnants of the regular army led by General Miaja, the defender of Madrid in 1936–1937. When the Communists were finally subdued, Miaja found that Franco still demanded unconditional surrender, and this had to be accepted (March 28, 1939). Franco then proceeded to bring to trial all the Loyalist leaders who had been unable to escape over the border into France, and numerous executions followed. Once more Spain had a military dictatorship, which, under varying social and political forms, has persisted to the present.

PORTUGAL UNDER SALAZAR

After the overthrow of the Portuguese monarchy and the establishment of a republic in 1910, the government was extremely unstable. There were numerous small revolutions and over forty changes of cabinet in the sixteen years of the republic's existence. Church and State had been separated in 1911, but many Portuguese would not accept either this or the abolition of the monarchy and plotted to restore the pre-1910 situation. General strikes fomented by syndicalists were common. Portugal, unlike Spain, took part in World War I. But although the parliament voted for war against Germany in 1914, not until February, 1917, after the Germans had declared war on them, did the Portuguese send to France an expeditionary force, which was severely mauled. Late in 1917 a dictator (General Sidonio Paes) took over the country for a year, but the old regime was re-established after his assassination. The condition of the country became worse after the war, and the economy was close to bankruptcy when a military coup again succccded in overthrowing the government on May 28, 1926. A month later General Antonio Carmona made himself dictator. After crushing a democratic rebellion the following year, he had himself elected president in March, 1928, and appointed a professor of economics from the University of Coimbra finance minister, with the task of bringing order into the chaotic economic affairs of the state. This man was Antonio de Oliveira Salazar, who in 1932 became prime minister and in effect dictator, protected and kept in office by the army, with General Carmona still as president until his death in 1951.

This durable dictator eschewed the flamboyant manners of his fellow European dictators. He ruled with a minimum of force, although he permitted only one party and maintained a secret police (the PIDE) and a number of corporative institutions, which functioned more effectively than in Italy. The Church, though remaining separate from the State, was systematically favored, especially in education. The finances were quickly reformed; the budget was balanced; and the *escudo* became and remained one of the soundest currencies in the world. But there was little real social progress, even in lowering the illiteracy rate, which was the highest in Europe and well over 50 per cent when Salazar took office. During the Spanish Civil War Salazar made no attempt to hide his sympathy with the Insurgents, and no aid to the Loyalists made its way through his country, but he did not intervene openly. During World War II Portugal, though maintaining friendly relations with Germany and Italy, did not break relations with the Allies, with the result that the country became the leading center for espionage in Europe. For most of the period up to the war it is probable that Salazar had the support of his people, though there was never any opportunity for them to express their opinions freely—as there has not been even in the years since.

CONCLUSION

By the outbreak of World War II the Iberian Peninsula had therefore fallen into the hands of somewhat clerically minded but by no means entirely fascist regimes. In some respects they resembled Austria before her absorption into the Third Reich, which will be dealt with in the next chapter. Although neither country came under Nazi rule during the war, their neutrality could not have been relied on by the Allies if Hitler had come closer to winning the war than he did. General Franco sent troops to Russia to fight on the German side, and withdrew them when the Germans began to lose. However, he refused to allow German troops to pass through Spain on the way to Africa, in spite of a personal interview with Hitler in which the latter tried to persuade him to join the Axis. Thus after all the Iberian dictators helped the Allied cause in a negative way, and this is in part the reason for their survival in a postwar world which was not inclined to view such supposed anarchronisms favorably.

6 SUCCESSOR STATES OF THE HABSBURG AND TSARIST EMPIRES

With the exception of the new state of Czechoslovakia, all the successor states of Austria-Hungary and tsarist Russia became authoritarian regimes in the interwar period, although they retained some democratic forms. Austria was unable to build a viable economy; Hungary continued to be dominated by her landowning aristocracy. Of the Habsburg successor states, only Czechoslovakia, who had inherited many of the industrial areas of the old empire was able to build a prosperous economy, but she still could not solve the problem of her minorities. Among the tsarist successor states, Finland became both democratic and prosperous and maintained her independence, whereas the Baltic states were all reabsorbed into Russia after World War II. Poland, never a democracy except in name, was conquered by Germany at the beginning of World War II and re-entered the Russian sphere of influence after the war, though remaining an independent state. Yugoslavia and Rumania may also be considered in large measure Habsburg successor states, but since they are also Balkan countries, they will be considered in the next chapter.

AUSTRIA

The entire interwar period was dominated by the question of the union of small German-speaking Austria with the still large and powerful state of Germany. Before the signing of the peace treaties Austria regarded herself as part of the German Reich and even assumed the name of German Austria. But the Treaty of St. Germain forbade the union with Germany, forcing Austria to become a separate republic. In the course of the depression a customs union (*Anschluss*) between the two states was negotiated, but the opposition of France, backed by Czechoslovakia and Italy, prevented this, and subsequently the World Court by a vote of 8 to 7 declared that the customs union was contrary to the terms of the Treaty of St. Germain. When the National Socialists came to power in Germany, there was much sympathy for their aims among certain classes in Austria. But the governments of Engelbert Dollfuss and Kurt von Schuschnigg, though authoritarian and to some degree fascist in complexion, preferred the type of fascism developed in Italy to that of the Nazis in Germany, and as long as Italy adopted a foreign policy different from that of Germany, they looked to Mussolini for help against Hitler. When Mussolini abandoned Austria it was only a question of time before Austria was absorbed by her larger neighbor. The two countries were finally united under German domination, on March 13, 1938.

The Democratic Period, 1919–1933.   Immediately after World War I the Bolsheviks attempted to create a revolution in Austria, but without success. In Austria the Socialists were strongly entrenched and were anxious to establish a Socialist, but not a Communist, state. A provisional government made up of the German-speaking members of the former Austrian Reichsrat established itself immediately after the abdication of Emperor Charles (see p. 5) and held elections for a constituent assembly. The Social Democrats won the most seats, and a Social Democrat (Karl Renner) became chancellor. It was this first government that signed the Treaty of St. Germain, and, in part for this reason, the Social Democrats were never again able to form a government in Austria until after World War II. A new constitution came into operation on October 10, 1920, under which Austria became a federal state, whose provinces retained considerable powers. One of these provinces was the former imperial capital, Vienna, which was ruled for more than a decade by the Socialists, though from 1922 onward the central government was in the hands of the right-wing Christian Socialist party, which was supported by the Nationalists. The Christian Socialists were a clerical party influenced by the social ideas of the Catholic Church. They were strongly anti-Marxist, as were the Nationalists, who, indeed, were primarily interested in union with Germany and later merged with the Austrian National Socialist party. Since elections were by proportional representation, no party had an absolute parliamentary majority during the republic.

By 1922 the Austrian economy had collapsed for lack of industrial raw materials, which she could not pay for by exports, since they were seriously hampered by the tariffs of her possible customers. She therefore requested help from the League of Nations, through which an international loan was floated, but at the cost of a virtual receivership administered by a Dutch commissioner-general. The loan was constructively used, and the receivership was withdrawn in 1926. Thereafter Austria was able to survive from her own resources for the next few years. Then the Great Depression struck, and she was unable to weather it without further support. The leading bank in the county, the Credit-Anstalt, failed in 1931, starting the chain of events that made the depression world-wide.

From Dollfuss to the Anschluss.   In February, 1930, Austria signed a treaty of friendship with Italy. For some years thereafter she was greatly influenced by Italian Fascism, and her leaders established cordial relations with Mussolini. In the same year Prince Ernst von Starhemberg, who had once been a National Socialist in Germany and had taken part in Hitler's Beer-Hall Putsch (see p. 63), began to organize a fascist militia (the *Heimwehr*), which in succeeding years played a part in Austria similar to that of the *squadristi* in Italy. It was supported by Italian money and arms. The Social Democrats in their turn organized a *Schutzbund,* mainly for purposes of defense against the Heimwehr. In May, 1932, Engelbert Dollfuss, a Christian Socialist with fascist and authoritarian inclinations, became chancellor of Austria. He ruled for a year with the usual precarious parliamentary majority. During this period he averted economic chaos by obtaining another international loan from the Bank of International Settlements.

Then in January, 1933, Hitler became chancellor of Germany. Though greatly opposed to National Socialism of the German type, Dollfuss nevertheless evidently came to the conclusion that a clerical fascist rule was desirable in Austria, and he set himself to achieve this goal, with the aid of the Heimwehr. In March, 1933, he therefore suspended parliamentary government and began a drive against the Austrian Nazi party by forbidding the wearing of uniforms. Subsequently, he dissolved the party and formed a party of his own which he called the Fatherland Front. With the encouragement of Mussolini, who regarded himself as Austria's patron among the Great Powers and who was as yet strongly opposed to Hitler, Dollfuss next turned against the Social Democrats, who were his rivals for power and popularity. They had ruled in Vienna and several smaller Austrian cities ever since the war, using their power to tax the rich heavily for the benefit of the poor. They erected blocks of apartments for the manual workers which were unique in Europe, and they built major public works of different kinds. In February, 1934, the government police and the Heimwehr raided the Socialist headquarters in Vienna, thus provoking the Socialists into calling a general strike. The Heimwehr thereupon went into action, using artillery to destroy the Karl Marx Hof and other new housing developments, and ruthlessly suppressed all resistance. The Social Democratic leaders were arrested, and in April, 1934, a new constitution was handed down for Vienna, which deprived it of self-government.

After this triumph, which resulted in the permanent embitterment of the working classes against the clerical-fascist dictatorship, Dollfuss decided that it was time to consult Mussolini again. His family were already in Italy staying with Mussolini and expecting the Chancellor daily when the Nazis struck in an ill-prepared *putsch* in Vienna (July 25, 1934). Although the *putsch* failed, Chancellor Dollfuss was murdered, perhaps unintentionally. Mussolini immediately sent four divisions to the Brenner Pass on the Austrian border in case it should be Hitler's intention to invade the country. Probably Hitler had as yet no such intention. In any event he disowned the plot, and allowed Kurt von Schuschnigg to take over the Austrian government and continue substantially the same policies as Dollfuss. Starhemberg and his Heimwehr continued to be a useful prop to the regime until 1936 when Schuschnigg felt strong enough to dismiss him from the vice-chancellorship. Later in the same year the Heimwehr was absorbed into the Fatherland Front militia.

Meanwhile Hitler was growing stronger, and Mussolini, isolated during his Ethiopian War, had begun to turn toward him as an ally. Thereafter he did not oppose Hitler's designs on Austria. Indeed, in April, 1937, Mussolini, now engaged in intervening actively in the Spanish Civil War (see p. 93) together with his fellow dictator in Germany, quite frankly urged Schuschnigg to make his peace with Hitler. When the Austrian Chancellor, still unwilling to do so, made attempts to join the French system of alliances, the Germans began to step up agitation against him. He was summoned to Germany to a meeting in which Hitler demanded that he make a Nazi (Artur Seyss-Inquart) minister of the interior (February, 1935). This had to be accepted, but Schuschnigg immediately afterward ordered a plebiscite to determine whether the Austrians wished to maintain their independence. Rather than permit this to come to a vote under the conditions proposed by Schuschnigg, which made a pro-independence vote almost inevitable, Hitler sent him an ultimatum and massed troops on the Austrian frontier. Schuschnigg was left with no alternative to resigning, and Seyss-Inquart became chancellor. Union was then proclaimed with Germany (March 13, 1938). A special envoy sent to Mussolini by Hitler sent back the news that Mussolini had no objections to the coup and offered his congratulations.

HUNGARY

After the suppression of the Communist regime of Bela Kun (see p. 5), Hungary was declared a monarchy with the throne vacant. Admiral Nicholas Horthy became regent (March, 1920). The following year the emperor Charles attempted to obtain the restoration of his "rights," but the National Assembly, influenced by the hostile attitude of Hungary's neighbors, turned down his application. Later in the same year Charles attempted to seize the crown by force but was captured and sent into exile. He was then officially dethroned, but Horthy remained regent for some future king.

The government, led by Count Stephen Bethlen, instituted a severely restricted franchise, which, accompanied by open voting in many parts of the country, especially in rural areas, gave the Count a conservative parliament to work with. There was no serious attempt to introduce a democratic system. The main platform of Count Bethlen's party was opposition to the Treaty of Trianon (see p. 12); this policy naturally aroused the opposition of those nations which had profited by the treaty.

The outstanding problem in Hungary was the need for land reform. But the government, which drew its strength from the large landowners and richer peasants, made no attempt to solve it. When in the 1930's Count Bethlen was looking for a platform which might bring him back to power, he proposed some land and electoral reform, but nothing came of it. Two strongly authoritarian leaders, General Julius Gombos (1932–1935) and Kalman de Daranyi (1935–1938), in the main continued Bethlen's policies.

In the late 1930's Nazi propaganda, inspired by Germany, made considerable progress in Hungary. As a consequence a number of political leaders from several parties began to urge a Habsburg restoration as an alternative greatly preferable to Nazism, but this movement also came to nothing. When Hitler took Austria in March, 1938, the Hungarians recognized that it might well be their turn next, and a new government came to power which made some half-hearted efforts to enlist popular support but without daring to make any really serious efforts to solve domestic problems. Under Bela Imredy's government, some electoral reforms were instituted, including a secret ballot; but on the other side attempts were made to curry favor with Hitler by instituting a strong anti-Jewish program. When Czechoslovakia was dismembered in October, 1938, Hungary, with Germany's consent, took part of the country though not as much as she desired. She took some more when Hitler seized the rest of Czecho-Slovakia (it had become a hyphenated country by this time) in March, 1939. By this time Hungary was under strong Nazi influence, although the official Nazi party came in a bad second to the government party in elections held under the improved franchise in May, 1939. Late in 1940 Hungary adhered to the Rome-Berlin Axis, and she declared war against Russia on June 27, 1941, taking part in the entire campaign. When the Germans were facing defeat in 1944, they installed a puppet government in Hungary, which lasted for only a few months until the arrival of the Russians.

CZECHOSLOVAKIA

The new state of Czechoslovakia was distinguished by a serious attempt to establish a government with truly democratic institutions. Unfortunately, the country contained many minorities, none of which was wholly satisfied with the composite state, largely controlled by its most populous group, the Czechs. Eventually the nation was destroyed by Hitler, in large part because he was able to use the German-speaking minority of more than three million to disrupt it. In this task he enlisted some support even in the democratic nations, where it was thought that Germans had a right to live in a German-speaking state.

Problems of the New Nation.   Three days after the Armistice (November 14, 1918), a national assembly held at Prague confirmed Thomas Masaryk, head of the provisional government, as president and Eduard Benes as foreign minister. These men worked together during the regimes of various prime ministers until the resignation of Masaryk at the age of eighty-five in 1935. From that time until the dismemberment of the country after the Munich Conference, Benes was president. He resigned October 5, 1938 and went into exile in the United States, to return as president once more after World War II.

The first task to which the provisional government addressed itself, even before the promulgation of a democratic constitution in February, 1919, was the burning question of land reform. Many large landowners had held their estates since the seventeenth century, when Czech independence had been crushed by the Habsburgs. The large landowners were now dispossessed, but received compensation, while the former crown lands reverted to the state. Under the Land Reform Act all these lands were distributed to the peasants, who cultivated them in small holdings of from 15 to 25 acres. These peasants were the major beneficiaries of the new state and were naturally the strongest opponents of any projected Habsburg restoration, whether in Hungary or Austria. In foreign policy Czechoslovakia relied on alliances with France (1924) and with Rumania and Yugoslavia, the other beneficiaries from the breakup of the Habsburg empire (1920–1921). These three states became known as the Little Entente. In 1935 Czechoslovakia also concluded a pact with the Soviet Union, under which the latter agreed to come to her aid provided that France did also.

The various minorities in due course received some measure of autonomy. They included Ruthenia, inhabited by Ukrainians, and Slovakia, whose inhabitants constituted the second most important people in the state. Most of the Slovaks were strict Catholics; the Czechs honored the memory of Jan Hus, the religious reformer who was burned at the Council of Constance in 1415. The Czechs (Bohemians) resented their domination by the strictly Catholic Habsburgs and their enforced reconversion to Catholicism during the Counter Reformation. Neither Ruthenia nor Slovakia was content with such autonomy as they were granted; still less were the dissident German and Magyar minorities, who were separated from the main body of their people. They also resented the centralizing efforts of the Czechs, though they obtained material benefits from them. Most of the country's industry, which was quite considerable and included the famous Skoda armament factories, was located in the Czech and German sectors. It enabled the whole country to achieve the highest standard of living in eastern Europe, but at the same time made her vulnerable to the depression, which hit Czech exports hard and led to increasing disaffection among the minorities.

The Dismemberment of Czechoslovakia. When Hitler came to power in Germany, there was at once an increase in agitation among the German-speaking minority, who called themselves Sudeten Germans. A National Socialist party was organized under Konrad Henlein, which began to agitate for union with Germany (the Sudetenland had of course never been part of Germany but part of the Austro-Hungarian Empire). Nevertheless, for some time the other German-speaking groups in the country remained loyal to Czechoslovakia and opposed Nazism. Even Henlein's group, faced by solid opposition in the country, dissolved itself in preference to being dissolved by the government (October, 1933), thereafter calling itself the Sudeten German party in competition with the other German-speaking parties. In 1935 it won a resounding majority in a general election in the Sudetenland, actually winning more seats than any other party with the exception of the Czech Agrarian party, which outnumbered it by a single seat. A Slovak (Milan Hodza) was chosen as prime minister. He made a serious effort to improve the position of the minorities in the hopes of blunting the Nazi propaganda for secession —which it was recognized would be disastrous for the state since most of its fortifications were in the Sudetenland, bordering on the German Reich.

Hitler, however, was determined, and Henlein's party, which took its orders from Berlin, followed his lead faithfully and showed itself totally unwilling to compromise. Whenever the Czechs agreed to any demands, Henlein raised them; and it soon became clear that only secession would satisfy the German dictator. When Germany incorporated Austria into the Third Reich in March, 1938, all the Sudeten Germans except the Social Democrats joined Henlein in demanding an eight-point program (Karlsbad Program) which included full autonomy for the Sudetenland. To this the Prague government could not agree. The British and the French, who had alliances with Czechoslovakia, in the interest of peace ("appeasement") began to put pressure on the government to make the maximum concessions; but the Czechs, as a demonstration of their will to resist, mobilized 400,000 men on the frontier early in May, 1938. This act, as is now known, so infuriated Hitler that he was no longer willing to accept only German-speaking Sudetenland but determined to take the whole country. He fulfilled his ambitions in two stages. The Pact of Munich (September 29, 1938) gave him the most strategically important parts of the country (including, of course the Sudetenland), leaving the remainder virtually defenseless. The second stage was accomplished in March, 1939, when Slovakia was permitted to become "independent," and German troops marched into Prague. These events will be treated in more detail as part of the background for World War II in Chapter 11.

SUCCESSOR STATES OF THE TSARIST EMPIRE

Although the Bolsheviks granted formal independence to Finland during the Revolution, they attempted to recapture the former duchy as soon as the war ended. They also tried to retain their outlying Baltic provinces. But when they met with serious military reverses in 1919 and 1920 they preferred to let them go rather than commit troops and supplies which were still much needed at home. On the outbreak of the Bolshevik Revolution all the Baltic states made preparations to win independence; but since the Germans were present in force in their territories at that period, they were willing to accept German hegemony as a step toward the independence they sought. Among these states only Finland became and remained a true democracy after independence. The others after a varying period as democracies succumbed to the prevalent tendency to become authoritarian dictatorships, whereas Poland, after the end of the Pilsudski military dictatorship, became an oligarchy of the Hungarian type, ruled by her landowning aristocracy and her army.

The Baltic States. The Finns declared their independence from Russia during the Kerensky regime, and at first the Bolsheviks acquiesced. But in January, 1918, a Communist rebellion broke out in the country, and for a time Finnish and Russian Communists fought side by side against the non-Communist Finns, led by Baron Karl Mannerheim and the Germans who backed them against the Bolsheviks. The German-Finnish alliance prevailed and the revolution was suppressed. War broke out again, however, as soon as the Germans left at the end of 1918, since the Bolsheviks, though willing to recognize Finnish independence, refused to accept the boundaries claimed by the Finns. A compromise solution was accepted in October, 1920, and the Russians withdrew. Under the Treaty of Dorpat (1920) one important question was not settled—the ownership of the Finnish-populated area of Eastern Karelia, which had never been part of the duchy of Finland. The Russians kept this area, but granted the Finns the ice-free port of Petsamo by way of compensation. They took this back in 1947.

In July, 1919, the Finns adopted a democratic constitution with power divided between an elected president and assembly. In 1922 they enacted an important law dividing up the large estates and distributing them among the peasants. Throughout the interwar period there was much fear of Soviet Russia and of Communism, which tended to make Finnish foreign and domestic policy rather more conservative than it otherwise would have been. Nevertheless two fascist coups, both claiming to be directed against Communism, were suppressed by the government (1930, 1932), which then enacted severe laws both against Communism and against parties organized along military lines whose members wore uniforms. By 1935 the Finns also were beginning to recognize a danger from Nazi Germany and tried without success to organize a Scandinavian bloc which would stand between Germany and Russia. In 1938 all the Scandinavian states declared their neutrality and increased their armaments to enable them to fight to defend it. A fascist group, the Patriotic National movement, was suppressed; and the following year, when a European war appeared likely, Finland refused German offers of a nonaggression pact, and at the same time refused a guarantee by the Soviet Union. In the secret clauses of the Russo-German nonaggression pact of August, 1939, Finland was acknowledged by the Germans to come within the Soviet sphere of influence. The Russians thereupon attempted to obtain some strategic concessions, and when these were refused they invaded the country—evidently with the limited aim of improving their strategic position against Germany in the event of war. After a brave but hopeless defense the Finns accepted the inevitable. They ceded the Karelian Isthmus and the city of Viipuri (Vyborg), and leased the naval base of Hango to the Soviet Union. (Hango was returned in 1944 in exchange for a similar base near the capital of Helsinki.)

Lithuania proclaimed her independence in February, 1918, whereupon the Bolsheviks invaded the country. The following month, after the signature of the Treaty of Brest-Litovsk, they recognized its independence, and for a brief period Lithuania became a monarchy, ruled by a German duke. When the Germans withdrew at the end of 1918, the Bolsheviks attempted to regain the country but becoming involved in a war with Poland, preferred to recognize Lithuanian independence (June, 1920). Events followed a similar course in Estonia. The Germans helped the Estonians against the invading Bolsheviks, but abandoned them after the Armistice. The Estonians then fought a war on their own against the Bolsheviks, receiving only some aid from a British fleet. The Russians abandoned their attempt to reconquer the country and in February, 1920, signed a treaty recognizing Estonian independence.

The Germans tried to keep Latvia even after their defeat by the Allies. The Latvian upper class was largely of German ancestry and gave them some support, although the country as a whole desired nothing but independence. The Bolsheviks invaded the country and captured Riga, the capital, but were driven out of the city by the Germans and Latvians. Late in 1919 the Germans left, as they had promised in the Treaty of Versailles, and soon afterwards the Latvians expelled the remainder of the Russians. In August, 1920, the Russians signed a treaty recognizing Latvian independence.

Lithuania, Estonia, and Latvia all suffered from their lack of experience in self-governing political institutions; from the loss of their great Russian market; and from a permanent danger that the Soviet Union, once she became again a major power, would try to regain her lost provinces by force. Lastly, all being somewhat artificial states created on the principle of self-determination, they had within their borders minorities of varying sizes (Lithuania, 16 per cent; Estonia, 12 per cent; Latvia 20 per cent). Before the war most of the best land had been held by foreign nobles. These lands were soon divided among the peasants, who in fact seized them in Estonia and Latvia, dispossessing the (German) Balt landlords who had held them for centuries. Later legislation gave the peasants legal title to the land. In Lithuania it was the Polish landlords and the Church who were dispossessed by a law passed in 1922.

Lithuania, due to her geographic location, was more concerned with Poland and Germany than with Russia. During almost the whole interwar period she had no relations with Poland, who had taken Vilna, her proposed capital, from her by force of arms. Poland "legitimized" her conquest by a plebiscite supervised by

Poles, which the Lithuanians, not unnaturally, refused to accept. By way of compensation Lithuania took the Memel area which had been separated from Germany, who had possessed it before World War I. The territory was then administered by the League of Nations; but in 1923 it was seized by the Lithuanians. The Council of Ambassadors (see p. 17) finally allowed the Lithuanians to keep it in return for an agreement to grant it autonomy —a promise which they had no intention of honoring fully, although they did permit separate elections there. In 1926 the democratic government which had functioned feebly in Lithuania since 1922 was overthrown by Antanas Smetona, who with military support made himself dictator. He obtained some political backing from the Nationalist Union party, which in the 1930's became frankly a fascist party. In 1936 Smetona suppressed all opposition parties, and in subsequent elections only the Nationalist Union party presented candidates. In 1924 a Communist uprising in Estonia was suppressed, and thereafter the governments were strongly conservative. The first democratic constitution of 1919 was abolished by plebiscite in 1934 as a result of which Konstantin Paets, who had founded the first provisional government after separation from Russia in 1918, made himself virtual dictator, backed by the army. He retained this position until the incorporation of the Estonian state into the Soviet Union in 1940. A plebiscite was held in 1936, in which the people voted by a 3 to 1 margin to abolish the constitution of 1934. Paets permitted a new constitution to be proclaimed, which gave very extensive power to the president. However, since he himself was then elected president, there was little change in the government.

In Latvia under a democratic constitution promulgated in 1922, the Social Democrats won the first elections and held power until 1928. Thereafter Latvia was ruled by conservative governments. In 1934 Prime Minister Karlis Ulmanis, with the aid of the army, suspended the constitution and arrested the Social Democratic leaders, who were accused of planning a left-wing coup d'état. In 1936 Ulmanis became president and continued as virtual dictator until 1940, when Latvia, too, was taken over by the Soviet Union.

The increasing strength of Nazi Germany presented all the Baltic countries with serious problems. The Germans in Memel won majorities in all elections held in the territory, and Hitler began to demand it back, eventually compelling Lithuania to cede it in March, 1939. In exchange Germany guaranteed the integrity of the rest of the Lithuanian territory. Meanwhile in 1934 the three Baltic countries signed a pact providing for common defense. Lithuania and Latvia had signed nonaggression pacts with the Soviet Union, and all three signed similar pacts with Nazi Germany in 1939. None of these arrangements did them any good. The nonaggression pact of August, 1939, between Germany and the Soviet Union permitted Russia a free hand in these countries, of which she took full advantage. She first signed agreements with them which gave her the right to station troops on their territories for their mutual protection; then she toppled their governments. The resulting pro-Soviet puppet governments next petitioned the Soviet Union to allow them to become Soviet Republics. Needless to say, the Soviet Union acceded to the request, and on July 21, 1940, all three countries exchanged their independence for the status of constituent republics of the USSR.

POLAND

By far the largest of the new nations was Poland, who, as described earlier (see p. 8), had to fight Bolshevik Russia for much of her territory and took Vilna from the Lithuanians through a rigged plebiscite. The Treaty of Riga between Russia and Poland (March 18, 1921) settled matters with Russia, but the Lithuanians never became reconciled to the loss of their capital to the Poles. The Polish leader throughout the war of independence was General (later Marshal) Josef Pilsudski, who was provisional president of the republic until the adoption of a new constitution on March 17, 1921. Until late in 1919 the famous musician Ignaz Paderewski was prime minister, backed by a coalition cabinet.

Abandonment of Democracy.   The new constitution provided for a president (Pilsudski held this position until his resignation in November, 1922) and a two-chamber parliament elected by popular vote. Though conservative parties won the election of 1922, a land reform bill was passed in 1925. During the entire period of attempted democratic rule there was considerable discord among the many parties. In May, 1926, Pilsudski (chief of the army staff) organized a revolt against the government, which at the time was headed by a Peasant party leader, and revised the constitution to give greater power to the president, Pilsudski's nominee. Even so, the opposition parties on the left, especially the Social Democrats, continued to oppose military rule. Pilsudski therefore arrested a large number of opposition members until at last an election gave the government parties a majority. They then proceeded to give the president the right to rule by decree. In 1935 the constitution was again revised to give almost complete power to the president. When Pilsudski died soon afterward, General Smigly-Rydz took his position as head of the army, and with it the control of the state. The opposition parties demanded a return to democratic rule, but nothing came of their efforts. The same presidential form of government, backed by the army, continued until the outbreak of war with Germany on September 1, 1939.

Minority Problems.   The minority problems of Poland were never solved in the interwar period, and perhaps were insoluble under the conditions of the time. The largest minority consisted of Ukrainians, who had been promised local autonomy after the war by a minorities treaty, agreed to by Poland and guaranteed by the League of Nations. But they did not in fact receive much autonomy and complained bitterly of their treatment by the Poles. The German minority, mostly in Upper Silesia, made similar complaints, which caused many difficulties between Poland and Germany, especially after the accession of Hitler with his policy of trying to protect Germans everywhere. The Poles counterclaimed with equal justice that the Germans mistreated the Polish minority in Germany at least as badly, and the latter did not have the right to appeal to the League of Nations for redress. Lastly the Jewish minority, which in Poland was a very substantial one, was given some rights by the Polish government in 1925. However, with the increase of anti-Semitism in Poland after the rise of Hitler to power in Germany most of these rights were lost.

The Problem of Danzig.   The Polish Corridor, which gave the Poles access to the sea, ended at the mouth of the Vistula with the great seaport of Danzig, a predominantly German city administered by a League of Nations commissioner with the aid of a popularly elected Assembly. For much of the 1920's Poland continued to use Danzig for her exports, which prospered accordingly. Then in 1925 she began construction of a new port of her own, Gdynia, to which she diverted as much of the traffic as possible. After an appeal by Danzig to the League of Nations, Poland agreed to channel 45 per cent of her trade through Danzig, leaving 55 per cent to Gdynia. In 1935 elections were held in Danzig in which the Nazis took a great deal of interest, since if the Nazi party won, the Germans in the city might be expected to petition for its return to Germany. The Nazis indeed won, if not overwhelmingly, and took over the government, proceeding to suppress the opposition parties. The League commissioner lacked power to prevent this, and by 1939 the League's presence in the city was largely formal. At the end of March, 1939, Hitler demanded the cession of Danzig to Germany. When the Poles refused to make any serious concessions an international crisis began, whipped up by Hitler and his propaganda ministry. Late in the summer Hitler sent troops into the city, but the Poles had still agreed to nothing by the time the war broke out. Danzig fell at once to the Germans and was incorporated into the Reich.

Foreign Relations.   Poland's foreign relations were dominated by her natural fear of both Germany and Russia, at whose expense her state had been created. Even so, she did not drop her expansionary ideas, and in October, 1938, took part of Czecho-Slovakia (Teschen) after the dismemberment of that country by Germany. Relations with the Soviet Union for most of the interwar period were correct but far from cordial. Until the rise of Germany Poland relied on alliances with France and Rumania, neutrality agreements with Czechoslovakia, Yugoslavia, and the Baltic states, and eventually a nonaggression pact with Russia. When Hitler offered her also a ten-year nonaggression pact in 1934, Colonel Beck, the Polish foreign minister, accepted. Poland now seemed to be as safe as treaties could make her.

The End of Polish Independence.   But it was only temporary German interests that had dictated the 1934 treaty. Hitler was left free by it to pursue his aggressive aims in the West. When he had nullified all the safeguards against German aggression written into the Treaty of Versailles, he turned his attention to Austria and Czechoslovakia. Poland was obviously next on the list, but for a long time the Poles would not recognize this fact, and they failed to improve relations with the Soviet Union until it was too late. After the final dismemberment of Czecho-Slovakia in March, 1939, the British and French, at last thoroughly aroused, offered Poland a guarantee of mutual assistance, which was accepted in April. Hitler thereupon denounced his nonaggression pact with Poland, which had by this time served its purpose. But Poland still would not permit Russian troops to enter Poland in any circumstances, thus making almost inevitable the breakdown of talks between Britain and France and the Soviet Union. The Soviet Union came to the conclusion that more was to be gained from an agreement with Hitler which gave her a share in a new partition of Poland. Thus Poland, in September, 1939, found herself with two major allies who had no access to her territories; and though they duly declared war on Germany in accordance with their obligations, Poland herself was forced to face the brunt of the German attacks alone.

CONCLUSION

World War II put an end to the independence of all the new states considered in this chapter with the exception of Finland. Hungary, it is true, maintained her formal status as an independent state, but she was in all essentials a German satellite during the war, as she became a Soviet satellite after it. Thus the 1919 peace settlement in eastern Europe collapsed after little more than twenty years. A new power structure was created after World War II, under which the Soviet Union was incomparably the greatest power in Europe, and second only to the United States elsewhere. Only Austria and Finland among all these nations escaped Soviet hegemony, at the cost of perpetual neutrality. As long as the Soviet Union retains her power, neither of these can be expected to enter the Western military orbit. The Soviet Union has therefore, in effect, become the successor state of the old Habsburg empire.

7 THE BALKAN PENINSULA AND TURKEY

At the outbreak of World War I, there were independent states of varying sizes in the Balkan Peninsula: tiny Montenegro, Albania, and larger Serbia in the west; Rumania, Bulgaria, and Turkey in the east; Greece straddling the whole peninsula in the south. Turkey had little remaining territory in Europe but still possessed a considerable empire in Asia. The remainder of the peninsula, consisting of Croatia, Slovenia, Dalmatia, and Bosnia-Herzegovina, was part of the Austro-Hungarian Empire, almost all of it under Hungarian control. (In this chapter we shall consider first the new composite state of Yugoslavia, then the other wholly European states that survived the war though with different boundaries. Lastly, the transformation of the old Ottoman Empire into the national state of Turkey will be considered; but only brief attention will be paid to the fate of her Asiatic provinces, since they will be dealt with in more detail in Chapter 10.)

YUGOSLAVIA

On July 20, 1917, the Pact of Corfu was signed. Under it the Serbian, Croatian, Slovenian, and Montenegrin leaders agreed to unite after the war in a single state to be ruled by the Serbian monarchy, which had gained prestige by its courageous and prolonged struggle with the Central Powers. Serbia and Montenegro were still under enemy occupation when the pact was signed. But it was assumed that after the war they would recover their full national territories and that Croatia, Slovenia, and Bosnia would be permitted to secede from the Empire. The Montenegrin king, Nicholas, was displeased by the action of his subjects in putting an end to their independent state and in not at least asking him to be king of the new one. But he was powerless to act and was deposed in November, 1918. Then, in accordance with the Pact of Corfu, the new Kingdom of the Serbs, Croats, and Slovenes was proclaimed, with Prince Alexander Karageorgevich as regent on behalf of his aged father, King Peter, who had been on the Serbian throne since 1903.

The Problem of Unity. Unfortunately, the act of union proved to be the last serious effort to build a united nation for more than twenty years. The crucial issue that confronted the kingdom was the degree of centralization that should be imposed upon it. The language of the Croats and Slovenes, though the same as that of the Serbs and Montenegrins, was written in different characters (Cyrillic); the former were Roman Catholics who used the Latin liturgy, the latter Orthodox, using a Slavonic liturgy; a large proportion of the Bosnian people were Muslim. Moreover, the Macedonians were a distinct minority who had no state of their own, though they had agitated for it for generations. Most of them lived in Bulgaria; there were others in Greece and Yugoslavia (as it was called from 1929). The Macedonians kept the whole peninsula in a constant turmoil through the terrorist activities of their national organization IMRO. The Serbs, who had been independent for more than a century, regarded themselves as the leading people in the new nation. The other peoples of the country had either been inhabitants of the Austro-Hungarian Empire or had remained in the Ottoman Empire for decades after the Serbs had successfully seceded. As a result the Serbs had every intention of dominating the new nation and were unwilling to permit any real autonomy to the separate peoples in a federal state. The Croats in particular were unwilling to submit to Serbian domination, since most of them regarded the Serbs as somewhat uncouth barbarians. They used their deputies in the national parliament almost solely to agitate for self-government; when this was refused, they usually boycotted the proceedings altogether.

Failure of Democratic Institutions. A constituent assembly was elected in November, 1920, for the purpose of writing a constitution. The Croat members under Stephen Radich, seeing themselves outnumbered, refused to take part in the discussions, thus leaving the field to their opponents, who voted for a centralist form of government. In the elections which followed, Radich and his Croat Peasant party won their expected number of seats, but they made no effort to unite with the other dissident parties against the veteran prewar leader Nicholas Pasich and his Serbian Radical party (founded in 1881). After a year, however, Radich changed his tactics and came to an agreement with the other opponents of the Radicals, and his party took its seats in the parliament, thus robbing the Pasich government of its majority and forcing its resignation. But even when it had been reconstructed, the Croats would not co-operate. In December, 1924, the government lost patience and imprisoned Radich, who had visited Moscow and considered having his party affiliated to the Bolshevist Peasants' International (*Krestintern*), formed the previous year. The Croat Peasant party was then banned.

Radich, finding that he had achieved nothing by his policies, decided in July, 1925, to accept the constitution. He was thereupon released, and soon afterward became minister of education in a coalition government. But the truce lasted for less than a year. He himself then quitted the Cabinet, but his Peasant party continued to sit in the parliament, usually making things as difficult as possible for the government. On June 20, 1928, Radich made a fiery speech denouncing a recent commercial treaty with Italy, and with several of his colleagues he was set upon in the parliament chamber by an angry Radical deputy and shot, dying shortly afterward of his wounds. Two other Peasant party deputies were killed outright. Not unnaturally, the Croat deputies again withdrew and decided to set up their own separatist government in the Croatian capital city of Zagreb. In this action they were joined by the deputies from Dalmatia.

Absolutism of King Alexander I.   At this point King Alexander, who had succeeded his father in 1921, decided to take a hand. With the aid of the army he dissolved parliament, abrogated the constitution, and placed a military man, General Peter Zhivkovich, at the head of the government. Zhivkovich was empowered to rule by decree (January 5, 1929) until a new constitution was proclaimed. Until 1931 the country was ruled by Alexander as virtual dictator, without the aid of parliament, and a thoroughgoing program of centralization was put into effect. One reform was the change of the name of the country to Yugoslavia, to de-emphasize its ethnic diversity.

The new constitution, when it was finally issued in 1931, was tailor-made to suit the King's policy. Only parties which had at least 60 members in each electoral district could take part in the election. This provision, apparently intended to make sure that no purely ethnic parties could participate, effectively prevented the earlier parties, which were all ethnic, from fighting the election. As in Italy (see p. 78) the party with the largest number of seats would be granted two-thirds of the deputies, making possible a government backed by a stable majority. Lastly, the voting was to be open, which by itself might well have ensured the victory of the government party. The result, a foregone conclusion, was that the National party, organized by the government, won the elections of November 9, 1931. The new Croat Peasant party leader, Dr. Vladko Machek, and several other Croat and Slovenian leaders were arrested, and Machek himself was sentenced to three years' imprisonment for treasonable activities. The dictatorship continued until 1934, when King Alexander was assassinated at Marseilles, while visiting that city in company with French Foreign Minister Louis Barthou, who was killed at the same time. The murderer, who was killed on the spot, was proved to belong to a Croat terrorist organization whose headquarters were on Hungarian soil. The Yugoslav government blamed Hungary for permitting the existence of such organizations, and tension rapidly mounted until the League of Nations took the matter in hand and mediated successfully.

Reorganization as a Federal State.   Alexander's place was filled by his cousin Paul Karageorgevich, as regent for eleven-year-old King Peter II. Prince Paul at first made a serious effort to bring the parties together, and Machek was released. But though there were new elections and a coalition civilian government was formed under Milan Stoyadinovich, the Croats continued to demand autonomy and the government was hardly less authoritarian than under Alexander and his army. However, Stoyadinovich did continue negotiations with Machek, who in every election was shown to have overwhelming support in Croatia. During the international crises of 1938 and 1939 Prince Paul attempted to maintain a wary neutrality between the Axis and the West. But German and Italian influence became stronger, and by 1939 the Serbs and Croats, both of whom feared German expansion, came to recognize that without internal unity in their country Germany might well make use of their divisions to destroy Yugoslav independence—as she had successfully destroyed Czechoslovakia's. As a result the Serbs, under a new leader, Dragesha Cvetkovich, came to an agreement to reorganize Yugoslavia as a federal state. Democratic government and the secret ballot were restored in August, 1939, and Dr.

Machek became vice-premier of Yugoslavia and head of the new antonomous government of Croatia. But the *Ustachi,* the terrorist group led by Ante Pavelich which had assassinated King Alexander in 1934, remained active. It was seeking the complete independence of Croatia and was prepared to co-operate with Nazi Germany to achieve its aims. Pavelich reached his goal during the war when he ruled Croatia on behalf of his German masters.

Foreign Policy.   In foreign policy Yugoslavia, as noted earlier (see p. 103), relied upon the Little Entente alliance with Czechoslovakia and Rumania. This led to a treaty of friendship with France in 1927. For a long time relations with Italy were difficult, until the question of Fiume (see p. 6) was settled. This was followed by a treaty of friendship (1924–1929) which was not renewed. But in 1937 Prince Paul, in pursuit of a policy that would lessen the danger from the Rome-Berlin Axis, signed with Italy a nonaggression pact, which also called for an improvement in the treatment of the fairly large Yugoslav minority in Italian Dalmatia. Italy and Germany tried to maintain friendly relations with Yugoslavia, since Hitler's plans did not originally call for war with her. Prince Paul indeed under strong pressure agreed in 1941 to join the Tripartite Pact of September, 1940, between Germany, Italy, and Japan, in exchange for the cession of the Greek port of Saloniki, which Yugoslavia had always coveted and in which she already possessed a separate area under her own jurisdiction. This action by the Regent was too much for the strongly anti-Nazi Yugoslav army, which ousted him in favor of the seventeen-year-old Peter, who was now proclaimed king in his own right. This military intervention convinced Hitler that Yugoslavia must be "punished" in the most spectacular manner possible, to teach the world that agreements with Germany were sacrosanct. His attack on Yugoslavia in 1941 delayed his planned invasion of Russia by some weeks, thus perhaps changing the entire course of history.

For the rest, relations with Greece, Bulgaria, and Albania were all difficult. Yugoslavia tried to get the right to build a railroad to Saloniki and to be granted special arrangements in that city to enable her to trade freely into the Aegean. What she won was far from being, in her view, adequate. Macdeonians living in Bulgaria made frequent raids into Yugoslavia from 1929 onward, causing the latter to close the frontier between the two countries for several years. Difficulties with Albania arose during the years immediately following World War I; but when Ahmed Zogu established himself in power the Yugoslavs, who had backed him, were reasonably content. They accepted the frontiers of Albania in 1926, and the last real troubles occurred in 1927. Thereafter Yugoslavia tolerated Italian supremacy in Albania.

ALBANIA

This little mountainous country, whose inhabitants were mostly Muslim in religion, had achieved independence from the Ottoman Empire in 1912 but the following year had to accept much less territory than she desired. During World War I the Serbs and Montenegrins occupied a part of the country until they were driven out by the Austrians, and toward the end of the war Italy occupied the greater part of it. The best Albanian seaport, Valona, was used as a naval base by Italy for almost the entire war. After the war Italy wished to annex Albania, or, at the very least, receive Valona. But, in part at President Wilson's insistence and in part because the Albanians themselves took action to expel the Italians, the independence of Albania and the integrity of her territories were again recognized. Even so, her boundaries were not fixed for some years after the war, and the Yugoslavs made incursions into Albanian territory to such an extent that the League of Nations threatened them with sanctions. The frontiers were finally accepted by all the interested powers in 1926. Ahmed Zogu, a tribal chieftain, was chosen president in 1925 under a constitution which provided for a bicameral legisature but left most of the power in the president's hands. Zogu used this power to have himself proclaimed King Zog I on September 1, 1928.

Albanian independence was always to some degree nominal. Unable to survive without outside assistance, she entered into close relations with Italy, and under two treaties of Tirana (1926 and 1927) she accepted a defensive alliance and agreed to co-operate in economic matters with Italy. In the early 1930's Zog attempted to escape from Italian domination, under which Albania had little short of protectorate status. But Mussolini replied by making a demonstration with his fleet. Thereafter Albania submitted, and economic and military co-operation between the two countries became closer than ever. In April, 1939, Mussolini, anxious to win a victory that would in some degree offset Hitler's expansion in central Europe, sent troops to Albania, compelling King Zog to flee the country; whereupon a subservient assembly requested King Victor Emmanuel III of Italy to accept the crown, and a few fascist institutions were imposed. Late in 1940 Mussolini used Albania as a springboard from which to launch his attack on Greece—from which adventure he had to be rescued by Hitler. Various groups of resistance fighters kept up guerilla warfare against the Axis powers throughout the war. The most radical of these, led by Enver Hoxha, took advantage of the confusion at the end of the war to set up a Peoples' Republic (Communist), which has survived to this day.

BULGARIA

Bulgaria, which had greatly increased in size through the Balkan Wars just before World War I, joined the Central Powers during the war and shared in their defeat. By the Treaty of Neuilly (see p. 12) she was shorn of most of her prewar gains and lost her opening onto the Aegean Sea. Her only outlet was now to the Black Sea, making her dependent on passage through the Dardanelles Straits for her sea trade with the rest of Europe. By this treaty Bulgaria also lost much of her population; more than a million Bulgarians were included in neighboring countries after the war. Many thousands of these returned to Bulgaria as refugees and spent much of the interwar period intriguing and engaging in acts of terrorism that they vainly hoped would bring about the retrocession of their lost homelands.

The Bulgarians had made most of their prewar gains in the First Balkan War when they had fought on the Serbian side against Turkey. In the Second Balkan War Bulgaria lost part of her gains to the Serbs, and her main reason for joining the Central Powers in World War I was that she (or her King and government) came to the conclusion that by a victory of the Central Powers she could regain this territory. When the war was lost great numbers of Bulgarians blamed the King (or Tsar) Ferdinand, whose ancestry was German, and he abdicated at once rather than face their wrath. His young son Boris III came to the throne, and for many years acted as a constitutional monarch, in contrast to his father, who had been a strong and authoritarian ruler.

A marked contrast prevailed between the standard of living and culture in the few cities, especially Sofia, the capital, and the countryside, where there was an almost unrelieved stark poverty. A giant peasant leader named Alexander Stamboliski had founded a Peasant party, or Agrarian Union, which by the end of the war had become the largest and best-organized body in the state and was thus in a position to win the first elections held under universal manhood suffrage. Once Stamboliski had become head of the government, he executed a ruthless purge of the opposition middle-class parties and established a dictatorship which was frankly hostile to all groups in the state except the peasants. A land law broke up all crown lands and estates over 75 acres, and a heavy income tax was levied from which peasants were excused. Stamboliski closed the University of Sofia and instituted a severe censorship. In spite of these measures the second largest party, first known as the "Narrow" Socialists, refused to join him, stating that a peasant-led revolution must be reactionary and would never lead to their cherished dictatorship of the proletariat. These Socialists soon began to call themselves Communists, like their counterparts in Russia.

There was no way of getting rid of Stamboliski by an election. He continued to be venerated by the peasants, and he was to some degree approved of by the Communists since the workers had benefited, if less than the peasants, by his measures. A conspiracy was therefore organized by army officers, middle-class political opponents of the regime, and Macedonian terrorists. The coup was successful and Stamboliski was killed. The government was then taken over by Alexander Tsankov, a professor of economics, who ruthlessly suppressed an uprising by the peasants and Communists in September, 1923. In 1925 two Communists exploded a bomb in Sofia Cathedral in the hope of killing King Boris and members of the government who were worshiping there. Though more than one hundred persons were killed the King was not among them. Ferocious reprisals were then visited on all known Communists by the Tsankov government, and the Communist party was outlawed. Meanwhile the Macedonian terrorists who could not be controlled by successive coalition governments and were frequently at odds among themselves, raided into Greece and Yugoslavia causing trouble with those countries. They were not brought under reasonably effective control until 1930.

In 1932 elections were again held, in which the Communists participated. They won control of Sofia, but elsewhere the still radical peasant parties triumphed. The government, backed by the army, again took steps against the Communists (June, 1933) and arrested considerable numbers. The following year a group of fascists and army officers overthrew the government and abolished all political parties (May, 1934), but King Boris succeeded in taking over from them in a coup of his own, and in April, 1935, he proclaimed a royal dictatorship. He disciplined the military leaders and condemned many of them to imprisonment. In 1938 Boris, in response to appeals from political leaders of all parties, agreed to elections provided that no candidate ran in the name of any of the old parties. When the new parliament was elected Boris gave it few responsibilities, and he himself continued to rule the country.

Like all other eastern European countries, Bulgaria felt herself threatened by Nazi Germany, but her leaders could not make up their minds how to deal with the threat. The official National Socialist party in Bulgaria was suppressed, but another pro-German party under former Prime Minister Tsankov flourished. In May, 1939, the Bulgarian prime minister was invited to Germany and given a friendly reception there, but no commitments were made. For some years Bulgaria had, in fact, been virtually an economic dependency of Germany. In 1940 the Russians, who had traditionally been friendly to Bulgaria, attempted to undermine the excessive German influence in the country, and Foreign Minister Molotov frankly brought up the subject in conversations with Hitler late in that year. But he could obtain no assurances. When Italy invaded Greece and Hitler decided on his Balkan campaign, King Boris, against the vocal opposition of the Bulgarian Communists and in spite of warnings from Moscow, bowed to superior force and chose to permit the Germans to pass through his country. On February 28, 1941, Boris joined the Tripartite Pact (Germany, Italy, Japan), and later declared war on Britain and the United States, though not on the Soviet Union.

RUMANIA

In spite of Rumania's overwhelming defeat by the Germans in World War I, the postwar settlement gave her a vast increase in territory, mainly at the expense of Hungary (Transylvania) and the Soviet Union (Bessarabia). Indeed, the new country was more than double the size of prewar Rumania. Bessarabia was won as the result of action taken before the end of the war by the Bessarabian leaders, who, like the peasantry, were mostly Rumanian. Their main purpose was to escape from Bolshevik rule. For many years the Russians refused to recognize the change in sovereignty which was confirmed by the Great

Powers. But in July, 1933, when it began to seem likely that Hitler would prove dangerous, the Soviet Union decided to patch up a settlement with Rumania. The two countries signed a non-aggression treaty, which by implication recognized the Rumanian possession of Bessarabia. As noted earlier (see p. 5), in April, 1919, Rumania invaded Hungary and occupied Budapest during the Communist regime of Bela Kun, but thereafter relations to some degree improved, and disputes were mainly over the treatment of the 1,250,000 Hungarians within the borders of Rumania, which treatment was often far from being in accord with the minorities treaty signed by Rumania in 1919.

Political Developments to the Restoration of King Carol. Before World War I the king was already supposedly a constitutional monarch, and there was thus no need for a new constitution. But a very liberal electoral law was passed (July, 1917) which provided for universal manhood suffrage. This meant that the peasants, who were in an overwhelming majority in the country, could control any parliament provided that their allegiance were given to a single party. This situation was not at all acceptable to King Ferdinand I and his aristocratic and middle-class advisers, chief of whom was Ion Bratianu, who had been prime minister for almost the entire war period. Ferdinand did not in fact recognize any constitutional duty to appoint as prime minister the leader of the majority party in the parliament, and both he and his successors (Michael and his regents, and Carol II) chose prime ministers as they wished. The result was that much of the interwar period was a more or less disguised royal dictatorship. This was especially true in the reign of Carol II (1930–1940).

With the aid of King Ferdinand, Ion Bratianu dominated the government, whether or not he was prime minister, until his death in 1927 a few months after that of the King. In the first postwar elections the Peasant party, led by Julius Maniu, a moderate and responsible Transylvanian of peasant stock, was the victor, but Ferdinand would not permit Maniu and his party to rule. Nevertheless, the Liberal and People's parties, which formed a smaller bloc in the parliament, passed a far-reaching land reform program. Land in foreign and crown hands was expropriated, and estates over 1,250 acres were divided and sold to the peasants on easy terms. When in 1928 Maniu was at last permitted to form a government after the death of Bratianu and won the subsequent elections by a large majority, he inaugurated many laws looking toward social reform and completed the land distribution. But he was faced by economic difficulties rising from the depression and began to lose support. He therefore decided to win some favor by bringing back the former Crown Prince Carol, who had renounced his right to the throne two years before his father's death as a consequence of his refusal to abandon his mistress Magda Lupescu and take back his divorced wife Princess Helen of Greece. An issue had been made of this liaison largely because the Bratianu faction had concluded that Carol could not be controlled as easily as Ferdinand. The result had been that Carol left the country and Michael, his eldest son by Princess Helen, became king in 1927, with Carol's brother Nicholas as regent. It was during the regency that Maniu and his Peasant party were permitted to take office.

The Reign of Carol II, 1930–1940.   Carol had remained popular with the army, and Maniu's proposal to bring him back was acceptable to the army and to most other elements in the state. In return for an empty promise to reconcile with Princess Helen, he was allowed to return and was proclaimed king. But he did not reconcile himself with the Princess, now Queen, and he did not abandon Mme. Lupescu. Nor did the move help Maniu recover his popularity; when he objected to the King's failure to keep his promise he was dismissed (officially he resigned due to ill health). Soon afterward he was replaced by Carol's former tutor, a professor named Nicholas Iorga. Once Iorga was in charge of the government, he held the customary manipulated elections, and the Peasant party was defeated. But his government had no more success than its predecessor in overcoming difficulties arising from the depression, and the financial deficit became almost unmanageable. When Iorga resigned Carol was obliged to recall the Peasant party under another leader Alexander Vaida-Voevod, whom the King preferred to Maniu. This new government stayed in office long enough to arrange a pact of nonaggression with Russia and a League of Nations loan accompanied by League supervision of Rumanian finances. The Peasant party, however, split on the issue of the rivalry for leadership between Vaida-Voevod and Maniu. This gave the King a chance to bring back the conservative Liberal party under Ion Duca at the end of 1933. But Duca was soon afterward assassinated, and George Tartarescu took over the government.

Duca's assassination had been the work of a native Nazi party called the Iron Guard that had been growing rapidly in Rumania under the leadership of Corneliu Codreanu. It was highly nation-alistic and anti-Semitic. At first the King was inclined to support it because of its nationalism; then he realized that it might present a serious danger to the state in view of Hitler's ambition and the growing German domination of the Rumanian economy as a re-sult of the Schacht Plan (see p. 74). However, Carol did not object to other, less pro-German, fascist groups in Rumania, and he gave some support to a new rightist bloc, which contained the Vaida-Voevod faction of the former Peasant party and various extremist anti-Semitic groups. In 1937, after an election in which this bloc was soundly defeated, he took the unprecedented step of appointing one of its members, the poet Octavian Goga, as prime minister, allowing him to issue extreme anti-Semitic legis-lation by decree before his hostile parliament had even convened. This brought strong protests from abroad, especially from Rumania's titular ally, France (then led by the Jewish Léon Blum) and from the native Rumanian business community. King Carol (who was perhaps well aware of what the reactionary Goga's government would do) dismissed him before he ever met his parliament, dissolved the latter, and himself became virtual dicta-tor. The consitution was suspended and a plebiscite arranged which duly ratified Carol's act (February, 1938).

Rumania as a German Satellite. Carol then chose a royal gov-ernment made up of distinguished men from many parties, includ-ing several former prime ministers, and he made a serious attempt to meet the Nazi threat, which had by this time become acute. Codreanu was arrested and imprisoned, then "shot while trying to escape," and the Iron Guard was dissolved. (These events natu-rally infuriated the Germans.) The country was administratively reorganized with the purpose of giving the non-Rumanians equality with the old Rumanians, and other long-overdue reforms were inaugurated. Rumania accepted the Anglo-French guarantee of her independence in April, 1939, as had Poland, but it was in the short run of no more value to her than it was to Poland. The Rumanian oil, wheat, and minerals were of too great value for Hitler to be willing to see the country escape from his grasp.

As stipulated in the Russo-German agreement of August, 1939, the Russians were permitted to take back Bessarabia and North Bukovina. This was achieved through an ultimatum which Hitler advised the Rumanians to accept (June, 1940). Hungary there-upon demanded back Transylvania, and Bulgaria demanded

Dobrudja. Both were quite willing to make war upon Rumania to achieve their ends, hoping that Germany would remain neutral. But the Germans, who proposed to control all three countries, in which event it did not particularly matter who controlled what for the short time that remained, made an award (Vienna Award, August, 1940) which stripped Rumania of much, but not all, the territory she had won at the end of World War I. Meanwhile, in hopes of appeasing Hitler, Carol repudiated the Anglo-French guarantee (July, 1940). In September, 1940, Carol, recognizing that he could do nothing more to prevent German occupation of his country, appointed as prime minister General Ion Antonescu, a pro-German officer who had close relations with the Iron Guard. Two days later Carol abdicated in favor of his son Michael and went into exile. Antonescu accepted Hitler's demands and joined the Axis (September 23, 1940). In October a German military mission entered the country, officially for training purposes. The Germans then rapidly took over the country but left Michael as king and Antonescu as dictator.

The Rumanian coup deeply offended both Italy and the Soviet Union. It was largely responsible for Mussolini's ill-fated decision to attack Greece later in the same month. Molotov discussed the matter with Hitler at length in November, 1940, but could elicit from him only the assurance that German interests in Rumania were temporary. However, according to the German records, Hitler found Molotov's awkward questions so irritating that this meeting contributed greatly to the decision that Russia must be attacked.

GREECE

During the World War I there had been great difficulties between Greece and the Allied powers as a result of the apparently pro-German outlook of King Constantine I (1913–1917), who was married to Princess Sophia, sister of the German Kaiser. Constantine refused to go along with the policy of his leading statesman, the Cretan-born Eleutherios Venizelos, who wished to join the Allies and accept what they offered for such participation (including an offer by Britain to cede the since much-disputed island of Cyprus). Constantine eventually did permit the landing of an Allied force at Saloniki (September, 1915). In 1916 Venizelos rebelled against Constantine, and with Allied support established a provisional government in Crete and Saloniki, which duly declared war on Germany and Bulgaria. But the main government could not be persuaded to enter the war until an Allied ultimatum forced the abdication of Constantine in favor of his second son Alexander (June 12, 1917). Venizelos then again became Greek prime minister and his government entered the war on the Allied side on June 27. The following year the forces at Saloniki broke out of their enclave and forced the Bulgarians to sue for an armistice.

The Greco-Turkish War.   As a result of these events Venizelos emerged from the war as prime minister, and with the presumed support of the Allies for an expansionary policy, primarily at the expense of Turkey. He succeded in securing more definite support for his views at the Peace Conference. The Treaty of Sèvres (see p. 13) gave Greece the Anatolian city of Smyrna, which had a large Greek population. But the changed situation in Turkey due to the ascendancy of the Nationalists under Mustapha Kemal meant that the Greeks would have to fight for what they had been promised, even though the Sultan had reluctantly under Allied military pressure agreed to the cession. The Venizelists did not hesitate to fight, but the venture was unpopular in the country, and they lost a general election in December, 1920. When Venizelos resigned as a result, the military decided that Constantine (whose son Alexander had recently died), should be invited back. Against strong protests by the Allies, who could not forget his pro-Germanism, a plebiscite was held, which showed close to unanimous support for the restoration. Constantine after his return pursued the war with vigor, but a great offensive which almost reached Kemal's headquarters at Ankara (Angora) was checked there. A Turkish offensive in the summer of 1922 almost drove the Greeks out of Anatolia, and Smyrna was burned. As a result the Venizelists in mainland Greece rebelled and demanded the abdication of Constantine, who gave up his throne for the last time in September, 1922, and died soon afterward. George II, his eldest son, succeeded him, but for the present the military remained the real rulers of the state.

In July, 1923 the Treaty of Lausanne was signed (see p. 13), settling the boundaries of the country. A supplementary agreement called for the evacuation of Anatolia by the Greeks and of mainland Greece by the Turks. This delicate operation was carried out under the supervision of the League of Nations. Two months later the Italians seized Corfu off the west coast of Greece, but they were compelled by the League of Nations to evacuate it (see

p. 17). This series of reverses suffered by the Greeks discredited both the military and the King, with the result that Venizelos won the elections held in December, 1923. George II then left the country. Venizelos tried to prevent the establishment of a republic, which the military desired, and went into exile when he failed. Three successive generals then ruled the state as presidents, but without showing any conspicuous capacity or winning much popular support.

Efforts to Restore the Monarchy. In May, 1928, Venizelos, who had now been converted to republicanism, returned to the country, won the necessary election, and attempted to make the republican system work. He was more successful in his foreign than in his domestic policy. He improved relations with Italy and Yugoslavia and signed agreements with them, as well as with Turkey. But sentiment was growing for the return of the King. When Venizelos resigned in October, 1932, he compelled his successor Panyoti Tsaldaris to renounce any plans he might have had for the restoration. But Tsaldaris was no more successful than Venizelos in his efforts to overcome the depression, the effects of which were particularly severe in Greece, a largely trading nation. After Venizelos himself had made another effort to surmount the difficulties, elections were held and the Tsaldaris group won, whereupon the government began to propose openly that the King should be brought back. Venizelos then raised a revolt in Athens and in his native island of Crete, but it was put down by General George Kondylis, who ousted Tsaldaris and then held a plebiscite to determine whether or not the King should return. Since the plebiscite was efficiently managed by the General it showed the desired majority and George returned (November 24, 1935). Kondylis remained in power as virtual dictator until early in 1936, when he died, as did Venizelos also, a short time later, in exile.

The Dictatorship of General Metaxas. Elections were held a few days before the death of Kondylis, with the unexpected result that the Venizelists who won were still unable to obtain a majority. The small Communist party had won fifteen seats, all in the north of Greece, and held the balance of power between the two political groups. This was a situation made to order for the military, who wished to rule the state; and when the Communists showed signs of preparing a general strike the King and the army, now led by General John Metaxas, struck swiftly. Parliament was dissolved and political parties were abolished. Metaxas himself became dictator. He set himself to improve the administration of the country, engaged in programs of public works, and instituted a rearmament program—all of which necessitated a considerable increase in taxation. Since Greece by this time was emerging from the depression, as was the rest of Europe, the country was more prosperous than it had been for many years. In 1938 General Metaxas became prime minister for life, and he remained in control of the country until his death in 1941.

In 1939 the British and French guaranteed Greek independence at the same time that they extended similar guarantees to Poland and Rumania. The Metaxas regime had tried to be neutral, trading with Germany but maintaining good relations with Britain and France. However, after the Italian occupation of Albania in April, 1939, Italy appeared to present the greatest danger, and Metaxas did his best to prepare for the defense of Greece—though the most fortified areas were in the north (the "Metaxas Line") against the perennial enemy, Bulgaria, in spite of an agreement signed with the latter in July, 1938. With no provocation, Mussolini invaded Greece from Albania in October, 1940. But he was badly defeated, and the Italian troops had already been driven back into Albania by the time Hitler was able to rescue his ally. Meanwhile Metaxas had died, and the British had sent troops to reinforce the country, giving Hitler a better excuse for invasion than Mussolini had had the previous year. The Germans attacked with such power that the Greeks were quickly defeated. George II went into exile, to return only after the liberation—when the question arose once more as to whether the nation should be a monarchy or a republic.

TURKEY

The old Ottoman Empire came to an end with the defeat of Turkey in World War I. Ever since the deposition of Sultan Abdul Hamid II in 1909, the real power had been exercised by Enver Pasha, though Abdul Hamid's brother Mohammed V occupied the throne. The reverses of the last year of the war robbed Turkey of all her possessions except her small European territory and Anatolia, and Enver's government was naturally discredited and unpopular. Indeed, the war hero Mustapha Kemal so consistently attacked Enver during the last period that he was lucky to escape with his life. Kemal's opposition to Enver and his well-known antagonism to the chief German adviser, General von Falkenhayn, served to dissociate him from the defeat. When Enver

Pasha fled the country early in November, 1918, Kemal was sent to Anatolia as the representative of the new sultan Mohammed VI.

Treaties of Sèvres and Lausanne.   Once away from the capital Constantinople, where the Allies held sway and the Sultan was their virtual prisoner, Kemal organized resistance against the Greeks and Italians, who had been promised Turkish territories in Anatolia, and eventually against the Sultan himself, especially after the latter had signed the (to Kemal) iniquitous Treaty of Sèvres (see p. 13). The Sultan was advised by a National Assembly meeting in Constantinople, which accepted the treaty, but a considerable number of Assembly members preferred to go to Anatolia to join Kemal. As duly elected deputies they expected to run the government, and they did form a provisional government. When they hesitated to choose Kemal as their president, he intimidated them with his troops, and was duly chosen president by the Assembly on April 23, 1920.

When Constantinople at last accepted the Treaty of Sèvres in August, 1920, Kemal and his government refused to accept it. They organized the war effort against the Italians and Greeks who were already in the country. The Italians withdrew in March, 1921, in exchange for economic concessions, and three days later Kemal signed a treaty with Bolshevik Russia, which settled their immediate problems and left him free to concentrate on the Greeks. Even so, the Greeks almost succeeded in taking his capital, and it was not until August, 1922, that the Turks were able to mount a counteroffensive which drove them out of the country. The British, who had been consistently supporting the Greeks, landed a force at Chanak on the eastern side of the Straits to bar the Turks from crossing over into Europe. Kemal prudently refused to tangle with them, and the Lloyd George government, which had been responsible for the intervention, fell soon afterward, in large part on this issue. An armistice with the Greeks was arranged soon afterward through French mediation, and the Allied troops withdrew from eastern Turkey, in exchange for an agreement neutralizing the Straits. Finally, in July, 1923, Turkey was granted a much more favorable settlement by the Treaty of Lausanne than had been imposed upon her at the 1920 Treaty of Sèvres. For this Kemal was entitled to a large share of the credit.

The Ascendancy of Kemal Atatürk.   Meanwhile Kemal had declared the sultanate at an end, and sent Sultan Mohammed VI into exile (November 1, 1922). The republic was officially proclaimed on October 29, 1923, and Kemal became its first president, with extensive powers, while his friend Ismet Pasha was appointed prime minister. Ankara replaced Constantinople as the capital. Turkey was now free and independent and, though shorn of her former provinces, had a compact state capable of being defended. It was almost entirely Turkish in population, with the exception of Turkish Kurdistan and Turkish Armenia, which Turkey had refused to let go in the peace settlement.

Once firmly in power and ready to deal with domestic affairs, Kemal turned his furious energy to the task of modernization of his country and the emancipation of his people, especially from the demands of Islam, which he regarded as a backward and medieval religion, quite unsuited for the modern world. New law codes were promulgated, based on European models; the symbolic fez was prohibited; polygamy was abolished, divorce made difficult, civil marriage made compulsory; the Latin alphabet was substituted for the Turkic. There was serious, often violent, opposition to all these measures, but it was always, equally violently, suppressed. For a time Kemal permitted the existence of only one party. Then, thinking it would be an advantage for the government to experience some opposition in the Assembly, he allowed a Liberal Republican party to come into existence. When it became obstreperous, and criticism of the government's unpopular policies became violent, and all this was followed by a Kurdish rebellion, Kemal concluded that he had gone too far. But he contented himself with taking strong action only against individuals, and the party system survived. Democratic forms, with free and contested elections, persisted after World War II. In 1934 Kemal instituted a five-year plan which helped the country out of the depression and provided it with many new industries. In the same year he assumed the title of Atatürk ("Father of the Turks"). He died in 1938, and was succeeded by Ismet Inönü, his first prime minister.

Turkey refused to be drawn into the German orbit during the Hitler era, in spite of her close trade connections with Germany. In 1939 she preferred to enter into agreements with Britain and France, which reinforced her neutrality. She persisted in this neutrality throughout the war, and it was not to Hitler's interest to take on her tough and well-trained army. Turkey likewise resisted victorious Russia's threats and blandishments as the war drew to an end. There was never any doubt as to where Turkey's sympathies lay during this period, and she eventually joined NATO as a postwar ally of the Western powers.

TURKISH PROVINCES

The former Turkish provinces will be dealt with in detail in Chapter 10. The Arab revolt of 1917–1918 succeeded, with British aid, in throwing off the Turkish yoke just before the Armistice. Difficulties at once arose as to the disposition of the territories thus liberated. The Sykes-Picot agreements (see p. 199) of 1916 between Britain and France provided for the allotment of some of the Arabic lands between these two powers. Syria (including the later independent state of Lebanon) thus became a French mandate; Iraq, Transjordan, and Palestine became British mandates; while Yemen, previously semi-independent under its Zeidi rulers, now became fully independent. The Sherif Husein, father of the two kings who eventually took over the mandates of Iraq and Transjordan, ruled Mecca for a few years until he was overthrown by King Ibn Sa'ud of Arabia. Cyprus and Egypt, nominally Turkish but ruled by Britain, severed their last ties with Turkey. They became respectively a crown colony and a protectorate with (beginning in 1922) an Egyptian king descended from the former Khedives. The Treaty of Sèvres established an independent state of Greater Armenia, made up of the sectors of Armenia hitherto in the Russian and Ottoman Empires. But neither the Russians nor the Turks accepted the arrangement, and Armenia was again divided by a treaty between Bolshevik Russia and Turkey in 1921. This the Allies had to accept in spite of the Treaty of Sèvres and the principle of self-determination.

CONCLUSION

The interwar period saw the establishment of a strong and independent Turkey, by far the greater part of which lay outside Europe. But none of the other Balkan states was able to avoid being drawn into World War II, though none entered it willingly. After being incorporated into Hitler's New European Order, all except Yugoslavia and Greece had to submit to a new master in the person of Stalin. Yugoslavia was saved from satellite status in part because her new government was Communist, and in part because the Yugoslav partisans played a larger part in liberating the country from German rule than did the Russians. Greece was saved because Stalin initially honored an agreement to let Greece fall into the British sphere of influence; and Britain and the United States provided sufficient military aid to prevent a take-over by a Communist movement backed by Yugoslavia and to a lesser degree by the Soviet Union. These events will be described in more detail in Chapter 13.

THE OLDER DEMOCRACIES OF EUROPE AND THE BRITISH DOMINIONS

8

None of the well-established democracies of Europe succumbed to dictatorship during the interwar period. Nor did the British overseas Dominions (Canada, Australia and New Zealand, and the Union of South Africa). Indeed, in many of these countries, especially in Scandinavia, there was much social progress, and democratic institutions functioned effectively for the purpose of increasing both political and social democracy. In France and Belgium in the 1930's there were serious threats from the right-wing parties and factions sympathetic to at least some of Hitler's theories; but no threats of any importance materialized on the left, in spite of the election of some Communist deputies in countries where the Communist party was legal. But it must be admitted that no European democracy improved its world position in terms of either power or prestige during the period, and weaknesses of the democracies in face of the totalitarian threat contributed to the coming of World War II.

GREAT BRITAIN AND IRELAND

Although Great Britain emerged victorious from World War I, the cost had been high. The trench warfare that had dominated the four-year conflict in the West had been extremely costly in lives, and the delay in enforcing conscription until 1917 meant that the loss was disproportionately high among members of those social classes educated in the "public" school system, in which the tradition of service to "king and country" was stressed. From these classes also came the great bulk of the officers, and mortality among junior officers was extremely high in this kind of warfare.

The British economy had also been hit hard. Although production had soared during the war, relatively little new industrial capacity had been added except for armament production. Too many of the older plants had become obsolescent or completely worn out. A large proportion of her merchant ships were at the bottom of the sea, and many more were not fit for much use. Although only about 10 per cent of British overseas investment had been liquidated to pay for war expenses, this represented a considerable sacrifice since for more than a century Britain had been able to balance her international accounts only through the receipt of income from foreign investment. Lastly Britain was heavily in debt to the United States (see p. 21); and though she was owed much more by her Allies than she owed to the United States, there seemed little hope that the Allies would repay the debts unless Germany provided sufficient reparations to cover them. In the end, in spite of her default on debts to the United States during the 1930's, Britain paid out to her creditors approximately $150,000,000 more than she received in the form of reparations and repayment of war debts.

Unlike the United States, Britain was economically weakened by her participation in both the First and the Second World Wars. She did not have the reserves either of natural resources or of manpower to enable her to profit by the huge increases in production made necessary by the war. Nor did she acquire any new imperial possessions of substance. The Palestinian mandate, for example, proved extremely expensive both in the costs of administration and policing and in prestige. On the whole the British Empire was probably no longer a paying proposition, even when all the indirect profits to private industry are calculated. As will be discussed in Chapter 10, for the first time the most valuable parts of the Empire were no longer securely in British hands; and her attempt to keep them also proved expensive. Britain therefore in 1918 faced an uncertain future even while she gave her victorious wartime coalition government a new mandate for five more years of power.

The Settlement of the "Irish Question." For many years the relation of Ireland to the rest of the British Isles had been a divisive issue in British politics. The great nineteenth-century statesman Gladstone had staked his career on the question of Irish Home Rule, and been repudiated by the electorate. In the immediate prewar years the Liberal party had continued the attempt to pass a law granting local autonomy to Ireland. But the House of Lords, made up of hereditary peers and government-appointed higher clergy who held office for life, had rejected it. At last in 1914 the House of Lords had exhausted its powers of delay, and the bill became law without its consent (September 18, 1914). The struggle had, however, given birth to two compromises. The law was not to come into force until after the war, and Ulster (six counties of northern Ireland) was to be dealt with separately at that time. The Conservative party, however, continued to oppose Home Rule, and even adopted as its official name the "Unionist" party because it favored preservation of the Union (which had been imposed on Ireland in 1800). During the war some Irishmen intrigued with Germany in the hope of obtaining arms and setting up their independent state by force. This attempt led to the Easter Rebellion in Dublin and a few other areas of Ireland (April 24, 1916), which was put down by the British with considerable bloodshed. Several of its leaders were executed.

Under the Union system the Irish were represented in the British Parliament, where at times they had exercised considerable influence. But the sole interest of the Irish Nationalist members had been to win Home Rule or independence; not unnaturally they had little interest in British domestic legislation. The independence party, known as Sinn Fein, led by Eamon de Valera (at that time in an English prison) won almost all the seats allotted to southern Ireland in the 1918 election. But instead of taking their places in the British Parliament at Westminster, they organized their own Parliament in Dublin (the Dail Eireann) and declared the independence of all Ireland. This the British would not permit, and they sent troops and a large constabulary (Royal Irish Constabulary, known as the Black and Tans) recruited from English returned soldiers. Atrocities followed on both sides for the rest of 1919 and most of 1920, until the British Parliament passed the Government of Ireland Act, which called for two separate Irish parliaments, one meeting in Belfast (Northern Ireland) and one in Dublin. Elections were held under this act, but the Sinn Fein party won 124 of 128 seats in Southern Ireland, and at once rejected the imposed settlement.

De Valera, who had escaped from prison early in 1919 and returned to Ireland, held a conference with the British prime minister Lloyd George and other British representatives, in which he was offered Dominion Status (the autonomy within the British Empire enjoyed by the overseas Dominions). But de Valera rejected this, insisting on outright independence and union with mainly Protestant Northern Ireland, who had no desire to be united with the south under Catholic rule. De Valera boycotted a further conference in which several other leaders of Sinn Fein took part, including the two most important ones, Michael Collins and Arthur Griffith. These men agreed to a treaty under which all Ireland was to become a Dominion, but the northern counties were to be given the opportunity to contract out if they wished. As de Valera well knew, this in fact would mean the partition of the country, and this he was unwilling to accept even as a stage on the way to complete independence. He thought—apparently quite correctly—that the partition once accepted could never be undone. By a small majority (64–57) the Dail Eireann accepted the treaty, whereupon de Valera resigned his position as head of the executive council and began another insurrection, this time against his former colleagues. An Irish Republican Army was organized, pledged to fight for independence and the union of all Ireland.

During the next few years the more moderate Sinn Fein group, led by William Cosgrave (Collins had been assassinated and Griffith had died in the interval) established a government, and Northern Ireland, as expected, seceded to form its own local government. Cosgrave accepted the new boundaries of the Irish Free State, as it was called. During the whole period he had to struggle against the Irish Republican Army and try to suppress the rebellion. De Valera was captured and imprisoned for nearly a year. When he was freed, he still would not co-operate, now making an issue of the oath to the monarchy which was demanded of all the members of the Dail. In 1927 he and his followers agreed to take the oath, but he continued to agitate for its abolition and for the complete independence of the country. In elections held in 1932 his party, Fianna Fail, won a small majority and he himself became president of the executive council (the equivalent of prime minister); but not until the next year could he persuade the Dail to abolish the oath. He instituted a tariff war with Britain in 1932, which lasted until 1936, but no final settlement was obtained until 1938, when de Valera, who had previously enjoyed only the smallest of majorities in the Dail, won a major electoral victory.

Thereupon the outstanding questions between Britain and the Irish Free State were adjusted and Ireland was allowed to have her own elected president instead of a governor general appointed by the crown. Only a few months before, Northern Ireland had given even more overwhelming approval to the party which wished to keep Northern Ireland separate. Partition has continued to this day. The Irish Free State (or Eire) left the Commonwealth in 1948 and became a totally independent republic in 1949.

The Unemployment Problem in Britain. The major problem faced by the Lloyd George coalition government, as indeed by all its successors, was unemployment. This was not solved during the interwar period, although the rearmament program of the late 1930's contributed to its abatement. Unemployment never at any time fell below a million, and it reached well over three million in the depth of the depression in 1932. Immediately after World War I there was a brief improvement in the economic situation, since Germany was not yet an important competitor and there was a considerable pent-up demand for industrial products. But by 1921 the brief boom was over. In the later 1920's while the United States was enjoying substantial prosperity, Britain's position improved slightly, but not enough to bring unemployment below a million.

Hardest hit was the coal-mining industry. British mines were technologically backward; the best seams were almost worked out; and there was so little prospect for improvement that it was difficult for the mines to raise capital for modernization. Most of the miners were unwilling to face the fact that theirs was a declining, even a dying, industry. To them, as to their fathers and grandfathers before them, mining was a way of life, and they could not face the idea of uprooting themselves from their homes (mostly in Wales, northeast England, and southern Scotland). Yet there was no other work available in these areas, which were dependent on coal, iron, and steel, all of which were depressed industries. In the 1930's the National government passed legislation to give incentives to new industries to settle in these "special areas," but not very much was achieved before the outbreak of war.

The textile industry was in hardly better condition, though here it was foreign competition that caused the decline. Before the war textiles had been the biggest earner of foreign exchange, and the huge market of India was supplied largely from Lancashire. But India now manufactured much of her own textiles, and the new government in India was allowed to place a tariff on English imports. Moreover Japan, with a more modern industrial plant, gradually took over many of Britain's former export markets, as did the United States in the Western Hemisphere. The economic nationalism of the new nations made exports difficult, but Britain herself remained largely a free market until the 1930's, though she did from time to time levy protective duties on certain imports in "key" industries, lest she be left without these industries in time of war. The free-trade barrier was broken by the McKenna duties of 1915, when automobiles, clocks, and similar items were for the first time protected by tariffs.

The "General Strike" of 1926. The Lloyd George government, faced with strikes in the mining industry, responded in 1919 with a 20 per cent wage increase. But this barely kept pace with the rise in the cost of living. When the mines were turned back to private ownership in 1921, the owners, in order to operate the mines profitably, felt obliged to lower wages. This resulted in another strike (March 31 to July 1), and the government provided the owners with a subsidy, so that they could pay a wage higher than economic conditions justified. There was a brief improvement in the industry while the Ruhr invasion was preventing the Germans from paying reparations in coal, but export markets contracted again thereafter. In 1926 the owners, who were about to lose their subsidy, served notice to the Mining Federation (the monopoly trade union in mining) that they would have to reduce wages again; and the Federation requested support from the Trades Union Congress (TUC), representing all the unions in the country.

For the first and last time the TUC responded to such a request. It called upon the unions in certain key areas, including transportation, to engage in a sympathetic strike to begin on May 3, 1926. This strike, although usually called a "general" strike, was not intended to be general; it differed in all essential respects from the kind of "general strike" so often called for political purposes on the Continent. About 2,500,000 workers were called out. This figure, including miners, was intended to include under half of the organized workers in the country. The government, now headed by Stanley Baldwin, was fully prepared for the strike (which had been announced well in advance), and skeleton services were maintained, mainly by volunteers from the upper and middle classes. It is far from unlikely that Baldwin wished to demonstrate to the labor unions they did not have the power to disrupt the life of the country.

The strike of unions other than mining lasted nine days (May 3–12). The miners' strike went on for many months until the Miners' Federation was bankrupt and the miners on the verge of destitution. On November 19, 1926, they surrendered; their wages were reduced, and their hours of work lengthened. The following year the Baldwin government passed a law making sympathy strikes (and certain kinds of lockouts) illegal and prohibiting the contribution of union funds to political parties except with the written consent of the workers. This law was not repealed until 1946 when for the first time a Labour government was voted into office.

Attempts to Solve the Unemployment Problem. The British government was, of course, greatly concerned with the unemployment problem and, in addition to trying somewhat fruitlessly to solve it, took many steps to palliate its effects. Before the war an Unemployment Insurance Act had been passed, under which both employers and employees contributed a percentage of wages to a fund, which was run on a true insurance basis and expected to be actuarially sound. The Act, however, applied to only a few industries, and the benefits were small. In 1921 and 1922, the Lloyd George government passed more unemployment bills which extended the coverage under the Act to almost all industries and provided for specific sums of money to be paid out in case of unemployment, including payments for dependents. This meant that in times of heavy unemployment the insurance fund could not remain actuarially sound, and it had to borrow from the Treasury to make the statutory payments. The additional payments above what was paid for by the insurance came to be called the "dole."

When unemployment rose to over three million and the dole payments continued on the same scale, it became clear that this borrowing would eventually lead to the bankruptcy of the state. As an alternative it was proposed that a "means test" should be substituted for the simple right to receive benefits. Under this test all members of a family who were earning would be expected to contribute to the support of the unemployed member, who was often an aging parent. The divided Labour government led by Ramsay MacDonald resigned on this issue (see p. 141), but even the National (mainly Conservative) government that followed, still led by MacDonald, did not feel able to enforce a rigid family means test because of the outcry against it and its obvious social disadvantages (e.g., breaking up of families, refusal of younger people to work). However, the National government did pass a bill in 1934 which separated unemployment insurance from public assistance and put the unemployment fund back on a sound insurance basis. In this policy the government was greatly helped by increased employment in the years following the Act.

Political Changes during the Interwar Period. In October, 1922, the Conservatives withdrew their support from the Lloyd George coalition government, in part because of the Chanak affair (see p. 129). Soon afterward an election was held, which was won by the Conservatives under Andrew Bonar Law. But Law soon had to resign because of ill health. He was succeeded as prime minister by Stanley Baldwin, who came to the conclusion that the only solution to the problems of British industry was the imposition of protective duties on imports. But this had been unacceptable to the electorate for almost eighty years. Baldwin therefore decided to "go to the country," as the English expression has it, and hold another election on this specific issue. As a result the Conservatives lost their over-all majority,* even though they still held the most seats. The Labour party had now become the second largest party. The Liberals were willing to try to work with the Labour, but not with the Conservative, party. The King therefore sent for Ramsay MacDonald, head of the Labour party, who became prime minister. Since MacDonald was always dependent upon Liberal votes for his majorities, he had to act in a very prudent

* It should be noted that British general elections do not always reflect the degree of popular support enjoyed by a particular party. A considerable increase in the popular vote for one party may nevertheless sometimes result in a loss of seats in Parliament, since it is possible for most of this increase to take place in constituencies where that party already has a substantial majority, so that the extra votes are wasted. When there are three or more parties, as there have been in Britain for the whole of the twentieth century, the least popular party may win only a few seats even though its total vote in the country may amount to several million. Thus there is always something adventitious in electoral victories in Britain. No party in the twentieth century has ever held an absolute majority of the votes cast, and in several elections a party has proportionately increased its vote even while at the same time it is voted out of office. The Liberal party, which since 1923 has been the least popular of the three main parties, has therefore wished to change the electoral system to proportional representation of the kind common to most of the countries on the Continent, since this would give the Liberals a far higher percentage of seats than they have ever won under the present system.

manner, and was unable to pass any of the legislation most ardently desired by his followers. In 1928 universal suffrage was finally granted, with the extension of the vote to all women over 21 on the same terms as men.

The government's greatest successes were in the field of foreign policy, but its diplomatic recognition of the Soviet Union and the negotiation of commercial treaties with her were opposed by the Conservatives and not popular with the Liberals. When the Labour government failed to prosecute a Communist on charges of subversion, the Liberals withdrew their support, making another general election necessary. A few days before the election a popular newspaper, the *Daily Mail,* published a letter purporting to be written by Zinoviev, head of the Comintern, calling upon the British Communist party (which was at the time extremely small and without any influence) to work for the overthrow of the government. Although the letter was almost certainly a forgery, it had the desired effect, and the Labour party was defeated. Stanley Baldwin, who now formed his second administration (November, 1924), denounced the new treaties with the Soviet Union and rejected the Geneva Protocol, which MacDonald had favored, for the purpose of strengthening the League of Nations (see p. 28). In 1927, following the "general strike," the government raided the offices of Arcos, the Soviet Trading company in Britain, and declared (without providing either Parliament or the public with the evidence) that it had found documents proving that the Russians were engaged in espionage and subversion. It then broke off diplomatic relations with the Soviet Union.

The Baldwin government stayed in office for almost its full term (five years), but on June 5, 1929, it was defeated in the elections. This time the Labour party won more seats than the Conservatives, but it still needed the support of the by now quite small Liberal party. The second administration of Ramsay MacDonald was called upon to meet the full force of the depression, but it failed to come up with any new plans for expanding industry and decreasing the number of the unemployed. It did, however, appoint a committee of experts to make suggestions. In July, 1931, this May Committee put forward a long list of economies and other deflationary measures, with the avowed purpose of saving the country from having to devaluate the pound sterling, which had been exchangeable for gold at the old prewar rate ever since 1925. (In contrast, other countries with few exceptions had devaluated their currencies, thus reducing the burden of internal debt.) The May Committee did not go so far as to suggest devaluation—which in fact proved to be inevitable—but preferred to make recommendations of a strictly orthodox nature. The most unpopular economy suggested was the imposition of the family means test, already referred to, and this caused a split in the Cabinet.

MacDonald himself was willing to accept the May recommendations, as was his chancellor of the exchequer, Philip Snowden, and one other Cabinet member, J. H. Thomas. The remainder refused, and the government had no option but to resign. King George V in these exceptional circumstances consulted the Liberal and Conservative leaders, and they concurred that a new National government should be formed and that the best person to head it was Ramsay MacDonald. The King therefore decided to ask MacDonald to form another government with a cabinet which would this time be united in favor of economies, including the means test and which would be prepared to impose protective duties. MacDonald accepted, and though he and his two colleagues were expelled from the Labour party, he could now rely on the backing of the Conservatives in Parliament, plus such Labour party members as would stay with him (who now included the Lord Chancellor, Lord Sankey) and such Liberals (few as they were) as were willing to abandon their opposition to protective duties.

The National government, nevertheless, had to face much opposition in the country, including some rioting and a very orderly "mutiny" in a part of the navy which thought that its already small pay would be still further reduced. There was also a prolonged run on the pound, as holders of sterling, expecting devaluation, sought to exchange it for gold before such exchange became impossible. In spite of loans from France and elsewhere, on September 21 the Bank of England abandoned the gold standard, and sterling fell precipitately. Thereafter England survived with a managed currency without gold backing, and no terrible consequence ensued. On the contrary for a time, until other countries, including the United States, also devaluated, Britain had a decided advantage in export markets and business began to improve.

A month later the government decided to ask for the support of the country and held elections, without offering any detailed program of how it proposed to overcome the depression, preferring to ask for a "doctor's mandate." This was granted overwhelmingly by the electorate, and Ramsay MacDonald continued to preside over a cabinet in which his party and the Liberal Nationalists were represented, but which, like the new Parliament, was made up mostly of Conservatives. The government then proceeded to impose a large series of protective duties, to provide farmers with a guaranteed price for their grain, to establish controls on foreign exchange, to organize marketing boards, to impose quotas, and to take other similar measures. Thus Britain completely abandoned the old laissez-faire policy and followed all the other European and most American countries, including the United States, in the general policy known as economic nationalism (neo-mercantilism). The policy almost certainly helped Britain out of the depression, although the unemployment problem was not solved until the war.

In 1935 another general election favored the National government, but Ramsay MacDonald personally was defeated in his own constituency. Although he was elected by another constituency shortly afterwards, Stanley Baldwin again became prime minister, with MacDonald remaining in the Cabinet with a sinecure position until his death in 1937. Baldwin retired to the House of Lords in the same year, leaving his chancellor of the exchequer, Neville Chamberlain, to succeed him. The last act of importance performed by Baldwin as prime minister was to ease out the new king, Edward VIII, who had succeeded his father in January, 1936. Edward, who was unmarried when he came to the throne, wished to marry an American woman, Mrs. Ernest Simpson, who was in the process of obtaining her second divorce. Baldwin, the Anglican clergy, and the Dominion prime ministers were all in agreement that Edward could not marry Mrs. Simpson and remain king. Nevertheless the King, who had become widely known while he was Prince of Wales and was popular in his own right, might well have brought the people over to his side. But most Englishmen knew nothing of the entire matter—which was widely bruited in the American press—until the last moment, by which time Stanley Baldwin had imposed his own solution on the King, who abdicated in favor of his brother Albert. The new King, who took the name of George VI, was eminently suitable for the ceremonial job of king, since he had an attractive wife and children.

There was little of importance in domestic affairs during the late 1930's, which were dominated by the aggressive tactics of Hitler on the Continent. Britain took the lead under both the

Baldwin and the Chamberlain governments in attempting to appease both Hitler and Mussolini. (These events will be described in detail in Chapter 11.)

THE BRITISH DOMINIONS

The British Dominions overseas had received their autonomy at different times, the last being the Union of South Africa in 1910. Since they did not control their own foreign policy, they were all automatically at war when the mother country entered World War I on August 4, 1914. They claimed the right to be treated as independent states at the Peace Conference, urging that their sacrifices had earned it. Eventually the Great Powers accepted their point of view, and each of the Dominions ratified the peace treaties through her own parliament. As duly authorized participants in the Peace Conference, they became charter members of the League of Nations. South Africa, Australia, and New Zealand were granted mandates. During the next few years several Dominions signed treaties with foreign powers, and they began to appoint diplomatic representatives in foreign capitals.

The evolving situation needed to be clarified and formalized. This was done at the Imperial Conferences of 1926 and 1930 and in the Statute of Westminster passed by the British Parliament in 1931. The Earl of Balfour in his report to the Imperial Conference of 1926 defined the relationship between Great Britain and the Dominions as follows: "They are autonomous Communities within the British Empire, equal in status, in no way subordinate one to another in any aspect of their domestic or external affairs, though united by a common allegiance to the Crown, and freely associated as members of the British Commonwealth of Nations." This Conference set up a committee to advise the next Conference, scheduled for 1930, on what legal steps were needed to complete the severance between the political structures of the Dominions and the mother country. The result was the Statute of Westminster of 1931, which gave legal form to this independence, removing the former right of the British Parliament to legislate for the Dominions and to disallow acts passed by the Dominion parliaments, as well as similar disabilities. The appeal to the Privy Council from the Supreme Courts of the various Dominions, was not mentioned in the Statute of Westminster; it could be retained or not according to the wishes of the Dominions. In 1939, when Britain declared war on Germany, the Dominions were free to enter war or not, as their own parliaments decided. All except the Irish Free State declared war within a few days of Britain's own declaration.

Canada. During the interwar period Canada increased her population by close to 40 per cent, largely through immigration from Britain, which was high in the 1920's but tapered off in the 1930's, when many British-born immigrants preferred to return home, where insurance and the "dole" lessened the rigors of unemployment. Canada became increasingly dependent for its prosperity on influxes of United States capital, since Britain herself no longer had much of a surplus to export.

Politically the period was dominated by the solid but unexciting government provided by the Liberals under William Lyon Mackenzie King, who was prime minister from 1921 until his retirement in 1948 (except for three months in 1926) and during the depression from 1930 to 1935. In the latter period Richard B. Bennett and his Conservative party were in power. It was Bennett's government which took the lead in arranging the Ottawa Conference of 1932, in which all the Dominions bargained with Britain for a differential tariff, granting them a preferred rate for their exports to Britain and to one another, in exchange for similar preferences granted by Great Britain. This was made possible by the recent coming into power of the National government in Britain with a program of protection. This system has been maintained to the present day. It was one of the reasons why France vetoed British entry into the European Common Market in January, 1963, since Britain, under pressure from the Dominions, demanded favorable treatment for them, which was opposed by France.

In 1935, when it appeared certain that Conservative popularity had so far declined that Bennett would lose the next election, he proposed a series of sweeping social and economic reforms, which were quickly passed before dissolution. Many of the reforms fell within the jurisdiction of the Canadian provinces, which had not been consulted by Bennett, and were therefore nullified by the Canadian Supreme Court. Mackenzie King, who returned to office in October 1935, obtained the consent of the provinces to new legislation in this field, and in the following years a program not dissimilar to Bennett's was enacted.

Newfoundland. This Dominion, an island east of Canada which had as its dependency (from 1927) a part of the mainland territory of Labrador, had refused to join Canada in the nineteenth century but was always closely connected with her. In the 1920's much social legislation was passed, particularly under the government of Walter Munroe; but it proved too expensive for the resources of the country, especially in the depression when its primary products, mainly lumber and fish, commanded very low prices. By 1933 the small country was headed for bankruptcy and petitioned Britain for help. As a result she lost her status as a self-governing Dominion, and was placed under a commission made up of three British and three Newfoundland officials, presided over by the British-appointed governor (1933). The Commission gradually restored the finances by orthodox deflationary measures, but Dominion status was not restored. In a 1948 referendum Newfoundland voted by a small margin to become the tenth province of Canada.

Australia and New Zealand.   Both Australia and New Zealand were pioneers of social legislation; most of their major reforms were made before World War I. In both countries trade unions were strong, and Labour governments had been in office since the early part of the century. But during the interwar period both, as producers of primary products, suffered very greatly from the depression, and many of their advanced social reforms had to fall into abeyance.

Australia was ruled by a Labour government during the early part of the war, until Prime Minister William Hughes of the Labour party formed a War Cabinet which favored conscription. The Labour party, which opposed it, then expelled him, but he continued as prime minister with the support of some of his ex-colleagues and a new Nationalist party. As Australian prime minister Hughes played an important part at the Peace Conference. After losing an election, he resigned in 1923, and thereafter governments of a conservative nature—though they never adopted the name of conservative—ruled Australia until World War II with the exception of the two years from 1929 to 1931. These conservative-style federal governments began to assume ever more powers hitherto exercised by the states, and they pre-empted all the best sources of taxation. This situation led to an attempted secession by Western Australia in 1933, and a serious quarrel between the federal prime minister, J. A. Lyons, and J. T. Lang, premier of New South Wales, over the latter's financial policies. When the New South Wales government defaulted on its obligations Lyons dismissed Lang, who was then repudiated in a general election in the state. Australia adopted an immigration policy which strongly favored the British above other would-be immigrants, especially the Italians, and totally excluded all nonwhites. She imposed very high tariffs to protect home industry, especially against Japanese competition.

The Labour government of James H. Scullin in Australia and the United (Liberal) party of George W. Forbes in New Zealand both met the depression mainly through drastic economies and deflation. Australia, however, devaluated her currency long before Britain and thus for many months had a considerable advantage over most other countries. This, combined with the fact that she was a major producer of gold, helped her to emerge fairly quickly from the depression. The conservative governments that followed Scullin's during the 1930's weathered the rest of the depression safely and with little loss of credit. The relatively conservative coalition government that held office in New Zealand during the depression soon turned to the customary deflationary methods, including exchange control, restriction of imports, and lowering of salaries. These measures proved adequate for the country's needs and in fact resulted in a budgetary surplus. At this point the New Zealand Labour party, which campaigned on a promise of relief from austerity, and in essence for the establishment of a true welfare state, won an overwhelming victory in the elections of 1935. The new government under Michael Savage instituted a social welfare program unique in the world of that time. The program culminated in a free national health service (1941). The Labour government continued in office until November, 1949.

The Union of South Africa.   Between the two wars the Union of South Africa was ruled by men who now seem very moderate in comparison with the Nationalist government that has held office since 1948 with ever increasing majorities. However, the Hertzog-Smuts governments were strongly racialist in relation to the native Bantu peoples, who outnumber both the white groups combined by about three to one.

In spite of this disparity in numbers, the country has always been ruled by its white elements. During the nineteenth century, when South Africa was a British colony, the British settlers naturally exercised an influence out of proportion to their numbers. In fact, they were outnumbered by the Afrikaners of Dutch and French descent, against whom they fought the "Boer" War at the turn of the century. Once that war was over, the Afrikaner leaders,

General Louis Botha and General (later Field Marshal) Jan Christiaan Smuts, decided that the best policy for their people was to co-operate with the British, and while they led the country, this was the policy pursued. But it was not acceptable to the more extreme Nationalists, who wished to rule in accordance with their own narrow views.

The Nationalist party won the elections in 1924, but it could not govern without the parliamentary support of the small Labour party. General Hertzog, the Nationalist who then became prime minister, had to postpone the fulfillment of his party's policies. In 1933 he and Smuts formed a coalition government which held together until World War II. But Hertzog opposed South African entry into the war, precipitating a showdown with his less nationalist colleagues. Smuts obtained parliamentary authorization for the declaration of war, and thereupon Hertzog left the government.

Some steps were taken during the period which brought South Africa nearer to *apartheid* (separateness between the races), a policy favored by almost all the Afrikaners. The Hertzog-Smuts coalition passed a bill taking away the right, which the Bantu in Cape Province had enjoyed since colonial times, of voting for members of parliament provided they could meet the high property qualification. Under this Act they could vote only on a separate roll and could choose only Europeans to represent them.

The South Africans were granted a C class mandate (see p. 16) over former German South-West Africa, which they administered as if it had been a South African province. It had a legislative assembly run entirely by the whites. In the course of the interwar period, British and Afrikaner immigrants came to outnumber the Germans in the legislative assembly, and at once tried to persuade the Union to annex the territory as its fifth province. This would have required either the permission of the League of Nations, which was not likely to be granted or outright defiance of that body, which General Smuts, as a founder and consistent supporter of the League, would not countenance. Today the Republic of South Africa still holds the territory as a mandate of the now defunct League, since it has consistently refused to convert it to United Nations trusteeship status. The World Court is considering the present legal status of South-West Africa, which is obviously somewhat unclear.

FRANCE

At the close of World War I, France was faced with a tremendous job of reconstruction, the cost of which she hoped Germany would meet in the form of reparations. If Germany had been required to bear only the cost of physical reconstruction in the countries which her armies had devastated, it is possible that she would have made a serious effort to pay. But since the other Allied countries, who had not suffered such devastation, also desired reparations, the "war guilt" clause was added, and Germany, as the declared aggressor, was required to pay not only the costs of physical destruction but also the indirect cost of the war, such as widows' pensions and the like (see p. 12). It was hoped that at least the reparations would also cover the Allied debts to the United States. The result, as already noted, was that Germany was assessed an astronomical sum, and in the first period after the war she paid relatively little. Thus France, who naturally wished to reconstruct her northern territories as quickly as possible, had to borrow to pay for the reconstruction. Since she had also met most of the costs of the war by borrowing, her debt soon became totally unmanageable, and her credit sank ever lower until the National Union ministry of Raymond Poincaré by rigid deflation and economy restored it at the cost of a devaluation.

Unfortunately, France did not derive as much advantage from the reconstruction of her devastated areas as she should have done. Too many of the new factories were little more modern than they had been before the war. Therefore, in spite of the restoration to her of Alsace and Lorraine, and the temporary cession of the Saar region (it was restored to Germany by plebiscite in 1935) which gave France ample supplies of coal and iron, she never became a great industrial power. Her agriculture, although it employed many people and supplied most of her needs, was relatively inefficient except in some specialties (such as wine). Not being so dependent on exports as Britain and Germany, France weathered the early years of the depression better. But in the later 1930's when, under the Popular Front government, she undertook a major social security program and reduced working hours, she did not have the resources to pay for it and became again beset by economic difficulties just at a time when other nations were recovering. Her great losses of manpower during the war and a declining birth rate afflicted her all through the period; and both were in large measure responsible for her defensive foreign policy, designed to prevent the recrudescence of German power. She failed in this attempt, in part because of her own political weakness and the strength of pacifism in the country, and in part because her allies underestimated the danger in which they all stood as the result of German revival. France was therefore compelled to face the full force of the German onslaught in 1940 with relatively little military support, and she went down to defeat as she had in 1871.

France against Herself. This title of a famous book by Herbert Luethy, a talented Swiss observer of the French scene, is an apt description of French politics during the interwar period. With the single exception of the Poincaré right-wing government from 1926 to 1929, which had substantial support while the financial crisis was being overcome, no government held a reliable majority in the Chamber of Deputies. Governments rose and fell with monotonous regularity. As a consequence of the system of modified proportional representation and the multiplicity of parties, all were of necessity coalitions. When a faction in the government objected to one of its policies, often even the budget which it had introduced, it withdrew its support, and the government fell. Continuity was provided by the civil service, which was extremely conservative but on the whole efficient, and occasionally by the presence of a particular minister, such as the perennial foreign minister Aristide Briand in the same office during many administrations.

The division in the Chamber of Deputies reflected the often virulent division in public opinion which had bedeviled the Third Republic since its beginning. Although the republic had been in existence for almost fifty years, a substantial number of influential persons had never accepted it, and there was still even a royalist group, the *camelots du roi*. In addition there were other right-wing movements such as *Action Française,* which was strongly Catholic, nationalistic, and anti-Semitic. This body became avowedly fascist in the 1930's and provided many of the collaborators with the Nazi regime after the fall of France in 1940. Another right-wing body was the veterans' organization the *Croix du Feu,* which became very powerful in the 1930's. On the left the Communist party split off from the Socialist party after the war—as it did in so many other European countries—and was always able to elect some deputies. Until 1935, when the party line handed down by Moscow changed, the Communist party invariably refused to support any government. It usually concentrated its attacks on the Socialists rather than on the right-wing parties, whose policies might be expected to foster a revolutionary situation. For most of the period the Communists controlled the largest labor union, the CGT (*Confederation générale du travail*). All these groups possessed their own tame press, which kept up scurrilous attacks on every government that was in power and upon the unfortunate politicians who had to exercise it. Lastly, big business in France (represented especially by the banks, the armaments industry, and the "two hundred families") very strongly opposed all increases in taxation, however necessary, and invariably gave its backing to the right-wing parties.

The French Political System. The constitution of the Third Republic provided for a president, a chamber of deputies, and a senate. The president, who was elected by the Chamber and the Senate sitting together for a term of seven years, had little power, hardly even as much as the British monarch, and as an elected official belonging to a particular party he lacked the latter's prestige. Although in theory he could dissolve the Chamber with the consent of the Senate, no president ever exercised this power during the interwar period. His task was virtually limited to the choice of a prime minister; but the latter had to be invested with his office by the Chamber. The Senate, indirectly elected for staggered terms for nine years, could delay and revise bills passed by the Chamber. The Chamber was elected for four years by proportional representation, and members could be virtually certain that they would hold their seats for that time, whether or not they supported their government or remained loyal to the party under whose label they had been elected. The Cabinet, which was responsible for the government, was always made up of ministers from two or more parties. But these ministers were chosen by the prime minister who had been given by the president the task of forming the government. If this particular government were defeated in the Chamber on a vote of confidence, it resigned, and a new prime minister would attempt to form a new combination. This might include the great majority of the ministers of the Cabinet that had just resigned, including the late prime minister himself, who might now hold a subordinate position.

Political Developments to the Popular Front of 1936. The first elections after the war, which were held in 1919, gave a large majority of the seats to the *Bloc National* originally led by the victorious wartime prime minister, Georges Clemenceau. However, the presidency was vacated the following year by Raymond Poincaré, and Clemenceau offered his candidature. But he was no longer so popular as at the end of the war, since he was widely regarded as having been too lenient toward the Germans at the Peace Conference. He was defeated by an undistinguished politician (Paul Deschanel) who was afflicted by mental illness and resigned later in 1920. Deschanel was replaced by Alexandre Millerand, a right-wing politician who had once been a Socialist. As president, Millerand displayed none of the impartiality expected of him in that position. So when the next elections were won by the *Cartel des Gauches* led by Edouard Herriot, the latter refused to take office under him, thus in effect forcing Millerand's resignation, since only Herriot commanded a majority in the Chamber.

When the National Assembly refused to elect Clemenceau president he resigned as prime minister, and the government was taken over first by Alexandre Millerand, and then by Aristide Briand after Millerand was elevated to the presidency. Briand was a staunch supporter of the League of Nations, and his influence, especially as foreign minister from 1925 to 1932, was always exercised in the direction of moderation, including an understanding with Germany. But in 1921 when he was prime minister such an understanding was not yet possible, since reparations had not been agreed to. Briand fell from office because he had been unsuccessful in making Germany pay. His successor, Raymond Poincaré, was responsible for the abortive invasion of the Ruhr (see p. 23). This failure was largely responsible for the defeat of the National Bloc in the elections of 1924.

Edouard Herriot, leader of the *Cartel des Gauches,* was faced with the fact that the Dawes Plan, accepted reluctantly by Poincaré (see p. 24), would not give France the kind of money from reparations that she needed to pay the tremendous cost of reconstruction, for which she had already borrowed the money from her own people. The Herriot Cabinet could not agree on any policy to halt the monetary inflation, and he resigned in April, 1925. Other governments had no success until the leading politicians, including Herriot, agreed to form a National Union government under Poincaré. This government was granted the right to rule by decree. It succeeded in stabilizing the franc at a low level (thus, in effect, defaulting on most of the internal debt) and returning to the gold standard. The 1928 elections confirmed the National Union government in office, but Poincaré for reasons of health had to resign in July, 1929. A number of short-lived governments followed. Meanwhile Briand's patient efforts to come to an understanding with Germany and promote peace in Europe had had some success, especially during the regime of Gustav Stresemann as foreign minister in Germany (see p. 28). The Locarno treaties had been signed in 1925, and the Kellogg-Briand Peace Pact in 1928. The Rhineland was evacuated ahead of time in 1930.

In 1932 new elections again gave a majority to the left-wing parties, and Herriot became prime minister once more. But this time, with the depression belatedly affecting France, Herriot tried to institute a severe deflationary policy to take care of the financial difficulties and unemployment. He himself resigned at the end of 1932 when the Chamber refused to meet an installment of the war debt to the United States that had become due after the expiration of the Hoover moratorium (see p. 25). There followed a series of exceptionally undistinguished and short-lived cabinets, during which the right-wing and fascist groups reached their peak of virulence. An unsavory scandal arising from the sale of an excessive number of bonds by Serge Stavisky, to finance a small municipal pawnshop provided the occasion for these groups to attack the Prime Minister, Camille Chautemps, and other politicians for having protected Stavisky—who committed suicide inconveniently, or perhaps was murdered by the police. Although Chautemps resigned and was succeeded by Edouard Daladier, the agitation continued and there was an attempt (perhaps not very seriously intended) to storm the Chamber of Deputies, which was bloodily suppressed by the police. The Communists through the CGT organized a successful general strike as a protest against the fascists, but for no other obvious reason. This also resulted in some bloodshed. But the real crisis was not settled, even though a coalition government under former president Gaston Doumergue was formed. It was followed by yet another government still further to the right, led by Pierre Laval, which undertook a program of deflation, including reduction of wages.

Failure of the Popular Front. In these circumstances the Communist party, whose Moscow mentors were now seriously concerned with the danger from Nazi Germany, proposed to the Socialists and the Radicals (left-center) that they form a Popular Front with a definite program of reform, and with the slogan "bread, peace, and liberty." This bloc, the first in which the Communists participated, won the elections of 1936. Léon Blum, who had been the leader of the Socialist party since 1919, became prime minister, with a cabinet which did not include any Communists, since they did not wish to share the responsibility for the government. Blum at once dissolved the various fascist leagues including the *Croix de Feu,* which was by this time the largest. Meanwhile a wave of industrial sit-down strikes had broken out, apparently not organized by the Communists, who were in fact embarrassed by them. Industry was brought almost to a halt.

This emergency frightened the businessmen, and they agreed to meet with labor union leaders and work out an acceptable program. This program, which included raises in pay, the nationalization of the arms industry, government control over the Bank of France, the forty-hour week, vacations with pay, and similar measures, was carried through by the Blum government. The leaders of industry at last agreed to recognize the union leaders and engage in serious collective bargaining (their previous refusal to do so had made strikes a first and not, as elsewhere, a last, resort). The strikes then subsided. But the government still had no means of paying for the reforms save by renewed inflation, and eventually in spite of promises to maintain the franc, it had to devalue it in terms of gold. But devaluation came too late to be stimulating to the economy. Blum was therefore forced to the conclusion that he had no option but to postpone the rest of his program.

This delay in no way appeased his critics on the right, whose press was even more venomous than in the past now that the government was headed by a Jew. The slogan "Better Hitler than Blum" began to be heard. Criticism also arose from the Communists, who objected to the slowdown of the social program and to the Blum government's policy of nonintervention in the Spanish Civil War (see p. 92). Sporadic strikes began again; the unemployment problem remained unsolved; production figures dropped as the workers worked fewer hours. When the flight from the franc was renewed and gold began to leave the country, Blum tried to win the power to rule by decree for the purpose of imposing emergency currency controls, but he was blocked by the Senate—whereupon he resigned in favor of the Radical Camille Chautemps, who took Blum into his cabinet as vice-premier. This combination, and several subsequent ones, did not produce a government strong enough to halt the economic crisis. Not until Edouard Daladier took over as prime minister in April, 1938, were the Chamber and Senate ready to give any government the power to rule by decree and impose the necessary controls.

It was Daladier who because of French weakness had to follow the British lead in appeasing Hitler, while trying at home to solve his economic problems and rearming, though in a somewhat half-hearted manner. After Munich the Socialists deserted Daladier, who thereafter drew his support only from the right and was granted almost completely dictatorial powers, some of which he used against protesting workers. Daladier was still prime minister when war broke out in September, 1939.

THE SMALL DEMOCRACIES OF WESTERN EUROPE

The three countries of Scandinavia (Sweden, Denmark, and Norway); the three countries which after World War II came to be called the Benelux countries (Belgium, the Netherlands, and the Grand Duchy of Luxemburg); and the tiny federal republic of Switzerland were all democracies, with varying constitutional forms. All except Switzerland were constitutional monarchies of the English type, although in some, for example, Belgium, the monarch had rather more power than in England.

Switzerland. Switzerland is a country made up of a number of cantons. Some of these joined together as early as 1291 to become a republican confederation; others were added during the following centuries. Their inhabitants speak the European languages of their larger neighbors. German, French, and Italian are all official languages of the country, though Italian is almost confined to one canton. The cantons still retain substantial self-government; but there is a Federal Assembly, made up of a house of representatives elected on the basis of manhood suffrage and a Senate chosen by the cantons, which deals with national affairs. Switzerland is a country dedicated to perpetual neutrality, and she was able to avoid becoming embroiled in either of the two world wars. She eschews military alliances with foreign countries but maintains a strong citizen army, and her frontier mountain passes are all fortified. Since the rest of the world has come to accept this neutrality, Switzerland was the natural home for the League of Nations; and the International Red Cross, founded by a Swiss, Henri Dunant, has its headquarters in Geneva. The Nazis attempted to convert the German-speaking Swiss to the notion that their true home was the Third Reich, but the Nazi movement that grew up in Switzerland did not present any serious threat to the state. It was, indeed, evident that popular opinion greatly preferred the existing status of the country, and the German Swiss continued to regard themselves as Swiss—on the whole in their own eyes a much superior breed to Germans.

Scandinavia. Each of the Scandinavian countries has her own language and national traditions, which do not grow weaker, so that there is little inclination toward unification. Sweden, the largest of the three, became mainly industrialized during the interwar period. Denmark organized her agriculture and dairying industry so successfully by means of co-operatives that she was able to maintain a high standard of living chiefly by exporting high quality foodstuffs. Norway, with less tillable land, specialized in fisheries and shipping, owning the fourth largest merchant navy in the world by the outbreak of World War II. Sweden and Denmark were ruled for most of the period by moderate Socialist governments, which enacted advanced social legislation. Norway, after more than a decade of conservative government, finally gave a strong mandate to its Labor party in 1935, which then brought the country up to the level of the others in social legislation, and by various measures of state aid overcame the difficulties still remaining from the depression. Leaders of the Scandinavian countries met frequently for economic discussions, and trade agreements between them were in operation for most of the period. But they did not unite for mutual defense, all preferring to work through the League of Nations, which of course failed them in the end. Sweden, backed as she was by a strong arms industry, built a small but well-trained and well-equipped army, and it is possible that its existence saved her from being attacked by the Germans in 1940. At all events when Norway, with her small army, and Denmark, who was virtually unarmed, were overrun by the Germans, Sweden agreed to continue shipping her high-grade ore to Germany, and this was apparently sufficient for the Nazi chieftains.

"Benelux" Countries. Luxemburg, the smallest of these three countries, is an independent grand duchy, closely allied with Belgium, having had a customs union with her long before the three countries united in a customs union after World War II. Although Luxemburg was overrun by the Germans in both world wars, the grand duchess was each time restored and the country of about

1,000 square miles became prosperous again since it possesses extensive ore deposits.

Belgium after World War I was faced with the task of reconstruction which was efficiently carried out, despite inadequate reparations from Germany, by means of borrowing and high taxation. Belgium is divided into two language groups and between Catholics and Protestants, roughly corresponding to the French-speaking Walloons and the Flemings. Many of the Flemings, even in World War I, felt akin to the Germans, and in the 1930's a Flemish National party arose, which was almost certainly subsidized by the Nazis. A more dangerous fascist movement of a somewhat mystical nature also arose, known as the Rexists, led by Léon Degrelle. This party won twenty-one seats in the Belgian parliament in the 1936 elections, but it made such a nuisance of itself through obstructing all constructive legislation that it could win only four seats in 1939. Both the Flemish Nationalist party and the Rexists collaborated with the Nazis during the occupation. In 1936, after the Germans had marched into the Rhineland, the Belgians came to the conclusion that the French, having failed to stop them, would be unreliable allies and returned to their pre-World War I policy of neutrality—which Hitler promised to respect. This decision threw the French military planners into confusion, since the French Maginot Line had been planned to be co-ordinated with Belgian fortifications. The Belgians continued with their fortifications, but without further close co-operation with the French. Belgian neutrality did not, however, save them from the German onslaught in 1940.

The Kingdom of the Netherlands had managed to maintain its neutrality during World War I, since invasion was not a strategic necessity for the Germans, and the Dutch maintained their armies in constant readiness and defended all their borders. As a commercial nation Holland was very severely hit by the depression, and as late as 1936 she had the highest unemployment percentage in Europe. But when the currency was devalued in 1936, a slow recovery began. From the time of the rise of Nazism in Germany, a parallel movement grew in Holland, and a Dutch Nazi party fought several elections, though it never won more than 8 per cent of the votes. The country was ruled through the whole inter-war period by coalitions, which were invariably of a conservative cast, since the Socialists could not govern by themselves and would not join any coalition. After 1935 when Hitler's bellicosity and aggressive policies became visible to all, the Nazi movement in Holland began to decline. The government, realizing the danger of war, began to rearm the country, eliciting several warnings from the Germans that collaboration with them would be safer. However, the Dutch continued to rearm, and refused to the end to come to an understanding with Germany.

CONCLUSION

Of these smaller countries only Switzerland and Sweden were able to save themselves from being sucked into the war; both of these, in their different ways, were useful enough to Germany to be spared the Nazi occupation, although in themselves they were not strong enough to have survived a determined German attack. As it turned out, even the occupation, severe as it was, proved to be temporary, and all resumed their course as free nations after the war.

9 THE WESTERN HEMISPHERE DURING THE LONG ARMISTICE

The United States entered World War I in April, 1917, the first of the independent American nations to do so. President Wilson then suggested to the various states of Latin America, which had hitherto been neutral, that they should reconsider their position. Cuba and Panama obliged at once and entered the war on the Allied side. Subsequently six other republics, some of which, including Brazil, had suffered from German submarine activity, declared war. All of these with the exception of Brazil were in Central America, and one, Haiti, was at the time occupied by United States troops. Four other republics broke off diplomatic relations with Germany. Seven maintained their neutrality. The last group included Mexico (who was still in the throes of revolution and had strained relations with the United States), Argentina, Colombia, Chile, and Venezuela. None of the formal belligerents except the United States took any active part in the war in Europe. The intervention of the United States, however, was decisive in its effects and ensured an Allied victory.

In the interwar period the United States became incontestably the greatest economic power in the world, but was as yet unwilling to play an effective part in international affairs, preferring to regard European problems as of no concern to her unless they impinged on her own immediate national interests. During the New Deal she began to modernize her domestic social structure, but Congress passed several Neutrality Acts designed to keep her out of future wars in Europe. Elsewhere in the Americas there was little change except in Mexico, where a violent revolution eventually led to a new political and social structure which has proved remarkably durable and provided effective government.

159

THE UNITED STATES OF AMERICA

The emergence of the United States on a world scene that had been dominated for the past century by Europe naturally had a profound effect on world politics. President Wilson's persistent attempts at the Peace Conference to make American views prevail, especially in the establishment of the League of Nations; his doctrine of self-determination as the principle for the peace settlement; the new role of the United States as the greatest creditor nation in the world; the tremendous increase in American industrial strength—all these changes in the balance of power and influence seemed to presage an era of American participation in world affairs. But, as it turned out, the United States was not yet ready for such a role. President Wilson did not have the support of Congress for the treaties he had helped to negotiate, all of which included the League of Nations—whether or not he had the support of the American people, a question which can never be decided. The United States was anxious to return to "normalcy," which meant the pursuit of private pleasures and profits at home without undertaking onerous commitments abroad. She had not yet come to the conclusion that her position as the leading creditor nation entailed certain obligations if the world was to prosper and thus pay its debts to her. At the end of World War II the United States took her obligations far more seriously—conceivably, even *too* seriously. But in 1919 the Americans had no intention of taking any active part in "making the world safe for democracy" if it involved any major deviation from the policies which had brought her to her present peak of prosperity—still less if it involved any serious sacrifices. President Wilson gained the plaudits of the crowds he addressed on behalf of the League of Nations; but neither he nor they knew just what would have been entailed by American entry into that body.

In fact, throughout the 1920's and 1930's the United States made little or no contribution to the efforts of the League powers, such as they were, to the maintenance of peace; nor did she have any constructive suggestions to make on how to deal with Hitler, Mussolini, Franco, and the other dictators. President Roosevelt torpedoed a World Economic Conference held in London in 1933 in his initial message to it, in which he made it clear that the nations should solve their own problems, and maintain what tariffs they wished without regard to other weaker national economies. The Washington Naval Conference of 1921–1922 (see p. 29) was successful, on American initiative, in reducing the naval forces of the various powers. But there did not seem any probable use for such large forces. President Roosevelt, however, did reverse the previous American policy of intervening in Latin America on behalf of United States interests and established a promising "good neighbor" policy which lasted until the 1950's. In the main, however, the achievements of the United States during these years were not in the field of international relations and the maintenance of peace, but in the field of technology, in which she established a commanding lead over all her competitors and demonstrated to the world the potentialities of a private enterprise economy—and it was her technical proficiency at least as much as her manpower that eventually liberated Europe from Nazi rule.

The "Roaring Twenties."   In the Congressional elections of 1918 control of both houses passed to the Republicans, marking the beginning of the end of the Democratic era that had begun in 1912. Both Congress and the presidency were in Republican hands from 1921 to 1933, when President Herbert Hoover's approach to the problems presented by the Great Depression was rejected by the voters. As already noted, the Republican-controlled Senate refused to ratify the Treaty of Versailles. The responsibility for this refusal must be shared by President Wilson himself (who compounded his lack of tact in not taking any Republican leaders with him to the Peace Conference by refusing to accept any reservations to the Treaty) and Senator Henry Cabot Lodge, chairman of the Senate Foreign Relations Committee, who demanded such sweeping reservations that it was doubtful if the European signatories of the treaty would have accepted them. However, it should be said that in the Harding-Coolidge era few Americans displayed any interest in the League of Nations, and it is therefore doubtful that the United States would have played an active part in it if she had belonged to it. In the course of his efforts to win the country's support for the treaty, President Wilson suffered a stroke which left him partly paralyzed.

During this period, in the United States as elsewhere, there was a series of strikes, including a three-day general strike in Seattle, a police strike in Boston, steel and coal strikes and others of lesser importance elsewhere. There was also a revival of the prewar violence by anarchists (which had cost the life of President Mc-

Kinley), and a number of bombs were even sent to distinguished persons through the mails. The press began to blame the Bolsheviks, foreign-born Socialists, and Communists. Attorney General A. Mitchell Palmer obtained the consent of the sick President to a series of raids, many of them brutal, against foreign-born persons whose views were suspect. Numerous deportations followed, including the return of anti-Bolsheviks to Russia. Although these raids died down before the end of 1920, the fear and dislike of immigrants from other than "Anglo-Saxon" countries persisted, resulting in the immigration acts of 1921 and 1924, which established quotas based on the ethnic composition of the country in 1890 (i.e., before the great waves of immigration from southern and eastern Europe). The Japanese were totally excluded. Not until 1965 did it prove possible to win Congress over to a more reasonable basis for immigration.

In 1919 an amendment to the Constitution had been ratified, prohibiting the manufacture and sale of liquor. This amendment, which was highly unpopular in the cities, demonstrated the continued influence of fundamentalist religion in rural areas, whose representatives controlled the state legislatures. Congress implemented the amendment by the Volstead Act, which was passed over the President's veto. Presumably the law limited drinking in rural areas to some degree, but it was little obeyed in the cities, where great ingenuity was expended in obtaining real liquor from abroad, or substitute home-made liquor. These beverages were consumed in illegal "speak-easies," since saloons were banned. The new "rum-running" from abroad and illicit distilling at home played into the hands of gangsters who made themselves fortunes from the trade; and the wholesale bribery of law enforcement officials added to the general corruption. Although the amendment was repealed in 1933, its effects in the form of organized gangsterism have persisted to this day.

Economic Problems.   The era was dominated by the values of the business community, or, as President Coolidge was to put it: "the business of America is business." And for several years, after a brief setback in 1920–1921, American business forged ahead to new records. The administrations of Harding (1921–1923), Coolidge (1923–1929), and Hoover (1929–1933) were anxious to promote the welfare of business. Measures were passed in Harding's and Coolidge's administrations that aided business and the growing middle class but did little for the poorer members of the working class and did relatively little for the farmers. Taxes were reduced, in part because of the extreme paucity of social services provided by the government. Tariffs grew ever higher to "protect" home industry against foreign imports, especially imports which were manufactured by much cheaper foreign labor. Yet these imports were vital for the foreign countries who could hope to earn dollars only by selling to the United States. The Fordney-McCumber Tariff of 1922 raised rates to the highest level in American history. The United States subsidized a large merchant navy which could not pay for itself, but prevented foreigners from earning some dollars, by transporting goods in their own ships. Even so, the United States still insisted that war debts had to be paid in dollars or gold. Since dollars could not be earned by trade, a large percentage of the world's gold flowed into American coffers and thus ceased to be useful as a medium of exchange for world trade.

What saved Europe was the willingness of American corporations and individuals to buy foreign bonds at high rates of interest, the proceeds of which eventually returned to the United States as payments against principal and interest. Few troubled to consider that the loans were not really based on foreign assets, but were simply paper obligations which in the end would have to be repudiated. In short, the United States, who for a century had exported more than she imported (especially agricultural produce) and thus repaid foreign investments in the United States, did not change her policy when she became a creditor nation (as Britain had done after 1846). The transition to the role of a creditor nation would certainly have proved difficult, and American agriculture and industry would have suffered severely if they had been made to face the full blast of foreign competition without "protection." But the failure to meet, or even to recognize, the problem was one of the most important contributory factors to the Great Depression. The problem persisted even in the 1960's. But the huge expenditures of American tourists abroad, the military establishments maintained abroad by the United States, the modified tariffs in certain industries in which European and Japanese products are competitive, and the large imports of foreign raw materials, especially oil, have helped the situation since World War II—even though the level of American investment abroad and the American ownership of so much foreign industry continue to give cause for concern.

The Great Crash.   The economic boom at home was never as strong as it appeared to be. From 1921 to 1926 there was a considerable growth in the automobile industry and its related industries such as steel; and throughout the 1920's the construction industry expanded, most spectacularly in the vogue for skyscrapers (many of which were half empty by 1932). But the maldistribution of the nation's wealth prevented large sales of home appliances, which were already in production. Industrial profits had begun to decline in the later 1920's in most fields. But this was not too widely known, and far too little attention was paid to the fact in the stock market, especially the New York Stock Exchange, where prices began to rise in an unprecedented manner from early 1928. The value of the shares bore little relationship to the actual profitability of the corporations that issued them, still less to the dividends they declared. But since the prices continued to rise, enormous paper profits could be made, resulting in an orgy of speculation. This was made possible by the extremely lax rules of the Stock Exchange, which permitted buying and selling on very low margins. Speculators could buy with a minimum down payment of 10 per cent, using this stock in a rising market as collateral on ever larger purchases—all ultimately resting on the small amount paid up at the beginning. Financial institutions investing depositors' money forgot the staid traditions of their profession and joined the rush.

It was therefore inevitable that there would some time be a crash when investors realized that what they had been buying was far from being worth what they had paid for it. Even so, the Great Crash which began in October, 1929, would not have had such devastating effects everywhere if the underlying economic situation had been sound, either in the United States or abroad. The margin buying meant that all the speculators were caught with huge obligations and rushed to sell what they had, driving prices down ever further. Businessmen lost confidence and began to retrench, throwing millions out of work. No more money was put into expansion of capital goods. The wages of those who were still employed were reduced; prices for farm produce, which had been depressed even during the boom years, dropped catastrophically; foreclosures on farm loans and mortgages multiplied. President Hoover for a long time issued optimistic statements which were soon shown to have been based on illusion, and when the depression deepened he, the businessmen who advised him, and the business-minded Congress were unwilling to take really drastic measure which would have involved federal intervention on a massive scale.

There was little provision in the early 1930's for dealing with destitution of the frightening scope that soon developed. There were then no social security laws such as existed in other countries, no unemployment insurance, no means of providing government income for the unemployed and underemployed to enable them to survive. Hoover believed that private charity, aided by some funds which would be contributed by the government to charitable enterprises, would take care of the unemployed. But the Hoover soup kitchens could hardly feed the thirteen million unemployed who were trying to find paying jobs in 1932. Numerous farmers lost their homes and took to wandering the highways in jalopies looking for areas where they could settle and make some kind of living. "Hoovervilles" grew up in the waste lands around the big cities, where the unemployed lived in conditions which today can hardly be imagined. Finally an army of "bonus marchers" consisting of some 200,000 unemployed veterans converged on Washington, hoping that Congress could be persuaded to grant them immediate payment of twenty-year endowment policies voted in 1924 for their war service. Although the House of Representatives passed a bill giving them the bonus, the Senate rejected it. Some of the marchers nevertheless stayed on in Washington, until Hoover called out the army, led by General Douglas MacArthur, with machine guns and tanks to disperse them (June 28, 1932). It was therefore not too surprising that Hoover lost the presidential elections of that year to the Democratic governor of New York State, Franklin D. Roosevelt, by the enormous margin of 472 electoral votes to 59.

Effects of the Depression Abroad. The depression in the United States affected the rest of the world mainly through the ending of foreign investment and the withdrawal of American funds from industry already established in foreign countries. The Hoover moratorium (June, 1931, see p. 25) was late in coming, and it was not accepted immediately by the French. Though useful as far as it went it did not touch the roots of the problem. Moreover the Hawley-Smoot Tariff Act of June, 1930, which was opposed almost unanimously by American economists, raised tariffs to such a height that even raw materials from abroad, on which so many countries depended, were now virtually excluded.

More than thirty nations found it necessary to retaliate; but the result was that fewer goods than ever crossed the Atlantic, and European countries one after another were plunged into the depression. Their banks failed; their unemployment figures mounted. But, with the exception of the Young Plan (see p. 25) for reduced reparations (which soon became outdated since both reparations and war debts were suspended by unilateral action) and the temporary Hoover moratorium, the United States for a long time did little to help the world emerge from the depression. Although President Roosevelt refused to co-operate with the World Economic Conference of 1933, his secretary of state Cordell Hull, under authorization of the Reciprocal Tariff Act of 1934, patiently attempted to negotiate reciprocal tariff reductions with foreign countries. This at least was a successful though small contribution to the world's recovery.

The New Deal.   After Roosevelt had been elected but before he took office (March 4, 1933), banks throughout the nation had begun to collapse. One state, Michigan, had closed all its banks in February, and few were open anywhere on the day of the Inauguration. Roosevelt at once closed all banks for four days and obtained the consent of his overwhelmingly Democratic Congress to allow the government to take charge of insolvent banks—whereupon the solvent ones soon reopened. There followed, especially in the first period (known as the Hundred Days), a spate of federal legislation unequaled in American history. Although some of the key legislation was later invalidated by the Supreme Court, as being beyond the powers of the federal government, so much had been done and confidence had been so far restored by then that the invalidation was not of supreme importance.

The major law declared unconstitutional was the National Industrial Recovery Act (June 16, 1933), which set up a National Recovery Administration, under General Hugh Johnson, to prepare codes of fair labor practices, including collective bargaining, and to supervise a program of public works. Johnson's duty also was to persuade employers and employees to accept the new standards, in which case they were entitled to display the "Blue Eagle" emblem. This Act was replaced on July 5, 1935, by the Wagner-Connery Trade Relations Act, which made provision for elections in industry to determine which union had the right to engage in collective bargaining and set up a National Labor

Relations Board with extensive powers of supervision and mediation.

The New Deal also regulated security exchanges and provided for a supervisory commission (SEC) to ensure that prospective investors would be provided with full and pertinent information on new issues. The Banking Act (June 16, 1933) provided for insuring the savings of depositors up to $5000 and enacted a number of stringent regulations for the behavior of deposit banks. To protect the currency the President was given the power to regulate all gold, silver, and foreign exchange transactions; to set up a stabilization fund for the dollar; and to devalue the dollar in terms of gold. An extensive program was adopted to relieve the plight of the farmers, especially under the Agricultural Adjustment Act of May 12, 1933. This Act authorized the government to fix farm prices on the basis of a "parity" figure (i.e., prices that prevailed from 1900 to 1914). Farm mortgages could be refinanced with federal aid; loans for processing crops were permitted. When the AAA was invalidated by the Supreme Court in January, 1935, it was in part replaced by the Soil Conservation and Domestic Allotment Act, which provided payments for those farmers who planted unmarketable crops which helped the soil instead of those which added to the surplus of farm products and depleted the soil.

Before going out of office the Hoover administration had passed a bill setting up a Reconstruction Finance Corporation to make credits available to industry in certain specified circumstances. This was greatly extended by the Roosevelt administration, which allowed the Corporation to make loans and grants to businesses suffering from the depression. A Civilian Conservation Corps was organized to give young people work on the land, in forests and national parks, and in similar areas. A Works Progress Administration was set up under Harry Hopkins which provided a remarkable number of varied opportunities for white-collar workers, such as a federal theater program, a federal writers' project, and a federal art project. A Public Works Administration, entrusted to Harold Ickes, the energetic secretary of the interior, was granted federal funds to set in motion new public works. Of a more permanent nature was the first American Social Security Act, which provided for old age pensions and unemployment insurance on a modest scale.

The major purpose of President Roosevelt and his advisers was to get business moving again. By pouring federal money into the economy they hoped to "prime the pump," after which business itself could take over and continue from where it had left off in 1929. At the same time, as a humanitarian, Roosevelt wished to make sure that no one starved; and, unlike his predecessor, who was no less of a humanitarian, he was prepared to use federal power and federal money to prevent starvation. In the process a great deal of work was accomplished that had been long neglected, especially in the conservation and improvement of natural resources. The most eminent and imaginative of these public projects was the Tennessee Valley Authority, which was empowered to develop all the resources of a seven-state region in a coordinated manner, while at the same time providing a "yardstick" by which prices of private utility companies could be measured. Naturally this provision raised an outcry from the utility companies, which charged that TVA power was subsidized by the government and therefore constituted unfair competition. In spite of the fact that, in the years since, similar projects have been planned that would be no less successful and socially useful, the TVA remains unique, for no subsequent president or Congress has sponsored any similar experiments elsewhere.

It remains doubtful how much the New Deal legislation really did contribute to the overcoming of the depression. But it is incontestable that it created a feeling among the people, especially the less privileged, that the government cared about them and was prepared to take steps to help them. In this the inimitable "fireside chats" of the President on the radio greatly assisted. The New Deal also passed laws which brought the social development of the United States closer to that of other nations, though she remained far behind such countries as New Zealand, the Scandinavian democracies, and Great Britain. One of the prices paid was the increase of federal authority and power in relation to the states, an increase which proved continuous and irreversible.

President Roosevelt was re-elected in 1936 over Governor Alfred Landon of Kansas with the loss of only two states (Maine and Vermont), thus demonstrating that his activist policy was to the taste of the nation. Social legislation slowed down in the second Roosevelt administration, and there was a mild economic recession in 1937 and 1938. The President attempted without success to win the right from Congress to add judges to federal courts where there were incumbent judges old enough to retire who refused to do so—a transparent attempt to "pack" the Supreme Court, which had invalidated so much New Deal legislation. This caused a revolt in the President's own party by those who felt that he was improperly tampering with the Constitution's separation of powers. The episode was probably partly responsible for serious Democratic losses in the Congressional elections of 1938.

Roosevelt's administration was also faced with the efforts of the Committee for Industrial Organizations (CIO), a large semi-syndicalist group of unions which wished to organize labor "vertically," that is, to organize all the workers in a particular industry into one great industrial union, in preference to the older system of organizing them by separate crafts. This plan threatened to give the unions a far greater bargaining power and was therefore resented and resisted by industry, especially when the workers engaged in sit-down strikes, some of which led to bloodshed. But the Wagner-Connery Act did not forbid such an organization, and when the largest steel company, United States Steel, agreed to accept a union of this kind and bargained with it, the other corporations had little choice but to follow its lead. The vertical union remains the union preferred by labor in the major heavy industries, including steel and automobile manufacturing.

Foreign Policy during the Roosevelt Administration. In foreign policy the United States continued to favor neutrality. All the presidential administrations and all Congresses resented the refusal of the European countries to pay their war debts. The Johnson Act of April, 1934, prohibited the granting of credits to any foreign governments that were in default on their payments. Neutrality Acts were passed in 1935, 1936, and 1937 spelling out American intentions not to take part in foreign wars. No arms could be sold to either side, and United States citizens could not travel in the ships of belligerent nations. Nevertheless, President Roosevelt and some of his advisers doubted whether the United States could keep out of any war started by Hitler in pursuit of his aggressive plans. In 1939 the Neutrality laws were modified to permit belligerents to buy planes and arms on a cash-and-carry basis (in effect supplying the Allies), and the United States armaments budget was greatly increased for the purpose of defending her neutrality.

At the same time isolationist sentiment in Congress prevented President Roosevelt from taking a strong line with the Japanese, who, in their war with China, were disregarding American interest and the traditional American "open door" policy in China. Secretary of State Stimson in the Hoover administration had stated that the United States would not recognize the results of aggression, but that was as far as he was willing to go. Even when the USS *Panay* was sunk by Japanese bombers in 1937, Roosevelt contented himself with an apology and an indemnity from the Japanese government.

President Roosevelt made a serious effort to improve relations with the states of Latin America (the Good Neighbor Policy). In this task the first great symbolic act was the abrogation of the Platt Amendment, which had authorized United States intervention in Cuba "for the protection of Cuban independence," and in other respects made her sovereignty even in domestic matters less than absolute. Since the United States had intervened several times under the rights conferred by the Amendment and against the wishes of the Cuban government, this was an important step forward. President Lázaro Cárdenas of Mexico expropriated United States oil concessions in 1938. But although the cry of "Communist" was raised against him, Cárdenas was not disciplined or subjected to "gunboat diplomacy" by the United States. In December, 1938, the Declaration of Lima bound twenty-one American states to consult together in case their security or territorial integrity were threatened. This beginning was in due course to lead to the Organization of American States, and the Pact of Rio, which will be discussed in Chapter 16.

LATIN AMERICA

Few generalizations about Latin America hold good for all the countries. Those that do in the main result from the long Spanish occupation which ended, except in the Caribbean, in the early nineteenth century. In every Latin American country the Spaniards bequeathed a pattern of social stratification which has in large measure persisted to the present day. All Latin American countries have a small aristocratic landowning class and an extremely large class of peasants, most of whom do not own their own land. The officer class of the armed forces is mostly drawn from the former. During the present century a middle class has also arisen in the larger countries, especially those in which there has been some industrialization. This class has tended to identify its interests more with the aristocracy than with the peasantry (with the exception, in some countries, of the intellectuals who have often tended to be politically radical). The military have almost always backed up the upper class and regularly intervened in political affairs when the privileges of this class or their own have been threatened. Thus the history of Latin America has been marked by a monotonous series of coups, followed by the establishment of military dictatorships or military oligarchy. Democratic institutions have taken root in few areas, although nearly all have formally adopted them. But when the president is either a military man or a civilian dependent on the good will of the military, and when the invariably weak legislature is either subservient to the president or interested primarily in the privileges of the class from which it is drawn, it is clear that democracy could hardly function in the same way as it does in countries where government rests on the consent of *all* the people.

North American capital is important in all Latin American countries, and North American corporations have been extremely influential in almost all. In the Caribbean and Central American countries they have frequently dominated both the economy and the government. Only in Mexico since the Revolution has there been a certain balance struck between nationalism and American infiltration and influence. Even so, the Mexicans had to fight hard to keep control of their economy, and it cannot be said that they have yet totally succeeded, since the withdrawal of American capital (and the absence of American tourists) would bring much of Mexican industry to an abrupt halt with untold repercussions on the rest of the economy.

By the end of World War I the United States had troops in most of the Caribbean and Central American countries, and their formal independence was somewhat illusory. By 1934 when the Platt Amendment was abandoned, these troops had all left except for the military and naval bases, such as the Panama Canal Zone and Guantanamo in Cuba. Meanwhile, Mexico had undergone the one important revolution that took place in Latin America before the advent of Fidel Castro to power in Cuba at the beginning of 1959. This revolution in Mexico will be considered in some detail in this chapter. All the other so-called "revolutions" in Latin America were merely changes of government imposed by unconstitutional means. In the period since World War II, on the contrary, there have been some significant changes, even though there has been no successful revolution of the Mexican type. (An account of the Latin American countries other than Mexico will therefore be deferred to Chapter 16, in which pertinent developments of the interwar period will also be considered.)

The Mexican Revolution and its Aftermath. In 1911 the long reign of Porfirio Diaz, which had achieved much of a material nature for the country but in the process had only aggravated its social problems, came to an end with a revolution which drove the aged dictator into exile. A well-meaning idealist, Francisco Madero, took his place. But Madero was dominated by his landowning family and achieved little before he was overthrown. The real revolution began with his murder in 1913. This time there was no single leader who was in a position to establish his rule, and fighting between different regional leaders occupied the next years. The first of these leaders to become president was General Victoriano Huerta, who might have established his position and put an end to the revolution if it had not been for the unrelenting hostility of President Woodrow Wilson, who blamed him for the murder of Madero. Wilson refused to recognize his government and after an incident in which Huerta refused to salute the American flag, he sent troops to occupy Vera Cruz. Huerta soon afterward left the country, while the various generals and their henchmen made and unmade presidents, and made a shambles of much of the country. One of the more disinterested leaders, Emiliano Zapata, at the head of a band of peasants, seized land and at one time controlled a large segment of the country. Although he was murdered in 1919, the movement that he had led continued to be influential, and agrarian reforms became and remained part of the program of all the revolutionary governments. General Francisco (Pancho) Villa, who controlled much of the north for long periods of time, gave lip service to a similar land reform program, but in effect he was little more than a bandit. Against him Wilson sent General Pershing and a body of troops who carried out some desultory reprisals after Villa had conducted a raid on Columbus, New Mexico. Eventually General Venustiano Carranza (who had revolted against Huerta) was able to secure his position with the aid of the best revolutionary general, Alvaro Obregón. In 1917 a constitution was written in six weeks, which is the key document of the Mexican Revolution.

Unlike so many of the liberal, even revolutionary, constitutions adopted elsewhere in Latin America, the Mexican Constitution of 1917 has truly represented Mexican aspirations, and with minor amendments it has continued in operation to this day. All subsequent presidents have attempted to put at least its major provisions into operation. The most important articles were Article 3, directed against the Church, which in Mexico was totally opposed to the Revolution and all its works, as it had been a mainstay of the established order since the time of the Spaniards. This article made all Mexican education secular, and in the primary grades compulsory—wildly impossible though it was at that time for the state to provide such education. Article 27 stated that all land, including its subsoil with its minerals and oil, belonged to the people and could be exploited only by Mexican nationals or by foreigners willing to recognize and abide by Mexican law. This was directed against the old landowning class which had ruled the countryside under Diaz and against American and other foreign companies which had been granted extraordinary concessions under Diaz and regarded themselves as scarcely bound at all by Mexican laws and regulations. These articles, which were a sincere expression of the ideals of the constitution-makers, could be expected to win the support of the peasants. During the Revolution, in many parts of the country the peasants had already seized the lands and burned the old hacienda houses—as they had also burned great numbers of churches. Article 123 gave expression to ideals long held by Mexican intellectuals which had already formed part of the reforms promised by Francisco Madero. It gave the industrial and other workers the right to organize, bargain collectively, receive a just wage, be compensated when they were sick, and similar benefits. The Constitution thus held something for everyone except the old ruling classes.

The Mexican Revolution dispossessed the old landowners almost completely, but not in all parts of the country equally; over the next decades land expropriated by the state was handed over either to individual peasants or to communes (*ejidos*), such as had been traditional among the Indians before the Spanish conquest. Some land even now continues to be distributed by each president. However, men had come to the fore, especially the numerous revolutionary generals, who acquired wealth and property to which they could never have aspired in more settled times; and the social system was not changed as much as it appeared to be. Only during the regime of General Lázaro Cárdenas (1934–1940) was there a continuous and sustained effort to carry out the agrarian provisions of the Constitution. Several labor unions were organized in accordance with the right granted by the Constitution. The largest in early years was CROM, run by Luís Morones. These unions were very closely connected with the government and supplied the government party with reliable votes, as well as armed bands of militants, when occasion demanded. Nevertheless, they did very greatly improve the lot of the workers, who now could appeal to their unions when they had grievances against their employers. The government, for its part, set up a Court of Arbitration and Conciliation whose services had to be used in cases of dispute. Its verdicts were generally believed to be overfavorable to the unions and the individual workers, so that employers were inclined to reach settlements directly whenever possible. During the regime of Cárdenas CROM was supplanted as the largest and most powerful union by CTM, led by Vicente Lombardo Toledano. At this time organized labor was extremely influential in the government and formed a distinct section of the government political party.

The main result of the Revolution was the dispossessing of a particular class of men who held their place by pride of ancestry and land handed down in their family from the time of the Spaniards and its replacement by another group of men who were self-made. Most of these men were mestizos, not pure-blooded descendants of the conquerors. These social gains were far more important than the democratic gains, which were more apparent than real. Universal suffrage was granted by the Constitution; but this has been an empty right in Mexico in view of the fact that the revolutionary party, first organized by President Calles in 1929, has always chosen the presidents in its own conventions. Opposition parties have been permitted as window dressing, but they have never had any chance of winning, since all the political machinery of the state has rested in the hands of the dominant party, which has changed its name several times, but not its functions or its relation to the government. Elections, when they have not been rigged, as they have certainly been on occasion, have therefore been foregone conclusions, and voting was merely an expression of solidarity with the government.

The Mexican system, in short, is a presidential dictatorship (originally for four years, then, beginning with the Cárdenas regime, for six). Presidents cannot succeed themselves, and only once was any president chosen for a second, nonconsecutive term (Obregón in 1928—he was murdered soon afterward). Policies therefore change in accordance only with the will of the president and not the will of the people, except insofar as this can be expressed within the party, both at the convention when he is chosen and afterwards in party councils. Lastly, it should be said that a crucially important change took place very slowly but now seems irreversible. Military men were gradually frozen out of the chief counsels of the party, and the army itself, which became more professionalized, ceased to be a factor in Mexican political affairs. It would probably be impossible now for the quite small but fully occupied army to overthrow the bureaucratic regime that has been securely in power since the late 1930's. When after World War II the army was anxious to receive arms offered by the United States government (which are almost exclusively used in Latin American countries to maintain internal order or to put generals in the seat of power), the Mexican civilian government refused, and the army leaders had no choice but to acquiesce.

Consolidation of the Revolution—Obregón and Calles. Mexico had a long history of unsatisfactory relations with the United States, who had taken half the country by force in the 1840's. It was not easy for the revolutionary government to come to any understanding with her northern neighbor, especially in view of the wording of the Mexican Constitution of 1917. President Obregón was able to obtain *de jure* recognition from President Calvin Coolidge (whose inertia was of great value to Mexico in a difficult period) in exchange for promises to respect American titles to land acquired before 1917 and to pay indemnities for American property damaged by the Revolution. This recognition stood Obregón in good stead when a serious revolt broke out against him which was favored by American business interests. Obregón was succeeded by General Calles, who ruled Mexico despotically for the next ten years, during the first four of which he himself was president. Calles quickly came into conflict with the Church as he endeavored to carry out Article 3 of the Constitution. The Church fought back by repudiating the Revolution and its Constitution. But Calles had the power, and he proceeded to deport foreign priests and nuns and close Church schools throughout the country. These events were followed by a general strike of the clergy in several states of Mexico and a violent uprising led by the priests (*Cristeros*) which was ruthlessly suppressed by the Calles regime. American Catholics tried to persuade President Coolidge to intervene, but he decided it was none of his business. However, he had the brilliant inspiration of sending the personable Dwight Morrow, known as a friend of the Mexicans, as ambassador to the Republic. Morrow negotiated a number of concessions both for American commercial interests and for the Catholics.

Renewal of the Revolutionary Impulse—Regime of Cárdenas. By the end of the Calles era, in the presidential terms of Pascual Ortiz Rubio (1930–1932) and General Abelardo Rodríguez (1932–1934) it seemed to many that the ideals of the Revolution were being abandoned. Little more land was being distributed to the peasants; revolutionary generals were more or less above the law; and the Calles-appointed bureaucracy and labor leaders were enriching themselves—while foreign interests, especially the great American and British oil companies, seemed as powerful and untouchable as ever. There was talk even within the party about the need for continuing the Revolution. But when Calles picked a young general named Lázaro Cárdenas as presidential candidate, he surely did not expect that his own influence would be swept away before two years were over. He himself was exiled by Cárdenas in 1935, and the latter, now in full command of the party and the government, was left supreme to do as he wished.

Cárdenas at once set to work to enforce the Constitution by expropriating and redistributing more land than had been distributed in all the years since the Revolution. Most of it was organized into *ejidos,* and capital was provided through the medium of the new *ejido* bank. Many thousands of peasants were settled in this way. The National Railways of Mexico were taken over by the new labor leader Vincente Lombardo Toledano; and though for a long time they were inefficiently operated, eventually state ownership resulted in an improvement. In 1937 Cárdenas precipitated a struggle with the great oil companies. Their subsoil domains were nationalized and they were instructed to raise the pitiful wages they paid to their workers. When they refused, Cárdenas raised the tariff on United States imports to a prohibitive level, and on March 18, 1938, he expropriated the oil properties of both the British and the American oil companies. He then proceeded to set up an all-Mexican corporation to handle the oil itself—an operation that took many years, but eventually became totally independent of American capital and technical aid. In order to offset the loss of American imports he entered into barter agreements with various European countries to exchange oil for manufactured products. In November, 1938, the United States government signed an agreement by which Mexico promised to compensate American nationals for their lands; but it was many years before any similar agreement was reached on the compensation to be paid for the oil properties.

In 1938 also a rebellion broke out in the province of San Luis Potosí, backed by conservative interests and led by a general, but this was quickly suppressed. However, when Cárdenas chose a little-known general Avila Camacho as the candidate of his party for the next elections, another, much better-known general, Juan Andreau Almazán decided to enter the lists against him, with the (now familiar) pretext that the Communists were trying to take over the country and would succeed if Cárdenas' candidate triumphed. When the party machine ground out the expected victory, Almazán tried to enlist support for his cause in the United States. But the war in Europe had already begun, and President Roosevelt preferred to pursue "hemispheric solidarity." Almazán received no support. The Good Neighbor policy had won a notable victory, and no defeated candidate has since thought it worth while appealing to American sentiment and interests to overthrow a president.

10 ASIA AND THE MIDDLE EAST BETWEEN THE WARS

In 1918 there were still few independent countries in Asia, and only Japan, one of the war victors, was a military power of any consequence. With the exception of Siam (Thailand), who had managed to maintain a precarious independence largely through the diplomatic skill of her rulers, all the smaller countries had been compelled to submit to the domination of the Western nations. Great Britain was the ruler of India, Burma, Ceylon, and Malaya in addition to several smaller territories won during the nineteenth century. France ruled the Indochinese peninsula (Vietnam). The Netherlands owned the richest possession of all, the Indonesian archipelago acquired before the nineteenth century in her palmy days of expansion. The United States ruled the Philippine Islands taken from Spain in 1898, while tiny Portugal still kept a few minor possessions won when she was a great maritime power. In western Asia, parochially called the "Middle East" by Western nations, several territories taken from Turkey at the end of World War I, fell into the spheres of influence of Britain and France and for a time were ruled as mandates of the League of Nations. Persia and Afghanistan retained the semi-independence they had enjoyed in the nineteenth century. In Africa, only tiny Liberia and the ancient kingdom of Ethiopia (Abyssinia) were independent, and even Ethiopia was conquered by Italy before World War II. (In this chapter we shall deal first with the independent nations of Asia, turning afterward to the colonial world. In Africa attention will be given only to Egypt, who can be regarded as a part of the "Middle East," leaving the rest of Africa for discussion in Chapter 19, when the African independence movements will be considered.

CHINA

China was opened up to Western influences during the nineteenth century, when the imperial powers of the West did much as they wished. Whenever the Chinese attempted to resist their encroachments they were defeated by superior Western armies and military techniques. Each time that the Westerners, mostly British, defeated them, they were forced to make concessions and pay indemnities. The Manchu dynasty, which was regarded as foreign by the Chinese themselves, lost so much prestige from its inability to defend the integrity of China that it collapsed in 1911.

The Chinese Revolution. The year 1911 thus marks the beginning of the Chinese Revolution, which may not have been completed yet, although the People's Republic of China has securely established its rule on the mainland since 1949. Upon the fall of the Manchu dynasty in 1911, Sun Yat-sen, a distinguished intellectual, was chosen provisional president, backed by the Nationalist (Kuomintang) party, which soon afterward won the first republican elections. However, one of the Manchu generals, Yuan Shih-kai, harbored the ambition to become emperor himself, and Sun soon found his position and that of his party impossible to maintain. When Sun resigned, Yuan had himself proclaimed president. But Yuan's effort to establish himself as emperor encountered opposition from the Chinese republicans, including Sun; from the numerous semi-independent warlords throughout the country, who proposed to maintain their current lucrative status; and from foreign powers, especially Japan, who was not anxious at any time between the wars to see a united China emerge from the Revolution. Yuan therefore failed in his efforts, and, "made ill by shame and anger," died in 1916.

Early Communist Influence. Dr. Sun, who had gone to Shanghai (the commercial capital of north China), now attempted to restore himself to power and assert his authority over the military. He had some success when he returned the next year to Canton (the commercial capital of south China). There he established a functioning government which declared war on the Central Powers. But he was unable to make his will felt in the north, where a military government under Tuan Chi-jiu continued to function in the old capital of Peking, and again he went into exile. (This latter government also declared war on the Central Powers.) In the Peace Conference China was unable to persuade the Great

Powers to compel Japan to return the conquests she had made in north China during the war (see p. 185). This failure caused a rise in revolutionary fervor and a renewed determination to achieve unity and respect in the world. Sun took advantage of the new spirit to return to Canton in 1920, and he was once again proclaimed provisional president of all China. But he was unable to unite the country, and for a time lost even his home base of Canton.

Decisive aid came in 1923 with the arrival of Mikhail Borodin as the emissary of Bolshevik Russia. Borodin gave Sun advice on the organizing of the Kuomintang party, with its three principles long ago proclaimed by Sun, "Nationalism, People's Livelihood, and Democracy." A revolutionary army was also organized, which was advised by Russian military leaders. A military academy established at Whampoa outside Canton under the leadership of Sun's henchman Chiang Kai-shek, was to be the center of this new enterprise. Sun died in March, 1925, without having seen the unification of his country, but in death he became the great prophet of the Chinese Revolution, its first leader, to whose ideas all were later to pay tribute. However, warlords still ruled in the north. It fell to Chiang Kai-shek (with some Communist support and the full co-operation of Borodin) to launch the expedition which finally captured Shanghai and Nanking by March, 1927. Nanking became the Nationalist capital.

Partial Unification of China under Chiang Kai-shek. Chiang had no intention of permitting the Communist movement, which had acquired some strength among the peasants and the urban proletariat, to dominate him. Within a few months he expelled Borodin, and the Communists, already led by Mao Tse-tung, went underground, after a last desperate effort to seize Canton. In spite of this success Chiang was still opposed by the northerners, who briefly drove him into exile in Japan (August, 1927). He returned in January, 1928, and this time found enough support to establish a fairly solid Kuomintang government in Nanking. Later in the year his forces at last occupied Peking (which was renamed Peiping).

By this time by far the greater part of the country was reunited under Chiang and his Kuomintang government. But Chiang did not rule Manchuria, Sinkiang, or Outer Mongolia; and Tibet had escaped from central government rule during the civil wars. Moreover, the allegiance of most of the warlords within the Great Wall in the different provinces was largely nominal and depended on Chiang's willingness to leave them alone. Marshal Chang Hsueh-liang (the "Young Marshal"), warlord of Manchuria, decided in December, 1928, to recognize the Kuomintang, in spite of Japanese blandishments, thus greatly strengthening Chiang's position and enabling him to bring to a satisfactory conclusion a number of negotiations with Western powers. Some of the unequal treaties to which China had been subjected in the late nineteenth century were abrogated by mutual consent. But none of the powers was as yet sufficiently confident of the new China to be willing to abandon extraterritoriality and allow its citizens to be tried under Chinese law.

Chiang Kai-shek now decided that the time was ripe to recover by force some of the concessions in Manchuria granted by Imperial China to tsarist Russia, including the Chinese Eastern Railway built with Russian money in 1903. This railway provided Russia with a short route to the Russian port of Vladivostok. Chiang and the Young Marshal co-operated in the drive, expecting that the Soviet Union would be too weak to resist. They could not have been more wrong. Soviet armies invaded Manchuria at once and, after completely defeating the Chinese, dictated terms. This venture did not go unobserved by the Japanese, who drew the correct conclusion that Manchuria could be taken from the Chinese without much difficulty. On September 18, 1931, the Japanese Kwantung army in the Liaotung Peninsula, which had controlled the area since the Russo-Japanese war, drove into Manchuria and captured the Manchurian capital of Mukden. Chiang and the Young Marshal decided that they did not dare to take on the Japanese at this moment, and they entrusted their case to the League of Nations. The League debated the possible use of sanctions, but decided against it, and the subsequent Lytton Report (see p. 18), though condemning the Japanese action (and criticizing certain Chinese actions also), did not excite any of the Western powers to take on the Japanese. Japan soon conquered the rest of Manchuria, persuaded the young royal heir of the Manchus, Henry Pu Yi, to collaborate, and installed him as the puppet ruler of the new "independent" state of Manchukuo (March, 1932). He became "emperor" under the name of Kang Teh in 1934. The following year the Japanese conquered the rich neighboring province of Jehol and incorporated it into Manchukuo.

Meanwhile Chiang Kai-shek remained more interested in consolidating his position in China than in resisting the Japanese, whom he could not hope to defeat, at least until he was in full command of the rest of his country. Outer Mongolia had now fully escaped from Chinese rule and had become a People's Republic under Russian protection. Tibet was too far away, and distant Sinkiang was deeply penetrated by the Russians, who had backed an anti-Kuomintang rebellion there and established a regime along Soviet lines. Even closer to home, independent warlords still challenged Chiang's authority, and the Communists had begun to reorganize after the debacle of 1927, winning some support among the peasantry of the mountainous province of Kiangsi. Since the Russian-controlled Comintern (see p. 53) continued to urge them to organize the urban proletariat, Mao Tse-tung broke with it because of its dogmatism. He repelled a force sent against him by Chiang and in November, 1931, set up a provisional Soviet government in Kiangsi. In February, 1932, this "government" declared war on Japan, a step Chiang's government had so far refrained from taking.

Nevertheless, within China Chiang's military position was improving. He had now hired a number of competent military advisers from Germany, and the effect of their work showed in his armies. After several failures in earlier years he launched (October, 1933) a major attack on the Communist positions in Kiangsi. Although he did not destroy the Communist armies completely, he was able to clear the provinces of them. But some ninety thousand troops led by Mao Tse-tung marched for over six thousand miles from Kiangsi to the northwestern province of Shensi. Twenty thousand survived this epic Long March, and joined a group of ten thousand Communists already in Shensi. These men formed the core of the Communist armies which defeated Chiang in 1949 and drove him from the country. They were never dislodged from Shensi during the intermediate period.

The Japanese War.   Chiang continued his efforts at "bandit suppression," as he called his expeditions against dissident warlords and Communists. Late in 1936 while he was visiting the Young Marshal, Chang Hsueh-liang, in Sian in the hopes of persuading him to join forces with him in an expedition against the Communists, Chiang suddenly found himself prevented by his host from returning to his capital until he had agreed to co-operate with the Communist troops and all the other independent Chinese armies in a united effort to drive out the Japanese, from whom new attacks were expected, in view of the recent signature of the Anti-Comintern Pact between Japan and the Axis powers (see p. 213). Chou En-lai (now prime minister of Communist China) went to Sian to add his persuasions, since the policy of a common front against Japan had now, for obvious reasons, become that of the Comintern. After long hesitation Chiang Kai-shek, in spite of threats from the Japanese, accepted the terms, which included a Communist promise to cease attempting to overthrow the Kuomintang government. Thereafter the warlords who had agreed to the pact allowed their troops to be co-ordinated under the command of Chiang Kai-shek, while the Communists retained command of their own troops but took part in some joint operations. The Soviet Union granted credits and various war supplies to the Kuomintang government, and sent a considerable military mission, including elements of its air forces.

The Japanese, seeing their hopes of dividing and ruling China evaporating, and greatly disturbed by the possibility that a truly strong national government, fortified by nationalist and anti-Japanese sentiment, might emerge, began a full-scale invasion of China on July 7, 1937. They quickly seized Peking, Nanking, and Tientsin, the chief cities of northern China; Canton in the south fell on October 21, and Hankow a few days later. The Kuomintang government moved to Chungking in the west, and it refused to surrender. Although the Japanese controlled the seacoast and all the largest Chinese cities, they did not have the military strength to conquer the whole country; and since they could not compel Chiang to accept the terms they offered, they spent the next few years in consolidating what they had won without seriously attempting to win more. In 1938 and 1939 they tested the strength of Russian defenses in the Far East and discovered that no easy conquests were to be made to the northwest. No doubt partly as a result of this stalemate on the Chinese and Russian fronts, the Japanese militarists made the fateful decision to attack to the south in December, 1941, thereby bringing the United States into the war and destroying the empire which they did not possess sufficient power to maintain.

Nonrevolutionary Role of Chiang.   It will be recognized from the above that Chiang during the period when he could have made internal reforms was extremely busy in attempting to unify his country. If he had succeeded in this aim, it is possible that he might have been able (if he had been really willing) to put into effect

Sun's principles, to which he always paid lip service. But, in part because of his imperfect control of the country, no major reforms were accomplished. There was a considerable increase in education, a simplified style of writing was introduced, and finance and budgetary methods were modernized. Numerous automobile roads were constructed. But none of this came close to the revolutionary changes that were needed. No agrarian reforms were instituted to benefit the heavily taxed peasantry; industry was relatively little developed. And though a functioning government did operate with formal institutions borrowed from the West, it was the old bureaucracy inherited from the empire, somewhat modernized and more open to new talent than before, that continued to run the country. The regime remained an authoritarian oligarchy headed by a man who made all the major decisions himself—even though he was not all-powerful because of his dependence on the oligarchy and bureaucracy. Within the single party opposing voices could be heard, but no possibility existed for a true political opposition. In short, Chiang was neither a democrat nor a revolutionary, and his views on almost all subjects were conservative. Though he inherited a revolution, he did not show any signs of wishing to continue it. When during the war his government became corrupt, despotic, and relatively ineffectual against the Japanese, in spite of receiving enormous quantities of foreign aid, he laid himself open to the ideological as well as the military onslaught of the Communists, who were really revolutionaries and had a revolutionary program that they were willing to put into effect. So, in spite of the immense armies under his command, he was never able to re-establish himself after the war, and he was driven from the country by the revolutionary armies which until the very end were numercially inferior to his.

JAPAN

In contrast to China, Japan in the nineteenth century adopted a policy of learning from, instead of resisting, the West. Among other lessons, she learnt the techniques of imperialism, which brought her Korea and Formosa before the outbreak of World War I. By 1895 she was making demands backed by military force, and from 1904 to 1905 she fought a successful war with Russia. She declared war on Germany on August 23, 1914, and in the next few months occupied the German islands in the Pacific and captured Tsingtao, the German settlement on the mainland of China.

Relations with China. Japan, however, was not content with merely falling heir to Western influence in China. She regarded China as a country that ought to be completely under Japanese influence, since she was clearly decadent and incapable of maintaining her traditional position in the modern world. In January, 1915, Japan therefore presented to Yuan Shih-kai a series of demands (Twenty-One Demands) which, if they had been accepted, would have reduced China to the status of a Japanese protectorate. Opposition to the demands by the Western powers as well as by China caused her to modify them somewhat. But an ultimatum submitted in May, 1915, extracted the agreement of Yuan to a shorter list, which included Chinese acceptance of Japan as the legatee of German rights in Shantung (see p. 10); the extension of Japanese leases in Manchuria; a declaration that no more leaseholds would be granted to foreign powers; and an agreement that China's heavy industries should thereafter be exploited jointly by China and Japan. Japan had therefore staked out her claim to be the future protector of China, at the same time giving notice to the Western powers that she would not necessarily respect their own concessions won during the nineteenth century, since her own interests as a Far Eastern power must come first.

During the interwar period Japan took unilateral action in China whenever she wished to do so. In the 1930's she began to back up her demands on China by military force, and she created a puppet regime under her control in Manchuria (Manchukuo), China's northernmost province. Thereafter she attempted a full-scale conquest of China, which she was unable to complete. In all this she was opposed only by words from the West, and by such policies as nonrecognition of her conquests. She left the League of Nations in 1935 (after having given the required two-year notice of withdrawal in 1933). By the outbreak of World War II she was in possession of most of the larger Chinese cities, and the entire eastern seaboard, but she was unable to put an end to the Kuomintang government, nor did she destroy the Chinese armies and power of resistance.

System of Government. It is quite possible that at no time did the Japanese people approve of the imperial expansion, but they did not have the power to prevent it; nor was the question ever submitted to them or to the House of Representatives, which was elected by universal suffrage. This situation was in large part due to the peculiar system of government that Japan had adopted in the late nineteenth century, which in effect gave the military leaders a power to act independently of the civilian government, as long as they could win the consent of the emperor. The emperor was a constitutional monarch, but he regarded himself as bound to accept the advice not of the prime minister and his cabinet but of those military leaders and top officials who had access to him. The Cabinet, which should in theory have been dependent on a majority in the House of Representatives, could function without it. The extremely conservative upper house, the House of Peers, had an unlimited right to veto legislation passed by the lower house, as did the emperor. Moreover, the minister of war, who by law had to be a high-ranking military man, held a position in the Cabinet superior even to that of the prime minister; in fact he exercised more influence on the Cabinet than it did on him. Thus the emperor listened to the advice of his Privy Council; of the two high officials, the Keeper of the Seals and the Minister of the Imperial Household (who had to advise him in any case on the appointment of the prime minister); and of his military and naval advisers far more often than he listened to the prime minister and his Cabinet. Least of all did he have to listen to the advice of the Diet (the two houses of parliament), in spite of the fact that the House of Representatives was the only elected body, and thus might be expected to reflect the will of the people.

The leaders of the armies in the field, especially the Kwantung army on the Chinese mainland, did more or less as they wished because their military superiors in Japan could make use of the emperor's official powers as commander in chief of the army. The bombing of the USS *Panay*, for example, was carried out exclusively by the Kwantung army. The United States of course protested the bombing not to the army, but to the civilian government, which quite genuinely disapproved of the army's actions. It apologized and paid an indemnity; but it was beyond its power to discipline the army. The government could not even mold the military policy of the country by withholding funds, since the ordinary expenses of the military and naval establishment were beyond its control, and it did not dispose of all the country's revenues. Lastly, the armies in China and "Manchukuo" largely lived from the resources they controlled in their occupied territories.

Civilian Attempts to Control the Military.   It is therefore somewhat misleading to pay very much attention to Japan's numerous changes of government or to the activities of the parties and their electoral successes and failures during this period. At no time did the civilian government exercise the power and influence which it appeared to possess; nor did the governmental system ever approach at all closely to democracy, in spite of many efforts by civilian leaders to win more real power. There were two major parties in the House of Representatives, the *Seiyukai* (conservative) and the *Kenseikai* (liberal), which was reorganized in 1927 as the *Minseito* (Democratic) party. These parties alternated in office during the 1920's although not all the governments commanded majorities in the House. The Minseito government led by Yuko Hamaguchi which took office in 1929 was the only one that showed much ability to govern the country or possessed a secure majority in the House. It negotiated the London Naval Limitation Treaty in 1930 (see p. 30) and was even strong enough to obtain the dismissal of some high naval officers. As a liberal regime it favored laissez faire in economic matters; and the country was prosperous until the stock-market crash in the United States, after which Americans ceased to buy silk, the major Japanese export, in the quantities they had bought hitherto. The government then as part of an economy program attempted to retrench on military expenditures. Hamaguchi was shot by an assassin in November, 1930; and though he did not die for some months, his government lost the slight control it had won over the military. The foreign ministry under the moderate Baron Shidehara was forced to accept the army's independent actions in Manchuria in 1931, in spite of its strong disapproval.

In 1932 the Seiyukai party won the elections; but by this time the army was unwilling to accept any dictation from civilians, even conservatives. The Seiyukai prime minister was murdered by young army officers who destroyed the party's headquarters in May, 1932. For the next few years under two prime ministers who were admirals, little attempt was made to curb the military. Any divisions of opinion that developed were confined to the armed forces themselves, in which some elements favored an all-out war in China, whereas more moderate elements preferred to consolidate what had already been won. The series of assassinations continued.

Victory of the Militarists. The people were given their last chance to express their opinions in the elections of 1936 and 1937. In 1936 the Minseito, with a moderate platform which stressed democratic parliamentary rule as opposed to "fascism," won both elections easily. After the first one, extremists fell upon many of the civilian leaders in a wave of terrorism. In the next election, neither party favored the extension of the war. The new prime minister, Prince Konoye, a conservative court noble, who did not himself belong to either party, made many sincere efforts to limit the war. However, he had no option but to accept the demands of the military for extensive rearmament, and he could not prevent the field commanders from renewing the war and undertaking the full conquest of China in 1937. Konoye resigned early in 1939, to be followed by a number of ineffective bureaucrats and military men. He returned to office again in July, 1940, still hoping to moderate the aspirations of the military men, and to avert war with the United States, which loomed ever nearer. In the course of this second premiership he substituted a single party of his own for the traditional parties which were dissolved. He took into his Cabinet General Tojo Hideki as war minister and Yosuki Matsuoka as foreign minister. Both were in favor of further Japanese expansion.

Konoye, however, did enjoy some support among the high naval officers, who feared being dragged into a naval war with the United States. But the army was adamant against relinquishing any of its gains in China—though it was not yet fully committed to a drive to the south. Konoye therefore attempted to persuade the United States to accept the existing situation in China, knowing that it was only on this basis that war could be avoided. When he failed, he resigned, to be replaced as prime minister by General Tojo. Meanwhile an Imperial Council had decided that if the negotiations were not brought to a successful conclusion by November 25, 1941, they should be broken off, and the attack to the south, including the bombing of the American fleet at Pearl Harbor, would be initiated. Tojo, anxious for war, carried on the negotiations as a matter of form; when they failed the fateful orders were given which led eventually to the destruction of the Japanese empire.

SIAM (THAILAND)

The only other independent country in the Far East at the outbreak of World War II was Siam, who had the good sense to declare war on the Central Powers late in 1917. As a result, she was allowed to abrogate the extraterritorial rights she had been forced to grant to the Western powers during the nineteenth century. In 1932 she established a democratic civilian rule, and her hitherto absolute monarch became a constitutional one. But the democracy never functioned effectively, and during World War II the country had to submit to Japanese dictation, even though it maintained its formal independence.

COLONIAL EAST ASIA

It was in the years following World War I that the retreat from colonialism began that was to become a rout in the later 1950's. British India showed the way by persuading one colonial power to relinquish its rule and thus made it clear that for a nation capable of standing on its own no halfway house need be accepted between colonial status and outright independence.

The Independence Movement in India. In 1885 the Indian National Congress, destined to become the leading political party in India, was founded. At first it welcomed Muslims, but as it gradually became a vehicle for Hindu nationalism, most Muslims ceased to feel at home in it, and the All-India Muslim League was founded in 1906. This, in turn, eventually became a body which spoke for the vast majority of Muslims and after World War II insisted on the partition of India, thus enabling the Muslims to rule their own state of Pakistan.

In the early years of the twentieth century, the British decided to devolve some governmental responsibilities on the Indians. They permitted the election of Indian representatives to sit in provincial councils, but they had as yet no intention of granting them real power in the central government, which was dominated by the British viceroy and his nominated council. Unfortunately for the cause of Indian unity, the British were so much impressed by the differences between the Muslims and the Hindus that in all elections under their regime (beginning in 1909), they provided for separate Muslim and Hindu ("communal") electorates, each being permitted to elect its own members to the councils. A large measure of reform was granted in 1919 (Montagu-Chelmsford Reforms). Provincial legislatures were to consist of a majority of elected members; some tasks were then "transferred" to Indian ministers in the provinces, although not those like defense which the British wished to keep in their own hands. At the center a Legislative Assembly was set up with a majority of elected Indians, which was given a few important tasks to perform, including the discussion and approval of the national budget. It was this Assembly that placed a tariff on cotton goods imported from England (see p. 137). But executive power remained firmly in British hands.

The Indian National Congress, now led by Mohandas Gandhi, did not think these reforms (known as *dyarchy*) were sufficient, and it objected also to the British policy (which it regarded as insulting) of seeing how the Indians behaved (how they used their limited powers) before granting anything further. Congress members were therefore instructed by their leaders to boycott the elections and not to take office in the provinces. As a result only the members of minor parties and the Muslims attempted to work the system. Gandhi himself began a campaign of "nonviolent" civil disobedience, designed to force the early independence which the British were unwilling to grant. Gandhi and other Congress leaders therefore spent many of the interwar years in jail. It was found impossible to engage in civil disobedience without some violence, relatively little though it was.

In 1926 the British appointed a commission led by Sir John Simon to inquire into the working of the reforms, although they made the mistake of insulting the Indians again by not including any Indians on the commission. The commission recommended a federal system for India, with a modified "Dominion Status." But the system entailed autonomy for different groups in the state, one of which was the native princedoms. The princes were not at all anxious to lose the almost complete internal self-government that they already enjoyed under the British, who had always favored them. Now that they were given the option they refused to enter the federal system, and never did agree to do so, even later—although after World War II they lost their option and were forced into one or the other of the independent states of Pakistan and India.

Gandhi also was dissatisfied. He desired to keep India together as a single nation and insisted that Congress was the only party which welcomed members of all creeds and could speak for all

India. He demanded the abolition of the communal electorates which emphasized the separateness of the Indian peoples. In several Round Table Conferences he refused to compromise. Nevertheless, the British in 1935 passed a Government of India Act which put into effect most of the reforms recommended by the Simon Commission and granted full responsibility in the provinces to elected ministers. No substantial changes were made at the center because the princes had not accepted the changes recommended and the British refused to coerce them. Both Hindus and Muslims this time took part in the elections, and Congress as expected won power in most of the provinces. But the Hindus and Muslims nowhere formed coalition goverments. Each group ruled in the areas where it held a majority—though in one province in which the vast number of the inhabitants were Muslim a Congress affiliate won the elections. By this time the Muslims were beginning to think of partition as the only policy that could save them from Hindu domination; and the Muslim League refused to accept an offer from Congress to co-operate in drawing up a constitution for an independent and united India.

When World War II broke out India was brought into it by the central government—in which there were now several Indians—without obtaining the approval of Congress leaders. As a result the provincial Congress ministers resigned their positions. In 1942 Britain sent out another commission, led by Sir Stafford Cripps, but Congress refused to accept his proposals and insisted on immediate self-government. When it continued to refuse its support to the war effort and Gandhi threatened to collaborate with the Japanese, the British felt they had no choice but to jail him and the other Congress leaders, including Jawaharlal Nehru, who became the first Indian prime minister after independence. They remained in jail until all danger was past.

Burma. Burma had been a warlike empire until it succumbed to British might in the late nineteenth century. After the conquest the British ignored the fact that all the peoples of Burma were ethnically distinct from the Indians and made the whole country into a single Indian province, ruled, like India, by the viceroy in Delhi. This meant that there was unlimited immigration from India, and the Burmese, who were not commercially minded and did not even make good bureaucrats, found themselves swamped by Indians in their own country. However, the minor peoples of Burma, especially the Karens, many of whom had been converted to Christianity (unlike the Burmese, who remained Buddhist), may well have preferred British to Burmese rule, especially since they were usually favored by the British over the disgruntled and unco-operative Burmese.

When it came time to grant the Montagu-Chelmsford Reforms to India, the British hesitated to extend them to Burma, which as an Indian province would have to be granted a substantial measure of autonomy. The British did not doubt that the Burmese would use their autonomy to tyrannize over the Karens and others, as they had done in the days of their empire. While the British hesitated the Burmese unleased a storm of protest over the proposed discrimination, and the British decided that it would be best to extend the reforms to them. Even so, few Burmese were willing to become ministers under the new system, though they won the elections. None of the governments could therefore command a stable majority, and they rose and fell with monotonous regularity.

The Simon Commission took note of the dislike of the Burmese for the Indians and recommended a full separation of the country from India. The Government of Burma Act of 1935 therefore separated Burma from India and gave the former the same powers that were given in 1935 to the Indian provinces. Thereafter the Burmese formed governments, but all were ineffective and corrupt coalitions, and the more extreme Burmese nationalists agitated for independence. Some of these decided that their best hope was to be found in Japan, who, they believed, would soon take over Burma and would be more willing than Britain to grant independence. Several of these nationalists made their way to Japan, where they were given some political indoctrination, and returned in 1942 in the wake of the Japanese armies. (This development will be discussed in Chapter 17.)

Ceylon. This island off the south coast of India had at one time belonged to the Dutch, who ceded it after the Napoleonic Wars to the British. It had never been ruled by India, in spite of its proximity to the Indian mainland. Its native inhabitants were Sinhalese. The Tamil Indians, who formed the largest minority in Ceylon, were immigrants from southern India. As in India, a national party was organized (in 1919), namely, the Ceylon National Congress, which opened its membership to all the peoples of Ceylon but soon became dominated by the Sinhalese. After World War I the British permitted elections to the Legislative

Council, but used the same system as in India of communal electorates, with the result that the minority peoples were grossly overrepresented. This gave rise to considerable agitation on the part of the Sinhalese, and in 1927 the British sent out the Donoughmore Commission to advise on necessary changes which would lead toward true self-government. As a consequence, universal adult suffrage was granted, and thereafter the minorities were merely guaranteed a certain number of seats, whose occupants would be nominated by the governor. A complex governmental system, unique in the British colonial world, was then put into effect, which gave the Ceylonese many governmental tasks to perform, as ministers. The Ceylonese were dissatisfied with the system, but had not made any further progress by the outbreak of World War II. Just before the war the British governor made a series of important suggestions and recommendations which would, if accepted, have devolved far more power on the Ceylonese and given them the kind of responsible parliamentary system that they obtained after it. But the war was too imminent for the British to give the attention to them that they deserved, and nothing was done to implement them.

Malaya. The Malay Peninsula, the last of Britain's large possessions to be considered here, lies to the south of Burma and Thailand. The British annexed a few urban areas of the country during the nineteenth century, including the island-seaport of Singapore and the ports of Penang and Malacca. The rest of the peninsula was divided into federated or unfederated sectors (depending on the type of treaties originally signed with the British). In the four protected states (known as the Federated Malay States) the Malay sultans were allowed to keep their thrones, but had purely ceremonial functions. The country was ruled by a British high commissioner who was also governor of the Straits Settlements (the crown colony which included Singapore). The remainder of the peninsula was made up of the "unfederated" states, ruled internally by their sultans, who were, however, bound to accept the advice of the British Residents attached to their courts.

The country was populated by a slight majority of Malays, a very large minority of Chinese, mostly congregated in Singapore, and a smaller group of Indian (Tamil) immigrants. Few members of either of these minorities regarded themselves as permanent inhabitants of the country, and the Chinese continued to look upon

China as their real homeland. They virtually monopolized the commerce of the country, which lived from its (mostly European-owned) rubber planations and its tin mines (some of which belonged to the Japanese), and its locally consumed agricultural products. It was prosperous in the 1920's, but suffered severely from the depression when the price of rubber and tin dropped precipitately. In view of the ethnic composition of the country, the British devolved little power on the native inhabitants during the interwar period.

Across the Straits of Malacca on the (otherwise Dutch) island of Borneo, the British controlled North Borneo, which was administered by the British North Borneo Company, an independent chartered company. They also took under their protection the neighboring territory of Sarawak, which was ruled by a "White Rajah," one of whose ancestors had been ceded it by the local sultan in the nineteenth century. Lastly there was a British-protected sultanate of Brunei. The first two of these territories were incorporated in the independent state of Malaysia in 1963, as will be discussed in more detail in Chapter 17.

Netherlands East Indies. This extremely rich colony was an archipelago, the various islands of which were taken by the Dutch at different times from the seventeenth century onward. The richest and most thickly settled island was Java, where the Dutch had their headquarters at the capital of Batavia (now Djakarta). The Dutch maintained a strictly authoritarian rule in their colony, which was exercised in the interests of commerce. Like Malaya, the islands were rich in rubber and tin, but unlike Malaya, also in numerous other tropical products. The Dutch did not keep a very extensive governmental apparatus in the East Indies. They worked through the native chiefs, who were responsible for local taxation and similar matters but were always kept in order by their masters. The fact that most of the internal commerce of the islands was in the hands of the Chinese prevented the growth of a middle class which might have proved dangerous. Even so, some Indonesians studied in Holland and became strong nationalists, while a Communist party was organized in the 1920's with some support from Russia. In 1926 the Communists prematurely attempted to overthrow the colonial government. The effort was a complete failure, and the party was dissolved and its leaders imprisoned.

The Great Depression hit the islands very severely, and the

Dutch were unable to do much to relieve the situation, especially that of the small proprietors whose credit was cut off by the Chinese merchants. The nationalists blamed the Dutch and succeeded in frightening them into a more repressive policy than they had adopted hitherto. Several nationalist leaders including the present president, Sukarno, were exiled or imprisoned. But this did not put an end to the revolutionary activity, which continued and became especially strong after Holland was overrun by the Germans in 1940. This event, though it did not involve the collapse of the Dutch government in Indonesia, had the effect of giving the Indonesian nationalists self-confidence and hope. Just before the Japanese invasion the Dutch released the imprisoned nationalists in the anticipation that they would support them against the new invaders. But when the Dutch themselves put up such slight resistance, the Indonesians decided to throw in their lot with the Japanese to obtain what they could from them. They used the war years effectively to build a political organization and gain experience in administration under the Japanese. Just before the Japanese left, the Indonesians proclaimed a republic (August 17, 1945).

The Philippine Islands. The Filipinos, who were freed from Spanish rule in 1898, did not expect to have to submit to a new colonial rule by the conquerors of the Spaniards. But the Americans were unwilling to hand over the government at once to the natives, and they soon convinced themselves that the Filipino resistance fighters could not be entrusted safely with the task of governing themselves. Even so, the United States never did regard her possession of the islands as permanent, and she endowed the islands with an elected legislature, whose powers were fairly extensive. President Woodrow Wilson had come to the conclusion before he left office that the Filipinos should be granted their independence and were fit for it. But the Republican administrations of the 1920's, which favored the American commercial interests that were active in the islands, disagreed. Congress, however, did not look upon the matter in the same light as the administrations. Other business interests unfavorable to duty-free imports of Filipino sugar and to unlimited Filipino immigration were influential in Congress and persuaded it to vote for independence.

The result of the tug-of-war between President Hoover and his Congress was that the latter passed an independence bill, which the President vetoed in January, 1933. Congress passed it over his veto, but the Filipino legislature did not ratify the Act, since it feared that the United States would impose a tariff on its exports. It also disliked a provision in the Act for American bases in the Philippines. A new bill passed in 1934 (the Tydings-McDuffie Act) was accepted by President Roosevelt. Since this bill did not provide definitely for the bases, the Filipino legislature ratified it, and the islands became a Commonwealth under their own president, Manuel Quezon. Independence was promised after a twelve-year-trial period. During World War II the islands were overrun by the Japanese, but were reconquered by the Americans in time for independence to take effect on the promised date of July 4, 1946.

French Indochina.   When the French took Indochina in the late nineteenth century, they annexed only the southern part of the peninsula, Cochin-China, leaving an "emperor" on the throne of Annam and Tonkin in the north and kings in Cambodia and Laos to the west. These potentates were, of course, under French domination, but the fact that they kept their thrones had considerable significance during the struggle for independence after World War II. All of them could count on a certain loyalty from their subjects. They and the Vietnamese leaders whom the French allowed into their councils collaborated willingly with their masters in the hopes, not often well founded, that they could temper the rather oppressive regime, which was to a large degree dominated by French commercial interests.

In the interwar period the nationalist movement in French Indochina was mainly in the hands of the Communists. They organized several insurrections in the 1930's and attempted to build up an underground party in all the main centers of the country. Nguyen Ai Quoc, who was the acknowledged leader of the Communists, spent almost all the period in exile, much of the time in Moscow. At the end of World War II, he emerged with a new name, Ho Chi Minh, and was backed at the time by the Chinese Nationalists who did not know his history as a Communist. The independence movement led by Ho Chi Minh in the north will be dealt with in some detail in later chapters, since a unified independent Indochina (Vietnam) has still to come into existence. (See pp. 324–327 for a discussion of the independence movement and pp. 367–371 for a discussion of the Vietnamese War.)

THE MIDDLE EAST AND EGYPT

At the outbreak of World War I the countries of western Asia either formed a part of the Ottoman Empire or enjoyed a somewhat precarious independence made possible by the rivalry of Russia and Great Britain. The Germans had also been attempting with some success to penetrate the area, but had as yet no firm basis of power in it; they were compelled to abandon their interests by their failure to win the war. The territories that had been part of the Ottoman Empire either became fully independent at once (Yemen), or became Class A mandates of the League of Nations (see p. 15). Persia (officially Iran from 1935 onward) and Afghanistan, influence in which had been disputed between tsarist Russia and Britain in the nineteenth century, became strongly influenced by Western nationalism and achieved a real independence of the West in the interwar period.

Persia. This ancient empire had virtually lost its independence in 1907 when the Russians and the British agreed between themselves to divide the country into their respective spheres of influence. The Bolsheviks abandoned their rights under this treaty soon after coming to power; but the British (who had obtained important oil concessions in the country in 1901) attempted to strengthen their influence by signing another treaty with Persia in 1919. The Persian parliament (*Majlis*), however, refused to ratify it, and the growing strength of the Bolsheviks after 1920 persuaded the British that they could not hope to maintain their position indefinitely. In 1921 an army officer named Reza Khan organized a coup by which he made himself ruler. He became shah (king) in 1925. His first important act was to conclude a treaty with the Bolsheviks, followed by another one with Turkey before the end of 1921. The treaty with the Soviet Union permitted her to send troops into Persia if the latter was unable to prevent a third power from entering the country for the purpose of invading Russia.

The Shah made a determined effort to modernize his country, in which task he had the valuable support of an American financial mission. In 1933 he compelled the Anglo-Persian Oil Company to pay far greater taxes and royalties than had been contemplated in 1901 before oil had actually been discovered. In the struggle with the Company, Reza Shah was strongly supported by the

Russians, and trade thereafter was greatly increased between the two countries. The Russians also supplied military and technical experts. They continued to maintain good relations with the Shah's government until the Germans invaded Russia in June, 1941, even permitting Persian exports to flow freely to Germany through their country. In August, 1941, a joint Anglo-Russian military invasion of Iran met little resistance. The northern zone was then occupied by the Russians until they evacuated it in May, 1946.

Afghanistan. This mountainous and desert country in central Asia was left under British influence, exercised from India, by the Anglo-Russian agreement of 1907. But being Muslim, Afghanistan objected to British participation in a war against the Turkish sultan, who was also the caliph of Islam. After the war an Afghan army briefly invaded British India in the vague hope of "liberating" Indian Muslims from British rule. Although the attack was soon beaten off, the British did recognize the Afghan desire for full independence and ceased to play as important a part in the country as hitherto. The Emir Amanullah (1919–1929, king from 1926) secured his position by cultivating the friendship of the Soviet Union, and he signed treaties with her and with Persia and Turkey (before the war such treaties with foreign powers had been forbidden by the British). Amanullah then began a determined effort to modernize his country with the help of foreign capital and technical aid; but he attempted to go too far too fast, and was deposed. Mohammed Nadir Shah (1929–1933) and his son Zahir Shah, who succeeded to the throne after his father's assassination, continued to modernize at a less breakneck speed under a new constitution, which provided for a two-chamber assembly, one house elected and one appointed. Although the country remains far from modern even now, it has made considerable progress since 1919 and was able to avoid being drawn into World War II.

Southern Arabia. The southernmost country in the Arabian peninsula was Yemen, which bordered on the British colony of Aden (taken by the British in 1839) and the British-protected sheikdoms of the Hadramaut. To the east was the growing independent sheikdom ruled by the Wahhabi chieftain Ibn Saud. (The Wahhabis are a puritanical sect of Islam.) Yemen achieved independence from Turkey immediately after the war under the extremely conservative feudal Imam Yahya (a Muslim heretic of the Zeidi sect). Yemen was attacked by Ibn Saud in 1934, but, though defeated, was able to maintain independence at the cost of some territorial concessions.

Ibn Saud had conquered his original small sheikdom as early as 1901, and he enlarged it by force of arms whenever opportunity permitted. The Sheik Husein of Mecca, father of Feisal, king of Iraq, and of Abdullah, king of Transjordania (both British mandates), had given his support to the Arab revolt against Turkish rule during World War I. As a reward he was recognized as king of the Arabs by the Allied powers in November, 1916. But even though after the war his kingdom became independent of Turkey, he was unable to maintain his position against the determined hostility of Ibn Saud, who persisted in capturing portions of his territory until Husein was compelled by his subjects to abdicate in favor of his son Ali in 1924. This still did not save his country, and at the end of 1925 Ibn Saud had conquered the whole country and reached the sea at Jidda. He had himself proclaimed king of the Hejaz early in 1926. The conquest was recognized by Great Britain in 1927, and in 1932 the name of the country was changed to Saudi Arabia in honor of its warlike ruler. The Arabian-American Oil Company was granted concessions to prospect for oil the following year, and today Saudi Arabia is one of the richest undeveloped countries per capita in the world, even though until recently relatively little of the money was used for the benefit of the country.

The Class A Mandates. The Arabs had expected to be able to create an all-Arab state in the territories taken from Turkey, in spite of the presence of fairly extensive Christian minorities in Syria and a growing Jewish minority in Palestine. But the British and French, who had oil and other interests in the areas, were extremely hesitant to allow them to escape from their protection unless the new countries were closely tied to them by treaties. The French, who had fewer interests than the British, were quite openly hostile to the growing Arab nationalism, which was likely to have a disquieting effect on their own Arab territories in North Africa. During World War I they had signed an agreement (Sykes-Picot Agreement, May, 1916) with the British under which they would receive Syria, while the rest of Arabia would be divided into British and French spheres of influence. This agreement conflicted with promises made to the Arabs in 1915 by the British High Commissioner in Egypt, Sir Henry McMahon, to the effect that Britain would "recognize and support" the independence of

Arabia, Syria, and Mesopotamia, with some named exceptions. The coast lands of Syria were not included in the McMahon promises. In 1917 Arthur Balfour, British foreign minister, issued a declaration stating that the British government "views with favor the establishment in Palestine of a National Home for the Jewish people." This promise was regarded by the Arabs as contrary to the undertakings made by the British on the strength of which they began their revolt against Turkish rule.

By the end of the war, the Emir Feisal, who expected to become king of the Arabs, was already in Damascus, slated by the French to become the capital of Syria. When the French insisted on the letter of the Sykes-Picot Agreement, the British had no option but to back them, and in due course they were awarded Syria as a mandate. They drove Feisal from the country, but he was compensated by being granted his own kingdom to be called Iraq, with its capital of Bagdad. The Emir Abdullah was granted Transjordania, a British mandate, of which he duly became the king. Iraq, in fact, though it was intended to become a British mandate, never formally became one, since the League of Nations concluded that by its becoming a kingdom protected by the British and scheduled to become completely independent, the purposes of the mandate had been fulfilled. After signing a treaty with the British granting them the right to maintain military forces in the country, Iraq became formally independent in 1932 and entered the League of Nations. Transjordania, almost totally dependent on Britain for enough funds to balance her budget and defended by a British-trained Arab Legion, remained a Class A mandate until 1946.

France at the time she took over Syria had very little except historical connections (dating from the time of the Crusades) with the country, which was bitterly divided by struggles among the Maronite Christians, the orthodox Sunni Muslims, and various Muslim sects such as the Druses. Although France was able to establish some kind of order by military means, her rule was never accepted as legitimate by any sizeable group of Syrians. The Christian Maronites originally welcomed the presence of a Christian power as mandatory, but they were offended by the high-handed methods of the early military governors and the anticlerical views of almost all. In 1925 a great rebellion was started by the Druses, which was not put down for two years. In 1926 Lebanon was separated from the rest of Syria and made into an "independent republic." This area, which is now the independent state of Lebanon, was inhabited by both Christians and Muslims, and was therefore not in complete sympathy with Arab aspirations. The Popular Front government in France, under Léon Blum (see p. 56), promised the Syrians an early independence (Syria too had been a "republic" since 1930), but the treaty that was negotiated was not ratified by the Syrians. Syria therefore entered the war years greatly disaffected toward France, and most Syrians welcomed the joint conquest of the country by the British and the Free French (the de Gaulle adherents) in 1941.

The most difficult problem that fell to the British to solve was that of Palestine, which was an overwhelmingly Arab country, but which was required by the Balfour Declaration, and by the terms of the mandate, to maintain a Jewish National Home within its boundaries. The Arabs, like the inhabitants of the other former Turkish possessions, naturally looked forward to a time when they could rule an independent state. But Jewish immigration and the success of Jewish land settlement (the lands for the settlement were bought from the Arabs), together with the obvious ambition of the Jews, and their supporters throughout the world, to have a state under Jewish control, created an insoluble problem for the British who were supposed to administer the country.

Until the rise of Hitler to power in Germany, which was followed by the persecution of the Jews in the Third Reich, the immigration by the Jews into Palestine remained of manageable proportions, even though it greatly disturbed the Arabs. But the persecutions had the effect of increasing the pressure on Palestine, which the Jews regarded as their natural homeland, until it became intolerable. The British restricted immigration but could not prevent it altogether. They could not win the agreement of the Arabs for any increase at all, since the latter felt, correctly enough, that they were likely before long to be outnumbered in the country they regarded as theirs and wished to rule. In 1937 a British Commission (Peel Commission) proposed the partition of the country, which plan was vehemently opposed by the Arabs. It was conditionally accepted by the Jews, who above everything else wished to have control over immigration and thus permit refugees from Nazi Germany into the country. In 1939 the British issued a white paper, proposing a limited immigration for the next few years and promising eventual independence for the whole country under Arab rule. The Jews naturally rejected this solution and opposed it by all means at their disposal, and the Arabs likewise rejected it because its promises of independence were too vague. Disorders increased as the policy was put into effect. Although the Jews recognized that Hitler's Germany was a greater adversary than Britain and therefore co-operated with the British war effort, they remained determined to win their independence as a separate state after the war. This was achieved in 1947, as will be discussed in Chapter 18.

Egypt. This ancient land had been "leased" from the Turkish sultan, who had not controlled it for many decades, by the British in 1882. Thereafter both Egypt and the Sudan, which was nominally subject to the Egyptain pashas, were administered by the British as a protectorate. During World War I British troops had been constantly on duty in Egypt to protect the Suez Canal, which since its opening in 1869 had become of vital strategic importance to Britain. Nevertheless the façade of Egyptian independence had been maintained, and an heir of the former ruling family was available in the person of Ahmed Fuad Pasha. After the war Britain decided to make him king under the title of Fuad I. He was expected to act as a constitutional monarch working through a parliament and cabinet headed by a prime minister.

This government was far from satisfactory to the Egyptain nationalists, most of whom belonged to the Wafd party. The country had been totally freed from Turkish suzerainty by the war, but the British were still in control and would remain so until the Egyptians agreed to sign a treaty which would grant Britain sole responsibility for Egyptian defense and external security, as well as make provision for the protection of foreign interests. The Wafd party might have accepted a treaty along these lines. Several such treaties were submitted to the Egyptian government. But it refused to accept the loss of the Sudan, which the British were not willing to cede to Egypt, in part because of the fact that they were in the process of developing major schemes for the improvement of the Sudanese economy and in part because of previous Egyptian mismanagement there and the apparent irresponsibility of so many Egyptain officials. As long as the treaty was not accepted by the Wafd, which won all the elections in Egypt for many years, the British intended to remain, and the Wafd would not sign any treaty unless the question of the Sudan was settled in their favor. The murder of the Governor-General of the Sudan by Egyptian nationalists in 1923 resulted in the expulsion of all Egyptian officials from the Sudan. They did not return until after the signature of the treaty of 1936.

In 1928 King Fuad grew tired of his Wafd-controlled governments, which did very little for the country. He decided to take a hand himself by appointing a prime minister who did not command a majority in the parliament, and then changed the constitution in such a way that this man won a majority. Fuad ruling through his prime minister was virtually absolute until 1935. Then the Italian invasion of Ethiopia (see p. 210) brought home to most Egyptians the danger in which they stood and the need for the continued presence of the British. At this point the British prevailed upon Fuad to restore the earlier constitution of 1923, and elections were held. The Wafd government that resulted ratified a new treaty negotiated by Foreign Minister Anthony Eden. The status of the Sudan was still left unsettled, but the Egyptians were permitted to emigrate there if they wished. The military clauses of the treaty permitted Britain to maintain armed forces in the country to protect the Canal and to defend Egypt in time of war. These clauses came into operation in 1940 when Egypt was in direct danger from the Italians, and later from the Germans. In 1938 the Wafd party in Egypt at last lost power since it had always thrived on the disputes between Britain and Egypt, and a more moderate government held office during the war under the new young king, Farouk I, who had succeeded to the throne in 1936.

CONCLUSION

During the course of the interwar period, Asia had begun its long process of entering the modern world created by Western technology and imperialism. The major export in the realm of ideas that Asia took from the West was nationalism, not consciously exported but accepted by the Asians as something both desirable in itself and capable of being used against its originators. In this India showed the way; and her methods, devised by Gandhi, were to be used to win independence by numerous colonies in the years following World War II, not only in Asia but also in Africa. One nation, Japan, took also from the West the idea of imperialism, backed by modern technology. But her empire was short-lived, and after the war she settled down again into an enforced military quiescence, accompanied by ever greater technical accomplishment. China, her much greater neighbor, was unable during this period to establish herself as the world power to which rank her population entitled her. It was left for the Communists to unify China in 1949 and succeeding years, though it remains to be seen whether she will yet imitate Japan in her career of imperialism. If so, she will surely use other means than the naked militarism of Japan, which could never again succeed in a nuclear-armed world.

11 THE COMING OF WORLD WAR II

It is usually difficult to assign reasons for the outbreaks of war that have afflicted man throughout history. In the case of the second world war of the twentieth century, however, it seems difficult to escape the conclusion that the major, almost the exclusive, responsibility rests with Adolf Hitler, Reichsfuehrer and Chancellor of Germany, whose will unleashed it; and that a secondary responsibility must rest with those powers which by their policy of appeasement permitted him to take so much that he believed himself capable of conquering and holding all Europe. The United States, a nation far greater in resources and manpower than Germany and Italy combined, must bear some responsibility inasmuch as she felt she could remain aloof from European affairs. She had been unable or unwilling to heed her experience in World War I, which should have made it clear that she could not live peacefully in a world in which one hostile power dominated Europe, and that in such a situation sooner or later she would be compelled to intervene.

The war in the Far East was precipitated by Japan, who, like Germany, believed she could dominate her sector of the world. Even before she joined the Axis she had already begun her war with China, as recounted in the preceding chapter. But if Germany had not been her ally in 1941, it is doubtful indeed that Japan would have taken on the full power of the United States by herself. Perhaps she would have contented herself with her conquests in China and attempted to consolidate, and possibly add to them, in the expectation that the United States would eventually learn to live with the new situation in preference to going to war. Nevertheless, the Japanese military leaders who extended the war to the south must bear a large part of the responsibility for the extension of the war until almost the entire world was involved in it.

UNDERLYING CAUSES OF THE WAR

The seeds of World War II can be found in the peace settlement which followed World War I. While it may be agreed that Germany could have lived with the Treaty of Versailles and accepted its provisions, the manner in which it was imposed upon her by the victorious powers made it a dictated rather than a negotiated peace. The Germans who signed the treaty were in fact compelled to do so by the continued blockade and the threat of invasion if they refused. The German people therefore did not regard it as binding on them. Although she was the largest of the European nations outside Russia, Germany was nevertheless condemned to a position of military inferiority in relation to France who had only two-thirds of her population—and it was impossible to escape from this position except by unilateral action and the threat of force. The League of Nations had been organized in such a way that it was bound to uphold the peace settlements. Any nation that wished to change these settlements would be faced by opposition from those who had benefited from them; and the latter could call upon the League to take steps to prevent changes imposed by force.

There was thus no incentive for any nation that had gained from the peace settlements to relinquish any of its gains. If therefore Germany (or any of the other nations) determined to take back what she had lost, there was no way open to her but to use force—and this fact was fully appreciated by the victorious powers. They recognized too that they might at any time be required to defend their newly acquired territories. Hence they dared not disarm, and the Disarmament Conference when it finally met could hardly be expected to come to any agreement. "Collective security" under the League of Nations was only a cloak for the determination to maintain the peace settlements and hence could not be accepted by those who were resolved to change them. The policy of appeasement, which was primarily a British policy, though France in her weakness had to go along with it, was regarded by the British as a means for abrogating those clauses of the Treaty of Versailles which bore most heavily on Germany. They were perfectly well aware of the fact that they were making concessions under the threat of force; but they regarded at least the earlier concessions as not unreasonable in themselves. However, it became difficult for them to stop, and Hitler naturally drew the conclusion that they would pay any price he asked. Eventually the British and French did make a stand and refused any further concessions. War followed because by this time Hitler had his powerful war machine, and had no scruples—indeed the evidence shows that he positively desired to use it. He did not even seriously attempt to coerce the Poles, the first victims of his armies, to cede the Corridor or Danzig by the means he had used hitherto.

Aside from the inequities of the Treaty of Versailles, the other peace treaties created an artificial Europe of small nation-states that could barely manage to exist in a dangerous world in which their armies counted for little and in which there was as yet hardly an attempt to escape from the economic nationalism that made none of their economies viable. Each state protected its own infant industries, however uneconomic they were, in preference to buying from those countries which could supply them far more cheaply. They lost the secure market for their own primary products that the old Austro-Hungarian Empire, whatever its other defects, had provided. Germany took advantage of their lack of markets during the Great Depression, and by providing a market on her own terms she made several of them into her economic satellites. Although the small states of eastern Europe have lost their freedom since World War II, at least they have their secure market within the Soviet bloc, and this particular problem has been solved, even if temporarily. The European Economic Community (the Common Market) and the European Free Trade Union (the Outer Seven) have likewise provided markets for the remaining free nations of the West.

Economic nationalism was not a direct cause for the war, but it (like political nationalism) undoubtedly contributed to the general weakness of Europe during the interwar period. If the New Order imposed by Germany had been a genuine attempt to unify Europe under German auspices, and not a simple tyranny in which all the conquered nations were compelled, as "inferiors," to serve the German "master race," it might even have survived, if not for the "thousand years" predicted by Hitler, at least for more years than the five which proved to be its total life span.

SUCCESSIVE STEPS LEADING
TO WAR

When Hitler became chancellor of Germany his first care was to consolidate his own position at home. This phase may be considered to have been completed with the blood purge of June 30, 1934 (see p. 72). By this time Germany had withdrawn from the League of Nations and the Disarmament Conference (October, 1933), and the other European nations had begun to consolidate their alliances or negotiate for new ones. No one doubted that Hitler would soon begin to fulfill his many promises to the German people that he would free them from the shackles of the Treaty of Versailles. But as yet he had not openly thrown down the gage to the former victors.

The Early Years—to the Ethiopian War.   It seems clear that when Hitler gave thought to the timetable for his abrogation of the Treaty of Versailles he concluded that the last and toughest nut to crack would be Poland. It was therefore logical that he should seek an agreement with Poland which he would keep for a good many years, meanwhile making the most of his apparent willingness to give assurances to those nations who had profited at Germany's expense by the peace treaties. In January, 1934, Hitler therefore signed a nonagression treaty with Poland which was to run for ten years. This treaty made a breach in the French alliance system. France had been allied with Poland since 1921, and the alliance was still in force. But the treaty suggested that Poland was no longer willing to rely on this alliance alone and preferred to hedge her bets by coming to terms with resurgent Germany.

At this time the Italian dictator Mussolini had little enough respect for his fellow dictator in Germany, and German and Italian interests clashed in central Europe, especially in Austria. Throughout the early months of 1934 there were rumors of a Nazi coup in Austria, since it was of course well known that almost all Germans desired the union, and Hitler himself, as an Austrian, had every reason to back it. It was in July, 1934, that the abortive Nazi coup took place (see p. 100). Mussolini, who at the time of Dollfuss' murder by the Nazis had as guests Dr. Dollfuss' family, was quite naturally furious. He at once sent troops to the Brenner Pass, to guard against the possibility that the Germans would try to take over Austria. Hitler disavowed the coup, and the crisis subsided.

In early 1935 Hitler was still far from friendly with Mussolini. Mussolini himself was trying to find a basis of agreement with the Western powers by which he could make some gains, perhaps at the expense of France, in Africa. He was as much concerned as the other powers when Hitler, who, as was common knowledge, had been rearming contrary to the Versailles Treaty, came to the conclusion that he might as well admit the rearmament and elicit what sympathy he could by pleading necessity to escape from the strangling disarmament clauses of the treaty. He gave a virtuoso performance along these lines, especially drawing attention to the fact that France had just doubled the period of service for her conscripts and that all other nations were rearming, not disarming. On March 16 he formally denounced the disarmament clauses of the treaty, reintroduced conscription, and mentioned the figure of thirty-six divisions as the total at which he was aiming.

France was more alarmed than Britain since she was more likely to be affected by German actions and by the collapse of the treaty. But even she did not propose sanctions through the League and contented herself with obtaining from the League a resolution condemning Germany's action. A conference was held at Stresa, Italy, in which Britain, France, and Italy attempted to build a common front against further unilateral actions by Germany. The conference, however, did not do more than reaffirm their continued adherence to the Locarno treaties (see p. 28) and their determination not to allow Austria to fall victim to German aggression. The French, however, in May signed a treaty with the Soviet Union, and the Soviet Union two weeks later concluded a treaty with Czechoslovakia under which the Russians bound themselves to support the latter if France did the same (see p. 103). But these efforts were to some degree nullified by British actions. Hitler in several speeches had made it appear that his armament would be limited and need be no cause for alarm. In particular he did not desire naval rearmament and recognized that Britain should remain the mistress of the European seas. Britain fell into the juicily baited trap and invited German representatives to London to put this into writing in the form of a naval treaty. Thus the Anglo-German Naval Agreement was signed on June 18, 1935, by the British government, which had just been reorganized with Stanley Baldwin as prime minister and Sir Samuel Hoare as foreign secretary. The agreement may be considered as the opening salvo in the British policy of "appeasement." It permitted the

Germans to build a navy not more than 35 per cent of the size of Britain's, although she was permitted parity in submarines. The agreement constituted a tacit acceptance by Britain of Germany's right to rearm. It had been concluded without consulting France or Italy, and thus contributed to the breakup of the unity which the three powers had achieved at Stresa.

The Ethiopian War and Its Consequences. In December, 1934, a frontier incident occurred on the boundary between Italian Somaliland and Ethiopia (Abyssinia) as a result of which about thirty Italians lost their lives. During almost the whole of 1935 this incident was discussed by the League of Nations, and both France and Britain attempted to settle the problem by making concessions to Italy in East Africa, which the Ethiopian emperor Haile Selassie I would not accept. It was widely recognized that Mussolini was not greatly interested in a settlement which would give him less than the entire country, and he was anxious to win military victories which would avenge the great defeat Italy had suffered at the hands of the Ethiopian emperor Menelik in 1896. For this reason many expected that the Ethiopian question would ultimately involve the full prestige of the League. In Britain, in particular, sentiment in favor of the League and its system of "collective security" was very strong, and a "peace ballot" held during the course of 1935 appeared to show that British public opinion would be willing to support the use of severe economic sanctions against any aggressor. When, therefore, Italy invaded Ethiopia in October, 1935, the British at once took the lead in the League in demanding economic sanctions against Italy, in which the other members (France, led by Pierre Laval, with considerable reluctance) followed. But the sanctions imposed were not likely to be effective unless oil was included, and an oil sanction was viewed with alarm by several of the powers, including Britain—although the United States agreed to cut off all exports to Italy and Ethiopia if League members did the same. The British government did not wish in any circumstances to become involved in a war with Italy over Ethiopia, and there were misgivings over the possibility of driving her too far in view of the weakness of the Mediterranean British fleet.

The British action in support of the League was very popular in England, and Stanley Baldwin therefore decided that this was the best moment to renew his government's mandate from the electors. The policy on which he "went to the country" was limited rearmament and collective security through the League—the armaments proposed being just enough to enable Britain to fulfill her League responsibilities. The campaign was extremely successful and the "National" government found itself with a strong majority in Parliament. But, instead of putting renewed pressure on the Italians through the League, and perhaps putting an end to the invasion, Sir Samuel Hoare, the British foreign secretary, met with Pierre Laval and together they arrived at a scheme which would give Italy her "just demands" and would save Ethiopia from being completely defeated. Ethiopia would merely lose one province which she had held for a relatively short time.

Whatever the merits of the Hoare-Laval agreement if it had been accepted by Mussolini and Haile Selassie, it suggested to the British people that they had been hoodwinked in the recent election and that the government they had just elected was not serious about collective security. When a French journalist leaked the supposedly secret agreement to the French press there was such an outcry that the British government had to disown the agreement and dismiss Hoare from the ministry, while Laval fell from office in France a month later. But meanwhile Mussolini was making progress with his conquest. In May, 1936, his armies moved into the Ethiopian capital of Addis Ababa, and Haile Selassie fled. The oil sanction had still not been imposed.

Clearly this episode was not lost on Hitler, who perceived its significance at once. He did not at first openly support Mussolini, nor did he object to the sanctions, and indeed he expressed himself as willing to do his own part in imposing them. If Mussolini should lose his war, then he would be in dire need of an ally. If he should win it, then this would demonstrate the feebleness of the resistance to be expected from the British and French. It might be possible to make a deal with Mussolini in either case. The only result that Hitler could gain little from would be if Mussolini accepted such an agreement as had been devised by Hoare and Laval, which would keep him securely in the Anglo-French camp. The League also had lost much prestige, not by attempting sanctions, but by not pressing them to the point where they were likely to be effective. The Soviet Union had recently entered the League (September, 1934), but her presence had in no way stiffened its fortitude.

The End of the Treaties of Locarno and Versailles. Hitler
therefore decided on his most provocative step. Complaining that
the Russo-French treaty of alliance had put an end to the Locarno
treaties, to which Germany had freely agreed in 1925, Hitler sent
his troops into the Rhineland in March, 1936, thus breaking both
the Versailles and Locarno treaties and giving an opportunity to
the Western allies to take action provided for by the treaties. In
giving the order to his troops, Hitler had rejected the advice of
his generals, who were afraid that the French, who had the power,
would send their own troops in, backed in this action at a minimum
by Czechoslovakia and probably by Poland and the other powers
who were in alliance with France. As it turned out this was the
last chance the Allies ever had of stopping Hitler cheaply, and
perhaps of encouraging his own army to overthrow him. At the
very least he would have lost much prestige at home if he had
withdrawn without a fight and by retreating would have demonstrated to all that his army was as yet no match for the French.

Yet the French did not march. The prime minister of the
day, Albert Sarraut, and his foreign minister, Pierre-Étienne
Flandin, were both aware of the crucial nature of the decision to
be made, and they sounded out their own general staff, led by
Marshal Pétain. The military leaders had staked everything on a
defensive war and hesitated to change their ultraconservative
notions. Even so, the decisive factor was the attitude of the British,
who found it possible at this juncture to agree that the wording
of the Locarno treaties, which Hitler had denounced and broken,
did not require their military intervention if Germany invaded
the demilitarized territory of the Rhineland. When the British
Cabinet, over the dissent of Anthony Eden, refused to give the
French any backing, France accepted the inevitable. Hitler had
triumphed over his own generals and the French at the same
time—and the French allies this time had no difficulty in understanding the significance of his victory. The Belgian declaration
of neutrality on October 14, 1936 (see p. 157) was a direct consequence of French acquiescence in the German march into the
Rhineland and was strategically disastrous for France, since her
famed Maginot Line could now be turned through Belgium. On
July 11, 1936, Austria decided to put her relations with Germany
on a more friendly footing and signed an agreement with her,
under which Germany promised not to intervene in Austrian

affairs, while Austria among other things agreed to relax restrictions on the Nazi party in Austria.

On July 17, 1936, the Spanish Civil War erupted (see p. 91), in which both Germany and Italy intervened from the beginning on Franco's side. This parallel intervention brought Italy and Germany closer together. There were no longer any major differences over Austria, and Mussolini evidently felt there was nothing further to be gained by supporting France and Britain, an alliance from which he could get little. Late in the year the Italian foreign minister, Count Ciano, visited Germany for conversations with the Fuehrer, as a result of which protocols were signed. The following month for the first time Mussolini spoke of a Rome-Berlin "Axis," "around which all those European states which are animated by a desire for collaboration and peace may work together." The word Axis was to become the favored term for the collaboration between Germany and Italy. On November 25, 1936, the Germans signed an agreement with Japan to oppose international Communism, to which the Italians later adhered. This was the famous Anti-Comintern Pact which first established an understanding between these three aggressor powers, although it did not yet amount to a military alliance.

The Spanish Civil War.   The Popular Front government had now taken office in France (see p. 153). It was strongly in sympathy with the similar Popular Front government in Spain, which was now under attack from General Franco and his insurgents. The French leftists were in favor of giving unlimited aid to the Loyalists, as was Prime Minister Léon Blum. But the more moderate members of Blum's Cabinet were seriously worried about the possibility of intervention not only by Italy and Germany, who had helped Franco from the beginning, but also by the Soviet Union, who was hesitating. It therefore occurred to the French government that the safest plan would be to prevent the Germans and Italians and perhaps the Soviet Union also, from sending aid by obtaining all their signatures on a nonintervention agreement. When this idea was broached to the British they agreed at once. The Soviet Union, believing that the Loyalists would win if the Germans and Italians agreed not to intervene and honored their agreement, quickly decided to sign. The Germans and Italians hesitated for some time—even while they were shipping large quantities of arms —but eventually signed. The agreement was not observed by the

Germans, the Italians, or the Soviet Union; but the other nations that had agreed, including the United States, in general observed the agreement, even though clandestine shipments of arms from France did reach the Loyalists from time to time. As noted earlier, the Italian and German aid, which was on a much larger scale than that supplied by the Soviet Union, turned the tide in favor of the insurgents. Germany in particular profited from the opportunity to test her pilots in genuine warfare.

The Anschluss. During 1937 Hitler was largerly preoccupied with internal affairs, including a purge of the army to bring its high command more into accord with his own plans. The rearmament program was now in high gear, and Hitler was planning what to do when his armies were ready. In England Neville Chamberlain, who had replaced Baldwin as prime minister, made it clear at once that he intended to take positive steps to maintain the peace. In pursuance of this policy in November, 1937, he sent Viscount Halifax to see Hitler and inquire into his intentions. Hitler did not reveal them to Halifax; but German archives record that he did reveal what was in his mind to a group of high officials and military men only two weeks before Halifax' visit. He intended to move against Austria and Czechoslovakia in the course of 1938, though he did not explain, and perhaps did not as yet know, how he was to do it. He was no longer seriously interested in Britain's views, as he had come to the conclusion that she would not fight.

The Austrian crisis in the spring of 1938 was carefully manufactured by Hitler. Since the 1936 agreement Austrian Prime Minister Kurt von Schuschnigg had been careful to avoid offending Hitler, realizing that his country, no longer able to rely on Italy, was defenseless. But he had not implemented that part of the agreement which called for him to grant some concessions to the Austrian Nazis. The party was still banned, and indeed in January, 1938, the Austrian police discovered some evidence of a planned Nazi coup. The German ambassador to Vienna, Franz von Papen, suggested in February that Schuschnigg might care to discuss personally with Hitler a number of problems of mutual interest. When Schuschnigg arrived at Berchtesgaden, however, he was treated to an angry tirade by Hitler, to which he had no opportunity to reply, and was then presented by Papen and German Foreign Minister Joachim von Ribbentrop with a series of demands and a time limit for acceptance. The demands included the legalization of the Nazi party in Austria and the appointment of a leading Nazi, Artur Seyss-Inquart, as minister of the interior. Schuschnigg had no option but to agree, but as soon as he returned home he tried to devise means by which he could escape the impending Nazi conquest of his country. Although he appointed Seyss-Inquart, as directed, he planned to hold a plebiscite in which the Austrians would be asked whether or not they favored a free and independent German and Christian Austria. No other choice was permitted.

Hitler, furious at what he regarded as an infraction of the recent agreement, at once gave orders to his army to be ready to march into Austria. Then he called upon Schuschnigg to cancel the plebiscite. He obeyed. But Hitler demanded his resignation, which after some hesitation was given. He was replaced by Seyss-Inquart, who was then required to request German troops. This he did, and Austria was thereupon occupied, bloodlessly. Hitler entered Vienna in a triumphal return to his native country. Meanwhile a special messenger had informed Mussolini of what had been planned, and to Hitler's delight he offered no objections. The other powers likewise accepted the situation—which was in accord with President Wilson's principle of self-determination, as Hitler demonstrated by holding the postponed plebiscite which went overwhelmingly in Germany's favor. Only the Soviet Union suggested that a conference be held to consider means by which Hitler's further aggression could be halted. The proposal was turned down by Prime Minister Chamberlain on the ground that it would divide Europe more than ever into two opposing blocs.

The Czechoslovakian Crisis. Doggedly determined to pursue peace, Chamberlain then entered into negotiations with the Italians for the purpose of settling differences between the two countries. Foreign Minister Anthony Eden bitterly opposed these negotiations, which began even before Hitler's move into Austria. He resigned in February, 1938, to be replaced by Viscount Halifax, whose views were in full accord with his leader's. The Italian negotiations came to fruition in April, 1938, with an agreement under which Britain would recognize Mussolini's conquests in Ethiopia—the League had withdrawn its sanctions only two months after the conquest had been completed—and Mussolini in return promised to withdraw his "volunteers" from Spain. France followed Britain's lead in recognizing Victor Emmanuel III as emperor of Ethiopia. But the Italians, far from being grateful for the recognition, at once raised demands for the "return" of Nice and Corsica.* France was bitterly humiliated by such demands, and her relations with Italy never thereafter became friendly.

In the summer of 1938, Hitler began to stir the Czechoslovakian cauldron (see p. 104). As noted earlier, the Sudetenland area in Czechosolvakia had a strong Nazi movement, led by Konrad Henlein, who demanded that the territory be ceded to Germany, although in fact it had never formed part of Germany, but had been taken from Austria-Hungary in the peace treaties. Prime Minister Chamberlain was so seriously alarmed by Hitler's evident intentions that he bent every effort toward making the Czechs co-operate in their own dismemberment. It was Henlein who was in charge of the operation, acting under orders from Berlin. Hitler himself did not make any demands until late in the year. In May the Czechs, acting on a rumor that the Germans were mobilizing troops, for use against them, themselves mobilized as a warning to Hitler that the Czech armies were still to be reckoned with. Britain and France protested to Hitler for his supposed mobilization and to the Czechs for their provocation. Hitler himself, as is now known, determined from that moment that he would teach the Czechs a lesson.

Meanwhile in Czechoslovakia itself the farce of negotiations between Henlein and the Czech leaders went on. The Czechs agreed to virtually complete home rule for the Sudeten Germans, but nothing would satisfy Henlein, and he kept raising his terms, according to plan. The British, by August very seriously concerned, sent out a mission headed by Lord Runciman to negotiate with the Sudeten-German leaders to see if there were any grounds for agreement. Runciman put pressure on the Czechs, but at the same time Britain and France informed Hitler that he could not count on their neutrality if he pursued matters to conclusions with the Czechs. The French called up about a million men. Meanwhile Hitler himself was busy trying to ensure that the Russians would be in no position to honor their agreements with France and Czechoslovakia. He was assured by the Poles and Rumanians that they would not permit the Russians to cross their frontiers to aid Czechoslovakia.

---

* Nice had been ceded to France by the King of Piedmont and Sardinia in 1860, during the wars of reunification; Corsica had been ceded by the Genoese in 1768. Neither had ever been part of the kingdom of Italy, which came into existence in 1870.

In mid-September Hitler announced publicly that nothing less than complete self-determination for the Sudeten-Germans would satisfy him, whereupon serious disorders broke out in the Sudetenland, and the Czechs declared martial law. Chamberlain thereupon flew to Berchtesgaden to a face-to-face confrontation with Hitler (September 15), but he was informed that Germany would accept only Sudeten self-determination. Chamberlain and Daladier, prime minister of France, then made it clear to the Czechs that if they did not accept, they could not count on their aid. The Czechs then yielded, but the government resigned and a new ministry was formed under a popular military leader (General Jan Sirovy). Chamberlain paid a second visit to Hitler at Godesberg (September 22–23) to inform him of Czech willingness to accept his terms. But Hitler then promptly raised the terms to include immediate surrender of Czech fortifications intact, as well as the Sudetenland, and the holding of plebiscites in other areas with German minorities. The Czechs refused even to consider such terms, and Chamberlain was bitterly disappointed at Hitler's attitude and apparent ill faith. France and Britain then concluded that Hitler was bent on war and there was nothing to be done but prepare to fight. Hitler himself took no further action, but President Roosevelt appealed to him to hold a conference, and Mussolini, who himself was afraid that Hitler had at last overreached himself, likewise made an appeal to which Hitler graciously consented.

The conference of Munich followed. Neither the Russians, who had consistently promised that they would honor their alliances, nor the Czechs, who were most concerned, were invited. The participants were simply the Big Four, Hitler and Mussolini, Chamberlain and Daladier. The two latter were so anxious for peace that they were willing to accept the very slight concessions agreed to by Hitler; in effect they accepted the demands put to Chamberlain at Godesberg. Chamberlain believed he had made Hitler back down, and he was greeted as a hero by his countrymen, whom he informed that he had brought back peace. All the European peoples were relieved except the Czechs, who had been ready to fight but could not do so without any allies at all, as it was clear they would be compelled to do. The Poles and the Hungarians also took the opportunity to put forward demands of their own, and these too had to be accepted by the hapless Czechs. President Benes of Czechoslovakia resigned and departed for the United States. Slovakia and Ruthenia, component parts of Czechoslovakia, at once received autonomy, leaving little but Bohemia to the now defenseless Czechs.

The Last Year of Peace. Hitler after his great victory was disposed to be magnanimous toward Britain and France, and relations appeared to be improving. A pact with France was signed in December providing for the peaceful settlement of all disputes. The British government, in spite of its belief that peace was now assured, and in spite of some fatuous remarks from Sir Samuel Hoare, who had re-entered Chamberlain's cabinet as home secretary, to the effect that Europe was now entering on a new Golden Age, nevertheless did make renewed preparations for war, though hardly on the scale needed. Nor were the preparations comparable with those being made by Hitler. Some planes were ordered from the United States. Opposition, for which Winston Churchill was the chief spokesman, grew in Parliament to the Munich Settlement.

In March, 1939, Hitler without the shadow of an excuse marched into the remainder of Czecho-Slovakia, and annexed the country, paying no attention at all to the guarantee of the new frontiers which had been made by the British and the French. The latter were helpless to prevent it. A few days later Hitler sent an ultimatum to Lithuania, as a result of which he annexed Memel (see p. 17). It was now clear to the British and French that Hitler was not merely trying to incorporate all Germans into a single Reich, as he had so often claimed. This time he had annexed a territory peopled by non-Germans. Chamberlain came to the conclusion that Poland would be next on Hitler's program, and he offered an Anglo-French guarantee to the Poles (see p. 208). Finally Mussolini, who had greatly disliked having to sit by with no new conquests, took Albania on Good Friday, April 7, 1939, meeting no resistance (see p. 118). A few days earlier the Franco forces had at last won the final victory in Spain. On April 7, 1939, Franco joined the anti-Comintern pact.

The best hope of stopping Hitler now seemed to be to improve relations with the Soviet Union. But Stalin had been deeply offended by the way in which the Soviet Union had been treated and the low estimate the French evidently had of their alliance with her. He was suspicious of both Britain and France, who approached him now only at the last moment. Moreover, he was not at all certain that they were not trying to turn Hitler in his direction in order to save themselves—a policy which would certainly have been popular enough in many sectors of British and French opinion. When the British sent a minor Foreign Office official to begin talks looking toward joint action against the Axis, Stalin was far from mollified, and the talks dragged on for months, while he put forward several of his own demands, as for instance a free hand in the Baltic countries. It can hardly be doubted that the British and French were, at best, halfhearted over the possibility of joint action, and they were doubtful whether after the great army purges of the past years, the Russian armies would be of much use to them. Moreover, Soviet aid to the Spanish Loyalists had been both ineffective and disruptive. Nevertheless, they were surprised when the Nonaggression Pact of August 23, 1939, between Germany and the Soviet Union (see p. 57) was announced. The Anglo-Russian talks were naturally broken off at once, and few continued to believe that war could now be avoided.

Meanwhile the British and French had had some success in persuading Turkey to stay aloof from the coming war, and each had signed a pact with her, the British pact calling for mutual assistance but not for military involvement. Germany and Italy, on the other side, had signed the Pact of Steel (May 22, 1939), and the informal Axis had now become a full military alliance.

The Invasion of Poland. On August 20 the final crisis began. Hitler demanded the return to the Reich of the Free City of Danzig (see p. 8) and complained of Polish "atrocities" committed against the German minority in Poland. President Roosevelt appealed to Hitler, to the Italian King, and to the President of Poland to take their differences to arbitration; the British and French repeatedly warned Germany that if she attacked Poland it would mean war with them. Hitler assured them that he meant them no harm and there was no need for them to fight in a lost cause. Poland began to call up reserves and signed a full treaty of mutual assistance with Britain. But to the end she was never willing to admit Russian troops into the country, and thus could never have been assisted directly by the Western allies. Hitler, of course, was well aware of this fact. Having protected himself against Russian intervention, and certain that his armies could conquer Poland within a few weeks, he was no longer interested in whether or not the Poles would accept his terms. He reiterated extreme terms to the last moment, which there was no possibility that the Poles would accept. Then on August 31, he sent an ultimatum which included much more moderate terms but did not leave time for the Poles to reply. The next day his armies crossed the frontier, and World War II began. On September 3 the British and French declared war on Germany.

From the German archives made available after the war, it was clear that nothing could have stopped Hitler at this point. It was for this reason that Hitler was held responsible at the beginning of this chapter for the unleashing of World War II. It is true that the Poles were far more determined to resist him than the Czechs had been, and they were unwilling to compromise. But they had had the example of Czechoslovakia before them, and no trust whatever could be put in Hitler's promises or guarantees. To the last moment they were willing to negotiate, but Hitler never gave them any real chance to discuss specific proposals, for the obvious reason that he desired war. However, he would have preferred a localized war, and even after the pact with the Soviet Union, great efforts were made to persuade the British to agree to keep out of it. The British and French had learned from the previous year's crisis that no good would come from putting pressure on their ally to agree to impossible demands. This time, therefore, they quietly reiterated that the Germans must negotiate with the Poles directly, and they would be willing to guarantee the settlement. But they would not abandon their alliance. Since Hitler did not desire a settlement that the British could have guaranteed and in fact desired to conquer Poland in warfare, no basis remained for compromise, and the war became inevitable.

12   WORLD WAR II

The Germans had counted on conquering Poland quickly, and Hitler had hoped that Britain and France could be persuaded to accept the conquest and make peace. If they did not, he was fully prepared to conquer France, and, if necessary, Britain also. Nevertheless, it is now known that his main objective was always the Soviet Union—even though Ribbentrop, his foreign minister, and others entertained many remarkable and far-ranging ideas on how the Germans and Russians together could conquer and rule the world. Hitler by his pact with the Soviet Union had bought time, but he disliked having to do it and had absolutely no interest in further collaboration with the Russians, whom he regarded as racial inferiors (and treated as such after the invasion). For this reason he did not object to letting the Russians have the Baltic countries, Bessarabia, and half of Poland; nor did he in any way interfere with the Soviet Union in her war with Finland. When the time came, he could easily take them back (as he in fact did).

By the middle of 1941 he was so confident of the invincibility of his armies that, unlike his generals, he did not even mind having to fight in a two-front war. It was this obsession which cost him whatever chance he had of defeating Britain after the fall of France. By failing to reinforce General Rommel in North Africa, he lost the opportunity to take Cairo and Alexandria, then move on to seize control of the Suez Canal and the British sources of oil in the Middle East. He did not seize Gibraltar and seal the Mediterranean, which should have been well within the capacity of German troops if they had been adequately reinforced. Such ventures he regarded as side shows, distractions from his main objectives. He gave no support at all to Japan. In short, he never really regarded the war from a global point of view, but looked upon it as an affair of gigantic armies crushing their opponents in huge land operations—in spite of the success these armies had when engaged in operations of a different kind (such as the amphibious operations in Norway and the victories won in the desert). This failure in over-all strategy must be laid to the debit of Hitler as supreme commander, and suggests a fundamental irrationality, a *preference* for certain kinds of warfare, the roots of which can be found in his own personality. The same irrationality dictated the behavior of the Germans toward the peoples they conquered, which made impossible the development of an enduring empire.

By contrast the Allies made mistakes only in detail. Once the United States and the Soviet Union were in the war as allies, it was only a matter of bringing their overwhelming resources and manpower into operation. From the end of 1941 it was physically impossible for the Germans and Japanese to win as long as the American-Russian alliance held together. Sooner or later their resistance would necessarily be worn down, and the result would eventually have been the same, whatever strategy and tactics were used. Even if the Germans had captured Stalingrad in 1942, or driven the Allies into the sea in June, 1944, when they invaded Normandy, it still cannot be doubted that the Russians would have survived and the Allies would have tried again. The war could have been prolonged, but the end would not have been different. The crucial years were therefore 1940 and 1941; and in this chapter more attention will be given to these years than to the details of the later campaigns, interesting though these may be to military historians, and important though they were to the participants.

THE FIRST YEAR

The Polish campaign, for which the Germans were thoroughly prepared, was over in under a month. The Poles were totally unable to deal with the weight of German armor, and the many-pronged attack known as the *blitzkrieg*. Before the war was over the Russians had taken their sector of the country by arrangement with Germany. Meanwhile the British sent their army over to France, and a small advance was made into German territory by the Allies. But the latter were not prepared for a war of offense. The French generals, in particular, were defense-minded and preferred to see their troops hold off the Germans in their prepared fortifications, especially the Maginot Line.

After the conquest of Poland Hitler's peace proposals were half-hearted. Having tasted blood and seen how effective German military tactics were, he was now confident that he could defeat and conquer France—on which point his generals disagreed with him —and planned an attack to begin as soon as possible. However several hitches developed, and eventually the campaign had to be postponed until the spring.

The Russo-Finnish War. Meanwhile the Russians incorporated Lithuania, Latvia, and Estonia without fighting (see p. 109) and took Bessarabia from Rumania. When the Finns, alone among the Baltic countries, refused to accept the Soviet terms, the Russian armies attacked, believing that the war would be over very quickly. But the Finns resisted the ill-planned invasion, and the Russians suffered very severe losses until they changed their tactics and brought an overwhelming weight to bear on the Finnish prepared defenses, known as the Mannerheim Line. This attack the Finns were unable to sustain, and they sued for peace. The Russians dictated terms which were not much more onerous than the demands they had made before the war. All these efforts on the part of the Russians were, of course, directed against the Germans, whom they did not trust, and the new territories under their control were intended to become buffer states against an eventual German attack. They did not wish to provoke such an attack, but they were apprehensive that it would come when the Germans were ready. Meanwhile the Germans did not interfere with them; while the Russians, for their part, provided the Germans with the economic support and the raw materials for which they had covenanted in an economic treaty concluded just before the war. There was great sympathy for the gallant Finns everywhere in Europe, even among the Italians, who would have greatly preferred the Germans to attack Russia rather than the West. But the war was over (March 12, 1940) before the volunteers from various European countries could be organized to give them aid. No country declared war on Russia because of her venture in Finland, but she was expelled from the League of Nations for her aggression.

The Norwegian Campaign. On April 9, 1940, the Germans launched an attack on Norway and Denmark. Denmark, completely incapable of defending herself, submitted at once. But Norway, attacked by sea and airborne forces which seized her main centers of population, resisted as effectively as she could with her small army, and several German ships were sunk during the operation. Britain and France sent an expeditionary force, and the British navy occupied the northern port of Narvik, driving out the Germans who had taken it. But the invasion had been such a surprise that the entire Allied operation had to be improvised, and it was close to being a complete failure. At all events Germany succeeded in bringing all resistance to an end except in Narvik by May 1. The Germans were assisted by a number of collaborators, including Vidkun Quisling, who was made "minister-president" of the country in 1942, with complete authority delegated to him by the Germans. The British withdrew from Narvik in June, 1940, by which time the Germans had already invaded France.

The Fall of Holland, Belgium, and France.   Meanwhile the Western Front had remained immobile, although several actions had taken place at sea, and the relatively few German submarines that were available had already begun to take a severe toll of British shipping. Germany, however, had lost one of her few battleships when the *Graf von Spee* was scuttled by her crew in preference to being sunk off the coast of South America.

On May 10, the Germans invaded Holland, Belgium, and Luxemburg in a many-pronged attack, which made use of parachutists and glider-borne troops to seize all the key points of the countries. (This crisis brought Winston Churchill to power in England.) German shock tactics prevented the Dutch from opening their dykes and completely undermined their plan of defense. The demoralization was completed by a savage attack on the undefended city of Rotterdam. The Dutch capitulated after four days. The Belgians resisted for fourteen days, and received some Allied help. But the defense plans with France had not been co-ordinated as Belgium since 1936 (see p. 157) had preferred to attempt to remain neutral. King Leopold III requested an armistice from the Germans on May 27. The cessation of hosilities in Belgium was a severe blow to the British and French, and they blamed Leopold for his action, both then and later, contrasting it with the fortitude of his father Albert in World War I. It remains doubtful that Belgium's prolonged resistance would have changed the course of the war in any important respect; but for the moment it meant that the British army was cut off by the German advance in the south.

The British were extremely fortunate in being able to evacuate from Dunkirk. The Germans had almost complete command of the air and could have damaged the British-improvised flotilla which took the troops over to England so severely that the operation could not have succeeded. Also Dunkirk itself could surely have been taken if Hitler had not issued orders to his armies to press on. Nevertheless, the Dunkirk evacuation (May 27–May 29, 1940) was a stirring episode in British history, even though the armies had to leave all their equipment behind.

Meanwhile the speed of the German advance demoralized the defense. The roads became clogged with refugees, and it was impossible for the French armies to re-form and resist. On June 10 Italy declared war on France and Britain; three days later Paris was evacuated and the government moved to Bordeaux; and on June 17 France requested an armistice, which was signed on June 22 in the same railroad car in which Marshal Foch had received the German capitulation at the end of World War I.

During the retreat the French government had been undecided as to what its policy should be. Prime Minister Paul Reynaud had proposed that the government itself should go to North Africa, leaving the army to make what terms it could. To this the army leaders objected, and Reynaud evidently could not count on the support of enough deputies to enable him to carry out his plan. Marshal Pétain, a World War I hero, minister of war in Reynaud's Cabinet, was willing to become prime minister and take the responsibility for requesting the armistice, in which he had the support of most of the deputies, who could see no alternative. It was Pétain therefore who asked the Germans for an armistice on June 17, and accepted their terms, which included the submission of about three-fifths of the country to direct German control, leaving "unoccupied France" to be ruled by Pétain from his new "capital" of Vichy (a noted French spa). Pétain, with the approval of the Germans, appointed Pierre Laval (see p. 153) as his vice-premier. The Pétain regime was authoritarian, and it commanded some voluntary support from the numerous right-wing groups in France. Other right-wing leaders remained in Occupied France and collaborated with the Germans.

Meanwhile an acting brigadier general, Charles de Gaulle, a military officer with a distinguished record, escaped to England and called upon all Frenchmen who wished to continue the struggle against Germany to rally to him. As time went on numerous

Frenchmen managed to find their way to England and joined him. The Churchill government gave de Gaulle its support and broke relations with the Pétain regime in France. Although relations with the prickly de Gaulle were never cordial, and usually difficult, the facilities provided by the British made it possible for him to maintain a rallying point for the Free French, as they called themselves; and the Free French took an active part in all overseas operations thereafter as far as their numbers and resources permitted.

The Battle of Britain. The British were now alone without allies except for members of the Commonwealth outside Europe. But the United States, under the leadership of President Roosevelt, was sympathetic to the British cause; and though there were great numbers of Americans who were against United States intervention in the war, very few indeed were pro-Axis. After the Fall of France the United States agreed to transfer fifty over-age destroyers to the British in exchange for the lease of a number of bases in the British colonies. The following year, after the Battle of Britain had been won, Congress passed the Lend-Lease Act (March 11, 1941), which gave the President authority to sell or lease or transfer war material to any country whose defense he considered essential to that of the United States. This all-important act enabled the United States to become the "arsenal for democracy," since it was quite impossible for Britain to pay for American war supplies on the scale needed. Thus there was to be no repetition of the war debt imbroglio of World War I. The United States also began to make extensive preparations for her own defense and mobilization of manpower and resources in case she was drawn into the war.

Nevertheless, it was Britain alone who had to stave off the determined German assault of 1940. Hitler intended to invade Britain if possible. But it soon became clear that as long as the British navy was intact the North Sea and the English Channel would be closed to German seaborne troops; and the losses sustained would render Germany incapable of invading Russia. At this period the Germans did not have enough airborne troops to make an air invasion feasible. Hitler therefore decided to try to knock Britain out of the war by bombing the country so severely that she would sue for peace. The German air force under the command of Marshal Goering was far larger than the British; but it had not been designed for this kind of work, and the bombs, though large for the period, were far smaller than later ones. Moreover the German air force, which had been intended mostly for the support of ground troops and had performed most effectively in that role, lacked fighters. The British, on the other hand, had two excellent fighter planes, the Hurricane and the Spitfire, and the RAF pilots had been trained for defense.

The Germans therefore inflicted very great, but not intolerable, damage during their months of saturation bombing, first of military and then of civilian targets, including the great cities. But they received irreplaceable losses. It was they who in the end had to call off the assault. If they had had larger and more effective bombs, just possibly they might have destroyed the British capacity to fight on or to resist a paratroop invasion. If they had been able to destroy enough of the British fighter planes so that their own bombers thereafter could have controlled the British air, the result also might have been different. But, as it turned out the indomitable will of the British people and their refusal, under Churchill's leadership, even to consider submitting, succeeded in turning back the German attack, which never could be renewed in the same way through the remaining years of the war.

THE SECOND YEAR

The second year of the war was marked by Italian efforts to win victories comparable to those of Germany. Italy had entered the war just as France was falling to Hitler's armies, but she won no laurels in France, and in fact was defeated by the French armies in the south. Nevertheless France was compelled by German successes in the north to conclude an armistice with Italy also (June 24, 1940), and Italy shared in some of the occupation duties. In North Africa Italy mounted a campaign, which netted her British Somaliland and a small sector of the Egyptian desert. She kept these for a very short time, and was enabled to reconquer the sector of Egypt from which she had been expelled only when she received heavy German reinforcements and a talented German, General Rommel, as campaign commander. Lastly Italy invaded Greece toward the end of 1940, but was badly beaten by the Greeks who drove her back into Albania, from which country the campaign had been initiated. Once more Germany had to rescue her ally. If the Italians had never invaded

Greece, Hitler might have been able to avoid a Balkan campaign altogether, with incalculable advantages for his over-all strategy and his planned campaign in Russia.

The African Campaigns.   British Somaliland, captured by the Italians in August, 1940, was a protectorate inhabited mostly by nomads and of little material or strategic value. It fell to Italian arms only because the British could not spare the troops to defend it. The British resistance to General Graziani's advance into Egypt was also rather light for the same reason, whereas the Italians, with no other front to defend, had upwards of half a million men available. Even so, they could not advance beyond Mersa Matruh, a relatively short distance inside the Egyptian boundaries. Instead of driving back the Italians on land, the British, who were still supreme in the Mediterranean sea (they had destroyed the potentially dangerous French fleet soon after France's surrender), successfully attacked Italian supply lines from the sea.

On November 11, 1940, a British fleet destroyed a considerable number of Italian ships in the Italian harbor of Taranto. By December the British had acquired sufficient reinforcements to enable them to make a counterattack against the Italians in Egypt. This attack, led by General Archibald Wavell, was unexpectedly successful, and drove the Italians not only out of Egypt, but right across the Libyan province of Cyrenaica, into Benghazi. Meanwhile, a mixed army made up mostly of Commonwealth and colonial troops invaded Italian East Africa (the former Ethiopia) and the old Italian colony of Italian Somaliland. As a result of this drive the entire Italian empire (and, of course British Somaliland) fell into British hands before the end of 1941.

In the Western Desert, however, the Italians were reinforced, and the British, who had been compelled to use some of their troops to defend Greece, which was under attack from Germans as well as Italians, had to retreat back the way they had come four months earlier. Only the fortified city of Tobruk in the former Italian territory remained in their hands when Rommel's drive ground to a halt at the Egyptian frontier (May 29, 1941). In December, 1941, the British tried again, and once more drove back the Germans and Italians to Benghazi. But the Germans provided reinforcements, and in May, 1942, they drove the British armies out of Egypt, reaching their furthest point of penetration into Egypt itself at El Alamein, only seventy miles from Alexandria. However, they could not supply enough troops to complete the advance with the conquest of Alexandria and the Canal. By this time they were heavily engaged in Russia, and the British had the logistical advantage. General Bernard Montgomery carefully prepared for the next advance and received enough reinforcements to outnumber Rommel's forces. The drive which began on October 23, 1942, was the last which was necessary. This time the attack was completely successful, and Montgomery reached French North Africa a few days after the Anglo-American invasion of November 8 (see p. 234).

The Balkan Campaigns. On October 28, 1940, Mussolini's armies invaded Greece. Hitler had not been warned of the impending invasion, and in fact was on the way to meet Mussolini in order to warn him against any such plan at the time of the attack. It was difficult for him to give any support directly to Mussolini, unless he sent troops to Albania, Mussolini's own jumping-off place. Hence he had been carefully working on the intervening nations, Hungary, Rumania, Yugoslavia, and Bulgaria, for some time in case it should be necessary for Hitler himself to invade Greece. By October, 1940, Hungary and Rumania had agreed to permit the Germans to use their territories. However, Bulgaria was hesitant because of Russian influence in the country, and Yugoslavia still believed she could remain neutral. When the Italian armies were driven back into Albania in early December, 1940, the Germans knew that they would have to rescue them, since Italy was Germany's one reliable ally. But the great damage had been done in that the Greeks had offered bases to Britain as soon as the Italians attacked their country. Greece was therefore no longer defenseless, and it would take a hard campaign to defeat her.

Bulgaria joined the Axis on March 1, 1941, and on March 25 Prince Paul, regent of Yugoslavia, agreed to join also (see p. 117). But Paul was immediately thereafter overthrown and driven into exile, and General Simovich took over the government on behalf of the young King Peter. On April 6 the Germans invaded both Greece and Yugoslavia in overwhelming force, and by mid-April both countries had capitulated. The British troops, for the most part, escaped, but many went to Crete, which was invaded and captured by German parachutists late in May. Thus the Germans now controlled the Aegean Sea, although Cyprus remained in British hands. The cost of the Balkan campaign, however, had been high, in casualties and in time.

RUSSIAN AND AMERICAN INVOLVEMENT

Hitler had long planned the invasion of Russia, and none of the events of the war hitherto had given him any reason to believe that the conquest would be any more difficult than his earlier ones. He did not plan, however, to conquer Asiatic Russia, to which the Russians were welcome, as far as he was concerned. What he desired was to destroy the Russian capacity to resist and to take Russian lands stretching from Archangel to the Caspian Sea along the river Volga.

The United States through her support of the British had shown herself far from neutral. But by the end of 1941 she had given no signs of entering the war voluntarily. She was content to be the arsenal of democracy; and since Britain was no longer in immediate danger of losing the war, she had no occasion to make an immediate decision. However, for a long time she had been coming to the conclusion that there would have to be a showdown in the western Pacific. She could win no assurances such as she desired from negotiations with Japan (see p. 188). Nevertheless, it was the Japanese who made the decision to attack first, whereupon Germany and Italy joined their Far Eastern ally and declared war on the United States.

The Russian Campaign (Operation Barbarossa). On June 22, 1941, the Germans invaded Russia in the greatest of their blitzkriegs, backed by an army of close to three million men, including Italian, Rumanian, Hungarian, and Finnish contingents. Although they made prodigious advances, reaching as far as Rostov on the Don in the south, the main objective was not attained in 1941. This was the capture of Leningrad and Moscow, and the destruction of the Russian armies and their will to resist. Stalin soon showed himself to be a patriotic leader as well as a Communist, and he roused national feeling to such an extent that the Russians were willing to "scorch" their earth as they had done when Napoleon invaded in 1812. And very few Russians willingly collaborated with the Germans; those who did, as in the Ukraine, conquered by Germany in 1941, soon ceased to do so in view of the ruthless policy and arrogant racialism of the Germans.

Since every effort had been made to win an outright decision before the onset of winter, and Hitler had been supremely confident that he would succeed, no serious provision had been made to equip the troops for fighting in winter. Hence the German com-

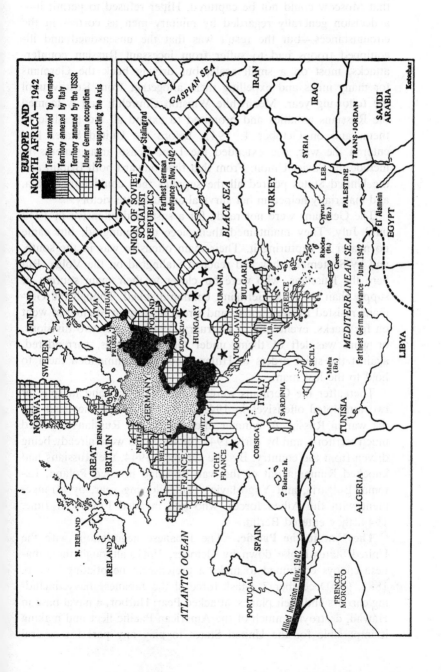

EUROPE AND
NORTH AFRICA—1942

■ Territory annexed by Germany
▤ Territory annexed by Italy
▥ Territory annexed by the USSR
▨ Under German occupation
★ States supporting the Axis

Farthest German advance – Nov. 1942

Farthest German advance – June 1942

Allied Invasion – Nov. 1942

manders wished to retreat to "prepared positions" when it was clear that Moscow could not be captured. Hitler refused to permit it—a decision generally regarded by military men as correct in the circumstances—but the result was that the unseasoned and ill-equipped troops had to suffer from incessant Russian counterattacks, most on a small scale, but driving back the Germans for many miles and expelling them altogether from Rostov until the following year. Meanwhile Winston Churchill had welcomed the Russians as allies and promised to extend all aid possible to them, and on October 1, 1941, before the United States had entered the war, she extended the Lend-Lease arrangements to include the Soviet Union. From that time onward both Britain and the United States poured all the supplies they could into Russia, and materially helped in her survival and ultimate victory.

The Germans were not ready for a sustained offensive in 1942 until July. They maintained their siege of Leningrad, but came no nearer to capturing it. Their main offensive was in the south, and by September they had reached Stalingrad on the Volga. But here the Russians, who were far closer to their main sources of supply than were the Germans, counterattacked. Though the Germans resisted to the utmost, and street fighting in Stalingrad went on for weeks, eventually in February, 1943, twenty-two divisions, or what was left of them, under General Paulus, surrendered, against the strict orders of Hitler, who had commanded them to hold to the last man.

Thereafter the Germans were on the defensive, and in spite of two attempted offensives in 1943, it was clear that they had lost the war in Russia. A summer offensive by the Russians regained much territory, and by early 1944 the Germans were already being driven from the country. By late summer, 1944, the Russians had knocked Rumania out of the war, and had invaded Poland, Estonia, Bulgaria, and Yugoslavia. The following year, by arrangement with the Allied forces, who had invaded France in June, 1944, they entered Berlin.

The War in the Pacific. The Japanese negotiations with the United States broke down by October, 1941, although the Japanese envoys continued to make a pretense at negotiating (see p. 188). On December 7 a task force of the Japanese navy, including carriers and their planes, attacked Pearl Harbor, a naval base in Hawaii, destroying much of the American Pacific fleet and making it impossible for the United States to play any part for several months in the Pacific war which the Japanese now launched. Before the end of 1941 Japan had obtained the consent of the French Vichy government to let her use French Indochina as a base of operations and had made agreements with Thailand similar to those of Germany with the Balkan satellites. Following the attack on Pearl Harbor, the Japanese seized Malaya, Indonesia, and the Philippine Islands, whose colonial administrators were almost helpless before the massive assault. The American islands of Guam and Wake were captured; Burma was also taken; and an expeditionary force was sent into India. But the United States navy was able to prevent further conquest in the Pacific. It won the battle of the Coral Sea (May 7, 1942), thus frustrating any further advance of Japan toward Australia, and a month later defeated a Japanese naval force attacking the island of Midway.

On August 7, 1942, the Americans began their counterattack, with a landing by marines in the Solomon Islands. Despite stubborn resistance, the Japanese were driven from their various Pacific islands, most of them acquired at the end of World War I as mandates (see p. 15). The Japanese navy was unable to win any more major engagements and was whittled down so that by the middle of 1944 it no longer presented a danger. It fought a losing battle on October 21 and 22, 1944, when the Americans began their invasion of the Philippines, which were soon recaptured. Then the United States air force began its massive assaults on the mainland of Japan. In February and April, 1945, the islands of Iwo Jima and Okinawa were captured by the Americans, still against heavy resistance and at high cost in lives. But thereafter the mainland of Japan was at the mercy of the superior air force. Although no American landing on Japanese soil took place until the war was over, a British-led army with American and Chinese forces attacked the Japanese on the mainland, freed Burma, and destroyed several Japanese armies.

After the collapse of Germany in May, 1945, the Japanese were left without allies and with almost no hope of avoiding the unconditional surrender demanded by the Allies. At the Potsdam Conference (see p. 241) the victors in Europe sent Japan an ultimatum but did not obtain a firm decision to capitulate, although the question remained under discussion. On August 6, 1945, the first atomic bomb was dropped on Hiroshima in Japan, destroying more than half the city and killing close to 80,000 persons. Two days later the Soviet Union declared war on Japan and invaded

Manchuria. Since no official surrender had been received by August 9 another atomic bomb was dropped on the industrial city of Nagasaki, killing a further 75,000 persons or more, and wreaking about as much destruction as had the first bomb on Hiroshima. The following day the Japanese offered to surrender, and the offer was accepted four days later, by which time the Russians had won a complete victory in Manchuria. The Japanese armies in China surrendered on September 9, and the war in the Far East was over.

VICTORY IN THE WEST

The Russians throughout the war years continued to demand that the Western powers initiate a "second front" to take the pressure off them. But the Westerners were determined not to invade until they were virtually certain of success, and had the necessary logistical support. They were in part led to this conclusion by the failure of a heroic reconnaissance in force carried out at Dieppe by Allied troops in August, 1942. This experience showed that the defenses, at least in that area, were extremely strong; it was probably responsible for the decision to invade on the beaches, in preference to attacking a defended port city. The decision was therefore made to attack the Axis by a different strategy, and first to drive Germany's weaker partner from the war.

The End of Italian Resistance. On November 8, 1942, an Anglo-American force under the command of American General Dwight D. Eisenhower landed in North Africa, which had previously been under the control of Vichy France (unlike French colonies to the south, especially in Equatorial Africa, which had declared for de Gaulle). The former Vichy admiral, Jean-François Darlan, gave some assistance to the Allied force, but was assassinated soon after he had helped to induce the various Vichy-controlled local governments to co-operate with the Allies. Three days after the landing the Germans occupied the remainder of France, which had been hitherto "unoccupied," in order to forestall a possible assault in southern France.

German resistance in Africa was stubborn, but it had come to an end by May, 1943. In July the Allies moved on to Sicily, which was conquered by August. Meanwhile the Fascist Grand Council (see p. 78) had forced Mussolini to resign as premier. Though he was placed under arrest, German parachutists rescued him in

September and thereafter he was a puppet minister under German control in northern Italy, which had not yet fallen to the invaders. Mussolini's successor, Marshal Pietro Badolglio, promptly opened negotiations for an armistice, which was signed on September 3. The Italian government was therefore no longer at war with the Anglo-Americans, but this did not mean that the war in Italy was over. By the time the Allies invaded the mainland of Italy the Germans had poured reinforcements into the country, and the Allies were unable to take Rome until June, 1944. Even after the invasion of Normandy, the Germans, with some Italians in their forces, continued to resist the Allied advance through Italy, and in fact they did not capitulate until the end of April, 1945, when the war was almost over in Germany.

The Conquest of Germany.   On June 6, 1944, the Allies invaded Normandy, with the greatest armada yet known to history. This invasion was also under the command of General Eisenhower, with British General Montgomery as his second-in-command. On August 15, 1944, another invasion of France was successfully accomplished on the Mediterranean coast. In spite of strong resistance the Allies liberated Paris before the end of August, and Brussels on September 2. French "resistance" forces, which had been growing in strength in the last year, rose against the German occupation forces just before the arrival of the Allies. General de Gaulle, returning from England, formed a provisional government in Paris on August 26.

In spite of these Allied successes, the Germans were able to prevent the invasion of their country in 1944. They manned their strong defense works known as the Westwall, or the Siegfried Line, and even launched a counterattack in the depth of winter, which had some initial success before being thrown back (the Battle of the Bulge, December 16–25).

By this time the Allies had almost complete command of the air in western Europe, and the Germans had to submit to more than a year of "strategic" bombing, which was extremely destructive—although by itself it could never have won the war and doubts have been expressed since whether the bombing of civilian centers was worth its cost. In February the Allied attack from the west was resumed, synchronizing with the Russian drive into Poland which had begun the previous month. By a fortunate chance a key bridge at Remagen over the Rhine was found undamaged, and the fortifications on the east bank of the Rhine were made

useless. Russians fought their way into Berlin by April 20, but the
city did not surrender at once. Hitler was in his chancellery, and
refused to leave it. He committed suicide there on April 30, 1945,
two days after the execution by Italian partisans of his fellow dictator Mussolini. In his testament Hitler appointed as his successor
Admiral Doenitz, who proceeded to agree to the unconditional surrender demanded by the Allies (May 7, 1945). On June 5 an
Allied Control Council which included the supreme military commanders of the three Allied armies took over the country and
divided it into zones of occupation. The French were also granted
a zone in due course.

13

THE AFTERMATH OF THE WAR— POSTWAR DISAGREEMENTS AND THE FOUNDATION OF THE UNITED NATIONS

During the war a number of conferences were held among the Allied leaders. Some dealt exclusively with the war effort and the co-ordination of military plans. Others, especially the first one (before the United States was in the war) and the last two, were concerned with the future after the Axis powers should have been defeated. These last, held at Yalta and Potsdam, laid the basis for what was intended to be a temporary settlement; but in the absence of any basis for permanent agreement between the Soviet Union and the Western powers, much of it has persisted to this day.

THE WARTIME CONFERENCES

On August 14, 1941, President Roosevelt and Prime Minister Churchill met at sea off the coast of Newfoundland and issued a statement of peace aims which became known as the Atlantic Charter. The two leaders declared that they would seek no territorial aggrandizement; that no territorial changes should be made except by agreement of the people concerned; and that sovereign rights would be restored to all nations now deprived of them by force. They also declared their intention to work for freedom from fear and want, to respect the right of all peoples to equal access to essential raw materials, to maintain freedom of the seas, and to carry out similar general aims. Lastly, pending the establishment of a permanent security system, they proposed to disarm aggressor nations and those who threatened forcible aggression. This declaration, which was not an official document and not legally binding, was accepted in 1941 (October) by the Soviet Union and by all the Allied powers then engaged in the war, as well as by nine governments-in-exile. Obviously Stalin's acceptance of the Atlantic Charter contained numerous reservations, including his intention, which he soon made explicit, of retaining those territories that he had obtained by his agreement of August, 1939 with Hitler.

At the Casablanca Conference held in January, 1943, President Roosevelt and Prime Minister Churchill announced that they would accept nothing less than "unconditional surrender" from the Axis powers—which demand was intended at least in part to reassure Stalin against the possibility that Britain and the United States would accept a separate peace before Germany was defeated. A French Committee of National Liberation was also set up, with the participation of General de Gaulle, who soon succeeded in dominating it. Meanwhile Stalin, whose country was bearing the brunt of German attacks, repeatedly urged the Western powers to invade Europe quickly, thus lessening German pressure on the Soviet Union. However, this could not be promised until the Teheran Conference, held late in 1943, in which Stalin participated personally for the first time. The British and Americans at this conference gave Stalin some assurances regarding his objectives in Central Europe after the war, although as yet nothing specific was promised. The three powers agreed to take part in a new international organization which would replace the League of Nations after the war. Definite plans for this organization took shape at a conference held at Dumbarton Oaks, Virginia, the following year (September, 1944).

The Yalta Conference.   By far the most important of the wartime conferences took place at the Russian resort city of Yalta in the Crimea in February, 1945. At the time of the conference it was still widely believed that Japan would have to be invaded, and that this would result in the loss of possibly more than a hundred thousand lives. An invasion of Manchuria by the Russians in order to drive the Japanese out of North China was therefore considered desirable; and a price for this would be demanded by Stalin, which President Roosevelt was prepared to pay if at all possible. The Russians at the time were in control of almost the whole of prewar Poland and were not at all disposed to see Poland under a government sponsored by the West such as the Polish government-in-exile which had been functioning in England since the German conquest of Poland. In spite of the overwhelming strength of the Allies in western Europe and the certainty that

Germany would soon be forced to surrender, the Soviet Union could not easily be coerced into disgorging her gains if she proposed to keep them. In fact, she had the intention of annexing the part of Poland she had taken in 1939 and incorporating it in the USSR while making sure that the new government of Poland would be reliably pro-Russian, an aim which could best be achieved by seeing that it was run by Communists.

President Roosevelt and Prime Minister Churchill were not in a good position at Yalta to make strong demands on their difficult ally unless they were prepared to take on the victorious Russian armies and prolong the war indefinitely—a policy which would be likely to arouse much opposition at home. All that they could do to coerce the Soviet Union was to take possession of those parts of Germany and eastern Europe which were not yet occupied by the Russians—and by this time the Russians had taken, or were in the process of taking, most of what they wanted. It was therefore to the Western interest to obtain what they could by negotiation and reach whatever agreement was possible. They obtained at Yalta the maximum to which Stalin would consent—and if the Russians had kept to their agreements, the settlement would not have been too unfavorable to Western interests.

But Stalin in fact intended to interpret them in a manner quite unacceptable to the West, and contrary—as he well knew—to the intentions of the Western leaders who negotiated with him. As it turned out, there was very little they could do about it, and President Roosevelt's confidence in the good faith of Stalin was rudely shaken before his death two months later. President Harry S. Truman, who succeeded him, thus inherited a suspicion of Russian intentions which he maintained throughout his presidency—although even he could do nothing to prevent the establishment of the Russian satellite empire. He could only help keep it from spreading into areas where the Russian army was not yet in control. Stalin himself, of course, could not but remain suspicious of the West, since he held the fixed view that the "imperialist-capitalist" powers were only waiting for their chance to destroy "socialism"; and he had never doubted that they would gladly have encouraged Hitler to attack Russia in 1939 if he had not outmaneuvered them by his agreement with Hitler.

After World War I, Russia had been forced to accept an enlarged Poland (see p. 8) which contained several million Russians and Ukrainians. She had no intention of returning this area to Poland now that she had recovered it, and therefore intended to keep the so-called Curzon Line as her own western boundary with Poland. For this Poland could be compensated at the expense of defeated Germany, as long as she had a Communist government. But such a solution was totally unacceptable to the Polish government-in-exile, which was strongly anti-Communist and contained many who had formerly been as strongly anti-Russian. Under pressure by the Western powers Stalin agreed to take some of the London Poles into the new Soviet-oriented government; but no agreement was reached at Yalta on the western frontier of Poland. At the Potsdam Conference of August, 1945, the Oder-Neisse Line (except for East Prussia, which was divided between Poland and the Soviet Union) was accepted as the provisional western boundary of Poland, which it has remained to the present day—still unaccepted by the Federal Republic of Germany and the Western powers. The London Poles who were accepted into the Communist-dominated government were soon ousted; the "free elections" promised at Yalta were far from free when they were at last held in January, 1947; and Poland under its Communist government became a satellite state of the Soviet Union by 1948.

Agreement was reached at Yalta on a four-power control of Germany, with French allotted a sector carved from the areas assigned to the British and Americans. The former German capital of Berlin fell within the sector granted to the Russians, and by agreement the Russians were to be allowed the honor of capturing the city. Berlin was to be controlled by a four-power commission, with each power in charge of its own zone. No arrangements, however, were made for free access to the city, since it was assumed at the time that all four powers would have joint control of all Germany, and thus the question of access would not arise. Stalin made no difficulties about Russian entry into the Pacific war after the defeat of Germany; and he persuaded Roosevelt and Churchill to agree to terms (subject to the approval of Chiang Kai-shek) which in effect gave the Soviet Union substantially what tsarist Russia had possessed prior to the Russo-Japanese War of 1904–1905.

It had been agreed as early as the Teheran Conference of 1943 that a United Nations Organization would be set up after the war, in which the Soviet Union would play her part. President Roosevelt, like President Wilson before him, regarded a new international organization as of supreme importance for the future peace of the world, and he was prepared to pay a high price for the essential co-operation of the Russians. No details were agreed to at Teheran. At Yalta Stalin succeeded in persuading the other conferees that the Soviet Union should have three votes in the United Nations. The device of regarding the Byelo-Russian and Ukrainian Soviet Republics as independent states was accepted. Stalin also got adopted the Soviet position on the principle of unanimity in the Security Council. All the great powers desired the veto, but the Soviet Union wished to be able to use it for more types of resolutions than the other powers did.

Potsdam Conference. Only Stalin of the Big Three remained in power for the whole period of the Yalta and Potsdam Conferences. The Potsdam Conference was held from July 17 to August 2, 1945, after the defeat of Germany but before the surrender of Japan. Harry Truman had replaced Franklin Roosevelt as United States president; and during the conference the Churchill government lost the first general election held since 1935. Clement Attlee, the new British prime minister, took Churchill's place as chief British negotiator. By the time of the Potsdam Conference the first atomic bomb had been demonstrated in New Mexico. Truman informed Stalin of its existence in a guarded manner—he spoke of it as a new weapon of "unusual destructive force"—though without telling him exactly what it was. According to the President, Stalin did not show much interest, merely hoping that he "would make good use of it against the Japanese." Little was said at Potsdam about the Russian entry into the Pacific war, which had been so important a topic at Yalta, though there were some technical discussions on the coming Russian compaign among the military leaders of the West and of the Soviet Union. As noted earlier, a declaration was also issued at Potsdam in the name of Britain, the United States, and China, calling upon the Japanese to surrender or risk much heavier damage than had hitherto been visited upon them.

For the rest, the conference came to very few decisions on the subjects discussed. It did, however, decide on the "temporary" western boundary of Poland and agreed in principle to the division of the German navy and merchant marine between the three powers. There was agreement on the disarmament and "denazification" of Germany, the proposed trials of war criminals, and other matters which Stalin regarded as secondary to his main aims and on which he was therefore prepared to fall in with Allied views. All the more difficult subjects, such as reparations, were tabled for discussion in foreign ministers' conferences to be held over the next months. The foreign ministers were instructed in particular to draw up peace treaties for the lesser enemy powers, Finland, Bulgaria, Hungary, Rumania, and Italy. Although there was much wrangling in these conferences, treaties for these countries were finally accepted late in 1946 and ratified by September, 1947. There was very substantial disagreement among the powers on Austria, with the result that a four-power control was maintained, similar to that of Germany, until after the death of Stalin. A treaty restoring full self-government to Austria—except that she was required to maintain neutrality—was eventually signed in 1955, and the occupation troops of all the powers immediately left the country.

THE RUSSIAN SATELLITE SYSTEM

During the four years following the war the Soviet Union established a tight control over several European states, all except one of which (Poland) had to some degree participated in the war on the Axis side. In all of these states except Czechoslovakia and Albania (never fully a satellite of the Soviet Union, though it was a Communist country) Soviet army units were stationed by agreement with the Communist governments which controlled them. It has become the custom to call these states Soviet "satellites," divided as they are from the independent democratic nations by what is spoken of as an "iron curtain." With the exception of East Germany, however, all enjoy a formally independent status, are recognized as independent by foreign nations, and hold seats in the United Nations.

Poland.   It has already been noted that in January, 1945, the Soviet Union sponsored a Polish government with headquarters in Lublin. The establishment of this government was naturally opposed by the Polish government-in-exile with headquarters in London which had functioned under the leadership of the Peasant party leader Stanislaw Mikolajczyk throughout the war and had been recognized as the government of Poland by both Great Britain and the United States. At the Yalta Conference Stalin reluctantly agreed to permit the entry of some of the London Poles into the government, and an Allied commission was set up to supervise the formation of a government of national unity. Mikolajczyk then became vice-premier and minister of agriculture, but the most powerful positions in the government were held by Communists. The prime minister, Edward Obsubka-Morawski, was a member of the Socialist party. After promising free elections with a secret ballot, the government was recognized by the Western allies. However, the elections (held in January, 1947) were marked by governmental intimidation and were won by parties opposed to Mikolajczyk, whose party secured only 28 of 444 seats. Soon afterward he fled the country, and the remnants of his party and the various Socialist groups merged into a United Workers' party controlled by the Communists. The government accepted a close alliance with the Soviet Union, and in 1949 a Soviet marshal became commander in chief of the Polish army.

Hungary. In December, 1944, a coalition government was organized in Hungary which included several leading Communists who had spent the war period in Moscow. The government leader was General Bela Miklos, who had taken his troops over to the Russians two months before. This "Independence Front" government lasted until November, 1945, when genuinely free elections were permitted, in which the Communist party won only 67 seats as against 71 for the Socialists, and 246 for the moderate Smallholders' party, whose leader Zoltan Tildy became president of the republic. (The republic was proclaimed in 1946 and the long-standing "regency" for the absent Habsburgs abolished.) Ferenc Nagy, also a Smallholder, became prime minister. However, a Communist became minister of the interior, and several important local administrations fell into Communist hands. The titular leaders of the republic did not dare to take active steps against the Communists because of the proximity of Russian armed forces and Russian support for the Communists.

The Smallholders' party, which was the main target for Communist attack, began slowly to disintegrate. Some of its leaders were expelled from the parliament, while others went into exile. In January, 1947, the Communist-controlled press proclaimed an attempt to overthrow the government. This was followed by a purge, instituted mainly against the Smallholders. Premier Nagy resigned his position and went into exile in May, 1947, and his place was taken by a leftist Smallholder who was prepared to co-operate with the Communists (Lajos Dinnyes). New elections were held in August, 1947, and the Communists won the most votes, with the Smallholders coming third. Dinnyes remained titular prime minister, but by this time the Communists held most of the important positions in the government. In March, 1948, the left Social Democrats and the Communists merged into a United Workers' party. The Smallholders' party, whose remnants by this time were hardly distinguishable politically from their opponents on the left, dissolved itself, and its last dissident leaders went into exile. On February 1, 1949, Hungary officially became a Peoples' Republic. The Communist leader Matyas Rakosi, as deputy premier, supervised these events and was probably the real ruler of the country throughout.

Rumania. When the Russians were approaching Bucharest, the Rumanian capital, in the late summer of 1944, King Michael dismissed the pro-Hitler government of General Ion Antonescu and appointed a moderate coalition government, which included the durable Julius Maniu (see p. 122) of the Peasant party. This government, however, was not satisfactory to the Russians, and in March, 1945, Michael appointed Petru Groza, a leftist leader of the Plowmen's Front, as prime minister. Since Groza's government did not include the more moderate leaders and since its policy was regarded as excessively favorable to the interests of the Soviet Union, the Western Allies refused to recognize it. When Groza agreed to take a few moderate leaders into it and promised free elections, the Allies relented and recognized it. As in Poland the elections (held on November 19, 1946) were very far from free. As a result the government party was declared to have won four-fifths of the seats. Maniu's Peasant party and its leader were soon accused of plotting to overthrow the government, and Maniu was sentenced to life imprisonment. In December, 1947, Groza's government declared that a monarchy was no longer fitting for the reorganized state, and Michael was compelled to abdicate and go into exile. Thereafter all opposition was suppressed, and a new constitution, based on that of the Soviet Union, was promulgated in 1948.

Bulgaria. When the Soviet army entered Bulgaria late in 1944 a coalition government was organized with Communists in key positions, including the ministries of the interior and justice. Although the prime minister, Kimon Georgiev, was not a Communist, the regents of the young king Simeon II were headed by a veteran Communist. Among the non-Communist parties which formed part of the ruling Fatherland Front were the Agrarian National Union and the Social Democratic parties. In November,

1945, an election was held, marked by the usual intimidation, as a result of which the Fatherland Front won an overwhelming majority in the Grand National Assembly, though the Communist party itself was far from winning an over-all majority. Georgiev remained as prime minister, and the coalition façade continued for the following year. The Allies, however, refused to recognize the results of the election, or of subsequent ones.

In September, 1946, the monarchy was abolished by referendum, and the following month a People's Republic was proclaimed. A new election was held in which the Fatherland Front again won. But this time the Communist party held a majority over the other parties in the Front, and Georgei Dimitrov, a former head of the Comintern and one of the defendants in the Reichstag Fire trial in Hitler's Germany (see p. 69) became prime minister. Thereafter the opposition was systematically eliminated. The Agrarian party was dissolved in 1947, and its leader Nikola Petkov was tried on the charge of conspiring to overthrow the government, and executed. The following year a number of Socialist deputies were imprisoned, and by 1949 no opposition leaders remained at liberty. Nevertheless, the ruling party has continued to call itself the Fatherland Front, and some nominal Agrarians have always held positions in the cabinet.

Czechoslovakia. The conversion of Czechoslovakia into a Soviet satellite followed a different course. During the war former President Benes organized a government-in-exile, which was recognized by the Allies, including the Soviet Union, as the legal government of the country. Both Czechs and Slovaks rose against the Germans on the approach of the Russian armies in 1944. Benes resumed his presidency in 1945, and in 1946 free elections were held, as a result of which the Czech and Slovak Communist parties won the largest number of seats. Benes therefore appointed the Communist Klement Gottwald as prime minister, presiding over a coalition government which included Socialists and members of other left-wing parties. Meanwhile a treaty had been signed with the Soviet Union which gave her virtual control of Czechoslovakian foreign policy.

In spite of having a Communist prime minister, the government for the next years continued to observe Western democratic procedures. But a crisis blew up over Czech willingness to participate in the Marshall Plan (see p. 247). This the Russians would not permit, probably fearing that Czechoslovakia would escape their tutelage and they would themselves be deprived of free access to the Czech industrial goods that they needed. The Communists then began to increase their pressure on the democratic parties and succeeded in winning over enough Social Democratic deputies to have a secure majority and continue to rule, even though the non-Communist deputies resigned from the coalition. The Communist-controlled General Confederation of Labor also offered its support to the Premier. Benes was therefore left with little option but to allow Gottwald to continue in office. Now that he was leader of a more homogeneous group in the Parliament, he proceeded to take full advantage of his position. In May, 1948, a constitution was adopted based on that of the Soviet Union, and new elections gave the Communist-Socialist National Front party an overwhelming majority. In June President Benes resigned on grounds of ill health (he died shortly afterward) and was succeeded as president by Gottwald.

East Germany.   In the Russian zone of Germany the Socialists and Communists merged into a single Communist-controlled party (Socialist Unity party) in 1946. In 1949 when the Western Allies were on the point of promulgating the Federal Republic of Germany in their zones, the Russians began to sponsor a Democratic Republic of Germany in their zone. Elections were held for a People's Congress to write its constitution, but, in spite of widespread intimidation, the coalition won by a surprisingly small majority. The constitution was then written, and as might have been expected, proved not dissimilar to that of the Soviet Union. On October 7, 1949, five months after the establishment of the Federal Republic, a Communist German Democratic Republic was established under Soviet auspices and protected by Soviet armies, with Wilhelm Pieck as president. This state, which would have been quite unable to subsist without Soviet support, is still unrecognized by any of the Western Allies. Even the Soviet Union has not yet signed a peace treaty with it, although the threat to do so has often been made. East Germany is, in fact, less of an independent state than any other of the Soviet satellites.

THE TRUMAN DOCTRINE
AND THE COLD WAR

The United States and her allies naturally did not accept the establishment of the Soviet satellite states with equanimity, but they lacked the power to prevent it. The Communist coup in

Czechoslovakia, which had hitherto been regarded as a bastion of democracy in eastern Europe, was especially galling. It hardened the American attitude toward the Russians and toward "Communism" in general, since it showed how impossible it was for any democratic government to allow Communists to hold key positions. It was thereafter assumed that no coalition governments that contained Communists would be permitted by the latter to remain democratic and that they would always conspire to destroy the democracy and replace it with a single-party Communist dictatorship.

The Truman Doctrine. Meanwhile a civil war in Greece had been going unfavorably for the West, and there was a serious possibility that the pro-Western royal army would be defeated by the Communist EAM, backed by Yugoslavia, Bulgaria, and Albania. The British had been doing their best to contain the Communists, but by 1947 they felt that it was beyond their power and resources to continue the struggle without American aid. President Truman therefore decided to aid the government forces with money, arms, and technical equipment. His offer was extended to include Turkey, who, he felt, was likewise threatened by Communist imperialism. In the doctrine called after him, President Truman stated that "totalitarianism imposed upon free peoples by direct and indirect aggression undermines the foundations of international peace and hence the security of the United States."

This was the beginning of the so-called doctrine of "containment," which has since been applied in all areas of the world where there has appeared to be danger of expansion by Communist powers. The American aid to Greece and Turkey was provided for in a bill passed by Congress on May 22, 1947. It was not, however, immediately effective, though it was certainly of assistance to the Greek government. Late in the same year the United Nations General Assembly called upon Yugoslavia, Bulgaria, and Albania to cease their aid to the Greek guerillas (a resolution repeated the following year). These resolutions had no effect, and the civil war dragged on until 1949, when President Tito of Yugoslavia, who had quarrelled with Stalin, closed his frontier with Greece, preventing the guerillas from receiving reinforcements from his country and thereby bringing the war to an end.

The Marshall Plan. Three months after the enunciation of the Truman Doctrine, on June 5, 1947, the new United States secretary of state, General George Marshall, announced a far-reaching program of economic aid to Europe for the purpose of stimulating her recovery. The aid was to be made available to all the European countries who desired it, including those with Communist governments. Czechoslovakia and Poland both wished to participate, but pressure from the Soviet Union, who regarded it an imperialist trick, prevented them from doing so. Although the plan was immensely helpful to the western European nations (as will be discussed later, see p. 259), it did not improve relations with the Soviet Union, who was moving ever closer to open enmity with the West, especially the United States.

The Berlin Airlift. Relations were especially rancorous in Berlin, where co-operation among the Western powers was almost nonexistent. The Western Allies were anxious to devolve political responsibility on the Germans as soon as possible, both in Berlin and in their own zones of occupation west of the Russian-controlled area, and they also wished to speed German economic recovery. The Russians—who had after all suffered most from the Germans with the possible exception of the French (who were not themselves enthusiastic about the policy of their allies though they acquiesced in it)—were fundamentally opposed to this policy. But they were powerless outside their own zones of Berlin and East Germany. When the Westerners introduced a currency reform that was intended as the first step toward the development of a sound German economy, the Soviet Union blocked all rail and road traffic between Berlin and the Allied zones as a reprisal.

President Truman reacted by ordering an airlift of supplies into the Western zones of Berlin. The operation, which lasted for more than a year, was spectacularly successful and extremely damaging to Soviet prestige. The Russians dared not put an end to the traffic for fear of outright war (they did not yet possess the atomic bomb) but hesitated likewise to admit defeat by opening the land routes they had closed. Meanwhile the Western Allies went ahead with their plans for the establishment of the Federal Republic of Germany in their zones. Elections were held both in Western Germany and Western Berlin (the latter for a mayor and municipal government). All that the Soviet Union could do was to arrange for the establishment of a Communist government in East Germany, as described earlier in this chapter. In December, 1949, the Federal Republic of Germany became a full participant in the Marshall Plan.

North Atlantic Treaty Organization (NATO). On April 4, 1949, a treaty was signed in Washington which placed the capstone on the defense structure of the Western powers and created a formal defensive alliance known as the North Atlantic Treaty Organization (NATO). Its members were the United States, Canada, Great Britain, France, Belgium, the Netherlands, Luxemburg, Italy, Denmark, Norway, Iceland, and Portugal (Greece and Turkey, as well as West Germany joined later). A Mutual Defense Assistance Act was passed by Congress later in the same year, appropriating more than a billion dollars for the rearming of Europe. A central council for NATO was set up and a common military strategy was planned under the leadership of the American Supreme Allied Commander of NATO, who headed an integrated force directed from the Supreme Headquarters of the Allied Powers in Europe (SHAPE) in Paris. The NATO Council was made up of ministers appointed by the component governments.

Communists and many Socialists in the Western parliaments bitterly opposed the NATO treaty, but it was eventually ratified by all. Naturally the Soviet Union assumed that NATO was directed against herself, although the Western Allies intended it as a bulwark against the huge Soviet armies which were still within striking distance of western Europe. The result was an intensification of the Cold War, which had existed since at least as early as 1947. It was further intensified when the Allies decided to take the Federal Republic of Germany into military partnership in 1955 and permitted her to join NATO, on the grounds that the twelve divisions she could supply were essential if a strong enough counterpoise to the Soviet armies was to be maintained. (This development will be discussed in later chapters.)

THE UNITED NATIONS

Reference has already been made to the intention of all the powers that fought against the Axis to establish a more effective international organization than the League of Nations. This organization was agreed to at a conference held in San Francisco in early 1945. When its charter had been ratified by twenty-nine nations it came into being (October 24, 1945). Although its permanent seat was to be in the United States, the first meeting of the United Nations General Assembly was held in London on January 10, 1946, with fifty-one nations in attendance. The principal organs of the United Nations are the Security Council, the General Assembly, and the Trusteeship Council.

The Security Council. The Security Council originally consisted of eleven members, of which five were permanent members. The remainder were elected by the General Assembly. Only the Security Council was directly concerned with peace-keeping operations, and it was therefore the sole United Nations organ entrusted with the powers of coercion. For this reason before any action could be taken, the permanent members of the Council had to be in agreement (in effect, each of these had a veto). This veto was intended by most of the charter members of the United Nations to be applicable only to matters of substance, not to questions of procedure—for example, whether or not a certain matter should be put on the agenda. But in practice the Soviet Union has insisted on being allowed to cast a veto also on questions of procedure, and the other members have acquiesced in this, in preference to risking a Russian walkout.

Although all the permanent members of the Security Council approved of the veto in theory, and probably none (with the possible exception of China, who was made a permanent member only on the insistence of the United States), would have agreed to the United Nations Charter without it, in practice the Western Allies, with three vetoes between them, could almost always command the necessary majority for their viewpoint without having to use it. This was not true of the Soviet Union, who was usually in a minority on the Council. She therefore used her veto with a frequency that exasperated the Westerners and in effect paralyzed the work of the Council. During the Korean War, United States Secretary of State Dean Acheson took the lead in persuading the General Assembly, in which there is no veto, to assume the right (Uniting for Peace Resolution, November 2, 1950) of "recommending" peace-keeping operations when the Security Council had failed to act. Such operations of course had to be voluntary since the General Assembly lacked the right to require members to take part in them. Nevertheless, several peace-keeping actions have been initiated in recent years by the General Assembly (for example, in the Suez operation of 1956 when both Britain and France cast vetoes in the Security Council).

The question of payment for these operations was naturally a thorny one. The Security Council could have made such payments mandatory, but it was not at all certain that the General

Assembly could do this. In practice the General Assembly did assess members for the costs of the operations and tried to make all of them pay in the same way as they paid the regular assessments for the general expenses of the organization. Its right to do so was upheld by a majority of the judges on the World Court, but a minority, including all from the defaulting nations, dissented. The position therefore remained as before, while the financial deficit of the United Nations, mostly incurred for its very expensive peace-keeping operations, grew alarmingly. A bond issue authorized by the General Assembly proved far from sufficient to make up the deficit.

Since nations more than two years in arrears in their payments were supposed to be deprived of their votes in the General Assembly, an impasse arose in the regular General Assembly session of 1964, by which time several nations, including the Soviet Union and France, were two years behind in their payments. Not wishing to break up the United Nations on this issue, yet believing that as a matter of principle all nations should contribute to the costs of peace-keeping authorized by the General Assembly, the United States refused to give way on the question of principle. No resolutions requiring a vote were therefore introduced during the session, which was confined to speech-making. A committee was set up to try to resolve the issue. Eventually the United States, in deference to the majority on the committee, gave way and agreed not to press the matter further, in the hope that the defaulting nations would make voluntary contributions to reduce the United Nations deficit. At the time of writing it is still too early to say whether— as appears likely—the General Assembly will in future be hesitant to authorize peace-keeping operations which do not have the support of the Security Council, or whether it will continue to authorize them when it thinks them necessary, but will make more serious efforts to discover in advance which nations will be willing to make voluntary payments. At all events it appears that the Soviet Union has at last succeeded in weakening, if not nullifying, the Uniting for Peace Resolution of 1950.

Lastly, it may be noted that the Security Council was given the rights ordinarily belonging to the General Assembly in the case of trust territories deemed to be of strategic importance (in effect, only the Trust Territory of the Pacific under United States administration), and it organized an Atomic Energy Commission which was intended to bring atomic energy under international control.

The commission functioned for a few years, but was then dissolved when it became clear that no agreement could be reached.

The General Assembly. The General Assembly is composed of all members of the United Nations (now well over one hundred or more than twice the original number). Nevertheless, some important national entities are missing from it, since the Security Council veto is applicable to the entry of new members. A regular session of the General Assembly is held every September, and extraordinary meetings may be summoned at any time. Resolutions of a substantive nature require a two-thirds majority of members to pass. In view of the great increase in membership as a result of the independence of so many former African colonies there is now an actual majority of nations from Asia and Africa in the Assembly—although it does not include the greatest of the Asian nations, the People's Republic of China. Material and military power is therefore now divorced from political representation, since for example the tiny population of the Central African Republic carries as much weight (one vote) as the United States or the Soviet Union. Nevertheless, the vote for a given resolution of more than two-thirds of the members of the Assembly carries, if nothing else, at least some moral weight. Few nations are willing to put themselves on record as opposed to the moral opinion of the world, when it is expressed through General Assembly resolutions. There are some such nations, as the history of the attempt to persuade Portugal and the Republic of South Africa to change their policies in Africa demonstrates, as does also the effort to persuade the Soviet Union to mitigate her policies in Hungary in 1956, an effort which carried the backing of almost every nation in the Assembly. But most nations probably still hesitate to incur the displeasure of the General Assembly, and in almost all cases will incur it only when they believe their most vital interests are affected.

The Trusteeship Council. This body, which is called in the Charter a "principal organ" of the United Nations, is in a somewhat anomalous position, since two articles of the Charter (85 and 87) speak of it also as operating under the "authority of the General Assembly." In practice the colonial nations belonging to it have regarded the opinions of the General Assembly in trusteeship matters as requiring consideration but not as binding; and the Council has made its own decisions and carried them out as it has seen fit.

The General Assembly, however, without doubt had the final right to make provisions for the independence of the trust territories, and to decide whether or not the purpose of the trusteeship had been fulfilled, and whether the terms on which independence was to be granted (as proposed by the Trusteeship Council) were acceptable. Thus the Council could guide the trust territories up to the point of independence but could not take the final step. The composition of the Council assured the colonial powers of a virtual veto on all action unless at least one of them voted against its colonial colleagues. Each power administering a trust territory sat on the Council as of right; an equal number of powers which did not administer trust territories made up the remainder of the Council, with the added proviso that all permanent members of the Security Council should be represented on it. Since Nationalist China and the Soviet Union never had any trust territories, their representatives always filled two of the seats allotted to "nonadministering" powers. At the beginning there were seven administering powers (the United States, Great Britain, France, Italy, Belgium, Australia, and New Zealand). There were therefore five seats available for the minor powers which did not administer the trusts. When the votes were equal on the Council no action was taken. Thus the seven administering powers if they held together were able to block action, though such votes turned out to be rare.

The Trusteeship Council, which replaced the Permanent Mandates Commission of the League of Nations, was entrusted with the task of preparing the trust territories for independence. It did this by receiving and studying reports submitted annually by the administering powers, and offering comments and suggestions on them, which might or might not be put into effect by the powers. It could consider petitions presented in writing or in person by inhabitants of the territories, and it sent periodic visiting missions to observe progress and report back to the Council. It did not have the authority to demand changes in the territories, which remained, for practical purposes, under the complete control of the administering power. What the Council did therefore was primarily to put moral pressure on the powers to improve conditions in their territories, and particularly to confer ever increasing self-government upon them. There is no way of telling how effective the system was, or whether any advances were made that would not have been made in any event by the administering powers. At this epoch all the colonies, as well as the trust territories, were pressing for political reforms, and in fact the first to attain independence were colonies and not trust territories.

The colonies which were not trust territories did not fall under the jurisdiction of the Trusteeship Council but under the General Assembly, which under Article 73 of the United Nations Charter could require reports from the colonial powers which should contain "statistical and other information of a technical nature relating to economic, social and educational conditions." The signatories of the Charter agreed to ensure just treatment and protection against abuses in their colonies, and to take due account of the aspirations of the peoples. This carefully worded Article was thus drafted because the colonial powers were opposed to giving the United Nations any jurisdiction over their behavior in their colonies, whereas the noncolonial powers were anxious to exercise some pressure on them and to promote independence of the colonies. The General Assembly, which had a trusteeship committee (the Fourth Committee) of its own, with the job of considering all colonial matters, set up a Committee on Non-Self-Governing Territories which reported to the Fourth Committee, and took into account all the reports submitted in pursuance of Article 73. Some of the powers voluntarily submitted political information in addition to what was required by the Charter, with the inevitable result that the Committee began to request such information from those powers who did not submit it voluntarily. This kind of pressure had the least effect on those countries which had the most to hide. They as a rule did not therefore submit any political information at all, with the result that the Committees had nothing important to discuss when their reports were presented to it. Other colonial powers insisted that their colonies were not colonies at all. France, for example, claimed that Algeria was a part of metropolitan France, and Portugal claimed that her colonies were "overseas provinces" of the motherland. The Committee's pressure was therefore relatively ineffective. But it served at least to focus the attention of the world on the colonies which had not yet received independence; and this may not have been without some effect in the end.

Today the Trusteeship Council has little left to do. The only remaining trust territories are small and of small importance. They consist of: the island of Nauru in the Pacific and northwestern New Guinea, both under Australian administration; and the Trust

Territory of the Pacific, the former Japanese-mandated islands, now under United States administration.

The Specialized Agencies. In addition to the main organs described above, the United Nations set up a considerable number of specialized agencies, which performed, on the whole, most valuable work in fields where there was little controversy. They also gave the nationals of small countries an opportunity to serve the world body as individuals and make use of talents that could often not be utilized effectively at home. The World Health Organization (WHO), the Food and Agriculture Organization (FAO), and the International Children's Emergency Fund (UNICEF) are examples of such agencies. These agencies are under the jurisdiction of the Economic and Social Council, elected by the General Assembly, and have the expressed purpose of improving living conditions throughout the world. The United Nations Educational, Scientific and Cultural Organization (UNESCO) attempts to promote international co-operation and exchange information in these fields. One of the most noteworthy achievements of the Economic and Social Council was the promulgation of the Universal Declaration on Human Rights, which drew the attention of the world to those rights that should belong to all human beings, even though relatively few nations in fact have as yet provided them.

Lastly mention should be made of an agency which was for a time of the utmost importance. This was the United Nations Relief and Rehabilitation Administration (UNRRA) which undertook the tasks, on the whole performed with outstanding success, of resettling the millions of persons displaced by the war and of supervising the many exchanges of population made necessary by the new political arrangements agreed to by the great powers. UNRRA was dissolved in 1947, and its work was taken over by the European Recovery Program, which was set in motion by the Marshall Plan referred to earlier. The United States paid most of the expenses of UNRRA, but it was administered by citizens of all nations with available personnel.

Early Political Operations. Most of the political operations of the United Nations will be dealt with as a part of the history of the countries involved and will therefore be included in later chapters. (Mention has already been made of the resolutions passed by the United Nations in the effort to halt the Greek civil war.) One of the first and most important undertakings was to smooth over the transition of several colonies from their former status to that of independent states. The British mandate in Palestine (see p. 199) had clearly outlived its usefulness, and the British were anxious to give it up as soon as possible. But the Jews and the Arabs were unable to reach an agreement for a unified state, and it became clear that partition was the only possible, if not mutually acceptable, solution. The Jews were willing to accept partition, but not the Arab majority which wished to rule the whole country. The British, unwilling to coerce the Arabs, handed over the whole problem to the United Nations, whose General Assembly voted for partition by a relatively small majority (33 for, 13 against, 10 abstentions), and called upon the Security Council to enforce the decision. But the latter could come to no agreement, even though the British announced that they would leave on a definite date. On the appointed date the Jews took matters into their own hands and declared the independence of their state of Israel. The Arab nations at once launched an attack upon them but were badly defeated, with the result that the Jews obtained by conquest more than they had been allotted by the General Assembly.

The United Nations then sent out a mediator (Count Folke Bernadotte of Sweden, who was later murdered by Jewish extremists) and a truce team to supervise a cease fire that had been agreed upon. This team has not yet been able to leave the country, since even now no peace has been accepted by the Arab states and the state of Israel. The episode demonstrates two important truths. The first is that the services of the United Nations are more readily acceptable to the involved nations when negotiations have broken down and hostilities have begun than they are when agreement is desired on policies to be pursued which may prevent hostilities. Almost all the peace-keeping operations of the United Nations have been concerned with policing cease fires, patrolling temporary boundary lines, and the like. The second truth is that the United Nations is still, like the defunct League, a league of nations, with none willing to abate any of its sovereign prerogatives, and each acting as a nation with an eye on its national interests and national policies, even though it is part of an international body. The United Nations provides a forum for discussion, and it is sometimes possible for the Great Powers, on the rare occasions when they are in agreement with one another, to impose a solution on minor nations. But it is very far yet from being a supranational body, nor is it likely to become one until the peoples of the world devise some political entity other than the present nation-state.

When the war was over, the Netherlands government decided to take back its rich former colony in the East Indies, which had been captured by the Japanese. The native Indonesians declared their independence just before the Japanese departure, and the Dutch were therefore compelled to try to suppress the Indonesians by force of arms. The United Nations Security Council quite early took a hand, and appointed a Good Offices Committee to try to arrive at an agreement. But the Dutch did not take the Committee very seriously and consistently disregarded its advice. Even when the Security Council passed a resolution (January, 1949) setting up a United Nations Committee for Indonesia, with the power to recommend action to the Council, the Dutch went ahead with their own plans and almost succeeded in reconquering the whole country. Then their military position suddenly weakened, as a result of which they became more willing to allow the United Nations to play a role in the settlement. American pressure and threats to cut off Marshall Plan funds were also of importance. But it can never be known whether, if the Dutch had succeeded in imposing their will on the Indonesians by force, they would have bowed to the will of the United Nations which they had hitherto defied so successfully.

This example also illustrates the difficulty of obtaining agreement to take effective action against a country which was an ally of important members of the Security Council. At one time the French threatened to cast a veto against a resolution which would have imposed sanctions on the Netherlands, and the resolution was abandoned. In effect it was the Indonesian army that compelled the granting of independence, and until the Netherlands had concluded that the war could not be won, the United Nations achieved little. But once agreement had been reached between the two warring nations, the good offices of the United Nations proved to have some value.

Conclusion. The United Nations is an imperfect organization because it is required to function in a world of sovereign states, few, if any, of which are as yet ready to devolve any of their sovereignty on it. Moreover, it can scarcely function at all in the atmosphere of the Cold War when almost every nation has its champion among the permanent members of the Security Council, ready to cast its veto if a resolution with teeth in it, which can

be thought damaging to its protégé, comes before it. So, in the
last analysis, up to the present time both the Security Council and
the General Assembly have had to act mostly by moral suasion
and not by threats. It may be that this is the best way after all for
the United Nations to function, as long as the stress is on the
"Nations" rather than on the "United."

THE RECONSTRUCTION OF WESTERN EUROPE—MOVEMENTS TOWARD INTEGRATION

14

With the invaluable assistance of the Marshall Plan (see p. 247), western Euorpe made a spectacular recovery from the war. By the mid-1950's further United States economic aid had become unnecessary and, by the end of the decade, the European countries were providing the United States herself with stiff competition. The one partial exception among the active belligerents was Great Britain, some of whose problems (described in Chapter 8) have still defied solution. The European Coal and Steel Community (1952) and the European Economic Community, usually known as the Common Market (1958), have greatly strengthened the economies of the member countries.

GREAT BRITAIN

Britain's six-year participation in the war left her in the worst financial situation in her history. She had not only suffered severe physical damage, but she had also liquidated virtually all her foreign investments, and was in debt to the tune of over £1 billion. The exigencies of war had compelled her to neglect her export trade, which amounted to a bare £350 million worth of ordinary commercial goods in 1945. When President Truman abruptly terminated Lend-Lease in August, 1945, a month after Britain's new Labour government took office, her position became desperate, and she was compelled to solicit major loans, which were granted by the United States and Canada, and minor loans, which were granted by the British Dominions in the Commonwealth. Although the terms of the North American loans were generous, a condition was attached to them which greatly lessened their value. Sterling had to be made convertible within a limited time. As soon as this had been done, there was an immediate run on sterling which quickly used up the remaining dollars. Only the European Recovery Act (Marshall Plan) of 1948 enabled her to survive. Even so, sterling had to be devalued in 1949.

The Labour Administration of Clement Attlee (1945–1951). For the first time in British history the Labour party had won an over-all majority in a general election (July, 1945). (In all earlier elections it had been dependent on aid from the Liberal party.) Clement Attlee and his supporters were therefore anxious to put as much of their socialist program into effect as they could, while at the same time they were faced by the enormous job of reconstruction. Both projects were extremely expensive. They could be achieved only by establishing the most rigid controls over imports and heavy taxation for the purpose of keeping down consumption. A program of "austerity" was therefore launched, which was in the main successful, though at the cost of numerous financial crises. Exports were increased and imports kept to a minimum; wartime rationing was continued; and a high purchase tax prevented people from buying too quickly the available material goods of which they had been deprived during the war. The graduated income tax, which naturally fell most heavily on the rich, was used unsparingly to equalize incomes. At the same time the government put into effect a plan, drawn up by Sir William Beveridge in 1942, for a national health and security program which provided social security on a limited scale and a free health service for the entire population, irrespective of income.

In accordance with its long-held ideas the Labour government nationalized the Bank of England, the coal, electrical, and gas industries, and the railroads. It also nationalized the trucking, and iron and steel industries, but these were returned to private hands as soon as the Conservative party was restored to power in 1951. Faced by opposition from the House of Lords to the nationalization of the steel industry, the government proceeded to reduce the suspensory veto of the House of Lords from two years to one year, and thereafter, with little time to spare before it fell from office, it put through the nationalization bill. By the end of its first five-year mandate it had achieved much of its program, and had safely weathered most of its financial and economic difficulties.

Conservative Administrations of Churchill, Eden, Macmillan, and Douglas-Home (1951–1964).   The austerity program was extremely unpopular, even among those who considered it necessary.

In 1950, when the first term of the Labour government came to an end, an election was held in which its majority was greatly reduced. The following year the Conservatives obtained a majority, and Churchill again became prime minister. The new government gradually put an end to the most unpopular measures of its predecessor, especially rationing, in addition to undoing some of the nationalization, as noted above. But the health and social security programs were so popular that it did not touch these except to reform some of their abuses and impose a few charges for medical appliances and dentistry. The new freedom of the economy led to a decade of gradually rising prosperity in spite of continued difficulties over the balance of payments and occasional but less frequent financial crises. The war damage was at last fully repaired. Unemployment, which had plagued all the prewar governments, had virtually ceased during the war. Since the war Britain has had almost full employment. Indeed at times she has suffered from a labor shortage, in spite of immigration from the Commonwealth which was unrestricted until 1963.

Nevertheless, though Britain enjoyed a higher standard of living than before the war, she did not share in the great increase in prosperity experienced by West Germany, France, and Italy during the late 1950's. The Macmillan government (1957–1963) therefore gradually came to the conclusion that the success of these other European countries was due to their membership in the Common Market (see p. 271). Late in 1961 negotiations were initiated with the Common Market countries with a view to British entry. This possibility excited considerable opposition both from the Commonwealth countries, who enjoyed a preference in the British market, and from Britain's fellow members of the EFTA (European Free Trade Association). As a result Britain (who could have entered the Common Market in 1957 when the Treaty of Rome establishing it was signed) made many conditions for her entry, including associate membership for her Commonwealth partners. Negotiations were difficult and prolonged, but the obstacles would surely have been overcome if French President de Gaulle had not finally vetoed her entry in January, 1963.

In the 1964 elections the mandate of the Conservatives came to an end; the Labour party, under Harold Wilson, won a paperthin majority and returned to office. It could do relatively little to implement its program until 1966, when it won a substantial electoral victory. But the only nationalization it planned to carry out was that of the steel industry. Britain therefore remains a mixed economy, with some giant corporations publicly owned, but the vast majority of enterprises still in private hands. It is only in part the "welfare state" it has so often been called, scarcely more so than the Scandinavian countries, and probably less so than New Zealand, the pioneer in social legislation among the English-speaking countries.

FRANCE

When France was liberated from the Germans in 1944, General de Gaulle, who had led the resistance movement abroad, came to power at the head of a provisional government. He resigned in 1946, mainly on the grounds that he disapproved of the new constitution for the Fourth Republic. The Third Republic formally came to an end in 1946, but the constitution of the Fourth Republic differed relatively little from that of the Third. In both the legislature was almost all-powerful, and the executive was woefully weak. There was so much dissension in the National Assembly of the Fourth Republic, in part due to the presence of the Communist party, which usually was the largest single one, that stable government was impossible. In 1958 President René Coty, faced by an incipient army rebellion in Algeria, called General de Gaulle back to power. For some months de Gaulle ruled by virtue of an enabling act passed by the legislature giving him full powers to legislate by decree. Later in the same year a referendum was held on a new constitution which gave far more power to the president, and the Fifth Republic was born, over which de Gaulle has presided ever since.

The Fourth Republic (1946–1958). When the war ended, the Communists and Socialists between them were almost able to command a majority of the votes of the entire country, thus making possible a Popular Front government such as had come into power in 1936 (see p. 153). But the first constitution, drawn up by an elected Constituent Assembly, which called for a unicameral legislature as favored by the left-wing parties, was defeated in a popular referendum. Another constitution was then prepared which provided for a second chamber (Council of the Republic), as well as for a National Assembly. This was accepted by a small majority in a new referendum. By this time de Gaulle had resigned. Socialist Vincent Auriol was elected president and a left-wing coalition government took office, with a few Communists in minor cabinet posts. In 1947, after the Communists had fomented a political strike, these members were dismissed. No Communist has ever held office again in any French government, and the party remained almost always in opposition. Nevertheless the Ramadier government was able to put through much new social legislation, completing the work begun by the Popular Front government of Léon Blum.

Although there were few political parties at the beginning of the Fourth Republic, they soon began to proliferate, as under the Third. One of them was Gaullist in philosophy, although de Gaulle himself soon dissociated himself from it. No governments survived for much more than a few months, most of them falling on budgetary issues. As under the Third Republic, all were coalitions, most of them somewhat to the right of center. The major problem was inflation, which no government could halt, partly because of the large expenditures on colonial wars, especially in Indochina until 1954 and North Africa thereafter. But the Foreign Office in the earlier years was almost invariably in the hands of either Robert Schuman or Georges Bidault, whatever the government in power at the moment. Both of these rather conservative men, belonging to a Catholic center party (MRP), were good Europeans who wished France to play a leading part in European economic and military integration. But the Assembly was too much divided ever to be willing to provide a majority to ratify the Treaty on European Defense, signed by Schuman. This American-sponsored effort to create an all-European army was tabled indefinitely in 1954. But Schuman's plan for a Coal and Steel Community, which called for an integrated European production was accepted and became remarkably successful (see p. 270). It was the precursor of the Common Market, which came into existence following the signature of the Treaty of Rome in 1957.

Meanwhile in spite of (or, at least in part, because of) the inflation and the chronic budgetary and balance-of-payment deficits, physical reconstruction moved swiftly. As early as 1946 economic planning was placed in the capable hands of Jean Monnet, as head of the *Commissariat du Plan*. This commission has remained in existence ever since. It was a success from the start, giving direction to the reconstruction and expansion of the French economy which took place throughout the 1950's and 1960's. It was, indeed, a curious paradox that even as early as 1953 the French economy was forging ahead, though strikes continued to be numerous and governments rose and fell with monotonous regularity, thereby deceiving most of the rest of the world into the erroneous belief that France as a whole was as decadent as she had been before the war.

The Fifth Republic. In 1954 the Indochinese war, which had been a constant drain on French resources and manpower since 1946 (see p. 367), was brought to an end, mainly through the efforts of the most energetic prime minister of the Fourth Republic, Pierre Mendès-France, who also made a beginning toward the settlement of a rebellion in Tunisia (see p. 346). But in the same year the Algerians began their long struggle for independence, a war which the French were unable to win in spite of military superiority. The failure to put an end to Algerian resistance, coupled with the inability of the Assembly to agree on acceptable terms in face of the million or so French citizens who had settled there, led to the fall of the Fourth Republic.

Part of the army in Algeria mutined and threatened to overthrow the government in Paris by force (May 13, 1958). This crisis provided the opportunity for General de Gaulle, who was living in retirement, to announce that he was ready to return to power as prime minister under certain conditions. These included the agreement of the Assembly to grant him full powers for six months while constitutional changes were made. The army leaders, who believed that a de Gaulle government would back an all-out effort in Algeria leading to victory, joined with Gaullist deputies in applauding the General's decision. President Coty informed the Assembly that he would resign unless de Gaulle's terms were accepted. Faced by this pressure, the Assembly agreed (329 votes to 229). Although the Algerian war in fact dragged on until 1962, in other respects de Gaulle's government was successful. Stability was restored, followed by prosperity far beyond any previously known by France in the modern period. In September, 1958, a new constitution was approved overwhelmingly in a referendum. De Gaulle became the first president of the Fifth Republic, wielding a power not unlike that of the nineteenth-century French monarchs, as, in the words of the Constitution, "protector of the independence of the nation and of the integrity of its territory," with the right to preside over the Council of Ministers (Cabinet), to dissolve the National Assembly, and to negotiate treaties. In November, 1962, deputies of the National Union of the Republic (UNR), a party favorable to de Gaulle, won an over-all majority in the National

Assembly. Soon afterward the Constitution was changed by another referendum to enable the president (hitherto elected by a college of notables) to be chosen by direct popular vote. In December, 1965 President de Gaulle was elected to a second term of seven years in a runoff election, after having failed to win an over-all majority in the first.

ITALY

When the Italians were defeated in 1943 and Mussolini escaped to the north (see p. 234), a government was formed in liberated southern Italy by Marshal Pietro Badoglio under Allied supervision. In June, 1944, he was succeeded by Ivanoe Bonomi, but the government was not fully in Italian hands until the beginning of 1946. Meanwhile the end of the war had seen the formation of a new government under Alcide de Gasperi, who headed the Christian Democratic party. During 1946 the monarchy was abolished by referendum, and a new republican constitution came into force. The first postwar parliamentary elections were held in February, 1948. At the time it was widely believed that the Communists might win the elections and every effort was made both by the papacy and the Catholic Church and by foreign powers (especially the United States) to put pressure on the voters not to give the Communists the mandate. They in fact won 31 per cent of the total vote. But the vote in favor of the Christian Democratic party was close to 50 per cent, as a result of which it had an absolute majority in the Chamber of Deputies. Thus de Gasperi ruled Italy with the first freely elected over-all parliamentary majority since the unification of Italy in 1870. In 1953 this absolute majority was lost by the Christian Democrats, and de Gasperi and his successors have been compelled to form coalitions with other moderate parties since that time.

Following the war, an immense amount of reconstruction was necessary since much of central and southern Italy had been devastated. The recovery was greatly aided by UNRRA; and Marshall Plan aid together with outright grants by the United States eventually set Italy back on her feet. With the coming of the Common Market in 1958 Italy began to forge ahead, and her exports, in particular, were greatly increased. But much of southern Italy and Sicily remains depressed, even while the north has been booming. Land reforms have helped, but no permanent solution has been achieved.

WEST GERMANY

The formation of the Federal Republic of Germany in 1949 under the leadership of Konrad Adenauer, head of the Christian Democratic Union, has been described in the last chapter. In all the elections held since that time the CDU has won the most seats in the *Bundestag,* but during the last period of Adenauer's chancellorship (from 1961 onward) the party lost its over-all majority and had to form a coalition with the small Free Democratic party in order to carry on the government. Ludwig Erhard replaced the eighty-seven-year-old Adenauer as chancellor in October, 1963. The elections of 1965 did not materially change the situation, and Erhard continued to need the parliamentary support of the FDP in the Bundestag. The Federal German constitution provides for a bicameral legislature. Most legislation originates in the Bundestag, the lower house (equivalent to the Reichstag of the interwar years). The *Bundesrat,* in which the *Länder* (states) are represented, exercises the usual functions of an upper house; it can be overruled by a qualified majority in the Bundestag.

The major problems of the Federal Republic are concerned with the still unsettled frontiers to the east and the isolated position of West Berlin, separated from the rest of the Federal territory by over one hundred miles. No West German government or party has yet accepted as legal the Oder-Neisse boundary with Poland (see p. 240), even though relatively few Germans remain in present-day Poland on the far side of the boundary. Nor has the Federal Republic been willing to recognize the German Democratic Republic (East Germany) as a separate state, though trading with it. Any foreign power that grants diplomatic recognition to East Germany is automatically barred from diplomatic relations with West Germany. Since the Soviet Union would have to agree to any change in the status of eastern Europe and has as yet refused to do so, no progress has been made in solving this problem.

For years West Germany received numerous refugees from East Germany. These refugees were easily absorbed into the extremely prosperous West German economy, which is indeed now short of labor. But the inflow was reduced to a trickle when the East Germans in 1961 erected a fortified wall between the Western and Eastern zones of Berlin. West Germany, as a member of NATO (since 1955) and a member of the Common Market from the beginning, has been clearly oriented toward the West. She has achieved an unheard-of prosperity, in part because of the long period when she had to contribute little toward the cost of the defense of western Europe or of herself. Democratic institutions appear to have taken root for the first time in Germany. The parliamentary system has functioned well, with a stable ruling party and a fairly effective opposition provided by the Social Democratic party, although the latter has never come close to winning power.

THE LOW COUNTRIES

Long before the Common Market, Belgium, the Netherlands, and the tiny but industrialized grand duchy of Luxemburg formed a limited economic union, generally known as Benelux (1948), which greatly aided their postwar recovery. The Belgians, who did not adopt a program of austerity, preferring to try to expand their exports in an uncontrolled market, recovered very quickly, whereas the Dutch, who had far greater war damage to repair, adopted stringent emergency measures. However, even they were well on the way to complete recovery by 1950.

Belgium was soon faced with the decision whether or not to restore Leopold III to the throne. It was widely believed that he had surrendered unnecessarily soon to the Germans in 1940 and thus let down his allies. Although he was restored to the throne in 1950, he soon abdicated in face of Socialist opposition and left the throne to his son Baudouin. There have been continued struggles between the Catholics and non-Catholics (especially on the issue of religious schools) and between Walloons and Flemings (over the question of language). There was much controversy also over the manner and timing of the independence of Belgium's huge colony of the Congo (see p. 353).

The Netherlands remained a monarchy under the same dynasty (Orange) as before. Queen Wilhelmina, who had spent the war years in exile, returned but abdicated in favor of her daughter Juliana in 1948. The Dutch attempted to restore their rich East Indian colony to obedience by military means, but they were unable to succeed in face of opposition from the Indonesians and from almost all the countries in the United Nations (see p. 321).

SCANDINAVIA

Denmark submitted to the Germans in 1940 without fighting and suffered little war damage. Sweden remained neutral throughout. Norway, however, was subjected by force and resisted the German occupation as far as she could. As a result, Norway had to face a problem of reconstruction. This was successfully accomplished under a series of Socialist governments which remained in power until September, 1965. These three Scandinavian countries, Iceland (which became independent from Denmark in 1944), and later Finland entered into several important economic arrangements among themselves in the late 1940's, and all except Iceland and Finland joined the European Free Trade Association (EFTA) formed under British leadership at the end of 1959. Denmark, Norway, and Iceland belong to NATO, though only Iceland permits contingents of NATO troops to be stationed on her soil. All the Scandinavian countries have long been noted for their comprehensive systems of social security.

SWITZERLAND

Switzerland, who suffered to some degree during the war from her isolated position and dependence on German agreement for supplies, had to strengthen her central government at the expense of the cantons in order to enforce rationing and similar measures. She nevertheless managed to maintain intact her traditional neutrality. After the war, with her economy functioning successfully, she resumed her position as a manufacturing nation largely dependent on exports but earning a comfortable surplus in her international trade. She also provided extensive banking services for almost the whole world. Suffering from a shortage of native labor, she permitted the immigration of many thousand Italians, most of whom were eventually offered citizenship. Although Switzerland does not belong to the United Nations, on the ground that membership would compromise her neutrality, the old League of Nations buildings soon came to be used by the United Nations, and many specialized agencies have their headquarters at Geneva, which is often host to major international conferences.

AUSTRIA

From 1945 onward an independent Austrian government functioned with some success in spite of the Four-Power occupation and its Allied Control Council. All governments were coalitions without the Communists, whose last member left the Cabinet in 1947. For some years Austria had to pay most of the costs of the occupying troops, and the Russians sequestrated much of her movable capital goods as reparations. The result was that the Western powers, especially the United States, had to pour aid into the country up to the time of full independence in 1955 (see p. 242). Thereafter Austria made a strong recovery. She is a member of EFTA. But even if she wished to, she could not become a member of NATO, since under the treaty of 1955, she accepted perpetual neutrality.

THE IBERIAN PENINSULA

Spain and Portugal have remained authoritarian states under their prewar leaders, General Francisco Franco and Antonio de Oliveira Salazar. The Franco regime, in particular, was looked upon with considerable disfavor by the Allies, and the United Nations voted at once to keep Spain permanently out—a decision that was reversed in 1955 when both Spain and Portugal were admitted. Spanish economic recovery was for a long time very slow, but the exigencies of the Cold War led the United States to decide that Spain could be a useful ally against the Soviet bloc. She therefore entered into a military agreement with Spain in 1953, by which she obtained important bases. Thereafter American money and support greatly aided Spanish recovery, and by the 1960's she was making rapid economic progress, aided also by vast expenditures of tourists who found Spain a less expensive country to visit than most others in Europe. Spain, however, has never been permitted to enter NATO since most European countries in that organization still view the Spanish regime with distaste.

Portugal has moved slowly ahead, but the orthodox conservatism of her economic and financial policies and the poverty of her resources have prevented her from making progress comparable with that of other European countries. A rebellion in the Portuguese West African colony of Angola which began in 1961 has never been completely suppressed. The effort to do so has resulted in a considerable drain on Portuguese manpower and resources.

No firm provision has been made as yet for the succession to the two aging Iberian dictators, although Franco, who is chief of state for life, has several times indicated that he looks forward to the restoration of the monarchy when he retires or dies.

EFFORTS TOWARD EUROPEAN INTEGRATION

Intra-European co-operation has been much greater since the war than in any previous period. The Marshall Plan (see

p. 247) led to close relations among the European powers involved, since each country had to state its needs to the United States, and the various national requirements were worked out through the medium of a special Organization of European Economic Co-operation (OEEC), to which all the recipients of aid belonged. The Atlantic military alliance (NATO), described in the last chapter (see p. 249), came into existence as a response to Soviet expansion. In the opinion of French President de Gaulle and many other Europeans, this military threat is no longer of such importance as it was in 1949, and changes will certainly be made when the treaty comes up for its second renewal in 1969. Meanwhile France is giving the organization a minimum of co-operation. Nevertheless, during the period of its existence it has been instrumental in fostering co-operation within its limited field.

The Council of Europe.　In the other intra-European postwar institutions the United States has played no direct part, though she has usually given them her benevolent co-operation and even tried to stimulate the various European nations to take steps toward a political union. Some of these nations have welcomed the American initiative; others have been inclined to resent it. At all events it must remain doubtful whether American support has had any effect in bringing political integration nearer. The first important initiative was the formation of a Council of Europe created by statute in May, 1949. The founding members were Belgium, Denmark, France, Ireland, Italy, Luxemburg, the Netherlands, Norway, Sweden, and the United Kingdom. All the western European countries except Finland, Spain, and Portugal have since joined, as have Greece and the mostly non-European nation of Turkey. The Council is composed of a Consultative Assembly (which meets at Strasburg) of 200 deputies from the parliaments of the various component nations and a Committee of Ministers who are ministers also in their own countries. The Council represents the beginning of an all-European parliament; but since its decisions are not binding on anyone it has had relatively little influence. However, the machinery is there if the nations ever wish to make use of it.

The European Coal and Steel Community.　Far more important have been the economic organizations, especially the Coal and Steel Community which came into being in July, 1952, composed of the same six nations (France, West Germany, Italy, Belgium, the Netherlands, and Luxemburg) that were later to form the Common Market. Indeed the latter was envisaged in the convention which set up the CSC as the fruition of its labors. ECSC is in many respects independent of the national governments which nominate the members of the High Authority, the ruling body of the Community. However the High Authority was subject to supervision by a Council of Ministers, a Court of Justice, and a Common Assembly. The Assembly has been merged with the Assembly of the Common Market, which meets at Brussels, and is composed of 142 deputies from the component countries. ECSC is authorized to control prices, raise loans and credits, channel investments, and allocate coal and steel production in accordance with potential demand. Though limited to six member countries, the ECSC Assembly, in view of the more definite tasks it had to perform, tended to act as a more effective intra-European parliament than did the Strasburg Council of Europe. Divisions within this Assembly took on a genuine ideological character with Socialists and Christian Democrats from the different countries teaming up. ECSC and its High Authority, which meets at Luxemburg, have proved extremely successful in the tasks of integrating the various national coal and steel industries, of increasing production, and of improving distribution. However, Great Britain from the first refused to subject her coal and steel industry to ECSC, holding that it would derogate from her national sovereignty and the authority of Parliament.

The European Economic Community (Common Market).   As a result of ECSC's success, the European countries in 1957 took the next step toward integration by forming the Common Market and signing another convention for the sharing of nuclear information and facilities for civilian purposes. This latter organization, known as EURATOM, has functioned successfully enough within its limited scope. The Common Market in the view of its founders was intended to establish first of all a customs union, which would in turn lead by stages to a United States of Europe. The customs union itself was also to come into existence by stages, leaving the thorniest problem (agriculture) to the last. A common tariff, lower than had been in operation heretofore in most of the countries, would be imposed in due course. This common tariff against nonmembers was undoubtedly of importance in persuading the British to make their application in 1961—as it was also to form a bone of contention with the United States, who saw herself as possibly unable to sell her goods over the new tariff barriers. President Kennedy therefore took the initiative in persuad-

ICELAND

NORWEGIAN SEA

Faeroe Is.

Shetland Is.

Orkney Is.

FINLAND

NORWAY SWEDEN

G. of Bothnia

N. IRELAND

GREAT BRITAIN

NORTH SEA

IRELAND

Baltic Sea

DENMARK

UNION OF SOVIET SOCIALIST REPUBLICS

GER. FED. REP.

GER. DEM. REP.

POLAND

ATLANTIC OCEAN

NETH.

BELG.

LUX.

GER.

CZECHOSLOVAKIA

FRANCE

SWITZ.

AUSTRIA

HUNGARY

RUMANIA

BLACK SEA

YUGOSLAVIA

ITALY

Adriatic Sea

BULGARIA

PORTUGAL

SPAIN

Corsica

ALB.

GREECE

TURKEY

Sardinia

Aegean Sea

Sicily

Rhodes

Cyprus

Malta

Crete

MEDITERRANEAN SEA

Kotschar

EUROPE—1955

NATO Countries   Soviet Satellites

ing Congress to give him the power to vary American tariffs in accordance with any concessions he might win from the Common Market. All the Common Market countries had some reservations about the entry of Britain, since her low-priced food imports from the Commonwealth countries gave her an unfair competitive advantage in her costs of production of manufactured goods. But it was President de Gaulle who vetoed her entry in January, 1963 (as was permitted under the Treaty of Rome, which required unanimity among the members on important questions such as the admittance of new candidates).

President de Gaulle also showed himself antagonistic to the political integration of Europe favored by many Frenchmen, especially Jean Monnet, and by most other European leaders. His preference was for a much looser confederation of states, and he has shown no signs of budging from this position. He has also at different times issued several ultimatums to the Common Market in the effort to compel his fellow members to come to agreement on the long-postponed integration of European agriculture. In mid-1965 de Gaulle brought all further evolution of the Common Market to a standstill by instructing his ministers to leave the Council until such time as his terms were met. However, after his re-election in December, 1965, de Gaulle agreed to resume discussions, and even went so far as to state that his veto of the British entry might be withdrawn if Britain were to renew her application.

As long as de Gaulle holds office the Common Market is likely to evolve along the lines he charts, and further steps toward political integration will be postponed until at least after his retirement. European nationalism is still far from being a spent force even in countries other than France, and there is probably more support for de Gaulle's position than currently appears on the surface. It is likely that some time Britain will become a member of the Common Market; but it is highly unlikely that British nationalism would ever permit the country to join a political union of western Europe unless it were of the loose kind preferred by de Gaulle. Full economic integration, however, is already well on the way to becoming a reality; and when Britain's entry is eventually permitted, most of her fellow members of EFTA will surely follow her lead. In any event the economic nationalism which did so much damage in the interwar years is unlikely to return. This fact surely represents a great step forward in the direction of world peace.

15 THE SOVIET UNION AND EASTERN EUROPE

After World War II the Soviet Union was faced with a labor of reconstruction second only to that of Germany. Indeed she had lost about five million more men and women during the war than Germany herself. Beyond the Urals her wartime industry, which had been virtually untouched by bombing, was in full operation and ready to be converted to peacetime uses. But in European Russia the damage had been immense, and little reconstruction had been possible as long as the war lasted. Russia was greatly assisted in her postwar reconstruction by the capital goods which she insisted on taking from her former enemies, often against the wish of her recent allies, who were however powerless to prevent her. In view of her refusal to accept aid under the Marshall Plan and her insistence on being the sole source of foreign capital investment for her satellites, it was astonishing that she made so speedy a recovery. By the mid-1950's her recovery was complete, though the same prewar weaknesses, especially in agriculture, were still in evidence.

THE POSTWAR SOVIET UNION

No constitutional changes of substance have been made in the postwar years. The Soviet Union remains a totalitarian party dictatorship. But internal pressures were greatly eased after the death of Stalin in 1953. Nikita Khrushchev, party secretary from 1953 onward, even went so far in the Twentieth Party Congress as to condemn the tyrannous methods of his predecessor, with the implication that they would not be repeated under his rule. Indeed, from 1957 to 1964, the years during which he was in undisputed control of the regime, Khrushchev did exercise a far less oppressive, though scarcely less absolute, rule—at least as far as it appeared on the surface. But he himself was compulsorily retired in 1964 by the action of the Central Committee and the Praesidium. This action made it clear that the one-man dictatorship which had been the rule in the Soviet Union since the Bolshevik Revolution had come to an end. The Soviet Union had in effect become the self-perpetuating oligarchy envisaged by Lenin, and provided for (in spite of a ritual obeisance to "democracy") by the Constitution of 1936.

The Last Years of Stalin (1945–1953). At the war's end the domestic prestige of Stalin was at an all-time high, and he and his henchmen were not slow to attribute the victory both to his leadership and to the effectiveness of the Soviet system. At the same time the war itself had been won in large measure as the result of appealing to latent Russian nationalism, and there was little thought, as there was at the end of World War I, that the rest of the world would of its own accord turn to Communism. The aging dictator himself evidently had no illusions on this score. If he had had them he would soon have been disillusioned by the uniform failure of the Communists in other European countries to win sufficient electoral victories to place them in power. In fact it became clear that his purpose in establishing his satellite system, under Communist governments, was simply to bring them under Soviet control—a task which he could not have accomplished if they had been allowed governments of their own choosing. But the Communist minority governments were dependent on Soviet support, especially that of the Soviet army, to keep them in power. When, as in Yugoslavia, the satellite had an army of its own not subject to Soviet control, then the government escaped from Stalin's domination, and he had the choice only of acquiescing or fighting. In the case of Yugoslavia in 1948, when his displeasure proved insufficient to halt the secession, he evidently felt that more would be lost by fighting than by accepting the situation.

The Communist parties in countries not dominated by the Red Army soon showed that they were not strong enough to take power legally, and no overt efforts were made thereafter to overthrow the governments by force. Under the leadership of Andrei Zhdanov, a young Communist who died in 1948, a propaganda bureau was established in 1947 called the Cominform, one of whose tasks was to co-ordinate the efforts of these parties. But it had few successes to its credit, and was abolished by Khrushchev in

1956 as part of his policy of "peaceful co-existence" with the capitalist nations. Zhdanov was also largely responsible for the propaganda efforts within the Soviet Union which extolled the virtues of Russia and the Russians—as for example in his claims to Russian priority in most modern scientific inventions—and the virtues of the Soviet system. In this he continued to cater to the nationalism aroused by the war.

In the first years after the war it was clear to Stalin that he was in an extremely vulnerable position. In spite of the size of the Red Army, to his suspicious mind there was always the danger that the United States might use its nuclear weapons against him without fear of retaliation. All the resources of Soviet science and technology were therefore pressed into service for the purpose of making a Russian atomic bomb. Success was achieved in 1949, followed in 1953 by a thermonuclear bomb. Thereafter the Soviet Union was in a position to retaliate, and a nuclear stalemate followed, which has persisted to this day.

In spite of this nuclear weakness, from 1945 to 1949 Stalin did not adopt a policy of co-operation with the West, a policy which was open to him at the end of the war. Too much was to be gained, he thought, from expansion in eastern Europe, an opportunity which might never recur. Yet it was this policy which turned the United States from a potential friend to a dangerous antagonist. The price Stalin did not consider too high, the more so since his Communist ideology taught him that there could be no lasting peace between Communism and capitalism. But at the same time he played his cards very cautiously, never going so far that the United States would be tempted beyond endurance but continually testing her defenses by such actions as the Berlin Blockade (see p. 248). Though he gave material support to the North Koreans in their war with South Korea, he did not intervene with troops. He did not give any aid to the Chinese Communists until by their own efforts they had ousted Chiang Kai-shek. He did not force Finland into his satellite system, since this would have involved direct military intervention. His policies enabled the Soviet Union to maintain firm control over his satellites (with the exception of Yugoslavia), but at the cost of a Cold War with the West, further details of which will be discussed in Chapter 20.

Many improvements in the management of the Soviet economy were brought about during the last period of Stalin's rule, including a degree of decentralization which was enlarged by his successors. But in the last year of his life he became more personally tyrannical than he had been since the war, seeing conspiracies everywhere, even among the doctors who attended him. When he died he had held absolute power for almost thirty years. Whatever his shortcomings, he left his country indisputably the second greatest power in the world, with a system that was still functioning and an economy that was rapidly expanding, especially in heavy industry. He had also built a new kind of empire whose boundaries were remarkably similar to those of the nineteenth-century tsars (the Soviet Union controlled much of imperial Germany, but had lost the former tsarist duchy of Finland).

The Malenkov Interlude (1953–1955). When Stalin died, there was no precedent to follow in the matter of the succession. Stalin's personal power had never been seriously disputed since the exile of Trotsky, but he had not conferred any remotely comparable power on anyone else. As party secretary and prime minister he had held the two major positions of power in the country. A year before his death the former Politburo had been converted into the Praesidium of the Central Committee of the Communist party, and the Orgburo (see p. 47), had been abolished as had also the name Bolshevik. But such changes had little bearing on the succession. Any member of the Praesidium might have succeeded Stalin, but the most likely candidate was Georgi Malenkov, the deputy secretary general of the party, who at once became secretary. But Malenkov had powerful rivals, and it was apparently the consensus among the leaders that no one again should have the power that had been enjoyed by Stalin. After only nine days, Malenkov therefore relinquished the position of general secretary of the party to Nikita Khrushchev, thus being allowed to keep the position of prime minister. Perhaps even superior in power to Malenkov was Laurenti Beria, the head of Stalin's secret police, who assembled numerous police cadres in the capital immediately after Stalin's death. However, he did not attempt a coup d'état, preferring to share power with Malenkov and Khrushchev. Before the end of 1953 Beria was expelled from the Praesidium and the party by the combined efforts of his colleagues, and he was soon afterward executed.

During his brief period of power Malenkov announced a policy that was both popular and timely—the increase of consumer goods, even if this meant a slightly smaller allocation of resources to heavy industry. He also declared his intention of giving more attention to agriculture. However, there was relatively little improvement in either respect during his regime, a failure that probably contributed to his fall. The rearmament program, which was constant throughout the middle 1950's, consumed more than a still relatively weak economy could afford. There was, on the other hand, a noticeable cultural thaw, and Soviet scientists began for the first time to take part in international conferences.

The Regime of Nikita Khrushchev (1955–1964). By 1955 Khrushchev had used his office as secretary so effectively that he was in a position to demote Malenkov (who, however, was permitted to resign and given a lesser position) and controlled the premiership through the incumbent Marshal Nicolai Bulganin, who was not strong enough to take an independent line. In March, 1958, after Khrushchev had managed to defeat his enemies within the party, Bulganin was made manager of the State Bank, and Khrushchev became both premier and party secretary. From then until his fall he was the undoubted leader of the state, although not without vocal opponents even within the ruling circles. Khrushchev, who had the reputation of being an agricultural expert, had first attracted attention by his reorganization and consolidation of the collective farms. But in spite of heroic efforts throughout his regime, he was unable to solve the agricultural problem. The state and collective farms evidently did not enlist the support of the peasants who worked in them. They preferred to give far more of their attention to their private plots, small though they were, which indeed provided quite a substantial amount of the population's foodstuffs. Khrushchev's answer was only to try to improve the management of the farms and mechanize them further, while allotting more fertilizer to them from the state chemical industry. Communist ideology continued to prevent the peasants from doing what they clearly wanted, namely, owning and working their own land—as was permitted, for example, in Poland and to a large extent in Hungary under their Communist regimes. In the later years of Khrushchev's regime he was even compelled to use scarce gold and foreign currency to buy large quantities of wheat abroad in order to assuage the desire of the people for a higher standard of living.

In 1957 the regime had its first spectacular success, the launching into space of a man-made satellite (sputnik), thus demonstrating to the world the effectiveness of Russian science and its apparent superiority in some respects to that of the West, even the United States. But the United States soon made good the deficiency, so that today the Soviet Union is ahead only in the thrust of its rockets. Early in his rule (1956) Khrushchev was faced with a dangerous situation in Poland (see p. 283) and an outright rebellion in Hungary which had to be put down by the Soviet army (see p. 284). This evidence of discontent in the satellite empire, combined with various later domestic failures, almost toppled him from power in 1957. But though he lost his majority in the Praesidium, he managed to turn the tables on his opponents through the medium of the Central Committee and so strengthened his position that he thereafter had no visible rivals.

By 1955 the Soviet Union was so far advanced in the production of heavy industrial goods that she was in a position to set in motion an extensive program of foreign aid. As far as can be ascertained, most of this aid was in the form of short-term and long-term loans and there were few outright grants. The recipients of the credits were, as a rule, those countries where the Soviet Union hoped to gain some political capital, although a country did not have necessarily to treat its Communists any the better because of its trade relations with her. Egypt, for example, kept her Communists under strict supervision or in prison; but this did not prevent the Soviet Union from stepping in and financing the building of the Aswan Dam, when the Western powers, for political reasons, withdrew their agreement to help. The Soviet Union has given considerable aid to India and built a steel works in that country on generous terms. Until the late 1950's she granted extensive credits to Communist China; but most of it was on a short-term basis and new credits have been withheld ever since the quarrel between Khrushchev and Mao Tse-tung. Cuba has been almost totally dependent on Soviet aid and long-term credits since 1960, when the United States cut off all credit and broke off trade relations with her. However, most Soviet loans and grants have been used for armaments, which have been supplied both to "neutralist" countries and to regimes which were potentially or actually hostile to the United States.

Policy of "Co-existence" with the West. By the mid-1950's, when the Soviet Union had acquired the atomic and hydrogen bombs and was rapidly developing means for delivering them, her leaders came to the conclusion that it was impossible to engage in a war with the West without incurring damage far beyond any conceivable gains. Malenkov and Khrushchev therefore proclaimed as their future policy a peaceful competitive co-existence. This in no way meant that they would cease probing the defenses of the West or that they would adopt an unadventurous foreign policy. In later years, indeed, the Soviet leaders specifically stated that aid would be given in just "wars of liberation," as defined by themselves. It remained of course their proclaimed belief that the Soviet system was so superior to that of the capitalistic world that the latter would eventually be surpassed in production ("We shall bury you," as Khrushchev graphically put it). Time was thus assumed to be on the Soviet side, but it was necessary to be militarily prepared in case the "declining" capitalist world decided to attack the Soviet Union and destroy her by sheer military might before she had proved her superiority in straight competition. Therefore, the Soviet Union continued to take whatever steps were open to her to weaken the West and to improve her standing in the neutralist "third world."

As far as it is possible to detect, the policy of co-existence has had relatively little success from the Soviet point of view, and it has been criticized unmercifully by the Chinese, who have adopted (at least verbally) a tougher line toward the West. Khrushchev held numerous conversations with the Western leaders and even visited the United States. But the latter remained as suspicious as ever and no tangible results accrued to the Soviet Union. Late in 1962 Khrushchev was compelled to withdraw the missiles he had installed in Cuba when faced with an ultimatum from President Kennedy. The following year (August, 1963) he signed a limited test-ban treaty to which all the potential "nuclear" powers except France and China adhered. Even this was taken by the Chinese as evidence of Khrushchev's softness toward capitalism. If the Third World War has so far been averted, this fact owes less to the policy of co-existence than to the nuclear stalemate or "balance of terror," which indeed forces a policy of co-existence, proclaimed or not, as the only alternative to mutual destruction.

In October, 1964, Khrushchev was driven from office by his colleagues and went into retirement. The positions of prime minister and first secretary were again separated, the former being held by Alexei Kosygin and the latter by Leonid Brezhnev. No major policy changes appear to have been adopted as the result of the transfer of power. The foreign policy of President Lyndon Johnson, which involved the escalation of the war in Vietnam (see p. 367), was obviously not calculated to win the favor of the Soviet Union, whose prestige among her satellites and the "third world" necessarily suffered from her inability to give effective military aid to her fellow Communists in the east.

Conclusion—The Soviet Union as a Stable and Satisfied Power. The Soviet Union is no longer in most respects a "have-not" country, and her major attentions are now given to the long-deferred effort to raise the standard of living in her own country. The Russian people have indeed been led to believe that at last there will be more consumer goods to compensate for their many sacrifices and cheated hopes over the years since the Revolution. The Soviet Union is by no means an egalitarian country, since certain classes, especially the professionals and bureaucrats, obtain far more than the others of the available goods. But there is more freedom of opportunity to move up the ladder of promotion than in many countries, and the accident of birth carries far fewer privileges than elsewhere. The price paid for success, however, remains the willingness to accept the prevailing ideas and conform to the views of the ruling oligarchy without overt dissent. The government is stable and well entrenched. It shows little sign of collapsing or even of modifying its particular form of tyranny—and this would be true even if it lost its satellite empire, which is of little economic value to it. The Soviet Union, in short, now has too much to lose to be willing to carry its antagonism toward the West into armed hostilities unless it were pushed into it by the West and could see no alternative. Its new leaders therefore remain unfriendly but cautious, more cautious but no less unfriendly than Khrushchev—and it is doubtful indeed if any other leaders will be either more friendly or less cautious as long as the United States continues to possess her undisputed military superiority, and, rightly or wrongly, regards "Communism" as an enemy, and places "anti-Communism" at the center of her foreign policy.

THE SATELLITE SYSTEM

The satellite system built up by the Soviet Union immediately after the war, included East Germany (German Democratic Republic, GDR) Poland, Hungary, Czechoslovakia, Rumania, Bulgaria, Yugoslavia, and Albania, leaving in eastern Europe only Greece as an independent parliamentary democracy and Turkey, most of whose territories lie outside Europe. Yugoslavia soon escaped from the Soviet system, although she remained Communist. Little Albania preferred to take the side of the Chinese when the Russians and Chinese quarreled, and as a result won a precarious independence from the Soviet Union in which the latter has so far aquiesced. (Albania, Yugoslavia, and Greece will therefore be treated separately in this chapter.)

Unity and Disunity within the System.   The winning of control by the Communists in the satellite countries during the postwar period has been described in Chapter 13. However, political events did not move smoothly thereafter. In 1948 Yugoslavia, which had been freed from Nazi rule by native Partisans led by Marshal Tito (Josip Broz) rebelled against the high-handedness of Soviet officials and advisers. This revolt was not the result of any desire on the part of Tito to modify or abandon Communism. But he did not wish his country to be a Soviet satellite and accept Soviet dictation. Stalin reacted against this show of independence by making use of all the weapons of coercion at his disposal short of armed intervention. These tactics forced Tito into choosing either to submit or to resist. He chose the latter course, even going so far as to request economic aid from the United States, who granted it, in the hope of creating a rift in the Soviet empire. Thus fortified, Tito survived the Soviet onslaught and thereafter proceeded to develop a kind of "national Communism," geared to the needs of his particular country, as he saw them.

The advent of "Titoism" had widespread effects in the other satellites. All the Communist governments were compelled to break trade relations with Yugoslavia and denounce their military alliances with her. Titoist "deviationism" became a capital crime, and important Communist leaders fell from power—some of them were even convicted of treason and executed—for supposedly supporting it. Other leaders more loyal to Stalin took their place. After Stalin's death Khrushchev attempted to patch up the quarrel with Tito, admitting that mistakes had been made in the past. But Yugoslavia did not return fully to the Soviet fold and steadfastly refused to join the Warsaw Pact (1955), the Soviet answer to NATO, which tied the other satellites more closely to the Soviet Union and provided for a common army under Soviet leadership.

The Warsaw Pact was only one of the means used to yoke the satellite countries securely to the Soviet chariot. A Council for Mutual Assistance (COMECON) was formed in 1949 but did not play any effective part in co-ordinating the different national economies until after 1954, when a general policy known as the

New Course was adopted by the Malenkov regime. This plan was intended to put an end to wasteful duplication. It called for the industrialization of the various countries and the gradual co-ordination of production and inter-bloc distribution. In recent years COMECON has enjoyed considerable success, and it is by no means simply a façade behind which the Soviet Union dominates the economies of the different countries. Like the Common Market, it has numerous commissions which deal with common economic problems on which all the component nations are represented. The various commissions decide, in particular, which countries are to specialize in producing different items consumed by the bloc. COMECON does, however, make it more difficult for any country to achieve economic independence or to adopt a "Titoist" attitude should it ever wish to do so.

Aside from Tito's successful defiance of Stalin, there have been several unsuccessful attempts by the various countries to rebel against their own Communist governments, thus indirectly threatening Soviet supremacy. However, the last of these took place in 1956. The manner in which the Hungarian Revolution of 1956 was suppressed by the military might of the Soviet Union must surely have caused other potential rebels to hesitate—even though it is also true that the system itself has been liberalized in the last decade, especially in Hungary itself and in Poland, whose nationalist Communist leaders won considerable concessions from Khrushchev by defying him.

The death of Stalin and the Malenkov thaw encouraged some workers to take direct action against their governments. On June 17, 1953, the East Berlin workers began a strike against their working conditions. This was followed by further strikes throughout the entire country. The puppet government was in danger of collapsing altogether until it was rescued by the appearance of Soviet troops and tanks. In the same month some workers in Pilsen (Czechoslovakia) began a violent strike. But this was suppressed without much difficulty by the government. Another opportunity seemed to be presented by the famous Khrushchev speech to the Twentieth Congress (February, 1956) in which he criticized Stalin and Stalinism, and spoke of the possibly different "roads to socialism." To the Polish leaders this seemed to mean that "Titoism" had suddenly become respectable. Although they suppressed a workers' uprising in Poznan directed against themselves as well as indirectly against the Soviet Union, they had their own grievances against their masters in Moscow. One of the most important issues was Russian leadership of the Polish army, whose commander in chief, though born a Pole, was a marshal in the Russian army. Without consulting the Soviet Union, they made Wladyslaw Gomulka, a nationalist Pole who had been imprisoned by the Russians, head of their government. This dangerous situation was handled by a visit of Khrushchev and other top Soviet leaders to Warsaw, from which they emerged apparently satisfied that Gomulka would not deviate too far from the Soviet-sponsored line. He was therefore allowed to remain in power, and he has retained it. By granting several important concessions to Polish nationalism, he even acquired some popularity. All Poles are well aware that they cannot escape altogether from Russian domination and adopt a completely independent line, so long as their frontiers with Germany are guaranteed by the Soviet Union but not accepted as final by the West. Poland, like Yugoslavia, requested and received economic aid from the United States, an arrangement to which the Russians made no serious objections.

The Hungarian Revolution.   The situation was far different in Hungary, where in October, 1956, a full-scale insurrection broke out in Budapest directed against the native Communists who controlled the government and against the Russians who backed them. Even some Hungarian army units joined the rebels. The Communists bowed before the storm and chose as prime minister Imre Nagy, a nationalist Communist, who agreed to preside over a coalition cabinet that included non-Communists. Khrushchev at first appeared to accept the situation, as he had in Poland, and the few Soviet troops in the country withdrew.

Then Nagy made his fatal mistake. Still pressed by popular opinion he proclaimed a neutralist policy, apparently intending to ask aid from the West as Tito had. Khrushchev hesitated no longer but sent in regular army units, which in a few days of fierce fighting crushed the rebellion. The valiant Hungarians resisted as best they could, many of them hoping for aid from the West or from the other dissident satellite countries. But no aid came, nor was it evidently seriously contemplated. Although the United Nations General Assembly condemned the Soviet actions in the strongest terms, it too did nothing effective. The United States at the time was indeed fully occupied with the Suez crisis, and the disciplining (with the concurrence of the Soviet Union) of her allies who had invaded Egypt (see p. 337). All that she could do was allow the immigration of the numerous Hungarian refugees who had fled over the frontier to Austria.

Nagy was deposed and later tried and executed. Janos Kadar, a member of Nagy's cabinet, was promoted to the position of prime minister, and after a few difficult years his regime gradually won some popular acceptance. He made many concessions to the people which the Russians did not attempt to prevent—thus demonstrating that they had no vital interest in the domestic concerns of their satellites so long as they did not lead to outright defiance and overt resistance to Soviet policy.

Economic Development. All the satellite regimes attempted to collectivize agriculture along Soviet lines with scarcely greater success than had been achieved in the Soviet Union. The process of collectivization slowed up during the mid-1950's but was resumed in the later years of the decade and was almost complete by 1960 (except in Poland, where early attempts at collectivization were virtually abandoned after 1956). In most countries little private agriculture remained except for the private plots retained, as in the Soviet Union, by the collective farmers. They continued to produce, however, a disproportionate amount of the foodstuffs consumed in every country of the bloc.

All the satellite countries followed the example also of the Soviet Union in giving priority in the Four-, Five-, and Six-Year Plans to the development of heavy industry. This policy, as in the Soviet Union, led to a deficiency in consumer goods and light industry, a deficiency which was gradually being made good in the 1960's. Eastern Europe, as a result, has become a predominantly industrial area, in marked distinction from the overwhelmingly agricultural economy of most of these countries in the prewar years. The satellite countries no longer export much food or raw material, with the exception of Rumania, who still exports some oil. Indeed, they import most of the raw materials needed for their new industries from the Soviet Union. In return they export industrial goods to the rest of the world and undertake to supply a major proportion of the foreign aid contracted for by the Soviet Union. In 1960 both Czechoslovakia and East Germany exported almost the same amount of industrial finished goods as did the Soviet Union herself, with her far greater population. But without the importation of Soviet raw material this trade would come virtually to a standstill, thus again demonstrating the dependence of these countries on the Soviet Union and the unlikelihood of any major political changes in their relationship, however much desired these might be by the people concerned.

ALBANIA

At the end of the war the Communists were the only organized political group in Albania, and their leader Enver Hoxha at once took over the government, voluntarily adhering to the Soviet bloc. The Soviet army had never reached this wild and isolated little country, and was not a factor in the situation. But the protection of the Soviet Union was essential to her survival if she was to be saved from Yugoslavia, who had always coveted the country. Hoxha has remained in power to this day, after executing as a Titoist his only serious rival. An advocate of the policies of Stalin, Hoxha had no sympathy for the softer policies of Khrushchev, and he purged his own native "Khrushchevites" in 1960.

Khrushchev ignored this gesture of defiance and took no action beyond breaking off trade relations when Hoxha expelled his Russian advisers and sided openly with China in the Sino-Russian quarrel. Even the rift in trade relations proved to be only temporary. China supplied what little economic aid she could, which seems in fact to have been sufficient for Albania's modest needs. In return Albania has regularly supported Chinese policies and dutifully criticized the Soviet Union in accord with the wishes of her new patron, even adopting an independent line at the United Nations. The special case of Albania must present an exceptionally difficult problem for the Soviet Union, but it has not been of sufficient importance to exercise her unduly. By tacitly accepting co-existence with her dissident ex-satellite, she has probably lost no prestige and has rid herself of an economically useless appendage.

YUGOSLAVIA

When the Germans invaded Yugoslavia in 1941, two different groups were organized to resist them and carry on guerilla war against the occupation forces. The so-called Chetniks under General Mihailovitch (a Serb) were backed by the Yugoslav royal government in exile in London, but they did not greatly distinguish themselves in the guerilla warfare, sometimes collaborating with the enemy, and seldom resisting effectively. Indeed, too often they preferred to fight the other resistance group, the Partisans, because the latter were led by Communists. The Partisans, under Marshal Tito (a Croat), were far more active in fighting against the Germans, so that even the impeccably anti-Communist Winston Churchill switched his support from Mihailovitch to Tito in 1943. It was the Partisans who finally drove out the disintegrating German armies, and the government they established was a Communist one. Perhaps the greatest success of this government was the manner in which it put an end to the divisive prewar quarrels in the different parts of the country. It did so by establishing a stable federal regime, with each of the component "republics" enjoying a real if limited antonomy with its own parliamentary bodies.

For a few years after 1948, when Tito quarreled with Stalin, the Yugoslav economy faltered, and it was perhaps saved only by American aid. Then Tito began to move it away from the Soviet model, which he had enthusiastically adopted until that time, and in truth became the "deviationist" that Stalin had wrongly accused him of being. Agriculture was slowly restored to private hands, especially after 1950, when there were some riots and numerous demonstrations against the collectivization program. By 1960 only some 12 per cent of the agricultural land belonged to the state and was run collectively, but about half of the independent peasantry was associated with co-operatives, which supplied machinery, fertilizer, and expert advice. This half, incidentally, produced much more effectively than the remainder of the peasants who continued to use their primitive methods and equipment. Pressure is always applied to hold-outs, but not compulsion. Even so, there have been several famines in poor seasons, and grain has then had to be imported.

Although the "means of production" in industry have remained in state hands, many independent enterprises have been run by Workers' Councils which elect their own Board of Management. If these enterprises make a profit, the workers receive a bonus; if they show a loss, wages are cut. As in other Communist countries, there are also state enterprises which compete with these modified co-operatives. Most Yugoslav trade is with the Soviet Union. The Workers' Councils play a large part in the complex electoral system, which is somewhat less of a façade than in the Soviet Union, though membership in the League of Communists (formerly the Communist party) is still the highroad for political advancement in the country. There is also far more freedom of religion in Yugoslavia than in other Communist countries. Roman Catholic Archbishop (later Cardinal) Stepinac was an uncompromising opponent of the Communist state, but his successor has co-operated with it. Churches are allowed to own up to 25 acres of land, and they can open schools on the high school and university levels. Public criticism of the regime, however, is still not permitted.

Yugoslavia is not yet a mixed economy of the Scandinavian kind, nor is there any sign that she will turn away from Communism, as she understands it. Nevertheless, "Communism" in Yugoslavia is thus far different in so many respects from Communism elsewhere that it is difficult to classify. Moreover, it is still in a state of development and transition, and experiments (many of which fail and are abandoned) are constantly made. If nothing else, the country appears to have freed itself from Communist (Marxist-Leninist-Stalinist) dogma, and there has been no "Titoist" dogma to replace it.

GREECE

Greece is the only parliamentary democracy in eastern Europe. She is a member of NATO and has been securely in the Western camp since the end of the civil war (1949, see p. 247). With American economic as well as military aid, she has made considerable progress. A right-wing conservative government headed by Field Marshal Papagos until his death in 1955 was followed by a more moderate conservative government under Constantine Karamanlis, who resigned in 1963 over a difference of opinion with King Paul. A few months later the aged George Papandreou, who had headed the first postwar government, took office after winning a general election, at the head of a liberal coalition. This government, probably the most popular since the war, initiated some much-needed reforms. In July, 1965, Papandreou also resigned after a clash with the new young king Constantine II over the Premier's desire to purge the army of what he called right-wing elements. After several efforts to form a new government without holding another election (which it was conceded would have been won by Papandreou), the King proposed a government of "national emergency" and appointed Staphanos Stephanopoulos as its head. This government won a vote of confidence from the old parliament. The most divisive domestic issue has continued, as in the prewar years (see p. 125), to be the role of the crown in the government. In foreign affairs it has been the quarrel with fellow NATO member Turkey over Cyprus, which will be discussed in Chapter 18.

CONCLUSION

In eastern Europe many difficulties have been overcome, while others remain, as they do in the Soviet Union itself. But it now appears that the satellites can survive as long as they are economically tied to the Soviet Union. The Communist governments are certainly unpopular, and even in Yugoslavia it is doubtful that the regime would win a majority in a free election. Several of the satellites—notably Rumania in recent times—have shown a desire to increase trade with the West and adopt some policies contrary to those favored by the Soviet Union. East Germany's future is still obscure and there can be no doubt of both the extreme unpopularity of the Communist regime and the continued resentment of even the Communists at the dependence of their increasingly industrialized economy on decisions made in the Soviet Union. In December, 1965, the minister responsible for the economy committed suicide rather than sign an economic treaty with the Soviet Union which he regarded as unfavorable to the German Democratic Republic.

But all this is not to say that the satellite empire is likely to break up in the early future. Such an eventuality still seems far off and probably awaits an East-West agreement on the future of East Germany, which is no more visible, even on the horizon, than it has been in any of the years since the war.

The United States, whose economy had been greatly expanded during the war, if in a necessarily one-sided manner, emerged from it incomparably the most powerful nation in the world. The Soviet Union presented a constant military threat to her, which she soon took steps to counteract, but the Soviet Union was so far behind in economic strength that she was not a serious economic rival. Only in the realm of ideas did the Soviet Union, and later Communist China, offer themselves as competitors for the allegiance of neutral nations.

The military and ideological clashes between these powers and the actions of the United States as a global power will be covered separately in Chapter 20, devoted to the Cold War—although in the course of discussing the other American countries, in all of which the most powerful American nation has naturally played its part, these factors will of course have to be considered.

THE UNITED STATES

In this chapter it is impossible to discuss in any detail the postwar history of the United States. We will therefore cover only a few major trends and areas in which events of importance have taken place.

Economic Developments. The economic history of the postwar years is one of more or less constant growth, marked only by some relatively minor "recessions" and periods during which the gross national product increased more slowly than in some other countries which had more leeway to make up. There has been no labor shortage in the United States, as there has been at times in most European countries; and there has been much more unemployment, especially among the unskilled, particularly the Negroes. This has in part been the result of the ever increasing mechanization of industry and agriculture and the need for skilled workers who alone can operate the increasingly complex machines. The social security system inaugurated under the New Deal (see p. 166) has been extended and the benefits increased with some regularity under both the one postwar Republican president and the three Democratic ones. But it was not until the Kennedy regime (1961–1963) that there was strong presidential pressure to enact a more extensive program of services for the underprivileged. When President Kennedy was assassinated on November 22, 1963, Vice-President Lyndon Johnson succeeded to his position; but even Johnson, in spite of his experience at handling Congress, probably could not have persuaded this one to go very much further. However, when he defeated the Republican candidate Senator Barry Goldwater in the Presidential election of 1964, he carried along with him a reform-minded Congress, which proved itself willing to enact such measures as the extension of social security to provide large-scale medical and hospital care for the aged, a program that had been bottled up in Congress for years. This same Congress also passed bills to alleviate poverty and to train unskilled workers.

Civil Rights. The most important social movement in the first half of the 1960's was the effort by activists, especially students, both black and white, to overcome the various disabilities suffered by Negroes. In this they had the support of both the Kennedy and the Johnson administrations, and Congress passed laws in 1964 and in 1965 which went some distance in this direction, especially in preventing the systematic discrimination hitherto practiced by many Southern states against Negroes who tried to vote. This civil rights movement arose largely as the result of an epoch-making decision by the United States Supreme Court (1954) requiring the states to provide equal educational opportunities and outlawing as unconstitutional the segregated schools ("separate but equal") previously found acceptable by the Court. The affected states complied with the new ruling unevenly. Most of them resisted to some extent, and some passed laws continuing the practice in disguised form, which had to be fought slowly through the Courts.

It was this slow acceptance of what in the South amounted to a social revolution and what even in the North had not hitherto been the usual practice that spurred the activists to further efforts on their own. By various means some of the old discriminatory customs were swept away. Public facilities, lunchrooms, parks, and transportation were integrated gradually in most states. But everywhere there was resistance from some sectors of the white community, often backed by the local police. Although the federal government and courts, aided by the Civil Rights Acts, did what they could, it was not easy to make much progress since the federal form of government leaves local law enforcement and education to the states—so long as federal law and the federal Constitution are not contravened. It was often difficult, for example, to obtain convictions against white offenders, since juries are chosen locally, as required by the Constitution. White lawbreakers were often allowed to go free even though the weight of the evidence to an objective and distant eye appeared to favor conviction. Nevertheless, undoubtedly far more progress in civil rights was made in the postwar period than in all the preceding years since the Civil War.

The "War against Poverty." In spite of the vastly improved standard of living enjoyed by the great majority of Americans, there remains a very considerable number of Americans, both whites and Negroes, whose income is far below the figure accepted by sociologists and economists as sufficient to maintain a family. Indeed, it is not at all certain that the percentage of these "underprivileged" persons is any lower than it was when President Franklin Roosevelt drew attention to the "forgotten man" in the Great Depression. But in recent years there has been an increasing awareness of this discrepancy and the Kennedy and Johnson administrations attempted to do something about it. Legislation was passed by Congress in 1965 setting up an Office of Economic Opportunity in the effort to help the underprivileged to help themselves and to alleviate the worst results of their present poverty.

Civil Liberties and the Communist Threat. The Cold War has cast its shadow over all American life throughout the postwar period. The doctrine of "Communism," held as an official dogma by the Russian and Chinese governments, has been imperfectly understood and for this reason greatly feared by many as a threat to American institutions and the "American way of life." The danger that hidden Communists might be exercising influence within the federal bureaucracy was brought to the attention of the public especially by the trial and conviction in 1950 of Alger

Hiss, a former State Department employee, for perjury. The conviction implied (though this was not specifically pronounced upon by the jury) that he had given secrets to the Russians. The conviction in 1951 and the execution in 1953 of Julius and Ethel Rosenberg for transmitting secret atomic information to the Russians added fuel to the flame. President Truman and President Eisenhower issued executive orders as a result of which government employees were subjected to stringent security tests, and, if suspected of "subversion," defined in a very broad sense, they were dismissed.

This program, however, did not satisfy Congress. A committee of the House of Representatives (House Committee on Un-American Activities) undertook to expose suspected subversion publicly. Senator Joseph McCarthy of Wisconsin, chairman of a Senate committee on government operations, also issued numerous charges against employees in all areas of the government, during and after the Korean War. He used his power to wreak havoc among the government departments, especially the State Department, which even appointed a McCarthy adherent as its chief of security. Congress also passed laws requiring the tiny Communist party to register as a subversive organization, and successive attorneys general issued lists of similar organizations which were made available to all potential employers as well as to government agencies.

Gradually, with the fading into the past of the Korean War, this immediate furor died down, but numerous private organizations continued to flourish which purported to awaken the American people to the dangers of Communism. The leader of the most influential of these, the John Birch Society, accused even President Eisenhower of Communist sympathies. The choice of right-wing Senator Barry Goldwater by the Republican party as its presidential candidate in 1964 was in part the result of continued fear of Communism, fanned by extreme right-wing groups. Nevertheless, there was also progress in the direction of increased civil liberty, as the United States Supreme Court became increasingly libertarian under the leadership of Chief Justice Earl Warren. The Court was severely criticized by the John Birch Society and others, who regarded many of its decisions as going beyond its constitutional powers. The John Birch Society, which regarded Chief Justice Warren as mainly responsible for this trend, regularly called for his impeachment.

Conclusion. By the mid-1960's the United States had enjoyed five years of unexampled prosperity, with common stocks averaging an all-time high and corporations continuing to report ever increasing profits. Her social security program was now well entrenched, and its benefits were growing closer to those of the mixed economies of Europe and New Zealand. President Johnson, in spite of some vocal opposition to his foreign policies, enjoyed a very wide measure of support among all classes, even among businessmen, who are traditionally suspicious of presidents from the Democratic party. If the hard-core domestic problems remained, most of them, at least the more tangible ones, were recognized, and the will was present in the federal government to do something about them.

CANADA

At the end of World War II William Lyon Mackenzie King was still prime minister of Canada after the longest tenure of office of any prime minister in the Commonwealth. Although he resigned in 1948, his Liberal party continued in office until 1957. In that year the reorganized Progressive Conservative party under John Diefenbaker at last won a general election, though it did not command a sure majority in the House of Commons until the following year, when it won a landslide victory. But by 1962 Diefenbaker had lost his over-all majority, and had to rely on the support of the more conservative Social Credit party (30 seats). The following year he was defeated by the Liberal party, headed by Lester Pearson, who had succeeded in recovering most of the Quebec seats lost in 1958. But his government, like the preceding one, was a minority one, and was dependent for its parliamentary majority on the New Democratic party, which was avowedly socialist. Hoping to win an outright majority, Pearson called another election in 1965, but still failed to win an over-all majority, though his government remained in office.

There is not very much difference between the political philosophies of the two major Canadian parties. Both have maintained the social services and the family allowances inaugurated by prewar and wartime governments, but they have not extended the social security programs so far as most other democratic countries have. The Progressive Conservatives are inclined to make more of the British connection than the Liberals are. All Canadian governments recognize the economic dependence of their country on the

United States, a dependence which is accepted, though with some resentment, by the people as something they are powerless to change. It is American investment alone which enables the Canadians to balance their international payments; but the cost has been the American domination of much Canadian industry, a trend that both Conservative and Liberal governments have attempted to stem but with indifferent success.

In recent years the major problem in Canada has been the rise of a fairly strong and highly emotional separatist movement in French Canada (not backed by the Quebec provincial government). Although not yet presenting a serious threat to Canadian unity, it has drawn much attention to itself by local demonstrations, occasionally accompanied by some violence. It might become more powerful if the Liberal party were to lose its comparatively recent control of the provincial government of Quebec. In foreign affairs Canada has at times assumed the leadership of the "middle" powers in the United Nations and elsewhere, especially when her representative at the United Nations was Lester Pearson. She has provided troops for some United Nations peace-keeping operations and has made it clear that she is not to be relied on as an undeviating supporter of United States policies. Although she belongs to NATO and has other defensive arrangements with the United States, she has refused to have nuclear weapons on her soil. She maintains relations with Cuba, and she has sold large quantities of grain to Communist China.

Canada now has ten provinces. Newfoundland, formerly an independent dominion within the Commonwealth, voted by a small majority to join her in 1949.

THE SOUTH AMERICAN CONTINENT

In the postwar years there have been so many coups, countercoups, and changes of government in Latin America that few can be discussed here in detail, but some brief information will be provided on each country, with emphasis on the most recent period.

With the exception of the Guianas (British, Dutch, and French) and British Honduras, the whole of the American continent south of the Rio Grande is Spanish speaking and formed part of the Spanish colonial empire. The Latin American republics have always pictured themselves as struggling to maintain their independence against the "colossus of the north," whose actual military interventions in the Caribbean and Central America are still vividly remembered and whose economic policies cannot but affect them. Most of them are dependent on the expert of primary products, mainly to the United States. United States investments provide most of their industrial capital (both in manufacturing and in the extraction of raw materials), and the profits from American enterprises when repatriated to the United States are a constant drain on their slender currency resources.

Relations with the United States. The United States has a considerable interest in maintaining the stability of the Latin American countries. She naturally tries to discourage nationalization of American-owned properties, and has done her best (with considerable success) to prevent other countries from following the example set by Mexican President Lázaro Cárdenas, who in 1938 nationalized American oil properties (see p. 170). She was unable to prevent Cuba from becoming a Communist state, with the subsequent loss of all her investments in that island. She is therefore extremely wary of other possible Communist revolutions. In 1965 she intervened in force in the Dominican Republic when information was received suggesting that a movement to overthrow the Dominican president might lead to a Communist take-over.

The result of such policies has been that the United States has come to be widely regarded as an upholder of the status quo and a foe of all revolutions. Yet the social structure of most Latin American republics has changed relatively little from the days of the Spanish colonial empire. Although most of the European-born Spaniards left at the time of independence, the native-born upper classes retained their land and the semifeudal system continued. During all the twentieth century a sizeable middle class has been arising with interests closely tied to those of the United States. But on the whole this class has tended either to identify itself with the landowners and share power with them, or to attempt to take power itself. Scarcely anywhere until very recent times has there been much attention paid to the industrial workers or to the peasants. This condition has naturally resulted in the growth of extremism, even though Communism itself—a philosophy alien to the Latin American mind—does not appear to have made much headway, partly perhaps as a result of the continuing influence of the Catholic Church. The "forgotten" men and women of Latin America are therefore becoming increasingly desperate because of their inability to change the existing social structure by any legal means open to them. Although real revolutions have taken place only in Mexico and Cuba, with a partial revolution in Bolivia, they cannot be ruled out elsewhere so long as there is little serious attempt to improve the lot of these people. Trained Communists can certainly give direction to them and very possibly take them over when revolutions occur.

This situation, widely recognized in the United States, has led to two distinct and not altogether compatible policies. One emphasizes domestic stability and social reform, while the other is based primarily on considerations of the struggle against Communism.

There has been increasing industrial investment by the United States, which has of course led to an increase in employment in some sectors of the economy, and pressure has been put on the Latin American governments to persuade them to make social reforms. The medium for this policy is the Alliance for Progress, a program inaugurated by President Kennedy in 1961, which called for aid of the order of $1 billion annually, to be distributed only to those governments which gave priority to social reform. The governments were of course anxious to receive this largesse, but far less anxious to institute social reforms. Much of the money has been spent on useful social enterprises such as the provision of housing, but few governments have instituted any really fundamental reforms. Such reforms as they have agreed to are recognized as little more than palliatives.

The second United States program has involved the provision of military aid to the governments. Obviously no Latin American country is in great danger of external invasion from outside the Americas; but every country except tiny Costa Rica maintains an army which, even when account is taken of military aid given by the United States, still consumes far too much of the national budget. Moreover, in almost all countries the army officers belong to the same social stratum as the ruling classes which control the government. They are strongly conservative, as a rule (exceptions will be noted later), and if the democratically elected governments adopt a policy contrary to their wishes, they overthrow it, and either install a government more to their liking or take over themselves and rule through a military dictatorship or junta. American arms are therefore too often used by Latin American armies to suppress incipient or actual rebellions and thus tend to defeat the expressed purposes of the Alliance. Since it is a part of American global policy to "contain" Communism wherever it appears (and the danger of Communist revolutions in Latin America is not to be denied), the United States acquiesces in the use of her military aid to suppress domestic revolutions of any kind, and even to help military dictatorships to attain power, whether or not there was any real danger of a Communist (or other) revolution. President Kennedy did, it is true, withhold recognition for a time from a Peruvian government that had forcibly seized power. But when this action had no effect, he soon reversed himself in exchange for undertakings given by the new government. President Kennedy also refused to recognize a military coup which overthrew the recently elected Juan Bosch in the Dominion Republic. Bosch had served out only seven months of his term, and his election had undoubtedly been a free one. President Johnson, who succeeded Kennedy after the latter's assassination, recognized the new government after receiving assurances that a new election would be held in July, 1965. Bosch naturally protested against the recognition, since he had been overthrown by force, and in his view no new elections were necessary. If it had not been for the coup, he would have remained in office for several more years.

Organization of American States.   In 1947 a treaty was signed at Rio de Janeiro which set up a Pan-American organization known as the Organization of American States (OAS), providing for mutual defense against external aggression and peaceful conciliation in the event of intra-American disputes. All the independent American nations except Canada became members. It was clearly stated that there was to be no interference in the domestic affairs of the members, and that aggression against one would hereafter be considered as aggression against all. The Alliance for Progress was proclaimed at a special OAS meeting held in 1961 at Punta del Este in Uruguay.

The OAS has had a somewhat uneven history. It succeeded in settling several small but dangerous disputes between members which had led to armed intervention on a small scale. But since the Cuban revolution of 1959 and the establishment of a Communist state in the Western Hemisphere, it has experienced peculiar difficulties. All the Latin American nations do not regard Communism as quite such a danger to them as does the United States, and only in such exceptional circumstances as the missile crisis in Cuba in 1962 have they been willing to take extreme measures against a sister republic. Although the United States has hitherto been able to win the necessary two-thirds of the votes for her policies, the majority has never included Mexico, and as a rule the larger and more important states have belonged to the minority of opponents or abstainers.

In 1960 with great difficulty the OAS was persuaded to impose economic sanctions on the dictatorial Trujillo regime in the Dominican Republic, after it had been proved that an attempt on the life of the Venezuelan president had been carried out by Trujillo's henchmen. Even then, some of the Latin American governments did not put the sanctions into operation. With no votes to spare and after strong pressure had been exercised by the United States, Cuba was excluded from the OAS in January, 1962, the exclusion to last until her "Marxist-Leninist" regime was overthrown. Brazil, Mexico, Bolivia, Chile, and Uruguay opposed the action. The same governments, however, gave their consent to United States actions in the missile crisis of October, 1962 (see p. 312), when it was recognized that there was an actual military danger to all Latin America stemming from Cuban willingness to install the Russian missiles. However, they did not break relations with Cuba until much later, when evidence was supplied that Cuba had provided Venezuelan Communists with arms. Bolivia and Brazil did not take the decision until military coups in these countries had ousted their leftist governments. Mexico still retains diplomatic relations with Cuba.

When a rebellion broke out in the Dominion Republic in April, 1965, the United States at once sent troops, ostensibly to protect American lives. She then requested OAS military assistance to put an end to the rebellion and keep the peace between the two warring groups. The Dominican intervention was strongly opposed by some Latin American governments since it appeared to be a direct infringement of the Rio Treaty of 1947. This was a different group of governments from those that had favored Cuban exclusion from the OAS. Mexico was joined on this occasion by Chile, Peru, Ecuador, and Uruguay. Brazil took the lead in trying to win support for American intervention and herself sent some troops to bolster the American strength. Later in the same year the United States tried to win OAS consent to a permanent inter-American military force, in which effort she was strongly seconded by the military government of Brazil under General Castelo Branco. But when this proposal was obviously going to fail for lack of the necessary number of votes, the attempt was abandoned.

By the end of 1965 the intervention of the United States in the Dominion Republic and the passing in the House of Representatives of the Selden Resolution (calling for the United States to intervene unilaterally in Latin America whenever there was danger of a Communist-inspired coup) had renewed Latin American fears of the United States which had been dormant since the days of President Franklin Roosevelt's Good Neighbor Policy. The future of inter-American co-operation through the OAS must therefore be considered doubtful.

Colombia. On the South American continent Colombia was ruled with army support by General Rojas Pinilla from 1950 to 1957, when he was overthrown in a military coup. In the following year, an agreement was reached by which the two evenly matched political parties, the Conservative and Liberals, would supply the presidents alternately. As a result of this a Liberal, Dr. Lleras Camargo, became president in 1958 and was replaced by a Conservative, Guillermo Leon Valencia in 1962. The deal between the two parties had been decided upon in part because of a virtual civil war that had killed upward of 300,000 Colombians in the years prior to the rulership of Rojas Pinilla. A rebellion has been smoldering for many years also in a remote part of the country, which no president has yet been able to suppress. The oligarchy is firmly entrenched in Colombia with a little over three hundred individuals owning 56 per cent of the country's industrial capital and some 3 per cent of the people owning more than 65 per cent of the land.

Venezuela. In Venezuela, a country long plagued by military dictatorships, Rómulo Gallegos, the leader of the reformist party *Acción Democrática,* was deposed in 1948 by a military group who ruled for the next two years directly and after 1950 through a civilian president. The latter was deposed in turn by Colonel Marcos Pérez Jiménez in 1958. He ruled as an absolute military dictator until he was expelled from the country in January, 1958, in a popular uprising. Free elections were then held and Rómulo Betancourt was elected president. He was succeeded in another free election by Raúl Leoni in 1963. During the rule of these two leaders from the *Acción Democrática,* many reforms have been carried out in spite of right-wing and Communist opposition. The most important of these reforms have been in land distribution, although the problem is far from solved. With the assistance of the government the oil workers employed by the large United

States companies have also won many concessions on wages and working conditions. The government receives a higher percentage of oil revenues than in the past.

Brazil. Brazil, the most populous country in Latin America, was ruled from 1930 to 1945 by Getúlio Vargas, at first as a virtual dictator, then as constitutionally elected president. A military coup deposed him in 1945, but he was re-elected under a new constitution in 1950 and remained president until he committed suicide in 1954. The following year Juscelino Kubitschek was elected. He initiated many grandiose but expensive plans for economic reform, as well as building the new capital of Brasilia. He was succeeded by Jânio Quadros, who suddenly resigned only seven months later, declaring that opposition to him in the conservative Congress and elsewhere made government impossible. Constitutionally he ought to have been succeeded by his vice-president, João Goulart, who belonged to a different party. But army opposition to Goulart made his succession doubtful until he agreed to constitutional changes establishing a congressional form of government, which in effect meant allowing Congress to make all important decisions. In January, 1963, Goulart felt himself strong enough to risk holding a plebiscite on the form of government preferred by Brazilians. As a result of this, his presidential prerogatives were restored.

In 1964 his ineffective government was overthrown by a military coup, and General Humberto Castelo Branco, the army chief of staff, took over the government, later having himself proclaimed president by a subservient congress. His presidential term was to last until 1967, when he promised to hold elections again. The General instituted a purge of left-wing elements and other opponents and attempted to deal with the numerous problems of his country that remained unsolved. However, little success has as yet been reported, in spite of the resumption of United States aid, which had been cut off from President Goulart. In particular the problems of northeastern Brazil, one of the most poverty-stricken areas in the world, have defied solution, and many of the efforts made by former presidents have been slowed down or abandoned. Yet São Paulo in southern Brazil is one of the largest cities in the world and its economy is booming.

Uruguay. In Uruguay the presidential system which had been in operation since the beginning of the Republic was abolished in 1951 and replaced by a nine-man National Council of Government, chosen by Congress, six from the majority and three from the minority party. The chairman of the council acts as president. The Blanco party won the congressional elections of 1958, breaking the hold of its perennial opponent, the Colorado party, for the first time in 93 years.

Paraguay. It is not too much to say that Paraguay has never known a democratic government. It has been almost always ruled by the military, some of whom have favored fundamental economic and social reforms, but have been unable to put them into effect. The constitution itself, promulgated in 1940 by the military president of the day, legalizes what is virtually a presidential dictatorship, and the presidents have never had any difficulty in suppressing their political opponents. The current president, General Alfredo Stroessner, has, however, made a number of minor reforms which have in some degree helped the people. But the cost of his dictatorship has been high since, like his predecessor, General Stroessner has not hesitated to use methods of terror to suppress his opposition. All active opponents of his rule are therefore forced to live abroad, and it has been estimated that there are more Paraguayans living in exile today than there are exiles from any other Latin American country, including even Cuba.

Argentina. In Argentina, Colonel Juan Perón, former minister of labor, who was popular with the workers because of the legislation that he had introduced on their behalf, was elected president in 1946 and in due course had the constitution changed to permit his re-election. He established a virtual dictatorship and held office until 1955, backed by the urban proletariat and the General Confederation of Labor, the most powerful labor union in the country. Perón's policies were ruinously expensive, and in 1954 he began a quarrel with the Church. In September, 1955, he was overthrown by a military coup. Military rule continued until 1958, when Arturo Frondizi was elected president with the aid of most of the still powerful Peronists. He was ousted by the army in 1962, to be replaced by the president of the Senate, José María Guido, who completed Frondizi's term. A country doctor named Arturo Illia was elected president in October, 1963, and has so far retained his position while making a serious attempt to solve the numerous problems remaining over from the Perón era. But the groups that backed Perón (himself still in exile and forbidden to return) are still strong, and whenever elections are held in which they are allowed to participate, they show their strength. No one else has yet been able to attract the support of the workers or of their union; and the only hope for the more moderate leaders has been to provide a prosperity in which all can share—a goal still far from attained.

Chile. In Chile, whose social and economic problems are as severe as those anywhere else on the continent, there has been no usurpation of power by the military since 1932, although a real dictator of the 1920's, General Carlos Ibáñez, was legally elected again in 1952. Neither he nor his successor, Jorge Alessandri (a son of a former president), was able to do much with the severe economic problems that beset the country, aggravated as they were by an appalling earthquake (May, 1960). In the 1964 presidential elections two parties were competing, both with new and, for Chile, radical programs. One, led by Salvador Allende, was a left-wing party backed by the Communists, who have been active in Chile ever since World War II. Eduardo Frei, the leader of the other party, called himself a Christian socialist and was backed by Catholic intellectuals, who had for years been preparing a detailed program for the improvement of the lot of the common people. Since he easily won the election, he gained the opportunity to do what he could. Among the first fruits of his rule was a far-ranging agreement with American copper companies which raised wages in mines and gave the government a substantial share in the industry.

Peru. Peru is a country with much the same problems as Chile, mainly the concentration of the land and wealth in the hands of a few ancient families. No president has ever been willing to change the system and face the opposition of the oligarchy. A revolutionary party (American Popular Revolutionary Alliance, APRA), founded in the 1920's, is still in existence, led by the now aged Victor Raúl Haya de la Torre. It was strongly militant until after the war and its leader spent much time in jail or exile. His party almost certainly won the presidential election of 1931, but the official winner was General Sánchez Cerro, who then proceeded to outlaw APRA. Although the General was assassinated in 1933, all subsequent presidents backed the oligarchy and were in turn supported by the army. Again in 1936 APRA was robbed of an electoral victory by the incumbent.

After the war, Haya and the bulk of his party threw in their lot with some of the oligarchs, and the party ceased to be revolutionary though its violence continued. In 1948 President Luis

Bustamante was overthrown by a military coup led by General Manuel Odría, who ruled until 1956. Since he did not wish to continue in office an election followed, in which a former president, Manuel Prado (who belonged to the richest family in Peru), was elected with the support of APRA. Prado had served out most of his term when new elections were held in 1962. These were fought by APRA led by Haya, Fernando Belaúnde Terry (an architect, leader of the Popular Action party), and Odría. APRA apparently won the most votes, though the margin between all three candidates was small. The army, unwilling to accept Haya de la Torre as president, staged a coup, jailed and imprisoned President Prado, and forced him and the President-elect into exile. President Kennedy retaliated by withholding recognition for a time, but the junta swore in a provisional president and held new elections the following year, from which Belaúnde, who was acceptable to the army, emerged the victor. Belaúnde's policies, as far as they can be ascertained, are similar to those of Chilean President Frei, but the entrenched position of the oligarchs in Peru is difficult to breach. Not much has as yet been accomplished, in spite of much planning. Throughout 1965, Communist uprisings in the Andes regions plagued the government, which was constantly accused by its vociferous APRA and Odrista opposition of taking insufficient steps to suppress them.

Bolivia. Bolivia was for a long time the poorest country in all South America, with the lowest per capita income and the highest death rate. She had been plagued by a series of military presidents since the Chaco War (1933–1938) against Paraguay from which Bolivia came off second best. Little was done to alleviate the lot of the perennially rebellious and revolutionary tin miners until 1952. In that year a rebellion of farmers and miners, aided by elements of the police, against the military junta was successful. Victor Paz Estenssoro, who had been elected president the previous year but had been prevented from taking office, now became president. The chief mines (owned mostly by the British or the Bolivian Patiño family) were nationalized, and an extensive land reform program was inaugurated. But in spite of much aid from the United States the economy sank from bad to worse. The miners' union led by Juan Lechín was not disposed to insist on higher productivity, and violence became endemic in the countryside.

A moderate leader of Paz Estenssoro's party, Hernán Siles,

became president in 1956. He had some success in controlling the galloping inflation, and the lot of the peasants definitely improved. He was succeeded by Paz Estenssoro again, with Lechín as vice-president. The reforms continued, but the President himself became ever more authoritarian and generally unpopular. He insisted on taking full credit for the revolution and regarded himself as indispensable. Fearing a Communist uprising, he declared a state of siege, a procedure which enabled him to rule by decree. In these dire straits he revived the army which he had abolished during his first term. When the time came for new elections he became a candidate for his third term of office. Since no opposition presented itself, he was declared elected and assumed office again in August, 1964. In November of the same year he was toppled by a military coup and his place was taken by a military junta, headed by an air force general, René Barrientos Ortuña. Paz went into exile, and the junta soon afterward expelled Juan Lechín from the country. These events were followed by violent strikes in the mines which reached their peak in September, 1965. They were reported as having been broken by the military, who again declared a state of siege. Nevertheless Barrientos and the army chief Ovando, who seem to be ruling together, have not attempted to destroy the revolution and its achievements. For the first time a revolution in South America has therefore been put into effect by an elected government, and it is possible that its reforms, such as they are, may turn out to have been irreversible.

Ecuador. Although the economy of Ecuador has been fairly prosperous in the last decades, at least insofar as external trade is concerned, it remains a poverty-stricken country with 90 per cent of the cultivable land in the hands of a tiny minority of the population. The government and army are both extremely conservative, and very little effort has been expended in trying to make any fundamental changes. As a result there are frequent small uprisings, supposedly Communist inspired, though none has come close to success. The military interfere whenever any government does not suit them. For many years the dominant leader of the country was a strong man, a former law professor of outstanding eloquence who never lost an election, but succeeded in serving out only one of his four terms as president. This was Dr. José María Velasco Ibarra, whose policies were never clear even to his supporters, but who made sporadic efforts to cope with the problem of reform. His first term lasted from 1934 to 1935, when he was deposed by the military, who in turn made him president again in 1944. After being legally elected to a full term, he was ousted in 1947. From 1952 to 1956 he ruled with some success, in part because he followed the policies of his predecessor, President Galo Plaza Lasso, a mild reformer who balanced the budget and permitted more democratic practices than were customary in Ecuador. Elected again in 1960, Velasco Ibarra had served only one year of his term when the military replaced him by his vice-president, Carlos Julio Arosemena, who in turn was ousted in July, 1963, by a military junta led by (Navy) Captain Ramón Castro Jijon (on the grounds that Arosemena was too soft on Castroites and Communists and was too often publicly drunk). The junta ruled on its own, trying in fact to put through some social reforms—a task made difficult by the conservative views of their civilian supporters —until 1965 when demonstrations took place in Guayaquil, the commercial capital of the country, demanding an end to military government. After trying to suppress these by force, the junta bowed to the storm and appointed a civilian government, which, however, it continued to control. No elections were promised.

CENTRAL AMERICA

We now come to the Central American countries, which have formed a fairly effective, or at least promising, common market among themselves. The Central American governments present some strong contrasts.

Nicaragua.   Nicaragua has been ruled for decades, directly or indirectly, by members of the Somoza family. Its patriarch, General Anastasio Somoza, who first became president in 1936, only three years after the departure of the American marines, was assassinated in 1956. His two sons have divided the power between them ever since, in spite of efforts to overthrow them. A Somoza henchman, Dr. René Schick Gutiérrez, has held the actual presidency since 1963. The country is a tight dictatorship with a primitive economy, and little progress of any kind has been noted in recent years.

Honduras.   Honduras is hardly better developed than Nicaragua, and it too has known little freedom, democracy, or economic advance. To survive in office presidents must have the support of the military. They permitted Ramón Villeda Morales of the Liberal party to become president when he was elected to that office in 1957 but looked with disfavor on his efforts to legislate social and economic reforms, which would probably have been strengthened if his Liberal nominee Modesto Rodas Alvarado had been elected in 1963. To prevent this Colonel Oswaldo López, head of the armed forces, staged a coup ten days before the elections and had himself proclaimed president, with a cabinet drawn from the opposition ultraconservative Nationalist party.

El Salvador. El Salvador has not known a civilian president since 1931, and her society is as stratified as any in Latin America. A strongly reform leftist group of young junior officers, backed by pro-Castro workers staged a military coup in October, 1960, against the ultraconservative government of Colonel José María Lemus. But these men in turn were ousted by Colonel Julio Rivero the following January. However, Rivero was not a conservative, and he pushed through a program of reform so popular that he was able to restore constitutional government in 1962 and be legally elected to a five-year term as president. By 1964 the reform program had slowed down in face of opposition from the oligarchs and threats from more conservative officers. But Rivero seemed likely to last out his term safely.

Guatemala. From almost the time of her independence, Guatemala has been ruled by military strong men. The last of these durable dictators, General Jorge Ubico (1931–1944) resigned his office at the age of 66 in 1944 in preference to continuing to suppress violent demands for constitutional reform. The military provided the government until elections were held in December, 1944, as a result of which Juan Arévalo, a liberal reformist, was elected president by a large majority. He won enough support from certain elements in the army to enable him to serve out his full term. He was even successful in lessening to some degree the influence of the army as a whole, though he was succeeded in 1950 by another military man, Major Jacobo Arbenz Guzmán, the defense minister in Arévalo's cabinet. The moderate reform program of Arévalo was stepped up by President Arbenz, who received support from the fairly strong Communist party. Well aware of the threat posed by the army, Arbenz organized a worker-peasant militia to offset its influence, while he put into effect a drastic reform program. Unable to obtain arms for his militia from the United States or other Western sources, he accepted them from the Soviet bloc (Poland). When these arrived the army prevented their distribution, and a short time later exiled army elements, supplied with arms by the United States, led an invasion of Guatemala from Honduras, which drove Arbenz into exile. The

rebels, led by Colonel Castillo Armas, then took over the government and suppressed all overt Communist activity. Castillo Armas
did nothing further to enforce the reforms of Arévalo and Arbenz.
He was murdered in July, 1957.

After some months' delay following the assassination, the military permitted new elections, which were won by General Miguel
Ydígoras Fuentes. During his term of office Ydígoras did little to
satisfy the reformers, nor was his exceptionally corrupt rule popular with the army. Small, presumably Communist-inspired, uprisings marked his rule, and the President permitted Cuban exiles
to be trained in his country preparatory to an invasion for the purpose of overthrowing the regime of Castro in Cuba. Toward the
end of his term it became clear that the next elections, if freely
held, would result in the re-election of former president Arévalo.
This was unacceptable to the army in spite of Arévalo's proclaimed anti-Communism. Before the election could take place the
army overthrew Ydígoras and exiled him, and placed its own
leader, Colonel Enrique Peralta, in the presidential palace. Peralta
did not make any significant reforms during his regime, but he
permitted new elections to be held in March, 1966, in which neither
he nor Arévalo was a candidate. These elections were won by the
furthest left of the three candidates, the moderate Julio Cesar
Mendez Montenegro, leader of the Revolutionary party.

Costa Rica. This small country, whose population is almost
all of European descent, does not have so many problems as its
neighbors and most other Latin American states. Land is fairly
widely distributed, even though the great majority of the farms
are very small. The Costa Rican army was abolished in 1948 in
favor of a militia much more easily controlled by the civilian government. Two subsequent invasions by exiles were handled by the
OAS, which backed the government and put an end to the danger.
The leading figure in the country has for long been José Figueres,
who was president from 1953 to 1958. At the beginning of his
rule he nationalized the banks and imposed a capital levy, but
little else of a revolutionary nature has been done since. The
present president, Francisco José Bolmarcich, was a minister under
Figueres, and remains his ally.

Panama. Panama's main reason for existence as a separate
state is the Panama Canal, which newly independent Panama
permitted the United States to build in the early part of the twen-

tieth century. The country was separated from Colombia in a revolution sponsored by President Theodore Roosevelt, and in a subsequent perpetual treaty granted the United States the right to a zone under American sovereignty. In recent years this zone and the treaty have excited such opposition from the Panamanian people that riots broke out, first in January, 1963, and then more seriously in January, 1964. As a result of the latter, such pressure was put on the ultraconservative President Roberto Francisco Chiari that he broke off diplomatic relations with the United States. The OAS attempted to mediate, and President Johnson eventually agreed to negotiate a new treaty. It was announced in September, 1965, that principles of a new treaty had been accepted by both the new Panamanian president, Marco Aurelio Robles, and President Johnson. This issue ever since independence has dominated Panamanian politics, which have been exceptionally virulent. But it has not been the only issue. The need for land reform is an urgent as in most other Latin American states. One president, José Antonio Remón, a former chief of police, was assassinated in 1955 (after three years in office) by a political opponent who objected to his reforms (mild though they were). President Remón's was the last serious effort to solve the numerous problems. It is possible that if the Canal Zone with its installations is returned to Panamanian sovereignty a new beginning can be made with some hope of success—provided the military permit it.

MEXICO

Little need be said on Mexico, whose problems and revolution were discussed at some length in Chapter 9. She has enjoyed considerable economic advance since World War II and is probably now ahead of any other country in Latin America. Her governments under one-party rule have been stable, and no attempts have been made to overthrow them. At the same time, though there has been a great increase in the number of persons who have moved into the middle class, the poorest classes have benefited very little indeed from the general prosperity of the country. They complain that the revolution, which was to such a large extent made by them, has passed them by. Even though land has continued to be distributed by every president since World War II, there is not enough good land left, and the population meanwhile grows incessantly. So Mexico too, in spite of appearances, still has her problems, and even renewal of the revolution cannot be ruled out, though the government's power is such that it will surely be able to suppress it without difficulty.

LATIN STATES OF THE CARIBBEAN

The most outstanding event in recent Latin American history has of course been the Cuban revolution. But elsewhere in the Caribbean there have also been events of importance, in particular the intervention of the United States in the Dominican Republic, ostensibly to prevent a revolution similar to that in Cuba from falling under Communist control. Meanwhile the Commonwealth of Puerto Rico (a Commonwealth since 1953) has been making impressive economic strides with American aid under its elected governors, especially during the long regime of Governor Múñoz Marin (1948–1964).

Cuba. After the Spanish-American war at the turn of the twentieth century, Cuba became formally independent. But it was not until 1934 with the dropping of the Platt Amendment (which permitted legal intervention by the United States) that she became really independent. Even since then, under a perpetual treaty, the United States has retained the base of Guantánamo on Cuban soil. A year before the abrogation of the Platt Amendment, a group of army sergeants led by Sergeant Fulgencio Batista overthrew a dictatorial regime headed by General Gerardo Machado. Thereafter Batista dominated the various governments, though he himself did not assume the presidential position until October, 1940. After permitting two civilian presidents (Ramón Grau San Martin and Carlos Prío Socarrás) to rule, he intervened directly in March, 1952, on the ground that President Socarrás was planning to put a president of his own choice in power without holding the elections scheduled for later the same year. General Batista (the rank he now held) ruled as a military dictator during his second term. His regime became ever more oppressive while he strove unsuccessfully to put an end to a rebellion, led by Fidel Castro, which began in December, 1956, in the eastern part of the island. Batista's regime collapsed at the end of 1958, and Castro entered the capital of Havana on January 8, 1959.

Although it is certain that Castro would have won any election held at that time, he did not hold one, but became prime minister, leaving the presidency to a former judge, Manuel Urrutia. When the two men later quarreled, Urrutia went into exile and was replaced by the more pliant Osvaldo Dorticós Torrado. But all power rested with Fidel Castro, who directed the revolution himself, aided by his brother Raúl, and, until 1965, by an Argentinian revolutionary, "Che" Guevara.

At the time of the revolution the economy was dominated by the United States, especially in the field of sugar, the leading Cuban crop, which was permitted entry into the United States on a preferred basis. Over the next two years Castro nationalized the sugar plantations and almost all foreign enterprises, including all that belonged to American interests. When the United States protested and eventually retaliated, Castro requested aid from the only power able to give it to him against the wishes of the United States. The Soviet Union agreed to supply him with oil and arms and accepted Cuban sugar in return. Meanwhile at home a thorough-going revolutionary program was being carried out which soon became a Communist one, although Castro always kept the Communist party leaders under his control and at times disciplined them. Large numbers of men and women, especially from the upper and middle classes went into exile in the United States, who was prepared to welcome them all and altered her immigration laws for the purpose. Cuba, denuded of her most experienced professionals, increasingly turned to the Soviet bloc for advisers.

In March, 1960, President Eisenhower issued instructions for a band of refugees to be trained in Guatemala, so that they would be ready "to act at the proper time" against the revolutionary government. In July he cut back the Cuban sugar quota, and just before leaving office (January 3, 1961), he broke diplomatic relations. Well aware of the preparations for invasion, the Cubans continually brought the danger to the attention of the United Nations, but obtained no help from that source.

President Kennedy on assuming office was faced with the decision whether or not to continue the preparations for the invasion and the question of how far the United States should give military support to the refugees she had trained. He was hesitant to damage the reputation of his country in the eyes of the world, especially of Latin America, on whose behalf the Alliance for Progress was being planned. But at the same time he was no less anxious than his predecessor and most other Americans to see Castro's government overthrown. Misled by intelligence that the Cuban people would rise in favor of the refugees when they landed, he at length authorized the invasion, but he did not authorize the air cover and logistical support necessary for its success. The result was that the invasion at the Bahia de los Cochinos (Bay of Pigs) in April, 1961, was easily repelled by the Cuban government, and most of the invaders were captured. Castro's position was greatly strengthened as a result of the American intervention, which gave his people confidence that they could after all stand up to the greatest power in the world. In spite of numerous errors and failures in the improvised revolutionary program at home, the government remained stable. Soon afterward Castro declared that he had always been a "Marxist-Leninist" and would remain one to the end of his life, and he accepted ever more help, including arms, from the Soviet bloc. In seeking this aid he explained that the United States was certain to try again, and that Cuba would be overcome if she were not given enough arms to enable her to resist. Soviet Prime Minister Nikita Khrushchev proved sympathetic to this plea.

Toward the end of 1962 Castro accepted rocket missiles from the Soviet Union which could be directed against the eastern seaboard of the United States. President Kennedy, unwilling to tolerate this new threat, replied by "quarantining" the island with United States naval forces, compelling Khrushchev to risk the danger of nuclear war if he persisted. After a brief hesitation he ordered the missiles removed and their sites dismantled. Castro had no choice but to submit to this indignity. Since Khrushchev still promised to fight if the United States invaded Cuba, he had to be content with that assurance. He was still completely dependent on Soviet supplies, and his new economy would necessarily collapse if they were cut off.

As it happened the United States made no further moves against Cuba, and the revolution continued. In 1965 the sugar crop was almost as high as in the prerevolutionary years in spite of the fact that the Cuban economy was now much more diversified. Although the country continues to suffer from disabilities resulting from the American embargo and from domestic failures in some areas, the government now appears stable and the revolution may be irreversible. In 1965 also, Fidel Castro felt strong enough to permit the departure of dissident Cubans into exile in the United States if they wished to leave, so long as they were neither of military age nor irreplaceable technical experts. It is expected that the number of exiles will reach a total of some 300,000 persons.

Haiti. French-speaking Haiti, the western half of the island of Hispaniola, is a Negro republic ruled since 1957 by Dr. François Duvalier, who has been a dictator since 1961. Aided by a so-called "People's Militia" loyal to himself, he has permitted no opposition and ruthlessly suppressed all attempts, including invasions by Haitian exiles, to overthrow him. He had himself re-elected before even the expiration of his first term. The army (which used to interfere regularly in domestic affairs, on several occasions even ousting unpopular presidents) has been downgraded and the country is quiet. But its economy is in an appalling condition, and the standard of living is by far the lowest in the Americas.

Dominican Republic. The Spanish-speaking Dominican Republic was a virtual private preserve of the Trujillo family from 1930 until the assassination of its patriarch General Rafael Leónidas Trujillo Molina in May, 1961. Throughout the entire period Trujillo himself, members of his immediate family, or loyal henchmen had held the presidency, but the policy remained unchanged. Dr. Joaquín Balaguer, the incumbent at the time of the murder, attempted to carry on the government with the aid of the former dictator's son, who was chief of staff of the army. But in November, 1961, the remaining Trujillos were forced into exile by riots directed primarily against the family. President Balaguer resigned soon afterward, after another military coup, and free elections were held. As a result of these Juan Bosch was chosen president by a large majority on the basis of a program of far-reaching reforms.

The Bosch government, however, was unable to achieve much in face of the appalling problems that had accumulated and the corruption that had undermined Dominican life for over thirty years. It was overthrown in September, 1963, by the military, who accused Bosch of trying to move the country too far to the left and relying on the support of the Communists. The military installed a three-man civilian junta, but unrest continued, culminating in an uprising in April, 1965, led by Colonel Francisco Camaaño Deno with the avowed purpose of restoring President Bosch. The uprising met determined resistance from the army, led by General Wessin y Wessin.

At this point the United States government, acting on early reports from the island, decided that there was an imminent danger of a Communist take-over. President Johnson believed that only military intervention could save the Dominican Republic from becoming another Cuba. He therefore sent a considerable force to the island which kept the two sides apart, although incidents were numerous, until arrangements could be made for a new middle-of-the-road interim government. This was accomplished with the aid of an OAS mission at the end of August, when Hector Godoy-Garcia, formerly foreign minister under ousted President Bosch, became interim president pending the holding of new elections in 1966, which Bosch declared himself again ready to contest. As noted earlier, the United States was able to obtain the necessary majority at a meeting of the OAS to authorize an inter-American peace force to replace the American forces. Only Brazil supplied a significant number of troops. The majority was obtained in the OAS by counting the vote of the outgoing Dominican junta which had already ceased to exercise its authority at home.

EUROPEAN COLONIES IN THE WESTERN HEMISPHERE

At the end of World War II, in addition to the former Spanish colonies in the Western Hemisphere, Britain, France, and the Netherlands still possessed colonies, mostly in the Caribbean. On the mainland of South America the British possessed British Guiana and British Honduras, while the Dutch had Dutch Guiana (Surinam) and the French had French Guiana. French Guiana and the French West Indian islands of Guadelupe and Martinique remain under French control as "overseas departments" with some local government and representation in the French parliament. When the Dutch lost Indonesia they took steps to bind their remaining colonies more closely to them by permitting local autonomy while reserving some rights for themselves, including external defense. Their influence in all their territories which are united under the Dutch crown remains very strong. The territories include as well as Surinam the islands of Aruba and Curaçao in the West Indies.

British Honduras has been in British hands since the seventeenth century, but Guatemala disputes the right of Great Britain to grant it independence, which has been promised for the near future. It now has full internal self-government. British Guiana has presented many difficulties to the British in view of its mixed population of Indians; sugar workers imported from India, who form the majority; Negroes, most of them descended from slaves; and a small white population. The Indians under Cheddi Jagan regularly won all elections in the colony for many years. But since Jagan was a Marxist and did not rule with what the British considered to be a proper sense of responsibility, they changed the constitution in such a way that he could no longer command an over-all majority. This left the way open for Forbes Burnham, a non-Marxist Negro, to form a coalition government with the somewhat overrepresented whites. Independence was then promised to the new government to take effect in 1966.

For many years after the war the British attempted to form a federation of their many West Indian islands. In 1957 the Federation of the West Indies came into being, but it was not a success, and the largest island, Jamaica, in particular felt that it was not sufficiently represented in the federal legislature. When given the opportunity to opt out of it, Jamaica held a referendum and as a result became independent. The second largest island, Trinidad (with its dependency of Tobago), followed suit. Since these events in 1962 the British have continued to try to form a federation of the remaining islands, but the efforts have so far not come to fruition.

17 EAST ASIA—DECOLONIZATION AND THE RISE OF COMMUNIST CHINA

The Japanese conquests of 1941 and 1942 brought all the countries east of India into Japan's empire, demonstrating in the process that Western colonial powers were not invulnerable. Although Japan granted a nominal independence only to Burma, in other colonies the nationalists were given many responsibilities that they had never handled before. Their new self-confidence made it unlikely that they would tamely submit to reconquest. Only Malaya and the small territories that later were included in the Federation of Malaysia, together with the commercial outpost of Hong Kong, returned to British hands. The Dutch and the French vainly tried to reconquer Indonesia and Indochina. The Philippine Islands, which before the war had been promised independence by the United States, received it on July 4, 1946.

THE DISMANTLEMENT OF THE BRITISH EMPIRE IN THE EAST

The British lost all their Far Eastern possessions to the Japanese. With American military aid, they recovered Burma during the war, but the other colonies were restored to them only after the Japanese surrender. Since they still had considerable naval power and troops at their disposal, they also helped the French and Dutch to begin the reconquest of their territories.

India. During the war the British sent a mission to India authorized to make many concessions short of outright independence. Since the Indian National Congress was prepared to accept nothing less, the negotiations collapsed and Congress called for a program of civil disobedience. Churchill had its leaders imprisoned for sabotaging the war effort, but when the war was over they were released since it was clear that independence must soon be granted.

If the Indians themselves could have agreed on a constitution for independence, no difficulties would have arisen. But the Muslims, led by Mohammed Ali Jinnah, were by this time determined to have a separate state of their own, which Jawarharlal Nehru, the leader of the predominantly Hindu Congress, made every attempt within his power to prevent. It was the view of Congress, and also of Gandhi, who was no longer politically active in it, that the new independent India should be a secular state in which the Muslim minority would play its part. But there was too much distrust between the two communities to make such a solution feasible. In spite of determined efforts by the British to keep the two segments of the country together, the Hindus were compelled reluctantly to accept partition. The overwhelmingly Muslim provinces were ceded to Pakistan (the new Muslim state), and the two provinces in which Muslims and Hindus were close to equal in numbers (Punjab and Bengal) were divided after plebiscites in which each community voted to join its coreligionists. The princely rulers of the "native" states which had not formed part of British India were allowed to choose whether to belong to Pakistan or India or to remain independent. With the exception of Kashmir, all eventually chose to join Pakistan or India in accordance with the religion of the majority of their subjects.

Kashmir, which is overwhelmingly Muslim in religion, had a Hindu ruler who would have preferred to remain independent. But the Pakistanis at once sent an expedition to take over the territory, whereupon the Maharajah opted to join India. Nehru, himself a Kashmiri, accepted the offer with alacrity and sent troops to hold back the Pakistanis. The province was then *de facto* divided, with the Indians in possession of most of it. The Pakistanis appealed to the United Nations, which tried to make Nehru hold a plebiscite (which at one time he promised). When late in 1965 the Pakistanis tried to take it by force, they were unsuccessful. The United Nations imposed a cease fire, but there is still no sign that the Indians will give way and hold the plebiscite.

Since independence India has been ruled by the Congress party, which has always won the elections for the central government. No changes have been made in the parliamentary system inherited from the British. Although the Indians under Nehru (who died in office in 1964) and Lal Bahadur Shastri, who succeeded him, tried hard to solve their immense social and economic problems, the constant population increase has defeated their best efforts, and the country has been greatly dependent on aid from the West, especially the United States. After the brief frontier war with China in 1962 (see p. 333) Nehru, who had tried to do without military aid from this source, and to give a lead to the neutralist nations, was compelled to accept it and to rearm, thus making his economic problems more difficult than ever to solve. Shastri died in 1966 soon after signing a limited agreement to settle the Kashmir issue peacefully in Tashkent (USSR). He was succeeded as prime minister by Nehru's daughter, Mrs. Indira Gandhi.

Pakistan for some years attempted to rule in accordance with the parliamentary constitution but gave up in 1958 when President Iskander Mirza declared martial law and handed over control of the country to General (later Field-Marshal) Mohammed Ayub Khan, who in turn deposed him three weeks later. Since then Ayub Khan has held undisputed power in the country, though he granted a new constitution in 1962 under which he was elected president. The country has made some progress under his rule. Pakistan adhered to two military pacts (CENTO and SEATO) which brought him extensive military aid from the United States. But when India, with whom he was still quarreling over Kashmir, also received aid he began to foster closer relations with Communist China. It is not yet clear how valuable these relations will prove to be or whether pressure from the United States will persuade him to abandon them.

Burma.   During the war a group of young Burmese who had despaired of being granted independence by Britain, went to Japan, where they received military and revolutionary training in the expectation that they would accompany the Japanese army when it invaded Burma. Among these was Aung San, who organized a Burma Independence Army, which aided the Japanese in consolidating their hold on the country. When the Japanese set up a puppet government in 1943 Aung San became minister of war, but when the Japanese began to lose the war he offered his services and his army to Lord Mountbatten, the British commander. When they were accepted he aided in the British reconquest, expecting to be rewarded with independence for his couutry after the war was over. At first the British had different ideas, but when Aung San organized a political party which showed that it had overwhelming strength in the country, the Labour government in Britain gave way and quickly granted independence.

While the final constitution was being discussed, Aung San and several other leading Burmese were murdered at the instigation of a political rival. Fortunately, U Nu, the second in command of the party, was absent at the time, and survived to become the first prime minister after independence. Burma decided not to join the Commonwealth and adopted a neutralist policy, remaining friends with the Chinese even after the Communist take-over. She refused also to accept any foreign aid, a policy made possible by the self-sufficiency of the country in food. Later various efforts were made by native Communists to take over the country, and the Burmese also suffered from the presence in the north of the country of Chinese Nationalist refugees, whom they were not strong enough to expel. Claiming that U Nu's government was not dealing effectively with its enemies, and also that proposals for a federal union, if brought to fruition, would break up the country, General Ne Win staged a military coup on March 2, 1962. Since that time he has ruled Burma as a virtual dictator. The popular leaders, including U Nu, have remained in custody.

Ceylon. This island to the south of the Indian subcontinent received its independence after a brief interval during which the British had tried to keep some reserved powers in their hands. It became an independent Dominion within the Commonwealth in February, 1948. The small country has been bedeviled by divisions between the majority of Sinhalese and the minority of Tamils (immigrants from India) and by the multiplicity of parties, some of them strongly Marxist and Trotskyite. For some years Ceylon was ruled by a leftist coalition led by S. W. Bandanaraike, who was succeeded by his wife, the first woman prime minister in the world. This coalition was upset in elections held in March, 1965, after which a new coalition (without the Trotskyites) under Dudley Senanayake took office, and attempted to prove that a more moderate policy would pay greater dividends and help to solve the still pressing economic and social problems of the country.

Malaya and Malaysia. Following the war the British reasserted their control over the rich Malay Peninsula, but after 1948 they were faced by a persistent "insurgency" of Communist Chinese. Few though these Communists were, they compelled the British to put forth a long military effort, which was at length successful.

The Muslim Malays, who form the majority of the people in the peninsula, aided the British in the struggle. The island of Singapore to the south of the peninsula, inhabited almost entirely by Chinese, was separated from the mainland government in 1946 and granted limited self-government in 1955. In the north the dominant Malays formed an Alliance party which included Chinese and Tamil (Indian) leaders. This party, led by the Malay prince, Tunku Abdul Rahman, won 51 of 52 seats in elections held in 1955 under a new constitution. After a further election won by the Alliance party, independence was granted in August, 1957, with Abdul Rahman as prime minister. Singapore became a separate state in 1959 under the leadership of the Chinese Lee Kuan Yew, whose People's Action party won 43 of 51 seats in the last election before the formation of the new state. However, Singapore was not yet fully independent since the British wished to safeguard their important military and naval base on the island. A Council, of which only three of the seven members were appointed by Singapore, retained responsibility for defense.

During the next years this division of Malaya into a state of Singapore and an independent country of Malaya was recognized as unsatisfactory. Singapore was by far the largest city in the country and an important seaport. But the Malays feared that they might be dominated by the slightly more numerous Chinese if Singapore were admitted to the Federation. Tunku Abdul Rahman therefore suggested that the British colonies in northern Borneo (North Borneo and Sarawak) and the protected state of Brunei, ruled by its sultan, should be included, together with Singapore, in a new Federation of Malaysia, in which the Chinese would no longer have a majority. This solution except for the inclusion of Brunei was accepted in September, 1963, when the Federation of Malaysia, with Tunku Abdul Rahman as prime minister, came into being. Singapore however, continued to enjoy internal self-government, as did the newly emancipated colonies of North Borneo (renamed Sabah) and Sarawak. The Sultan of Brunei opted to continue as a protected state outside the Federation.

The Federation of Malaysia encountered many obstacles, the most important of which was the refusal of Indonesia to recognize it—understandably enough in view of the fact that Sabah and Sarawak formed part of the large island of Borneo, the rest of which belonged to Indonesia. Since the Federation had close military ties with the British, and Indonesia objected to the British presence as a form of "neo-colonialism," she did everything possible to disrupt the Federation, including sponsoring a secession movement within northern Borneo and staging hit-and-run raids on the Malayan coast. She left the United Nations in 1965 when the Federation was elected to a seat on the Security Council. Meanwhile the Philippine Republic under President Macapagal likewise refused to recognize the Federation, since she herself claimed a legal right to a part of North Borneo. (The newly elected president of the Philippines, Ferdinand Marcos, however, is likely to reverse this decision.) Late in 1965 Singapore, dissatisfied with the Tunku's government, decided to leave the Federation and became a separate independent state. It is not yet clear what effect this will have on the rest of the Federation.

Hong Kong. Lastly Hong Kong may be briefly mentioned. This island with a small hinterland on the mainland leased from Imperial China (and due to revert to the mainland government in 1998) has remained a British colony, generally prosperous, but incapable of resisting any serious attempt by the Communist Chinese to retake it. Hitherto the Chinese have refrained from doing so, since the colony is a useful "window" on the Western world and a source of scarce foreign currency.

INDONESIA

At the end of the war the Indonesians in Java and Sumatra, with the acquiescence of the local Japanese military, proclaimed themselves independent under their own president, Sukarno. The Dutch, however, were not willing to give up their rich colony without a fight, and they at once began to make difficulties for the Republican government. The British had been given the responsibility by the Potsdam Conference (see p. 241) of supervising the Japanese surrender in some areas of the East. An Anglo-Australian expedition, accompanied by some Dutch officials, therefore proceeded to Indonesia and attempted to restore the Dutch authority in the islands, which necessarily meant disarming the Republicans. The latter, however, refused to yield, even when the Dutch began to appear in force. For their part, the Dutch were willing to make some concessions, so long as they retained their sovereignty. Several agreements were entered into, which were not fully kept by either side, and it soon became clear that the Dutch were anxious to restore all the islands to their former obedient status. When the Republicans resisted by force of arms, the United Nations took cognizance of the problem and sent out a team of negotiators. Eventually the Dutch, unable to force a victory in the face of hostile world opinion and continued resistance by the Indonesians, settled for a United States of Indonesia under the Dutch crown. But by this time the prestige and power of the Republicans were such that they were able by 1950 to throw off the remnants of Dutch rule and proclaim their complete independence as the Republic of Indonesia. Only the western half of the island of New Guinea remained under Dutch control thereafter, a constant bone of contention between the Indonesians and the Dutch. The latter finally ceded West Irian, as the Indonesians called it, in May, 1963, although a plebiscite was scheduled for 1969 in which the New Guineans, a people ethnically distinct from the Indonesians, were to choose whether or not they will remain a part of Indonesia or become independent.

Indonesia, with a population in excess of 100 million, is potentially the dominant power in Southeast Asia, especially since she has an exceptionally large army, to equip which she had to go into debt to the Soviet Union for upward of $12 billion. But Indonesia is far from a united nation. The predominance of Java, with close to two-thirds of the population of the whole country, is greatly resented by the other islands, and a prolonged rebellion by most of the latter against the central government in 1957–1958 was suppressed only with difficulty. Moreover the Chinese community, with 3 per cent of the population, owns a virtual monopoly of the commercial enterprise of the country. The one idea on which the whole nation is united is that Indonesia must be a great nation and recognized as such. For this reason Sukarno has given more attention to his foreign than to his domestic policies. This fact accounts for his imperialistic gestures (as, for example, his drive for West Irian and his opposition to Malaysia).

The domestic problems of Indonesia appear insoluble as long as the upkeep of the army requires almost four-fifths of the annual budget and while inflation is not checked. Foreign currency reserves have dwindled almost to the vanishing point. President Sukarno, who is now president for life, has tried to tread a tightrope between the power of the army and the one countervailing political force, the Communist party of Indonesia, but recent events suggest that this force has been destroyed and that the President is now the prisoner of the army. The Communist party

(PKI) was until late in 1965 the largest and best-organized political group in the country, with over three million members, and it was widely thought that it might win free elections if they were ever to be held. It backed Sukarno's official policy, which he called "guided democracy," with its five rather vague principles (Belief in God, Nationalism, International Solidarity, Popular Government, and Social Justice).

However, an apparent effort on the part of PKI either to take over the government or at least to lessen the power of the army boomeranged badly, and it is difficult to see what else could have been expected in view of the size of the army. An uprising, apparently sponsored by PKI (October 1, 1965), resulted in the murder of a number of military leaders. The army reacted by arresting Sukarno and instituting a purge of the PKI, an example which was followed throughout the country by Muslim anti-Communists. As a result it has been estimated that the party has been completely broken, and that upward of 300,000 members have been murdered or executed. Sukarno was quickly released, and he remains the head of the government and the symbol of such unity as the country possesses. But there can be little doubt that his personal power has been broken and that it will be difficult for him, ailing as he is, to recover full control of his country's policy.

THE PHILIPPINES

After independence the Philippine Republic was faced with a huge burden of reconstruction, since the Japanese had followed a scorched-earth policy in the last months of the war. This work was handled by an American-Philippine Commission, and the United States contributed more than $1 billion to the program. But too much still remained in the Philippines from the Spanish colonial period, and the problems still to be faced in many ways resembled those of Latin America discussed in the last chapter. Land reform was an urgent necessity, and outside the area of endeavor presided over by the Reconstruction Commission, the government of President Elpidio Quirino was as corrupt as any in Latin America. A rebellion was started by a group called the Hukbalahaps (Huks), which the government was unable to suppress until it received direct American support in 1950. A strong government under President Ramón Magsaysay succeeded in putting an end to the rebellion and cleaned up the government.

But Magsaysay was killed in an air crash in 1956, and the governments that succeeded his did relatively little. The Republic is still to a large degree dependent on aid and various preferences granted by the United States, and, as in Latin America, American capital predominates in the economy. The land problems are far from solved, and the Huk movement has recently shown some signs of new life.

INDOCHINA (VIETNAM)

The French, like the Dutch, returned to their colony of Indochina (actually a colony, Cochin China, and three nominal kingdoms under their own rulers, Annam and Tonkin, Laos, and Cambodia) with the British forces. They found that a "national" government of Vietnam (the local word for Indochina) had been proclaimed in the north led by a Communist, Ho Chi Minh, with the support of many non-Communist nationalists. The government had some representatives active in the south. Ho Chi Minh's government had a claim to legitimacy, at least in the north, in that the legitimate "emperor" Bao Dai had abdicated in its favor and it had won an election in the only parts of the country where voting was possible. At first the French contented themselves with taking possession of Cochin China, while recognizing the provisional government of Ho Chi Minh. Then, as they grew stronger, they decided to make no more concessions and reconquered by force of arms the greater part of the country, including the major northern cities. Ho Chi Minh therefore began a guerilla war which slowly wore down the French in spite of the presence of over 400,000 French troops in the country. The climax came early in 1954 with the capture by the guerilla army (known as the Viet Minh) of the French outpost of Dien Bien Phu.

Meanwhile the costly war had been growing increasingly unpopular in France, and serious attempts had already been made to end it. In mid-1954 a conference met at Geneva, chaired jointly by Britain and the Soviet Union. From this emerged an accord whose main provisions were that the whole of Vietnam should be temporarily divided at the 17th parallel pending unification following elections to be held in 1956. French troops were to be phased out as soon as possible, except for a few French advisers if desired, and no side was to enter into any foreign alliances. The independence of Laos and Cambodia under their respective monarchs (which had been formally granted by the French the previous years, was now officially recognized. South Vietnam was to remain under the nominal rule of Emperor Bao Dai, while North Vietnam would remain under the Viet Minh government headed by Ho.

After 1949, when the Communists took over mainland China, and especially after the Korean War (1950–1953), the United States pursued a firmer line in Southeast Asia. In pursuit of her proclaimed policy of "containment" of Communism, she gave wholehearted support to the government of Ngo Dinh Diem for several years, until his murder in 1963. This nationalist, who returned from exile in the United States in 1954 to become Bao Dai's prime minister, requested and received American military advisers and large quantities of American arms for his country. In 1955 he held a plebiscite which deposed Bao Dai and made him President of South Vietnam.

For the first four years Diem succeeded in maintaining his authority in South Vietnam. But he was no statesman. He governed South Vietnam as a feudalist; he systematically favored his fellow Catholics, and in particular his immediate family whom he placed in positions of importance. Whereas Diem and his colleagues promised for 1956 in the Geneva Agreement he refused them, regarding himself as in no way bound by agreements he had not accepted. He could always claim to have a clear title since Ho Chi Minh could not challenge his position in his own held. He was regarded by almost everybody as the smaller evil of their countries. From the beginning once North Vietnam was a popular dictatorship and it was expected that they would be absorbed.

When it became evident that the elections were to be no unifying elections for a free South Vietnam, nationalists formed a National Liberation Front and in 1960 began guerilla war against Diem. Whereas Diem had stamped the war at once against the Communists, he was quickly to "communism." Diem continued to promise reforms which he did not implement. More and more resentment in the strong centralized machinery was in the hands of his troops in the hated secret police. The Communists exploited in greater part of the countryside and set up a functioning government which they controlled. In spite of ever greater

previous year) was now officially recognized. South Vietnam was to remain under the nominal rule of Emperor Bao Dai, while North Vietnam would remain under the Viet Minh government headed by Ho.

After 1949 when the Communists took over mainland China, and especially after the Korean War (1950–1953), the United States played a leading part in Southeast Asia in pursuit of her proclaimed policy of "containment" of Communism. She gave wholehearted support to the government of Ngo Dinh Diem for several years until his murder in 1963. This nationalist, who returned from exile in the United States in 1954 to become Bao Dai's prime minister, requested and received American military advisers and vast quantities of American aid for the reconstruction of his country. In 1955 he held a plebiscite as a result of which he became president of South Vietnam, and Bao Dai went into exile.

During the next four years Diem succeeded in consolidating his rule over most of South Vietnam. But his regime was extremely oppressive and as a Catholic he systematically favored his fellow Catholics, and, in particular, his immediate family whom he placed in positions of importance. When the time came for the elections promised for 1956 in the Geneva Agreements he refused to hold them, regarding himself as in no way bound by agreements which he had not accepted. In this he was backed by the Americans, since Ho Chi Minh would surely have won the elections if they had been held. He was regarded by almost all Vietnamese, north and south, as the liberator of their country from the French. In any case North Vietnam was more populous than South Vietnam, and it was expected that he would be able to control its votes.

When it became clear that the country was not going to be reunited by elections, a group of South Vietnamese nationalists formed the National Liberation Front, and in 1959 began a guerilla war against the Diem regime. North Vietnam did not back the war at once, since it was engaged in the difficult task of trying to "communize" the country. But later it did give an undetermined amount of support, including full moral support for what it regarded as a justified "war of liberation." The NLF and its troops, known in the United States as the Viet Cong (Communist Vietnamese), during the next five years took possession of the greater part of South Vietnam and set up a functioning government in the areas they controlled, in spite of ever increasing aid given to Diem by the United States. This aid included the provision of great amounts of war supplies and large numbers of military "advisers." But Diem's regime in the process of fighting the war became so unpopular that by the time he was murdered late in 1963 in a military rebellion, scarcely anyone but the Catholics supported him politically, though the military and an unknown number of civilians continued to support the war effort. When Diem died there was no one with comparable authority capable of replacing him. The government therefore fell into the hands of different groups of military men (with a few civilian interludes) whose support in the country was minimal. They were enabled to keep power by the Americans, who could not permit the country to fall into anarchy, or allow any government to be set up which might demand their withdrawal. The South Vietnamese army, mostly conscripted from unwilling peasants, was an uncertain fighting force in spite of its modern equipment; annual desertions were of the order of 20 per cent or more.

At the beginning of 1965 the United States began to enter the war openly and to bomb North Vietnam, while at the same time building up her own ground troops in South Vietnam. Since this is the major military effort in which the United States is currently engaged, and forms a part of the "Cold War" which she has been waging against the Communist powers since 1947, it will be dealt with further in Chapter 20.

JAPAN AND KOREA

After the Japanese surrender, General Douglas MacArthur was appointed military governor of the Japanese islands, with virtually full powers to do as he saw fit during the military occupation. Although the Japanese homeland had not been overrun with foreign troops, it had suffered greatly from American "saturation" bombing, as well as from the atomic bombs dropped on Hiroshima and Nagasaki. MacArthur supervised the necessary reconstruction, and in due course handed down to the Japanese a democratic constitution. This worked so well that by 1951 the United States was willing to sign a treaty with Japan, restoring her independence with the exception that the island of Okinawa was to be retained by the United States for an undetermined period as a military and naval base. The Japanese, forbidden by their constitution to rearm, have now only "Self-Defense Forces" comprising about 250,000 men.

Japan, freed from the expense of having to keep her armed forces, set to work on developing her economy, which expanded rapidly. Before long she had again become one of the major industrial countries of the world, with a thriving export trade. Her governments have been uniformly conservative in nature, but the land reforms and other changes carried out under the Mac-Arthur proconsulship have with few exceptions been maintained.

The former Japanese colony of Korea was not so fortunate. During the war the Allied powers had decided that, after forty years' occupation by the Japanese, Korea would not be at once ready to undertake the responsibilities of self-government. The country was therefore divided into two spheres of influence by the Soviet Union (North) and the United States (South). The Soviet Union established a Communist form of government which was headed by a Moscow-trained Communist, General Kim Il Sung; while the United States, as unwilling as the Soviet Union to let a self-constituted Republican government of resistance fighters take over the country, brought back an aged anti-Japanese exile named Syngman Rhee from the United States and gave him enough backing to make sure that he won the first elections (1948). The national assembly thus elected chose Rhee as president and wrote a new democratic constitution. The North Koreans held a "Soviet-style" election the same year. The Soviet Union trained the North Korean and the United States, the South Korean armies. In 1948 and 1949 both the Soviet Union and the United States withdrew their own troops.

New elections were scheduled to be held under the constitution, but Syngman Rhee, who feared with good reason that his oppressive regime would lose them, continued to suppress his political opponents on the grounds that they were "pro-Communist," and he tried to postpone the elections as long as possible. But the United States insisted on them, and a United Nations Commission was in the country to supervise them, so that at last he gave way. Held on May 30, 1950, they resulted in a decisive defeat for Rhee, although he remained president, since the elections had been only for the national assembly. Some of the opponents of Rhee attempted to enter negotiations with North Korea in the hope of reunifying the country peacefully under a coalition government. But Rhee had the three Northern representatives who crossed the border for this purpose arrested.

On June 25, for reasons that have never satisfactorily been

explained since events seemed to be running in their favor, the North Koreans invaded the South over the 38th parallel. President Truman decided at once to send Rhee military aid, in which he was backed by the United Nations (whose Commission did not observe the beginning of hostilities but gathered its information afterward). On the basis of the report from the Commission, the United Nations Security Council (in the temporary absence of the Soviet delegation, which was boycotting the Council) authorized military aid to the South Koreans (see p. 250).

As the local leader of an international effort to resist Communist aggression, Rhee of course gained immense prestige, and while the war was on he had no further need to work with his hostile assembly. The war at first went unfavorably for the South, but the United States was soon able to send enough reinforcements to turn the tide. Indeed, not only were the North Koreans driven out of South Korea, but General MacArthur, the United States commander, then invaded North Korea, and Rhee's objective of uniting all Korea under his rule was almost achieved. But when MacArthur's troops appeared at the Chinese border (the river Yalu), Chinese "volunteers" joined the North Koreans, inflicted a severe defeat on the United Nations forces, and recaptured the capital of Seoul. However, they were in turn driven back, and a stalemate ensued, as a result of which the country was again divided at the 38th parallel (1953). It has remained divided to this day. President Rhee stayed in office until he was overthrown by a military coup in 1960, and once more driven into exile. After an interval elections were held, but the army remained the most important influence in the country.

CHINA

The Chiang Kai-shek (Kuomintang) government, although part of the victorious coalition, never succeeded in consolidating its rule over the whole country after the war. The Communists, led by Mao Tse-tung, overthrew the regime in 1949, driving Chiang and his followers over to the island of Formosa (Taiwan), where they set up a government. Backed by vast contributions from the United States, who protects it and still regards it as the government of the Republic of China, the regime has many economic and social achievements to its credit and retains its seat in the Security Council. But it has not felt strong enough to submit to evaluation by the local electorate, most of them native

Formosans who are not necessarily favorable to permanent rule by mainlanders. About half of the last assembly elected on the mainland migrated with Chiang to Formosa, and these men continue to act as Chiang's advisers and regularly elect him president of China.

The Civil War. When the Russians invaded Manchuria in the last days of the war, they met little resistance from the Japanese. After Japan surrendered, the Russians looted much of the country, but declared themselves ready to yield the area under their control to the Kuomintang government. It was not an easy task for the Nationalists to take possession of the former Japanese protectorate of "Manchukuo," since the Communists were in control of much of the area. Although Chiang eventually forced the Communists to give up some of it, their main bases in the north remained undisturbed, and it was clear enough that their long years of working with the peasants had gained them much local support.

The Communists at no time had any intention of co-operating with the Kuomintang government. In their view it had done far too little against the Japanese during the war and at times had been more interested in fighting the Communists than the Japanese (cf. the situation in Yugoslavia; see p. 286). Chiang remained no less insistent in his determination to subject the Communists to his rule. There was thus no real basis for co-operation, but General George C. Marshall was nevertheless sent by President Truman as his personal emissary with the mission of trying to bring the parties together. Marshall never achieved more than a verbal agreement between the two parties while both were maneuvering for position. The Nationalist government was duly reconstituted and Chiang elected president. But by this time (1948) it was becoming clear that the Communists were far stronger, in spite of the war materials given to Chiang by the United States (a large proportion of which indeed fell into the hands of the Communists). Many Kuomintang leaders were corrupt, and so little democracy was in evidence that President Truman at last decided it was no further use trying to help Chiang (a decision very unpopular with some sections of Congress). In October, 1948, Mao completed his conquest of Manchuria, with the capture of Mukden, its capital. By early 1949 he had taken Peiping (which he renamed Peking), and in April of the same year he took the Nationalist capital of Nanking. By the end of the year all South China had submitted, and in October Mao proclaimed the People's Republic of China, which was soon converted into a Communist state.

The People's Republic of China.   Stalin had continued to recognize the Nationalist government until the end, and it is possible to speculate that he was not too happy that Mao had been able to conquer it without his aid. There were considerable differences between Soviet (Stalinist) and Chinese Communism, even though both claimed to be the rightful heirs of Marx and Lenin. It was therefore fairly certain that eventually there would be a clash between the two Communist groups, especially in view of the long common border between the two different countries and their divergent national interests. But at the beginning of 1950 the Soviet Union had no allies aside from her satellites; NATO had already been organized; and a marriage of convenience was thus a natural outcome, for just so long as the Soviet Union could remain the senior partner. A thirty-year defensive alliance was agreed to, and the Soviet Union gave China a number of short-term credits. But the cautious Stalin refused to grant anything but loans, and the term of repayment for these loans was short; China had to begin repayment by 1954 and complete it within ten years. As a result of these arrangements, numerous Russian and satellite advisers poured into the country, and over two hundred industrial enterprises were organized by the Soviet Union.

It was, however, clear to Mao (who had expected much more than the $430,000,000 that he received in exchange for his political support) that no major reconstruction and modernization of the country could be carried out, still less the creation of a heavy industry such as he desired except at the expense of the Chinese people, who must be compelled to tighten their belts to provide the necessary capital from domestic sources. Although the entire landlord class was wiped out at the cost of some two million lives, the confiscation of their property was of little help since it had to be divided among smallholders or organized into collectives. The First Five-Year Plan (1953–1957) therefore entailed very great hardships to the people; and though it did achieve much, there were also numerous breakdowns comparable to those of the first Soviet Five-Year Plan of 1928. The necessary imports had to be paid for mostly by the sale of agricultural products abroad which were scarce at home (as was also the case in the Soviet Union in the 1930's).

When the Plan was completed Mao tried again to obtain help from the Soviet Union for a second Five-Year Plan. But he could gain nothing but ordinary commercial credits to be paid for out of current production. However, instead of modifying his plan accordingly, Mao insisted on what he called a Great Leap Forward, which was to be attained by stretching the endurance of his people to the limit and depriving them of all but the minimum of consumer goods. Serious unrest and disturbances ensued, and he was forced in the end to modify the Plan. A concomitant effort to force almost the entire agricultural population into large communes (collective enterprises through which the peasants could be subjected to effective discipline and rationing) likewise met with such resistance that it too had to be modified. By 1960 the Great Leap Forward was evidently recognized in practice as a failure. Agricultural production, partly from natural causes, dropped seriously until 1963, and huge quantities of grain had to be imported from capitalist countries. But thereafter the reported general economic progress seems to have been genuine, and the system is now working tolerably, with a few more consumer goods at last reaching the workers and peasants.

The Sino-Soviet Quarrel. Relations between China and the Soviet Union had never been truly cordial, though both sides tried for a long time to keep up appearances. The Chinese have never in their history been willing to take second place to any "barbarian" rulers, and the similarity of Communist ideologies made little difference to this tradition. The Soviet Union was well aware that Russia had made territorial gains in the last century at Chinese expense when China was weak. If now China became strong she would surely demand them back, as well as other areas which had been seized by the capitalistic nations. Very early the Soviet Union therefore abandoned her outpost of Sinkiang, which she had virtually colonized during the war, although it was indisputably Chinese territory. But more than any possible territorial claims, the major differences between the two Communist powers were over their respective claims for leadership of the world's revolutionary forces and over the insufficiency of Soviet economic aid. The first difference became acute especially after Stalin's death. Khrushchev, after all, had been only a relatively minor henchman of Stalin and was not entitled to the respect more willingly accorded to Stalin. It soon became Mao's contention that co-existence was not possible between "imperialism" and Communism (a thesis more Trotskyist than Stalinist) and that the Russian acceptance of co-existence implied that the Soviet Union was ceasing to be revolutionary and was becoming a satisfied "bourgeois" power—as was, incidentally, evidenced by her refusal to grant unlimited economic aid to a fellow revolutionary. In particular, the Soviet attitude toward debts was, in Mao's view, in the worst bourgeois tradition. Khrushchev, on the contrary, had acquired a healthy respect for the military might of the United States, and had no wish to see his country overwhelmed by it, even if he could wreak return havoc. For him co-existence was the only sane policy. When China eventually became strong enough to do without the Soviet aid and the Soviet technicians, who were withdrawn rapidly from the country after 1959, she became more confident and presented herself as a competitor for the allegiance of the Soviet satellites (winning, however only poverty-stricken Albania) and of the neutrals, to whom she even offered economic aid that she could ill afford. The quarrel has been growing ever more acute in recent years and even under the Kosygin-Brezhnev leadership in the Soviet Union has shown no signs of abating.

The United States has never recognized the People's Republic of China, and ever since Chinese intervention in the Korean War the two countries have been more or less open enemies. Without American opposition it is certain that the PRC would long ago have been admitted into the United Nations. (More will be said on this subject in Chapter 20.) With India, China had fairly friendly relations until the Himalayan War in 1962 (see p. 318). In spite of the fact that China did not pursue her advantage, withdrawing her troops from all but the disputed territory after her military victory, India changed her attitude and accepted aid from the United States in the hope that she could offer more resistance if the aggression were renewed. China then offered friendship and aid (including economic aid) to Pakistan, India's perennial enemy. At the Bandoeng Conference of "uncommitted" nations held in 1955, Chinese Premier Chou En-lai won a great personal success and much prestige for his country. But since that time China has known few diplomatic successes. The combination of verbal bellicosity and cautious behavior, notably in the Vietnamese War, is not especially impressive, even to her fellow Communists in the "Third World," though her detonation of an atomic device has won some respect for her scientific achievements. But as the largest nation in the world under a single unified government, with the largest army and the greatest number of reserves, she can hardly be neglected in the future, as she was during the period of her weakness in the late nineteenth and early twentieth centuries.

18 WESTERN ASIA, EGYPT, AND THE EASTERN MEDITERRANEAN

At the end of World War II, Egypt, who was to provide much of the leadership for the postwar Arab world, was temporarily occupied by the Allied powers, as was much of the rest of North Africa. Iran was partly occupied, while the Near Eastern League of Nations mandates were not yet independent, with the exception of Iraq. Only Turkey had maintained both neutrality (until 1945) and independence during the recent war.

EGYPT AND THE FORMER NEAR EASTERN MANDATES

These independent countries of the Near East will be dealt with together here because since the Egyptian revolution of 1952 all the states have in some degree been influenced by Egypt and Egyptian policies. Egypt, indeed, still bears the official title of the United Arab Republic as a heritage of the short-lived (1958–1961) union between Egypt and Syria, which may yet be revived in more auspicious circumstances. However, we shall speak here of Egypt to distinguish it from Syria which will be dealt with separately.

Egypt. The British forces which occupied Egypt during the war left soon afterward (1946) except for troops occupied in guarding the Suez Canal under the treaty of 1936 (see p. 203). This treaty the Egyptians wished to revise, but the British refused to do so. A persistent problem in the postwar years was the future of the so-called Anglo-Egyptian Sudan, which King Farouk I and all his governments insisted should be returned to solely Egyptian authority. The British, however, preferred to lead the Sudan toward independence, especially after elections held in 1948 pro-

335

duced an anti-Egyptian majority. Eventually, in 1953, President Mahommed Naguib accepted the inevitable, and after further elections the Sudan became independent in 1956. When Naguib withdrew his opposition to the British solution for the Sudan, an agreement became possible on the question of British withdrawal of troops from the Canal area. The troops were withdrawn in June, 1956.

Meanwhile Farouk's government had been overthrown by a military coup, led by Colonel Gamal Nasser and a number of young reformist officers, together with an older officer, General Naguib (July, 1952). The following year Naguib became president, but he was forced out of office in 1954, Colonel Nasser then became president, a position he has held to this time. Military men have continued to hold most of the important posts in his government, but in recent years an Arab Socialist Union has been permitted to function as a political party, backed by the government. No opposition party as yet exists, and all effective authority is concentrated in the hands of the President.

Nasser has attempted to provide leadership for the entire Arab world. He has much the largest and best-equipped army among the Arab states, and the most influential Muslim university is in Cairo. The powerful Cairo radio has sounded clarion calls to all the Arab nations. Its propaganda, unmatched in any of the other states, is beamed to the other African countries, in whose affairs Nasser has also been active. He has constantly proclaimed the unity of the Arab world, but such unity is intended to come about only under his leadership. He has to a large degree placed his own still underdeveloped and grossly overpopulated country under a socialist regime, having nationalized the greater part of Egyptian industry in 1961. He has had some support from the Soviet Union, who provided most of the equipment for his army and undertook to build the Aswan Dam when the Western powers withdrew their offer to do so in 1956. But Nasser's policy remains strictly neutralist, and he has shown himself adept at playing the Soviet Union against the United States, turning to one for support when the other refuses. His socialist policies, however, have come up against the similar but somewhat more radical policies of the one international socialist Arab party, the Baath. This party has some support in several Arab countries, though its headquarters is in Syria, which it has been ruled at times during the postwar years.

The main unifying force in all Arab countries is opposition to the state of Israel which came into existence in 1948. This touched off a war in which the newly established state came off victorious, winning in fact more land than it had been granted by the United Nations, under whose auspices the state was formed. In 1956, when the United States finally decided not to support the building of the Aswan Dam, Egypt retorted by nationalizing the Suez Canal. After a period of desultory negotiations, the British and French launched an expedition against Egypt; the objective seems to have been the overthrow of Nasser's government. The French, indeed, were motivated less by their interest in the Canal than by Nasser's assistance to the Algerian rebels, whom they were trying to subdue. At the same moment the Israelis, who had for years been subjected to hit-and-run raids over the borders by the Egyptians, themselves sent their armies against Egypt. Once again the Egyptians were severely defeated by the Israelis, but the United States and the Soviet Union, acting together in the United Nations Security Council, compelled a cease fire, and the Anglo-French forces were withdrawn. The Israelis also retreated behind their frontiers, but they had made their point, and the raids were not renewed. A United Nations peace-keeping force patrolled the frontiers and cared for the refugees.

In spite of the growing strength of his army, Nasser has not yet decided to engage the Israelis again, although he has convened various conferences of the Arab nations looking toward a joint attack. Much of his army was occupied for three years in Yemen, where a revolution broke out in 1962, headed by General Abdullah al-Sallal. Though the Imam of Yemen was driven from his capital, he was not fully defeated and, backed by King Feisal of Saudi Arabia, continued to resist, until August, 1965. In that month Feisal entered into an agreement with Sallal and Nasser, under which Egyptian troops were to be withdrawn within ten months and a coalition government was to be formed in Yemen.

The union with Syria, already referred to, was the result of a request by the Syrian government of the day, which for the time was led by admirers of President Nasser. But it was never a happy union, in large measure because the Syrians desired a collective leadership, whereas Nasser intended to act as the senior partner and make all major decisions. However, "Nasserites" are still present in large numbers in Syria, as they are also in Iraq, which under its present leadership has undertaken to enter into a closer relationship with Egypt. This could lead to another attempt at Arab unity, although it would be somewhat impracticable unless Syria joined also. Prospects of uniting with Lebanon, the tiny state to the west of Syria, in which Christian and Muslim Arabs are almost equal in numbers, and with Jordan under its Hashemite monarch, remain slim.

The Former French Mandates. Syria and Lebanon were both granted their full independence immediately after the war. By a kind of "gentlemen's agreement" the Lebanese president was to be a Christian with the prime minister a Muslim. In 1958 it was widely believed that President Camille Chamoun was intending to have himself re-elected for another term after having had the constitution changed by the Chamber of Deputies. The latter was favorable to his aspirations since it had just been elected itself (fraudulently, its opponents claimed). When an uprising in May of that year threatened his position, Chamoun appealed to the United States for support in accordance with the so-called "Eisenhower Doctrine" (see p. 371). The State Department, doubtful whether the Doctrine was applicable, temporized until the revolution broke out in Iraq which claimed as its victims both the King and his prime minister Nuri as-Said. Uncertain what this might portend, President Eisenhower sent to Lebanon a large contingent of marines, who found they had nothing to do (they were greeted with American soft drinks offered even in the ocean by Lebanese traders). A few months later the marines were withdrawn. By this time Chamoun had stepped down, and an opposition deputy had been appointed prime minister.

Syria has been plagued throughout its period of independence by numerous military coups and has enjoyed little stable government. The union with Egypt collapsed in 1961; thereafter all governments were short-lived. The government was overthrown in December, 1965, by the army, which appointed Salah Bitar as prime minister.

The Former British Mandates. Iraq became independent in the interwar period (see p. 200), but British influence continued strong. A move to overthrow the regime in 1941 resulted in direct British military intervention. After the war Nuri as-Said, a friend of the British, was the effective ruler of the country through his control of the electoral process. As prime minister, he sponsored a considerable amount of social and economic reform and used most of the oil royalties accruing to Iraq for the purpose. But his regime was unpopular, and he was overthrown and murdered in 1958 in a revolution led by Abdul Karim Kassem, who ruled as virtual dictator until 1963. For a period in his regime the Communists were actively supporting him, but he later put an end to their activities. In 1963 he was murdered by dissident officers in alliance with the Baath party, and for some months a Baath government attempted to rule. Before the end of 1963 the regime was overthrown in a military coup led by Colonel (later Marshal) Abdul Salam Aref, who had been made president by the Baath but was allowed little power. Since that time the country has been under a tight military dictatorship.

Relatively little progress has been made in the country since the Kassem revolution, but Aref followed a modified "Nasserite" policy, nationalizing the major banks and larger private enterprises, and he announced a Five-Year Plan for development (1965–1969). He appeared to be interested in converting Iraq into a state not unlike Egypt with the intention of uniting the two countries when the time appears suitable. When he was killed in a plane crash in April, 1966, he was succeeded by his brother, whose policies were much the same.

The former mandate of Transjordania was converted soon after the war (March, 1946) into an independent state whose name was changed in 1949 to the Hashemite Kingdom of Jordan (after the name of the ruling dynasty). Its king, the former Emir Abdullah, was expected to be a constitutional monarch. But both Abdullah, who was assassinated in 1951, and his son Hussein, who succeeded to the throne on May 2, 1953, maintained most of the authority in their own hands. For many years the British kept up the armed forces of the country, especially the Arab Legion, an effective body of fighting men which played an important part in the 1948 war against Israel. Contrary to the wishes of other Arab rulers, who were still hoping for a Palestinian Arab state, King Abdullah annexed that part of Palestine that he controlled west of the Jordan River (1950). The British again sent troops to Jordan after the American intervention in Lebanon in 1958. For a few months in 1958 Jordan united with Iraq under the Hashemite king of that country, but the union was dissolved after the Iraqi revolution.

After the war the British were unable to maintain their rule in Israel owing to the opposition of both Arabs and Jews. Britain turned the problem over to the United Nations, whose General

Assembly, against the wishes of the Arab rulers, voted for partition. But when a war between the Arabs and Jews became imminent, the United Nations began to waver. The Jews therefore took matters into their own hands and declared their independence under the name of Israel. The announced policy of the new state was "the ingathering of the exiles," in other words unlimited immigration of Jews, who could at once become Israeli citizens. A United Nations commission attempted to mediate the war which followed, and policed the cease fire when at last it came into effect.

The state of Israel, the only real democracy in the area, has been ruled ever since independence by a socialist coalition, led for most of the period by David Ben-Gurion. She has been forced to maintain a strong army for the whole period of her existence as a protection against hostile Arab neighbors, especially Egypt and Syria. The present prime minister is Levi Eshkol, under whose leadership immense efforts have been made to develop the desert territories and bring water to them, both from the Jordan and from the Sea of Galilee. This policy has led to increasing tension, since Syria, in particular, feels that it is her water that is being diverted, and various plans have been put forward to cut off the water from Israel. As yet Israel has been able to carry out her policy without having to encounter serious armed opposition. But in view of the increased strength of the Arab armies, especially the Egyptian army, the situation remains dangerous.

Lastly, mention should be made of the British colony of Aden and the British-protected states of South Arabia. Aden experienced much disturbance because of the large number of immigrants from Yemen who worked in the oil refineries in the colony but were systematically excluded from voting when the time came for Aden to move toward internal self-government. Yemen itself, both under the former Imam and under the present revolutionary government, laid claims to the colony, Britain, however, preferred to attach Aden to the semi-independent sheikdoms to the east, and formed a Federation of South Arabia, which included Aden, in 1963. Independence has also been promised for the near future, but it remains to be seen whether this artificial arrangement can be carried to fulfillment. The Persian Gulf sheikdom of Kuwait, rich in oil, which at one time was protected by British arms, became an independent state in 1962 and associated itself closely with the Arab world, which it has aided from its oil revenues.

INDEPENDENT STATES OF WESTERN ASIA

There are three major states of western Asia which were independent before the war: Saudi Arabia, Iran, and Turkey. Saudi Arabia has remained an absolute monarchy, now under King Feisal, who dethroned his elder brother, the somewhat ineffective King Saud II, in November, 1964. Feisal has given little power to his ministers but is using his vast oil revenues for the first time with some effect for the purpose of modernizing his country.

Iran (Persia). As long ago as 1906 the Shah of Persia (as the country was called at that time) granted a constitution and undertook to rule as a constitutional monarch. A National Assembly (the *Majlis*) was brought into being, together with a Senate, half of whose members were appointed by the shah. The constitution was amended in 1949 to permit the shah to dissolve it. But the Majlis has continued to sit, and in the early 1950's it appeared for a time that it could keep even the shah under control. After the war the Russians occupied much of northern Iran, while the Western powers, especially the British, who had rich oil concessions, were influential elsewhere in the country. At first the Russians were unwilling to leave the area they controlled. Then an oil agreement was signed, and they withdrew. But the Majlis, which had been elected on a program calling for ratification of the Soviet treaty, then refused to ratify it under pressure from the United States. Thereafter Iran accepted military and economic aid from the United States.

In 1951 Prime Minister Mohammed Mossadegh, a radical nationalist, declared his intention of nationalizing the oil industry, thus bringing on a quarrel with the predominantly British Anglo-Iranian Oil Company, which accepted an agreement to pay higher royalties but would not submit to nationalization. Mossadegh, backed by a large majority in the Majlis, then nationalized the industry, whereupon the British closed down the refinery (the largest in the world); when the Iranians succeeded in producing some oil themselves, all the major oil companies in the world boycotted it. The quarrel dragged on for more than two years, leading to increasing violence in Iran. Mossadegh's government became ever more authoritarian and tyrannical at home, ruling by decree without further reference to the Majlis. He abolished the Senate.

In August, 1953, Shah Reza Pahlevi II dismissed the Prime Minister, but Mossadegh refused to accept his dismissal, in which defiance he seemed to have the support of the army. The Shah and his family then left the country, but an internal revolt in the army brought to the fore another group of officers. This group arrested Mossadegh and invited the Shah to return. Since that time the Shah has been virtually absolute, backed by an army which he has favored and which remains loyal to him. He has put into effect a thoroughgoing program of modernization of the country, in the process exciting much opposition from landowners and others affected by the program. It is still too soon to say whether this revolution imposed from above will succeed, and whether the Shah can keep under control the numerous opposition groups in the country—which include both the conservatives who oppose the reforms and the democrats and left-wing elements who demand the restoration of constitutional government.

Turkey. During the rule of Kemal Atatürk (see p. 128) there was no serious opposition to the government, and the sole political party was one created by the dictator (Republican People's party). After the war Kemal's successor, General Ismet Inönu, was still president, and the regime was more presidential than parliamentary. This situation changed with the elections of 1950, which were won decisively by the relatively new Democratic party, led by Adnan Menderes, who became prime minister, while another member of his party became president. Menderes' government was devoted to the improvement of the economic status of the country through the encouragement of private enterprise, and it had several important achievements in this field, though at the cost of a serious inflation. Political opposition was controlled by stringent laws against the press, and the government became increasingly authoritarian, though it continued to win elections. In May, 1960, a bloodless military coup overthrew it, and Menderes was later convicted of subverting the constitution and hanged. The military government had a new constitution prepared which was accepted in July, 1961. Thereafter elections were held (October) and RPP won a plurality. Former President Inönu became prime minister, leaving the presidency to General Cemal Gursel, leader of the military junta.

But the followers of Menderes were not content with the new arrangements. Many of them helped in the formation of a new Justice party which, like the former Democratic party, favored economic reforms under private enterprise in preference to the system of state-directed enterprise inherited from the time of Kemal. In February, 1965, the Inönu government was forced to resign after an adverse vote on the budget. It gave place to another minority government headed by Suat Hayri Urguplu. This government attempted to improve relations with the Soviet Union, though it continued to co-operate with NATO, to which Turkey belonged, and CENTO (a defensive alliance, which united Britain, Turkey, Iraq, Iran, and Pakistan, following the signature of the Bagdad Pact in 1955). The Justice party won a decisive victory in new elections held in October, 1965 (260 of 450 seats), and its leader, Suleyman Demirel, became prime minister. Thus for the first time since 1960 a government has been formed which can look forward to a period of stable rule.

CYPRUS

Although Cyprus has a population which is more than two-thirds Greek, it is far closer geographically to Turkey than to Greece, and there is an important Turkish minority on the island, dating from the period when it formed part of the Ottoman Empire. The Greeks have been trying for more than a century to bring the Cypriotes under their rule as part of a program for uniting all Greeks under a single government (*Enosis*). They have failed in Cyprus because of the continued presence of the Turkish minority which detests the notion of being ruled by Greeks. After World War II Cyprus was still a British colony, but the Greeks made the position of the British impossible by organizing an armed rebellion which they could never fully suppress, even though they temporarily exiled the Greek Cypriot leader, Archbishop Makarios.

In early 1959 the Greek and Turkish mainland governments decided that the problem must be settled and agreed to a constitution under which the island could become independent. Makarios, under severe pressure, agreed to the plan, and Cyprus became independent in 1960. But the constitution, which called for the presence of Greek and Turkish troops on the island and gave both Greek and Turkish Cypriotes the right to veto all measures that affected them, proved unworkable. Armed hostilities broke out in 1963, which still have not been settled, in spite of the presence of a United Nations peace-keeping force. The conflict has greatly embittered relations between the Turks and Greeks, who are both members of NATO. The other NATO powers have been unable to solve the problem. The two communities on the island are not geographically separated, and so partition (favored by the Turks) has not as yet been thought possible, since it would necessitate removing members of both communities from their homes.

CONCLUSION

The areas considered in this chapter constitute a continuing problem for the world. In spite of the efforts of Egyptian President Nasser and the uniform hostility to Israel, Arab unity seems as far away as ever, and an Islamic superstate seems out of the question for the near future, even though there may be some lesser unions, which could conceivably become permanent. But there is little in common between, say, Turkey or Iran and Egypt —not even Islam, which takes different forms in the different countries. Some of the nations are monarchies, while others are revolutionary republics. The area is therefore likely to continue to be disturbed. But in spite of various Soviet efforts under Nikita Khrushchev to play a leading role in the area, it is not the Cold War that causes the divisions, and even a settlement of the Cold War will not solve the problems.

19   THE END OF COLONIALISM IN AFRICA

Perhaps the most revolutionary of all postwar changes has been the abandonment by the Western powers of almost all their African colonies. Prior to World War II only Liberia and the Union of South Africa were independent, though recently conquered Ethiopia was restored to its independence during the war. By the end of 1965 every country north of the Zambesi River except Portuguese Guinea was under an indigenous African government. South of the river the Portuguese still retained their prewar colonies, but Rhodesia under its white minority had declared itself independent contrary to the wishes of Great Britain, while the remaining British colonies were enjoying substantial self-government and had been promised their independence. In all the Portuguese colonies there are active rebellions which have been held in check at considerable cost up to the present time. In the Republic of South Africa the white minority has hitherto had little difficulty in keeping its black majority under control (even in the former League of Nations mandated territory of South-West Africa), and no major change can be expected for the near future.

NORTH AFRICA

The French protectorates of Morocco and Tunisia won their independence in 1956, in spite of French efforts to keep them. In these the persecution of nationalist leaders (including the exile of the Moroccan Sultan and the periodic imprisonment of the chief Tunisian nationalist, Habib Bourguiba) proved insufficient to halt the movement. The former Italian colonies of Tripolitania and Cyrenaica, taken from Turkey just before World War I, were not restored to Italy in early 1951 after World War II. After a period of tutelage under the United Nations, they became two provinces of a new independent state of Libya, headed by King Idris I as a constitutional monarch. Algeria, held by the French for over a century and regarded as a province of France, achieved independence only after a long and bitter war (1954–1962).

Tunisia. The postwar system of the French Union, which will be discussed later (see p. 352), was not regarded as applicable to the protectorates of Tunisia and Morocco, whose relations with France were regulated by the original protectorate treaties. As early as 1922 Tunisia had been given a consultative assembly, of which half the members were French and half Tunisian. However, the French members in fact dominated the assembly, and Habib Bourguiba and his Neo-Destour party were usually proscribed. After the war it was a long time before the French were willing to make further concessions. In Tunisia, as elsewhere in French North Africa, it was the French colonists in the country (*colons*) who led the opposition to any concessions. In 1952 the nationalists appealed to the United Nations, which considered the Tunisian question. In December of that year in the absence of the French, who regarded the discussion as beyond the powers of the United Nations, the General Assembly recommended bilateral negotiations. But nothing was done, and the French government took strong measures against the rebellious nationalists who sponsored several minor uprisings. In 1954 French Premier Pierre Mendès-France began negotiations which resulted in an agreement the following year under which internal self-government was granted. In 1956 this was converted into independence, although the French were allowed to continue using their naval base of Bizerte. Bourguiba became president of Tunisia, an office he has held to this day. When the French refused to promise a date for the evacuation of Bizerte, Bourguiba sponsored direct action against them in the base area. Although the French at first resisted, they eventually withdrew in exchange for an agreement over compensation (1963).

Morocco. The powers of the sultan of Morocco were more real than those of the nominal ruler of Tunisia, the bey. After the war Sultan Mohammed V became a pronounced nationalist himself and gave his support to the nationalist Istiqlal party. Following a political strike in 1952, in the course of which several hundred persons were killed by the police, the Sultan was kidnapped from his palace and exiled. This experience made him into a genuine

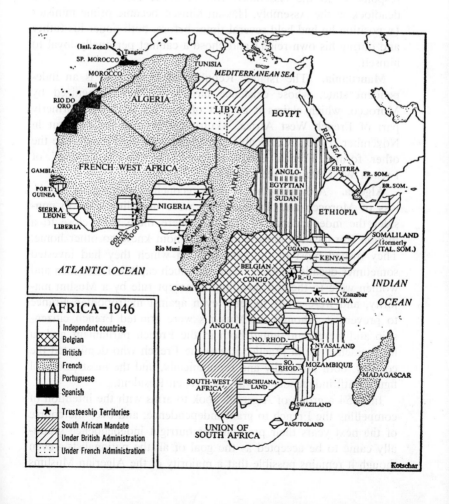

AFRICA—1946

Independent countries
Belgian
British
French
Portuguese
Spanish
★ Trusteeship Territories
South African Mandate
Under British Administration
Under French Administration

Kotschar

national hero, and the puppet ruler whom the French installed in his place owed such authority as he had entirely to the French army. Although the United Nations took cognizance of the case, it was not until 1955 that the French came to realize they could not hold Morocco indefinitely by such means. The protectorate became an independent kingdom in 1956 (adding most of the Spanish Moroccan territories by agreement with President Franco).

King Mohammed died in 1961, and was succeeded by his son, Hassan II, who at last promulgated a constitution long promised by his father. When elections were held in May, 1963, Hassan became a constitutional monarch, and the prime minister became responsible to the Assembly. But in June, 1965, in face of a deadlock in the Assembly, Hassan himself became prime minister (a position he had held several times before, both under his father and during his own reign) and chose a cabinet personally loyal to himself.

Mauritania. The Islamic Republic of Mauritania is an independent state, whose existence has never been recognized by Morocco, which claims it as part of its own territory. Formerly part of French West Africa, Mauritania became independent in November, 1960, by amicable agreement with the French, like the other former French Union territories in the "federation" of French West Africa (see below).

Algeria. Although the French reconciled themselves to the loss of Morocco and Tunisia, they were unwilling even to consider the independence of Algeria, where there were close to a million European colonists, many of whom knew no other home. They owned most of the best land, in which they had invested sometimes decades of their labor and much capital. These men and women were to the end unwilling to accept rule by a Muslim majority, and were ready to rebel even against metropolitan France to prevent it. Though the Muslims were granted French citizenship and were represented both in the French parliament and in local assemblies, in practice it was the French who dominated the country, both politically and economically, and the most powerful figure until independence was the French Resident.

In 1954 a group of Algerians took to arms with the intention of compelling the French to grant independence, and over the course of the next years their program for outright independence gradually came to be accepted as the goal of all the nationalists—even though it remains possible that a majority of the Algerian Muslims would have preferred internal self-government in union with France if they had ever been permitted to vote on it. But the French were far too late in offering substantial concessions, and the war was waged with so much ferocity on both sides that no alternative could be considered. When the colons and a sector of the army came to believe that the Fourth French Republic would come to terms with the nationalists, they staged a rebellion, as a result of which General de Gaulle came to power, and the Fourth Republic itself came to an end (1958). But even de Gaulle could not subdue the nationalists, though by very careful tactics he restored the army to its obedience. When he agreed to Algerian independence the colons resorted to terrorism, but the only result was that their position became untenable after independence. The vast majority of them had to abandon their lands and return to France or go elsewhere.

Algeria became independent in July, 1962, and after a brief struggle with his fellow nationalists, Ahmed ben Bella became president and virtual dictator of the country. He leaned strongly toward the Soviet bloc, and won some aid even from the Communist Chinese, at the same time trying to constitute himself the champion of all the remaining African nationalist movements. But he had little success in solving the domestic problems arising out of the long war with the French, and he was ousted in June, 1965, by his minister of defense, Colonel Houari Boumedienne, who thereafter tried to improve his relations with the West, even while not as yet repudiating the revolutionary policies that had marked the regime of his predecessor.

WEST AFRICA

West Africa was partitioned in the nineteenth century by the British, French, and Germans. The Germans lost their two West African colonies of Togo and Kamerun after World War I. Both became Class B League of Nations mandates and were divided unequally between the British and the French, the latter taking the larger share. These two territories (which were trust territories under the United Nations) became independent, like all the other West African colonies, in the years between 1957 and 1965 with relatively little acrimony.

Ghana. The path to independence was blazed by the Gold Coast, in which leadership was provided by a young nationalist, Kwame Nkrumah. The British had not intended to grant self-government as early as the nationalists proposed, but their hand was forced by Nkhrumah, who used the vantage point of secretary of a rather conservative party to found the more radical Convention People's party with mass participation. When the British handed down a constitution under which it was expected that leadership would be provided by traditional chiefs, Nkrumah (who was in jail for sedition at the time) won almost all the seats available for direct election, making it impossible for anyone to govern without his agreement (1951). The British therefore accepted the inevitable and made him Leader of Government Business and later prime minister, at the head of a government with an over-all majority in the Legislative Council. When he showed himself capable of governing, they granted first internal self-government and then outright independence (March, 1957).

At first the new nation (renamed Ghana) accepted Queen Elizabeth as monarch, but in 1960 it became a republic within the Commonwealth. Nkrumah became president under a new constitution that gave him considerable powers as president, while he was in fact virtually absolute as head of the only party of substance in the country. Ghana has attempted to give a lead to all the black African nations, and Nkrumah wielded much influence in the period before the other colonies had won their independence. But Ghana, though relatively prosperous and one of the best governed of African states, was too small to exercise either power or influence on the scale desired by her president; and the supression of political opposition within the country was viewed with disfavor in the West. Several attempts were made on Nkrumah's life, and at last a coup was carried out by the army in March, 1966, while the President was abroad. Since the coup proved very popular, and it was revealed that Nkrumah had amassed a vast private fortune at the expense of his country, it is unlikely that he will be permitted to return. Meanwhile President Sékou Touré of Guinea proclaimed Nkrumah co-president of Guinea, where he received asylum, though as far as is known this title remains honorific.

Nigeria. The most populous of African nations, Nigeria is a federation, whose component peoples are held together somewhat artificially by its constitution. It is still far from certain that a state which is the fortuitous result of nineteenth-century imperialism can survive intact in the long run. Nigeria, which became independent in October, 1960, could have achieved independence long before, if it had been able to solve its internal problems. The leading people in Western Nigeria are the Yoruba, in Eastern Nigeria the Ibo; and in the north the Muslim Hausa and Fulani still are to a large degree dominated by traditional Islam and its chiefs. Nevertheless, the population of the north exceeds that of all the other areas combined—a fact which is resented by the more energetic and better-educated southern peoples. The result was that the Eastern and Western Regions received internal self-government from the British before the Northern Region; but the latter was able to dominate the federal government and supply its prime minister until he was murdered in a military coup in January, 1966. Until this event the North always entered into electoral compacts with the East, and the two Regions provided the federal government with secure majorities. But this situation deeply angered the leaders in the West, especially when the federal government used its power to excise a new Region from the Western territories, and backed opponents of the popular Western premier, Chief Awolowo, who accused him of treason and had him imprisoned. Late in 1965 there were so many disorders in the Western Region that it began to appear that the federal government was losing control of the country, and the army decided to dispense with the civilian regime altogether. In a sudden coup a group of rebels murdered several important leaders, including the Prime Minister and the Premier of the Northern Region. President Azikiwe was deposed, and the office was assumed by Major General Johnson Aguiyi-Ironsi, commander in chief of the army.

The Smaller British Colonies.   Sierra Leone, originally founded as a haven for freed slaves, moved fairly smoothly toward independence under the leadership of Sir Milton Margai, in spite of quite acute divisions between the descendants of the former slaves and the less developed hinterland from which Margai himself came. The country became independent in April, 1961, with Margai as prime minister (he was succeeded on his death in April, 1964, by his brother Arthur, formerly his political opponent). Independence was delayed in the small colony of Gambia until February, 1965, largely because of the extremely artificial nature of the "country," an enclave completely surrounded by the French-speaking state of Senegal. Unable at any time to pay its way through its own resources, Gambia became a republic one year after independence and negotiations have been opened with Senegal looking toward a closer union.

French West Africa. The former colonies of Senegal, French Soudan (renamed Mali after independence), Guinea, Ivory Coast, Upper Volta, Dahomey, and Niger formed with Mauritania the so-called "Federation" of French West Africa until 1957. Thereafter they rapidly became independent as separate states, joined only by a customs union. They will be dealt with together here because under the French system reforms were granted to all colonies at the same time. Immediately after World War II a new system was instituted called the French Union, under which a consultative Grand Council was set up for the whole of French West Africa (FWA) in which all the colonies were represented. The Council had little power but was given some tasks in regard to the whole Federation. In each colony there was a local territorial council elected by two separate colleges, one composed of French citizens, the other of Africans. Each colony was also represented in the French parliament by deputies chosen in the same way.

In 1956 a considerable step forward was taken by the passing of an enabling act (*loi-cadre*), in the framing of which leading Africans in the French parliament played an important part. Under the *loi-cadre,* which came into effect in 1957, the "Federations" of French West Africa and of French Equatorial Africa were dissolved, and became simply Groups of Territories. The dual colleges were abolished and territorial councils were elected by universal suffrage. Each council now had an African vice-president and a French president. Soon after de Gaulle came to power in May, 1958, the French presidents were retired, leaving the Africans to become presidents of the councils (the equivalent of prime ministers). In September, 1958, all the colonies voted on a new French constitution under which they could choose between immediate independence and becoming part of the "French Community," in which each colony would have full internal self-government. All except Guinea voted to join the new Community (the most important feature of which for the Africans was the fact that French financial aid would be continued).

Guinea, led by Sékou Touré, who advised a "No" vote on the constitution, at once became independent, but had to suffer the financial consequences of the sudden breaking of economic relations with France. With the aid of other countries, especially the Soviet bloc, she survived. In part as a result of this demonstration, Senegal and Mali formed a federation between themselves and demanded outright independence as the Federation of Mali. This was granted in exchange for a treaty of mutual defense, and French economic aid continued. The other territories thereupon asked for independence as separate nations, and this was likewise conceded, bringing the new Community to a virtual end. All became independent and joined the United Nations in the course of 1960. The Federation of Mali did not long survive independence and was dissolved before the end of 1960. A new union between Mali (the separate state that dated from the dissolution of the Federation), Guinea, and Ghana likewise proved abortive and was dissolved. Most of the independent nations of the former FWA have been fairly stable, and the original presidents have remained in office. The most notable exceptions have been Dahomey, where the army has several times taken a hand in making and unmaking presidents, and Upper Volta, whose president was deposed by the army early in 1966.

French Equatorial Africa. The four colonies of French Equatorial Africa—Chad, Gabon, Ubangi-Shari, and the Middle Congo —followed a similar path to independence. In the process Ubangi-Shari became the independent state of the Central African Republic, and the Middle Congo became the Republic of the Congo, usually known as the Republic of the Congo (Brazzaville) to distinguish it from the former Belgian Congo which took the same name (to which is usually appended the name of the capital, Léopoldville). No difficulties were experienced by these colonies in winning their independence, but a revolution in the Congo resulted in a marked swing to the left and the deposition of former President Fulbert Youlou. President Dacko of the Central African Republic maintained his position until he was overthrown by the army late in 1965. President Leon M'ba of Gabon was likewise overthrown in a coup in February, 1964, but he was restored to power by the French army, whose aid was solicited by the government. The government of Chad has been unstable, but it has survived under the presidency of François Tombalbaye.

United Nations Trust Territories. The two former German colonies of Togo and Kamerun were divided, as noted earlier, at the end of World War I. The British-administered western sectors of both territories were not given separate governments, but were joined to the Gold Coast and Nigeria, respectively. Just before the former became independent a plebiscite was held by the United Nations, and the Togolese voted to join Ghana at independence—

though a substantial minority, mostly from the Ewe tribe, voted against the proposal. This minority would have preferred to join their fellow Ewes in French-administered Togoland. But this territory was not yet independent, and thus no choice was offered in the plebiscite. The French administered their sector of Togoland separately from their West African colonies and made preparations for an eventual independence somewhat earlier than in them. When they proposed a constitution under which they themselves would have retained the substance of power, the United Nations refused to accept it as the fulfillment of the terms of the trust agreement. But the French went ahead and for the first time permitted truly free elections, as a result of which the nationalist Ewe leader Sylvanus Olympio came to power. Soon afterward France granted full independence and the trust agreement was terminated (April, 1960). President Sylvanus Olympio was assassinated in January, 1963, and was replaced by Nicholas Grunitsky, his predecessor in office under the French.

The British sector of Kamerun (Cameroons) was permitted to decide whether or not to join Nigeria or the newly independent state of Cameroun, the former French trust territory. As a result of this plebiscite the northern part was united with Nigeria, while the southern part chose to join Cameroun. In view of the fact that the peoples of southern Cameroons spoke English as their sole Western language, this sector of the country entered into a federal relationship with the larger French-speaking sector, and it maintains a degree of self-government. In French Cameroun the path to independence was not so smooth as in other French West African territories. A strongly leftist party which had caused some disturbances during an election was outlawed and thereafter took to guerilla warfare. However, this was not allowed to interfere with the granting of independence, though the party itself was not permitted to take part in elections until after independence. As a result the dominant party, led by Ahmadou Ahidjo, won the postindependence elections without difficulty, and he has remained in office as president.

CENTRAL AFRICA

Central Africa is usually regarded as comprising two of the territories of former French Equatorial Africa already dealt with; the three states of the former Federation of Rhodesia and Nyasaland; the Democratic Republic of the Congo (Léopoldville);

and the former Belgian trust territories of Ruanda and Urundi (now the independent states of Rwanda and Burundi). Although all these are now independent (Rhodesia under a white minority), nowhere was independence easy to come by, and all have experienced difficulties since independence.

Federation of Rhodesia and Nyasaland. This Federation, formed by the British in 1953, comprised the three territories of Southern Rhodesia, a self-governing colony, and the protectorates of Northern Rhodesia and Nyasaland. Southern Rhodesia had been ruled since 1923 by its white settlers; Northern Rhodesia and Nyasaland were ruled by the British, with a very limited African participation. The Africans in all three states objected very strongly to being included in the Federation (which they believed, quite correctly, would be dominated by the white settlers of Southern Rhodesia), but were unable to prevent it. However, as a result of riots in Nyasaland in 1959, led by Dr. Hastings Banda (who was briefly imprisoned), the British decided that this territory, which was poor and lacking in valuable minerals, should be given internal self-government. This led fairly quickly to independence (July, 1964) and the breakup of the Federation, which had been economically successful but never acceptable to its African members. Nyasaland took the name of Malawi.

The white settlers did not particularly object to the departure of Nyasaland from the Federation, but they fought hard to persuade the British to refuse independence to Northern Rhodesia, which was rich in minerals, especially copper, the exploitation of which was in large measure responsible for the prospertity of the Federation as a whole. But the nationalists, led by Kenneth Kaunda, were adamantly opposed to the continuance of the Federation, and Northern Rhodesia was granted independence in October, 1964. The new nation took the name of Zambia. The Federation itself was then dissolved, leaving Southern Rhodesia (now called Rhodesia) still a British self-governing colony, under a constitution which made it virtually impossible for the African majority to win control of the government within the foreseeable future. In elections held in 1965 a party pledged to independence under the same constitution was returned to office. Although it entered into negotiations with the British Labour government in the effort to obtain British sanction for immediate independence, the Rhodesian government under Prime Minister Ian Smith refused to make any compromise which would bring majority

(African) rule nearer. On November 11, 1965, Smith declared the country independent, whereupon the British inaugurated economic sanctions against the rebels, in which they were joined by most of the United Nations. However, during the next months the newly independent state managed to survive, and it proved difficult to institute an effective sanction on oil, which continued to enter Rhodesia through Portuguese Mozambique and the Republic of South Africa. Britain therefore requested and received permission from the United Nations Security Council to prevent the oil from reaching Rhodesia, but it is uncertain whether this measure will prove effective enough to put an end to the rebellion.

Democratic Republic of the Congo.   The former Belgian Congo had been governed by the Belgians from 1908 under a policy of paternalism, according to which they attempted to develop the mineral-rich territory economically, providing a relatively high standard of living to the Africans. But even while the independence movement was growing strongly in other African countries, they hesitated to grant any political concessions, preferring to keep to a carefully planned timetable under which the Congo might have become independent by the 1980's.

However, once they had permitted elections in 1959, they were quickly forced to grant far more than they had intended. As a result they decided to take a calculated risk and grant independence in June, 1960, in the hopes that they could retain their economic control of the country afterward. In this they were completely unsuccessful (at least in the short run), for the Congolese cordially detested their former masters and took the first available opportunity to turn against them. A revolt of the army (*Force Publique*) a few days after independence was followed by an invasion of Belgian paratroopers intent on saving Belgian lives, whereupon the Congo prime minister, Patrice Lumumba, appealed to the United Nations Security Council, which authorized a peace-keeping force made up of neutrals and peremptorily commanded the Belgians to withdraw. Meanwhile, Moise Tshombe, premier of the richest province, Katanga, declared his province to be independent and accepted Belgian aid.

There followed several confused years during which the United Nations forces strove to keep order in the country while experts tried to keep its economy from collapsing. Lumumba was murdered in Katanga; prime ministers came and went in Léopoldville; and tribal wars broke out in many parts of the huge country. A

United Nations expedition succeeded in ousting Tshombe from Katanga in December, 1962, and the nation was again formally united. After spending eighteen months in exile, Tshombe returned to Léopoldville and was appointed prime minister at the head of a coalition government by President Joseph Kasavubu (July, 1964). By this time a new constitution had been promulgated and the United Nations forces had withdrawn.

During the Tshombe regime a substantial rebellion broke out in various parts of the Congo, and the prime minister called upon mercenaries, mostly South African, to suppress it when the still unreliable army was unable to do so. The rebellion was suppressed, in spite of winning some support from other African countries, notably Algeria, but Tshombe's government did not survive the year. Late in 1965 Premier Tshombe was deposed by President Kasavubu, but a short time later Kasavubu himself was ousted by General Joseph Mobutu, leader of the army, who declared himself president and suspended the new constitution. He then appointed a civilian as prime minister.

Belgian Trust Territories. When the Congo became independent in June, 1960, the trust territory of Ruanda-Urundi was still far from a similar goal. The position was greatly complicated by the fact that each sector had its own king (*mwami*) from the minority Batutsi tribe, which had conquered the other tribes in an earlier period and had until recent times held all the more important positions in the country. The majority of the people in both countries belonged to the Bahutu tribe. In Ruanda the Mwami (like the Sultan of Morocco) decided to become a nationalist, whereupon he was exiled by the Belgians. A Bahutu party, no doubt with some Belgian assistance, thereafter won elections in Ruanda, and the small country was permitted by the Belgians and the United Nations to become independent under the name of Rwanda on July 1, 1962. Meanwhile, the legislature had forbidden the return of the Mwami, so that the new nation was a republic. The Mwami of Urundi during this period had adopted a safer policy and decided to act as a constitutional monarch. For this reason his Bahutu subjects made no objections to his retaining his throne. A coalition party won the pre-independence elections, and Burundi became an independent constitutional monarchy. Since that time there have been many disturbances in the small nation, and several of its leading political figures have been assassinated.

EAST AFRICA

East Africa is made up of three states formerly under British rule, Kenya, Uganda, and Tanzania (the latter formed by the amalgamation of two separate independent states, Tanganyika and Zanzibar); the former Italian and British colonies of Somaliland, now amalgamated into the independent state of Somalia; and the large formerly French island of Madagascar, together with a few other smaller dependencies.

Kenya. The postwar history of Kenya was for a long time time dominated by the problem of the white settlers who during the early part of the century had acquired much of the best land of the country. The African tribe which laid claim to these lands —although it was temporarily not in possession of them—was the Kikuyu, by far the largest in number and the best educated of the Kenyan peoples. Although the whites at all times exercised a considerable influence in the colony, the British never handed over rule to them, as they did to the white Rhodesians. But it seemed to the Africans after the war that they were never likely to gain independence in face of the stubborn opposition of the settlers. Thus there broke out in 1952 a widespread rebellion (the Mau Mau), marked by atrocities on both sides, which held up all political advance and required many years to suppress. The Mau Mau rebellion was the work mainly of the Kikuyu, whose leader, Jomo Kenyatta, was condemned for his supposed part in it and sentenced to imprisonment.

In due course the British could postpone political reforms no longer and, over the opposition of the vast majority of the settlers, granted in early 1960 a considerable measure of advance, which in fact rapidly led to Kenya's internal self-government and then to independence late in 1963. This was made possible by the effective organization of the Kenya African National Union, which won an over-all majority in the pre-independence elections, in spite of the fact that the greater part of its membership was Kikuyu. Although the British for a long time kept Kenyatta in detention even when his sentence had been served, pressure from the Africans (and refusal to co-operate in running the country as long as he was detained) at last forced his release. He became the first prime minister after independence, and quickly won a reputation for moderation; he was, indeed, markedly successful in winning the co-operation and good opinion of those white settlers who had remained in the country.

Uganda. There were few white settlers in Uganda, which had, indeed, been one of the best governed of African states before the coming of the Europeans. But the march toward independence was complicated by the presence within the colonial territory of a native kingdom which contained the greater part of the educated Africans and a strong governmental system headed by a king, the Kabaka. The traditional leaders of this kingdom of Buganda did not wish to yield their power to elected politicians from outside Buganda, or even to Baganda politicians elected by persons opposed to the traditional administration. Eventually the issue was settled by allowing Buganda to retain its internal administration and enjoy a "semifederal" relation with the rest of the country. The prime minister at the time of independence was Milton Obote, who was not himself a Baganda. He was, however, backed by a Baganda party which owed its primary allegiance to the Kabaka but co-operated with the government in national affairs. After independence the Kabaka of Buganda became the official head of the state of Uganda, which is therefore a constitutional monarchy. The country became independent in October, 1962.

Tanzania. This country comprises the former United Nations trust territory of Tanganyika, and the former sultanate of Zanzibar, which was a British protectorate until independence.

Tanganyika's path to independence was relatively smooth, perhaps because it was a trust territory. This position gave its gifted leader Julius Nyerere the opportunity to address the United Nations on behalf of his people. Once Nyerere had organized the Tanganyika African National Union which won almost all the seats available for election by Africans, there was no further need to delay, and independence, the first for an East African state, was granted on December 9, 1961.

Zanzibar followed a different course. For more than a century most of the commerce of the two islands of Zanzibar and Pemba was in the hands of persons of either Persian or Arab descent, and it was the Arabs who had ruled the country before Britain established her protectorate in the late nineteenth century. But the Arabs were nevertheless a minority in the country, the majority being Negro African. When the British were planning to grant self-government to the islands, the electoral system favored the Arabs as against the Africans; and it was with an Arab-dominated government that Zanzibar achieved independence in December, 1963. The very next month the Africans in the new state, aided by various revolutionary elements and with some Communist Chinese support, staged a coup, as a result of which the leading Arabs were dispossessed of their property, and the Sultan was forced into exile. A new Revolutionary Council, headed by Obeid Karume, took over the government.

In the same month (January, 1964) a coup was attempted against President Nyerere of Tanganyika, led by some disaffected elements in the army, who objected to their British officers. The President thereupon appealed to Britain for help, and the revolt was put down. Soon afterward, agreement was reached between the Tanganyika government and the African Revolutionary Council in Zanzibar for a merger of the two countries. Later in 1964 the name of the united country was changed to Tanzania. On the mainland there is a single party, but elections held late in 1965 were nevertheless contested by individuals belonging to this party, resulting in a very large turnover of seats in the National Assembly. In Zanzibar, however, elections were not held except for the president. There is still no National Assembly in Zanzibar, which is internally self-governing. Karume is first vice-president of the Republic of Tanzania, but government on the islands is still in the hands of his Revolutionary Council. Tanzania has accepted help from whatever sources available to it, including substantial economic and military aid from Communist China, which has a large embassy staff in Dar-es-Salaam, the capital. Dar is also the headquarters for various political groups seeking to overthrow the remaining colonial governments in Africa.

Madagascar. The large island of Madagascar, which was ruled by a native dynasty until almost the end of the nineteenth century, became important during World War II because it was regarded as a possible outpost for the Japanese and it possessed a useful naval base. The British therefore dispossessed the Vichy French, who had administered it, and it was later turned over to the Free French. Madagascar became a component state of the French Union, but when the French systematically favored a particular party a bloody uprising occurred, which was ruthlessly suppressed by the French (1947). The leaders were exiled, and remained in exile even after the passing of the *loi-cadre*. This gave a more moderate nationalist, schoolteacher Philibert Tsiranana, the chance to organize a moderate party which won the subsequent elections. No hitch occurred thereafter on the path to independence, which was granted in June, 1960. Tsiranana became president of the Malgache Republic, as the country was then called. He has remained in office ever since. The exiles have returned, but the Republic has followed a notably moderate policy and co-operated closely with the other French-speaking African nations.

Somalia. After the war the former Italian colony of Somaliland, which had been conquered by the British, was handed over by the United Nations to the Italians to administer as a trust territory, with a ten-year time limit set for independence. As the time grew to a close the Italians instituted a crash program to train administrators, and elections were held. The United Nations permitted independence several months early, on July 1, 1960. The British Somaliland protectorate, its neighbor, was not similarly prepared, and the British did not appear to believe that its people would in fact opt to join the new state of Somalia (which Italian Somaliland was renamed) when given the opportunity. However, elections were held on the issue, and a party that favored union won easily. Thus the Protectorate from the beginning formed part of the new state.

The Somali people, however, are far from satisfied with the two territories under their control and are doing everything in their power to create a Greater Somalia, which would include Somalis now in Ethiopia, Kenya, and a French overseas territory called French Somaliland on the Red Sea. Somalia has accepted military aid from the Soviet Union, who has trained her army, and there have been several border incidents. The Somalis in the newly independent state of Kenya do not co-operate (if they can help it) with the African government of Jomo Kenyatta, in which they are permitted a limited local autonomy. Up to this time Somalia has had no success in either persuading or coercing her neighbors into yielding up their Somali minorities, and the Somali army remains far too large for her ordinary needs.

CONCLUSION

The decolonization of Africa has been one of the most dramatic events of the postwar period, and south of the Sahara it was accomplished with very little bloodshed. The ease with which it was achieved in the area was certainly due to the fact that the colonial powers lacked vital interests in Africa. Since Africa was strategically of minor importance, commercial interests, it was hoped, could be maintained after independence. But in the countries where African majority governments have not yet come to power, prospects of early change are not bright. The whites in South Africa and in Rhodesia have made Africa their home and have no present intentions of leaving or submitting to African rule. The South African whites have known no other home. Portugal, a very minor power in Europe, feels that her main title to greatness lies in her history as the oldest of the colonial powers, and that without her African "overseas provinces" she would carry little weight in the world. It may therefore well be a long time before the remaining colonial territories are ruled by their African majorities. It is, indeed, open to serious doubt that the Africans themselves will ever be strong enough to compel it, least of all in South Africa where the whites are outnumbered by fewer than four to one and have a monopoly of modern arms.

20 INTERNATIONAL RELATIONS— THE COLD WAR

Ever since the dropping of the atomic bombs on Hiroshima and Nagasaki, the two superpowers of the world, the United States and the Soviet Union, have been engaged in a diplomatic struggle so intense that it has given rise to the term the "Cold War" as a description of the conflict, which has never led to actual bloodshed between the two principals but has never ceased to threaten it. In this chapter an attempt will be made to trace the Cold War back to its origins and to deal with the most important manifestations of the mutual hostility between the two powers. In the course of the narrative, attention will also be paid to the intervention of a third great power, the People's Republic of China, its unremitting hostility to the United States, and its initial friendliness and later hostility to the Soviet Union.

THE NUCLEAR STALEMATE

Reference has already been made in Chapter 13 to the deterioration of relations between the United States and the Soviet Union after World War II, culminating in the Berlin airlift and the organization of NATO as an alliance among the Western powers to checkmate the supposed Soviet intention of overrunning western Europe. In retrospect it would appear likely that the Soviet Union never had any such intention, but in any case she certainly had no chance of winning a quick success once NATO was organized, and such an attempt would presumably have resulted in nuclear retaliation. After 1949 when the Soviet Union exploded her first atomic bomb, the United States herself was unlikely to escape unscathed from an all-out war. Since then both sides have devoted enormous sums of money to perfecting bigger and more destructive bombs and ever more improved methods of delivery. Bombing planes have now given place to intercontinental missiles powered by rockets, and it is no longer disputed that each side has the ability to destroy every industrial installation and almost all the human beings in the other's country. To engage in a full-scale nuclear war is therefore virtually to commit national suicide.

This fact, however, has not persuaded the powers to abandon nuclear weapons. The United States, in particular, has expended much ingenuity in devising other methods of responding to aggression than the use of megaton bombs. She has developed low-yield so-called "tactical" bombs with relatively little fallout, and has pursued the idea of a "graduated response" which, it is hoped, will not "escalate" to a full-scale nuclear war. If only these lesser nuclear weapons are used, neither country will be completely devastated, and destruction will be kept to an "acceptable" level. Needless to say, these theories have never been tested in practice, and for practical purposes a nuclear stalemate has subsisted ever since World War II.

THE TRUMAN DOCTRINE—
"CONTAINMENT" OF COMMUNISM

It seemed clear to the United States in 1947 that "Communism" was the major danger that threatened world peace. The Soviet Union had established her satellite empire in Europe and it was thought that she was supporting the Greek Communist guerillas, apparently in the hope that yet one more European country would succumb to Communism by military means. When President Truman announced the doctrine that bears his name (see p. 247), it became American policy to "contain" Communism by whatever means were available. In Greece, where the danger was a military one, it was clear that military means would have to be used.

Since it has always been difficult to formulate a counterideology to Communism which would be acceptable to all non-Communists, the "containing" of Communism in the last two decades has been almost exclusively military in nature. In order to be prepared to resist outright military aggression, the United States has leased numerous military and naval bases throughout the world wherever she has been permitted to do so; has signed several military treaties with nations willing to enter into an alliance with her;

has provided non-Communist governments with arms, either without payment or on easy terms (especially in Latin America); and has engaged in two substantial wars in Asia. (In neither of these wars did she have an obvious national interest, although in view of the fact that her enemy in each case was a Communist-controlled government, both could be regarded as part of her policy of containment.) Lastly, she has intervened in several countries, either openly or covertly, to overthrow governments that were either Communist-controlled (as she thought Guatemala was in 1954) or likely to fall under Communist control (the Dominican Republic in 1965). It is therefore not too much to say that her view of world affairs is that there is a gigantic struggle in progress between two ways of life, "freedom," of which she has constituted herself the champion, and "Communism," which she equates with unfreedom or slavery, an enemy that must be overcome by her power and resolution. Thus her policy is, in a sense, uncompromisingly ideological (as is presumed to be true also of both her major Communist adversaries); and the result has been a lack of flexibility characteristic of all firmly held ideological positions.

THE COLD WAR IN EUROPE

Europe has not been the scene of the most important of American confrontations of Communism. The one great unsolved problem in Europe is the division of Germany and Berlin, which is no nearer to solution than it was in 1945. West Berlin, a West German enclave within Soviet-dominated territories, has been defended not so much by Western troops (which, at least in Berlin, could not resist a sudden Russian thrust) as by the threat of nuclear retaliation. The Western powers have steadfastly refused to budge from the city in spite of periodic Soviet threats, and of occasional interference by Soviet troops with the free passage of supplies through East German territories. On each such occasion the Soviet Union gave way. The Russians regard East Germany as a buffer state between themselves and western Europe, and ever since West Germany joined NATO in 1955 and began to rearm, there has been no possibility that they would relinquish their satellite without a *quid pro quo* which would include, as a minimum, the disarming and neutralization of West Germany. (Such a suggestion, the Rapacki Plan, has indeed been put forward by Poland, whose western boundaries have never been recognized as permanent by the West.) Stalemate in Central Europe is therefore complete.

Since the advent of General de Gaulle to power in France, French official thinking appears to have veered toward the idea that at least the military purposes of NATO have been fulfilled. In this view, the Soviet Union presents little further danger to western Europe, and an accommodation should therefore be sought with her in the hope of unfreezing the attitudes adopted in 1949. France now plays little part in NATO affairs, and it is expected that when the treaty comes up for renewal in 1969 she will insist on major changes, in default of which she may withdraw altogether from the organization. Early in 1966, indeed, she demanded that all the NATO forces on French soil be put under French command, in default of which they must leave the country before the expiration of the treaty. Since none of her allies was willing to accept these terms, it may be that they will be modified. President de Gaulle has made it clear that France wishes to continue as an ally, and he does not want to bring the alliance to an end. His objections are to the existing military arrangements accepted by the Fourth Republic.

THE COLD WAR IN ASIA

The crucial event which froze American policy in Asia was the Korean War, described in Chapter 17. The war marked the entry of Communist China into world affairs. Already frustrated by her inability to prevent Mao Tse-tung and his Communists from taking over mainland China, the United States was infuriated by the initial defeat of her armies by Chinese "volunteers." Even though she counterattacked effectively and recovered that part of South Korea that had been overrun by the Chinese, she was forced to accept a stalemate and the continued division of Korea between a Communist north and a non-Communist south.

Consequences of the Korean War. The dismissal of General MacArthur, the American commander in Korea, by President Truman in 1951 was the signal for an outburst of recrimination at home which virtually destroyed the usefulness of Secretary of State Dean Acheson, who was regarded as responsible for United States failure to take effective steps to defend South Korea before the outbreak of the war, and even for the fall of China to the Communists. Both Acheson and President Truman were widely condemned for refusing to carry the Korean War into Chinese territory, as MacArthur had advocated. But the administration did succeed in "branding" Communist China in the United Nations as an aggressor, and from that time onward it became politically impossible for any administration either to recognize China or vote for her admission to the United Nations. The "Republic of China" on Formosa has remained in American eyes the legal government of China, and it has been defended unstintingly by American arms, especially by the Seventh Fleet. Even the offshore islands of Quemoy and Matsu, within sight of the mainland, have not been allowed to fall into mainland hands—though they are subjected to regular shelling by mainland artillery. The Communist Chinese attitude has likewise remained one of implacable hostility to the United States, although Mao Tse-tung has been extremely cautious about taking any steps which might lead to actual war.

The Asian Treaty System. The Eisenhower administration inherited these attitudes and policies from its predecessor, but its secretary of state, John Foster Dulles, took a series of new steps in the pursuit of the policy of containment. He arranged (1954) a treaty which gave birth to a new organization, the Southeast Asia Treaty Organization (SEATO), consisting of the United States, Britain, France, Australia, New Zealand, the Philippine Republic, Thailand, and Pakistan. (Australia, New Zealand, and the United States were already united in the ANZUS pact for joint defense.) The three Asian members, who were all that Dulles could enroll, were already firm friends of the United States, but they now became entitled to virtually unlimited military aid, with which they might hope to defend themselves against encroachments by the Communist powers. Secretary Dulles was also largely responsible for the CENTO treaty (see p. 345). The United States did not formally adhere to this unpopular pact, though she provided military and economic aid to the signatories. Iraq withdraw from the alliance in 1958 after the revolution of that year (see p. 339). All the possible allies of the United States in the containment of Asian Communism were now therefore enlisted in the Cold War and received such aid as they needed for the task.

The Indochinese War. In retrospect the most important of the foreign policy decisions of the first Eisenhower administration was the decision to support the French with arms and money in their colonial war against the Communist Viet Minh in Indochina. Secretary Dulles wished to intervene far more actively in the last stages of the war, but the President, backed especially by Britain, refused to do so. Whether such massive intervention would have succeeded will never be known. At all events, following the fall of Dien Bien Phu in early 1954, the French entered into negotiations with the Viet Minh and Communist China (Great Britain and the Soviet Union were the joint chairmen of the conference), from which emerged the Geneva Agreements of 1954 (see p. 324). Although the United States did not sign the agreements, her representative promised that she would not interfere with their execution. Meanwhile the mandarin Ngo Dinh Diem, as noted earlier, returned to Indochina (Vietnam) with the promise of American support, and was accepted as prime minister by Emperor Bao Dai.

In due course Americans replaced the French as military advisers to Diem, who had now disposed of the emperor and become president of the republic. After the outbreak of the Viet Cong rebellion in 1959 the number of these advisers and the military aid increased. This policy was inherited by the Kennedy administration, before the end of which American air force personnel were giving active aid to the South Vietnamese. After Ngo Dinh Diem was murdered, a series of military governments, none with any authority beyond what was conceded to them by the Americans, assumed power. When Lyndon B. Johnson became president at the end of 1963 he continued the policy of his predecessor except that the intervention became more open. Nevertheless, the Viet Cong continued to make progress, and were quite possibly within sight of final victory when President Johnson in February, 1965, decided to bomb North Vietnam as the presumed instigator and controller of the rebellion, and thereafter sent in enough ground troops to make a loss of the war virtually impossible. He informed the world that he was willing to enter into "unconditional negotiations" with any government (which of course excluded the National Liberation Front, the political arm of the Viet Cong), and at the end of 1965 he sent roving ambassadors to almost every neutral government of consequence for the purpose of explaining American aims in Vietnam and to see if they could put pressure on China and North Vietnam to "bring them to the conference table."

Whatever the outcome of this war, it should be noted that there has been much stronger opposition, especially among the academic community, to involvement in this war than there was in the case of Korea, where the North Koreans had clearly invaded South Korea, and the United Nations Security Council cast its aegis over the intervention. The main grounds for opposition are: (a) it was American backing of Ngo Dinh Diem's refusal to hold the elections for the unification of Vietnam envisaged in the Geneva Agreements (elections which would almost certainly have resulted in victory for Ho Chi Minh and his Communists) which brought on the rebellion; (b) the conflict is in fact a civil war, in which both North Vietnam and the United States have intervened on opposing sides (as did the Soviet Union, Germany, and Italy in the Spanish Civil War, an intervention condemned at the time by the United States (see p. 93); (c) the United States has little if any legal right to intervene in view of the fact that she is there by the invitation of the South Vietnamese government, which admittedly exists only because of United States support; (d) the intervention is contrary to the undertakings made when the United States agreed to the United Nations Charter, since the South Vietnamese government is not a member of the United Nations (only members are entitled to military support from other members, and even then only when it is authorized by the Security Council). Indeed, according to this view, the South Vietnamese government is not a permanent and legal government at all, but a temporary administration entitled to hold office only until the unification of the country, as envisaged in the Geneva Agreements.

However all this may be, both Communist China and the Soviet Union have been assisting the North Vietnamese and the Viet Cong with military and economic aid, even though they have not yet intervened militarily, as has the United States. From the point of view of these nations, the United States is an "imperialist" power, intervening with the unavowed intention of frustrating the unification of Vietnam under any auspices but her own, and with the avowed intention of preventing a Communist-dominated government from taking power in South Vietnam even if it comes to power through elections. If the United States is allowed to succeed in these aims a potential, and possibly an actual, Communist state will have been destroyed by American arms, perhaps the prelude to many similar "imperialist" wars.

This war is further complicated by the numerous differences that have arisen between the two major Communist powers in the last years, which were briefly alluded to earlier (see p. 280 and

p. 331). Communist China has been far more militant in its revolutionary efforts in recent years and has tried to foster "wars of liberation" (of which she approves in principle as the only justifiable use of military might) wherever she has been given an opening, as in some Latin American and African countries. Hitherto her aid has been only in the form of advisers and military supplies, but it is her avowed intention to continue this policy. She has no use for "co-existence" as long as there are "imperialist" nations seeking to expand (as, in her view, the United States is doing), and as long as there are any colored peoples subjected to white domination. The Soviet Union has been noticeably less revolutionary in her deeds, and even her words, in recent times. She is anxious to give more attention to domestic problems, many of which are far from solved, and she has a healthy respect for American military might. Most of the other Communist countries incline toward the Soviet view, since they too wish to solve their domestic problems; and, perhaps more important, the Soviet Union can give them far more effective economic aid than poverty-stricken China can.

In the Vietnamese war neither the Soviet Union nor Communist China can tolerate an American victory, but at present the need of the rebels is more for military supplies than for manpower. These the Soviet Union can provide, but China does not relish the notion that her rival is doing more for victory than she. Hence she has been reluctant even to permit the passage of Soviet arms through her territories. From China's point of view the longer the North Vietnamese and Viet Cong can prolong the war, the more damage will be done to the United States, whereas the Soviet Union would like the war to come to an end provided this does not mean a military victory for the United States, who as the champion of the non-Communist world remains her rival in world affairs.

In the United States the war is seen as a further effort to "contain" Communism, and it is widely believed, in spite of the conditions peculiar to this particular war, that the situation is similar to that of the 1930's when the Western powers refused to stand up to Hitler's expansion until it was too late. It is believed that the Asian Communist powers (and perhaps even the Soviet Union) both instigated and are backing the war in order to expand the area controlled by "international Communism"; and that therefore, at bottom, the war is ideological in nature. The United

States has thus been extremely hesitant to state her specific war aims and the kind of peace she hopes to see as the result of her efforts. If indeed the war is *not* ideological in essence, but a local war fought for local reasons, and China is involved, as far as she is, mainly to recover her traditional influence in this area and not because of her Communist ideology, then it is difficult to see how she can be prevented from achieving her aims in the long run. She is the most powerful nation in the area and she must exercise influence. The only reason that Chiang Kai-shek did not exert a comparable influence was simply because he never fully unified China under his own rule.

THE "EISENHOWER DOCTRINE" IN THE MIDDLE EAST

In July, 1955, President Eisenhower made a great effort to improve relations with the Soviet Union at a Summit Conference held at Geneva. He appears to have convinced the Soviet leaders that he personally was a man of peace and that his country was not in the least interested in "imperialist aggression." Although they were still distrustful of his Secretary of State, they celebrated the Conference as the beginning of a new era in Soviet-American relations. But nothing substantial came of this *détente*. Secretary Dulles continued to speak of the impossibility of a settlement without the unification of Germany and the abandonment of the Soviet satellite system. When Hungary attempted to escape from her satellite status in 1956 (see p. 284), the United States gave no material aid to the rebels, but American opinion hardened against the Soviet regime. At the end of the year the Soviet Union joined the United States in condemning the Suez expedition (see p. 337), but she gained most of the credit in the neutral world for putting such a speedy end to it. When the Soviet Union showed signs of wishing to fortify her newly won position in Middle Eastern affairs, President Eisenhower retorted with a new doctrine (Eisenhower Doctrine), under which he proposed that the United States assist any nation with economic aid if it were to be used "to strengthen its national independence"; to give military aid when requested; and to use the American armed forces, when requested, "against overt armed aggression from any nation controlled by international Communism."

In spite of some Congressional opposition the resolution was passed in substantially the form requested, and the Eisenhower

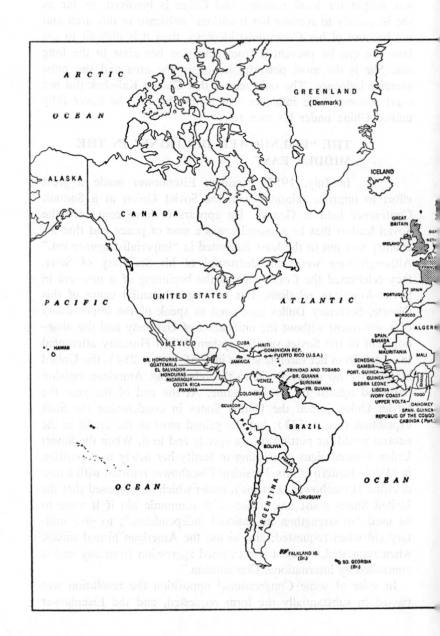

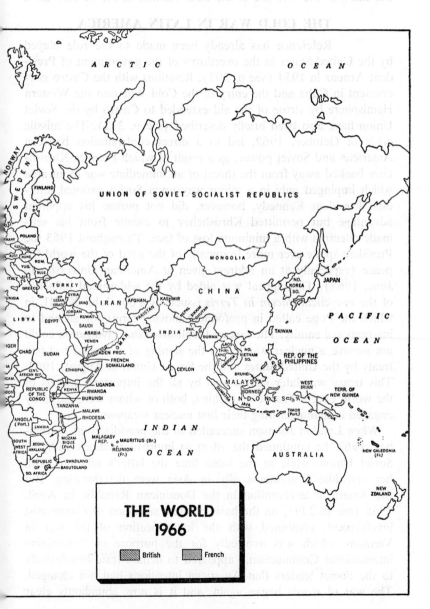

THE WORLD
1966

British   French

Doctrine became a part of United States proclaimed policy, an extension of the Truman Doctrine of 1947. Action was taken under the Doctrine in Lebanon in peculiar circumstances (see p. 338), but this was the sole use of the authorization in the Middle East.

THE COLD WAR IN LATIN AMERICA

Reference has already been made to the role played by the United States in the overthrow of the government of President Arbenz in 1954 (see p. 307). Relations with the Castro government in Cuba and the entry of the Cold War into the Western Hemisphere by virtue of the aid extended to Castro by the Soviet Union have also been briefly described (see p. 312). The missile crisis of October, 1962, led to a direct confrontation between American and Soviet power, as a result of which Premier Khrushchev backed away from the threat of an immediate war in an area which impinged only in a minor way upon Soviet national interests. President Kennedy, however, did not pursue his apparent advantage but permitted Khrushchev to escape from his self-made dilemma with a minimum loss of face. Throughout 1963 the President spoke ever more frequently of the need of the world for peace (especially at an address given at American University in June, 1963). This appeal was aided by the widespread influence of the encyclical *Pacem in Terris* issued by Pope John XXIII, in which the Pope called in profoundly moving terms for an end to international enmity. The renewed realization that civilization could not survive a nuclear war led to the signing of a limited test-ban treaty by the United States and the Soviet Union in August, 1963. This treaty was later signed also by all the important nations of the world except France and China, both of whom were currently engaged in manufacturing their first nuclear weapons.

When Lyndon Johnson succeeded to the presidency in November, 1963, he continued the effort to improve relations with the Soviet Union, while at the same time the latter's relations with her erstwhile Communist ally in Asia were deteriorating. But the American intervention in the Dominican Republic in April, 1965 (see p. 299), on the basis of mere suspicion of Communist involvement, combined with the intensification of the war in Vietnam, which was avowedly for the purpose of "containing international Communism," appeared to demonstrate conclusively to the Soviet leaders that American intentions had not changed. The war of words began again, and it is now abundantly clear that there will be no further let-up in the Cold War until the Vietnamese War is either brought to an end or escalates into a nuclear holocaust.

THE UNITED NATIONS AND THE COLD WAR

The United Nations has been virtually powerless in the Cold War between the two greatest powers in the world, even though almost every nation not allied to one or the other of these powers has expressed publicly the desire that it should end. Secretary-General U Thant, like his predecessor Dag Hammarskjöld, has shown himself willing at all times to mediate whenever he has been requested to do so, and various relatively small disputes have been handled effectively. Even as recently as the fall of 1965 the United States and the Soviet Union teamed together to bring an end to armed hostilities between India and Pakistan in Kashmir (see p. 317). The United States has not had to interpose her veto in the Security Council since she has usually been able to command a majority of the votes for her viewpoint. The Soviet Union, unable to win a majority for hers, has cast vetoes on numerous occasions. Only when the two powers have agreed on a proposed course has the Security Council been able to act effectively, while the General Assembly has necessarily had to confine itself to recommendations, except in the case of peace-keeping operations already authorized in principle by the Security Council. As noted earlier (see p. 250), the organization is still heavily in debt for former peace-keeping operations authorized by the General Assembly under the Uniting for Peace Resolution of 1950; and it is doubtful whether any similar actions will be taken in the future without the agreement of all the permanent members of the Security Council.

CONCLUSION

The Cold War has cast its shadow over all efforts at building a permanent peace; and though the world has so far escaped a nuclear war, it can scarcely be maintained that its thinking and its institutions have evolved as yet to the point where such a peace is even remotely feasible. Although the tendency in the immediate postwar world was to play down the importance of nuclear weapons and to insist that they were only an extension of conventional armament, it has now become clear that the ability to destroy the entire earth and all its inhabitants within the space of a few days has placed a heavier responsibility upon the possessors of these weapons than has ever been borne before by fallible human beings, and that *some* changes will be necessary in the institutional framework of mankind if the weapons are not to be used.

Up to the present time nations have continued to act as they did in the pre-nuclear ages. They defend their ideas and their institutions by military (though as yet not nuclear) means as they did before; they thrust and counterthrust in their political warfare just as if there were no nuclear weapons leering behind every diplomatic note and every gesture of defiance. In short, they resolutely refuse to "think the unthinkable" and to plan co-operatively the future of their planet. The time-lag between social thinking and technological advance has now become so great that it seems hardly possible to bridge it. But it must be bridged, if the planet is not to become as dead as the moon, which the technologies of the leading powers are bending every effort to reach in preference to solving the apparently insoluble problems that remain on earth.

21

SCIENTIFIC AND CULTURAL DEVELOPMENTS SINCE WORLD WAR I

Without question the greatest intellectual advance in this century has been in the field of science. It has been made possible by the Industrial Revolution, which has continued without break since the middle of the eighteenth century. This correctly called "revolution," by substituting the labor of machines for that of men, has provided the means of subsistence in all the industrially developed nations for a growing number of human beings who are not directly engaged in productive activity. These men and women staff on the one hand the service industries and on the other the ever growing educational establishment. Within the universities, and attached to some industries as an intellectual appendage, are to be found the greater number of scientists, who are thus provided with the means for organized research. It is this organization of research, which involves teamwork of the highest order, that has attracted scientists, who in an earlier age might have been solitary thinkers and experimenters, into engaging in a planned activity, the fruits of which are to be seen in twentieth-century civilization.

THE DEVELOPMENT OF SCIENCE

Under the general heading of science we shall here deal with not only the so-called "natural sciences" but also the social sciences concerned with human behavior, past and present, which only in recent times have come to be regarded as sciences in their own right.

Physics. Much of modern physics stems mainly from the work of such intellectual giants as Clerk-Maxwell, Einstein, Rutherford, Planck, and Roentgen, and such practical experimenters as Pierre and Marie Curie, all of whom did the bulk of their work before the period discussed in this book. Modern physics is mainly concerned with such problems as the mechanics of light and electricity, the ultimate constitution of matter, and similar questions. As the result of the work of the above-named physicists and of countless others, it began to be held that matter is composed of elementary particles which will never be seen by human eyes (and, according to the Heisenberg principle of uncertainty, they never can be observed at all, since the effort to do so will change their position); but they are certainly *there,* because only by the postulation of some such entities can the macrocosmic phenomena be explained and certain mathematical equations be solved. It was as a result of this kind of research that the atomic (fission) and hydrogen (fusion) bombs were manufactured by the technologists and engineers. The very fact that the bombs could be made was in a sense a proof of the theories which lay behind them, as the observation of an eclipse of the sun in 1919 confirmed Einstein's General Theory of Relativity, sprung on the world in 1915. Much of theoretical physics, however, is incapable of being proved by controlled experiments. It remains, nevertheless, one of the greatest theoretical structures in the history of mankind.

Biology, Chemistry, and Medicine. The grandfather of much of biological theory was the nineteenth-century monk Gregor Mendel, whose experiments in the field of heredity in the plant world were to give rise to the postulation of genes as the carriers of various hereditary characteristics. The nineteenth-century work of Charles Darwin, as developed by countless experimenters in twentieth-century laboratories, has in very large measure been confirmed. It is now almost universally accepted that Darwin's teachings about the "survival of the fittest" in the evolutionary process were basically correct and that the chance mutation of the genes is the mechanism by which evolutionary change comes about. This work has had many practical applications, especially in agriculture and husbandry.

Chemistry has not felt a similar need for new theory, although, like physics, it has made extensive use of mathematics. Much attention, in particular, has been devoted to the synthesizing of products which appear in nature in a form not always best adapted to human use. Synthetic rubber, for example, is in many respects better than natural rubber. Medicine makes use of numerous new drugs derived often from inorganic sources, while biochemistry has given us a whole group of so-called antibiotics, the first of which was penicillin (derived from a mold) discovered by Sir Alexander Fleming in 1928. Chemistry has also given us a wide range of pesticides from organic and inorganic sources which have wrought a revolution in agricultural practice as well as helping to eradicate such scourges of mankind as malaria. Only the virus has so far continued to defeat the best efforts of research scientists, since no substance has yet been found capable of destroying viruses. The sole method of dealing with viral infections therefore remains that of immunization discovered as early as 1796 by Edward Jenner, though the technique has improved out of all recognition in the twentieth century. Lastly, the great advances in surgery have been made possible by extremely sophisticated new methods of anaesthesia and an ever greater understanding of the mechanics of the human organism—itself the result of careful observation under controlled conditions and experimentation with laboratory-raised animals.

Psychology. The study of the human psyche has stemmed in the main from the work of Sigmund Freud (1856–1939) and his followers. Freud's theories, though suggestive, have been found to be of limited practical application, in part because of the enormous time required for the technique of psychoanalysis which he invented. But the attention given to the scientific study of human behavior in this century has borne fruit in numerous fields, including such diverse realms as literature and advertising, to say nothing of penology. Researchers have also been compelled to give more attention than before to the social conditions which give rise to deviant behavior of all kinds, with the result that professional social psychologists are in as much demand today as are psychiatrists and psychoanalysts. The major new treatment, largely developed during World War II, is shock therapy, which makes use both of drugs and electric shocks, though it is still imperfectly understood how such treatment in fact works in the human organism.

Social Science. Most historians have followed Ranke's nineteenth-century admonitions, spending their energies in discovering what happened and either fitting the results of their research within the accepted historical framework or using them to criticize and develop it further. However, two historians have made their influence widely felt by devising theories of history based on the study of past civilizations. These were Oswald Spengler and Arnold Toynbee. Spengler concluded that "cultures" rise and fall somewhat on the analogy of the life cycle of plants. Toynbee, less dogmatic than Spengler, enunciated a theory of challenge and response to account for the rise and fall of "civilizations." If a civilization, in his view, did not rise to a challenge with a suitable response, it was doomed to decay and disintegration. Other historians have followed with different theories to account for the same phenomena.

Sociologists and anthropologists have now staked out their respective fields of inquiry, the former dealing with present social structures and the latter with the societies of "uncivilized" or "primitive" peoples. Although both these groups of social scientists have observed and classified numerous societies, their theories have so far proved of limited practical application except in a few special areas—no doubt because of the notorious unwillingness of societies to reform themselves. Economists, on the contrary, have been in great demand in the industrial societies of the world, and the theories of the Englishman John Maynard Keynes on the manner in which governments can deviate from orthodox economic practice (i.e., balancing income with outgo) for the benefit of the economies they control have been paid the compliment of becoming orthodox themselves in the course of the postwar era.

Philosophy.　Although the intuitional philosophy of Henri Bergson had a considerable vogue for a time, especially in the interwar period, it has been the existentialists (Heidegger, Jaspers, Sartre, and numerous others) who have enjoyed the greatest esteem in recent years. In limited circles the "anti-philosophical" logical empiricism of Wittgenstein and Carnap, which declared that almost all philosophy is meaningless because it asks unanswerable questions, has held the field, especially in some of the major philosophy departments of the United States. According to this school, the only proper philosophy is concerned with the analysis of meaning through the use of symbolic and other kinds of logic. In the Soviet Union dialectical materialism has continued to be the only acceptable philosophy, although the form this philosophy has taken in recent years might well be unrecognizable by Marx.

Technology and Engineering.　The accomplishments of technology and engineering are far beyond possible listing in this chapter, or a chapter twenty times its length. If one were to study the technology involved in the orbiting of human beings around the earth at a height of two hundred miles, a feat now performed several times, or the technology involved in the photographing of the planet Mars from an unmanned satellite directed entirely from the ground, a kind of cross section of all recent technological developments would emerge. Most important of all would be the computers (based on the technique of the feedback and the almost miraculous advances in electronics combined with applied mathematics). Television photography, industrial chemistry with its specialized rocket fuels, and the engineering feats involved in the actual construction of space ships and rockets might come next, and then the numerous precision instruments, based in part on the development of the machine tool industry. The list could go on almost indefinitely, as could the list of other engineering advances in the industrialized nations.

LITERATURE AND THE FINE ARTS

The tremendous and continued advances in science have been the result almost exclusively of work done in the industrialized countries, which have in turn made them available to undeveloped and underdeveloped nations that have been able to use them. Such nations have, indeed, come to believe that they can solve their problems only through industrialization. But they do not sufficiently realize that the skills that have gone into industrialization in Europe and the United States are not acquired in an instant or that the possession of extensive mineral resources does not guarantee that they can be used effectively or even exploited efficiently by themselves.

However, there is no necessary connection between excellence in literature and the fine arts and industrial development. The achievement of such excellence may be favored by many factors, of which one of the least may well be the industrialization of the local environment—which provides, to be sure, a mass market for the consumption of literary and artistic "products," but not necessarily either the leisure for thought and contemplation, a cultured and critical audience, or life experiences likely to stimulate the imagination and summon up an overmastering desire to transmute them into art. Indeed, it may well be that an industrial civilization with its accompanying mass market tends to overstimulate the production of mediocre works designed primarily to entertain without evoking thought, works which are neither expected to, nor are likely to, endure. Few would probably claim that even the interwar period when some of the older masters of literature like Thomas Mann, William Butler Yeats, James Joyce, and André Gide were still producing was a great age in literature, still less the postwar era when one had to look far to find great names. (Even the Nobel Committee with the world to choose from has had to look far and wide for writers on whom to bestow its largesse, and among these often their best work had been done decades earlier.) Neither of these eras can remotely be compared with the ages of Pericles or Augustus or Renaissance Italy, in none of which was there any comparable advance in industry and technology. Artistic excellence, especially in sculpture and painting, was surely greater during and immediately after the revolution in Mexico, when such giants as Diego Orozco and Diego Rivera were working, than at any time since in any country.

Architecture, however, has been stimulated in the modern age, with the development of new structural materials and advances in engineering technique. The work of Walter Gropius and his Bauhaus school which was transplanted from Europe to Chicago, of the Swiss Le Corbusier, and of the American Frank Lloyd Wright has broken away completely from the older classical styles favored for centuries, not only in Europe but also in America. Yet it has not been in the larger industrial states that the innovations of modern architecture have flourished most strongly, but in the newer countries such as Brazil and Mexico. Brasilia, the capital city of Brazil, designed as a whole by Oscar Niemeyer, is architecturally surely the most exciting city in the world, even though it is so far from the main centers of population in the country that its future as a capital cannot be considered certain. Mexico now has many of the most daring of the world's architects, who are all trained at home. With the aid of the national government (and the drive of Ernesto Uruchurtu, long-time governor of the Federal District), the face of old Mexico City is being rapidly changed, and what may well be the most beautiful and functional modern museum was recently completed. Nothing comparable has been achieved in the United States or western (still less eastern) Europe, although there are some smaller areas, especially in Scandinavia, which have been wholly modernized and where town planning is at last becoming a respectable profession.

In music it is curious that if one leaves aside jazz and its various descendants and relatives, and dance music, which have their own popular appeal, the taste of what appears to be the overwhelming majority of concert-goers is still fixed on the classical music of the last three centuries. But among serious musicians there is far less enthusiasm for the past, and the great majority of them compose (and even prefer to play when given the opportunity) modern music, in which there have been many revolutionary innovations in recent times, including the twelve-tone scale of Arnold Schönberg.

CONCLUSION

The industrialized modern world is not one that encourages the rise of élite groups such as produced most of the world's art and literature in previous centuries. Far more men and women are receiving an education and are thus able to read masterpieces of literature and appreciate masterpieces of art. But it is mostly among the works of the past that they have found what they are seeking. Whether human beings working today, perhaps unknown, will be found as inspiring by posterity cannot be predicted with any degree of probability. But it is quite certain that the world has been changed for good by the achievements of the scientists and technologists, and that over the course of the next decades these achievements will be shared with those who did not originally make them.

It is likely that in time those peoples who are now in the earliest stages of the technological revolution will (like the Japanese) first learn by imitating, and then move onward to add to the sum of human knowledge and technical achievement. This at least must be the hope of men of good will. If, as J. M. Keynes used to remind us, "in the long run we shall all be dead," in the short run there is much to do to make the world into a more livable habitat for man, and the scientists—even while teaching us how to destroy the planet and all its inhabitants—have also shown us what may so easily be done, if we so decide, to make use of human skills to provide for all reasonable (and many unreasonable) human wants and human needs.

THE ACHIEVEMENT OF INDEPENDENCE

Colony (or protectorate)	Formerly ruled by	Date of Independence	New Name
Egypt [1]	Great Britain	February, 1922	United Arab Republic (since 1958)
Syria *	France	April, 1945	United Arab Republic (1958–1961)
Lebanon *	France	April, 1945	
Transjordania *	Great Britain	March, 1946	Jordan
Commonwealth of Philippine Islands	United States	July, 1946	Philippine Republic
India [2]	Great Britain	August, 1947	Republic of India
India	Great Britain	August, 1947	Republic of Pakistan
Burma	Great Britain	January, 1948	Union of Burma
Ceylon	Great Britain	February, 1948	
Palestine *	Great Britain	May, 1948	Israel
Korea [3]	Japan	August, 1948	
Netherlands East Indies	Netherlands	December, 1949	Republic of Indonesia
Libya	Italy	December, 1951	
Eritrea	Italy	September, 1952	Federated with Ethiopia
French Indochina [3]	France	July, 1954	Vietnam
Laos	France	July, 1954	
Cambodia	France	July, 1954	
Anglo-Egyptian Sudan	Great Britain	January, 1956	Republic of the Sudan
Morocco	France	March, 1956	
Tunisia	France	March, 1956	
Gold Coast	Great Britain	March, 1957	Ghana
Togoland *	Great Britain	March, 1957	Incorporated in Ghana
Federated Malay States	Great Britain	August, 1957	Federation of Malaya (Malaysia since 1963)
Guinea	France	September, 1958	
Cameroun *	France	January, 1960	
Togoland *	France	April, 1960	Republic of Togo
Madagascar	France	June, 1960	Malgache Republic
Belgian Congo	Belgium	June, 1960	Republic of the Congo [4]
Italian Somaliland *	Italy	July, 1960	Somali Republic
British Somaliland	Great Britain	July, 1960	Part of Somali Republic
Middle Congo	France	August, 1960	Republic of the Congo [4]
Ubangi-Shari	France	August, 1960	Central African Republic

384

Chad	France	August, 1960	
Gabon	France	August, 1960	
Dahomey	France	August, 1960	
Niger	France	August, 1960	
Upper Volta	France	August, 1960	
Ivory Coast	France	August, 1960	
Cyprus	Great Britain	August, 1960	
Senegal	France	September, 1960	(Federation of Mali,
Mali	France	September, 1960	1959–1960)
Nigeria	Great Britain	October, 1960	Federation of Nigeria
Mauritania	France	November, 1960	Islamic Republic of Mauritania
Sierra Leone	Great Britain	April, 1961	
Cameroons *2	Great Britain	June, 1961	Joined to Nigeria
Cameroons *2	Great Britain	October, 1961	Joined to Cameroun
Tanganyika *	Great Britain	December, 1961	Tanzania since 1964
Western Samoa *	New Zealand	January, 1962	
Ruanda-Urundi *2	Belgium	July, 1962	Two states of Rwanda and Burundi
Algeria	France	July, 1962	
Jamaica	Great Britain	August, 1962	
Trinidad and Tobago	Great Britain	August, 1962	
Uganda	Great Britain	October, 1962	
North Borneo, Sarawak, Singapore	Great Britain	September, 1963	Incorporated in Federation of Malaysia; North Borneo renamed Sabah. Singapore seceded from the Federation in 1965 and became an independent state.
Kenya	Great Britain	December, 1963	
Zanzibar	Great Britain	December, 1963	Incorporated with Tanzania, 1964
Nyasaland	Great Britain	July, 1964	Malawi
Maldive Islands	Great Britain	July, 1964	
Malta	Great Britain	September, 1964	
Northern Rhodesia	Great Britain	September, 1964	Zambia
Gambia	Great Britain	February, 1965	
Rhodesia	Great Britain	November, 1965	Independence declared but not recognized by Great Britain

* Mandate or trust territory
1 Independence nominal until 1936
2 Permanently partitioned by agreement
3 Temporarily partitioned pending unification
4 Usually distinguished from one another by adding the name of the capitals: The former Belgian Congo known as Congo (Léopoldville) and Middle Congo as Congo (Brazzaville)

IMPORTANT POLITICAL LEADERS

EUROPE

Albania. Ahmed Zogu. Premier, 1922–1924, 1925; President, 1925–1928; King Zog I, 1928–1929.

Enver Hoxha. Prime Minister-Dictator, 1945–.

Belgium. Paul-Henri Spaak. Foreign Minister, 1938–1949, 1961–1965; Prime Minister, 1938–1939, 1947–1949.

Czechoslovakia. Thomas Masaryk. President, 1918–1935.

Eduard Benes. Prime Minister, 1921–1922; Foreign Minister, 1918–1935; President, 1935–1938; President, Government-in-Exile, 1940–1945; President, 1948–1953.

Clement Gottwald. Prime Minister, 1946–1948; President, 1948–1953.

France. Georges Clemenceau. Prime Minister, 1917–1920.

Raymond Poincaré. Prime Minister, 1912–1913, 1922–1924, 1926–1929; President, 1913–1920.

Aristide Briand. Prime Minister, 1915–1917, 1921–1922; 1925–1926; Foreign Minister, 1925–1932.

Charles de Gaulle. Head French National Committee, 1940–1944; Head, French Provisional Government, 1944–1946; Prime Minister, 1958; President, 1958–.

Pierre Mendès-France. Prime Minister, 1954–1955.

Germany. Friedrich Ebert. President, 1919–1925.

Paul von Hindenburg. President, 1925–1934.

Gustav Stresemann. Chancellor, 1923; Foreign Minister, 1923–1929.

Adolf Hitler. Chancellor, 1933–1934; President and Reichs-fuehrer, 1934–1945.

Konrad Adenauer. Chancellor, Federal Republic of Germany, 1949–1963.

Great Britain. David Lloyd George. Prime Minister, 1916–1922.

James Ramsay MacDonald. Prime Minister, 1923, 1929–1935.

Stanley Baldwin. Prime Minister, 1923–1924, 1924–1929, 1935–1937.

Neville Chamberlain. Prime Minister, 1937–1940.

Winston Churchill. Prime Minister, 1940–1945, 1951–1955.
Anthony Eden. Foreign Secretary, 1935–1938, 1940–1945, 1951–1955; Prime Minister, 1955–1957.
Harold Macmillan. Prime Minister, 1957–1963.

Greece. Eleutherios Venizelos. Prime Minister, 1910–1915, 1917–1920, 1924, 1928–1932, 1933.
John Metaxas. Prime Minister–Dictator, 1936–1941.

Hungary. Nicholas Horthy. Regent–Head of State, 1920–1944.

Ireland. Eamon de Valera. President of (unrecognized) Irish Republic, 1917–1922; President, Irish Free State, 1932–1938; Prime Minister, 1938–1948; Prime Minister, Republic of Ireland, 1951–1954, 1957–1959; President, 1959–.

Italy. Benito Mussolini. Prime Minister–Dictator, 1922–1943.
Alcide de Gasperi. Prime Minister, 1945–1953.

Poland. Josef Pilsudski. Provisional President, 1919–1922; Prime Minister, 1926–1928; Dictator and Chief of Army, 1930–1935.

Portugal. Antonio de Oliveira Salazar. Minister of Finance, 1928–1932; Prime Minister–Dictator, 1932–.

Rumania. John Bratianu. Prime Minister, 1909–1911, 1914–1918, 1922–1927.
Carol II. King, 1930–1940.

Spain. Miguel Primo de Rivera. Dictator, 1923–1930.
Manuel Azaña. Prime Minister, Spanish Republic, 1931–1933, 1936; President, 1936–1938.
Francisco Franco. President-Dictator, 1939–.

USSR. Vladimir Lenin. Chairman, Council of People's Commissars, 1917–1924.
Josef Stalin, General Secretary, Communist party, 1922–1953 (Dictator, 1927–1953); Prime Minister, 1941–1953.
Nikita Khrushchev. General Secretary, Communist party, 1953–1964; Prime Minister, 1958–1964.

Yugoslavia. Alexander I. King, 1921–1934.
Josip Broz (Tito). Head of State, 1945–.

ASIA

Afghanistan. Amanullah I. Emir, 1919–1926; King, 1926–1929.

Burma. U Nu. Prime Minister, 1947–1956, 1957–1958, 1960–1962.
Ne Win. Prime Minister, 1958–1960; Chairman, Revolutionary Council, 1962–.

China. Chiang Kai-shek. Generalissimo and Chairman of Kuomintang, 1928–1948. President, Republic of China, 1948– (on Taiwan from 1949).
Mao Tse-tung. Chairman Administrative Council, People's Republic of China, 1949–.
Chou En-lai. Foreign Minister, People's Republic of China, 1949–.

India. Mohandas Gandhi. Independence Leader, 1915–1948.
Jawaharlal Nehru. Prime Minister, 1947–1964.

Indonesia.   Sukarno. President, Republic of Indonesia (unrecognized), 1945–1949; President, Republic of Indonesia, 1949–.
Iran.   Reza Pahlevi I, Shah, 1925–1941.
Reza Pahlevi II, Shah, 1941–.
Mohammed Mossadegh. Prime Minister, 1951–1953.
Iraq.   Feisal I. King, 1921–1933.
Nuri as-Said. Prime Minister, 1943–1958, intermittently.
Israel.   David Ben-Gurion. Prime Minister, 1948–1963.
Jordan.   Abdullah I. Emir of Transjordania, 1921–1946; King, 1946–1951.
Hussein I. King, 1952–.
Korea (South).   Syngman Rhee. President, 1948–1960.
Malaya.   Tunku Abdul Rahman. Prime Minister, Malaya (Protectorate), 1955–1957; Prime Minister, Federation of Malaya, 1957–1963; Prime Minister of Malaysia, 1963–.
Pakistan.   Mohammed Ayub Khan. President, 1958–.
Philippine Islands.   Manuel Quezon. President of Senate, 1916–1935; President, Philippine Commonwealth, 1935–1944.
Ramon Magsaysay. President, Philippine Republic, 1953–1957.
Saudi Arabia.   Abdul Aziz ibn-Saud. King, 1901–1953.
Singapore.   Lee Kuan Yew. Prime Minister, 1959–.
Turkey.   Mustapha Kemal Atatürk. President, Provisional Government, 1919–1923; President, Republic of Turkey, 1923–1938.
Ismet Inönu. Prime Minister, 1923–1924, 1925–1937, 1962–1965; President, 1938–1950.

AFRICA

Algeria.   Ahmed Ben Bella. Prime Minister, 1962–1963, President, 1963–1965.
Cameroun.   Ahmadou Ahidjo. Prime Minister, 1958–1960, President, 1960–.
Congo (Léopoldville).   Joseph Kasavubu. President, 1960–1965.
Moise Tshombe. Prime Minister ("President") of Katanga, 1960–1963; Prime Minister, Congo Republic, 1964–1965.
Egypt.   Fuad I. King, 1922–1936.
Nahas Pasha. Prime Minister, 1928–1930, 1936–1937, 1950–1952.
Gamal Nasser. President, 1953–.
Ethiopia.   Haile Selassie I. King, 1930–1936; 1942–.
Gabon.   Leon M'ba. Prime Minister, 1958–1960; President, 1960–.
Ghana.   Kwame Nkrumah. Prime Minister, Gold Coast, 1952–1957; Prime Minister, Ghana, 1957–1966 (also President after 1960).
Guinea.   Sékou Touré. Prime Minister, 1958; President, 1958–.
Ivory Coast.   Félix Houphouet-Boigny. Prime Minister, 1958–1960; President, 1960–.
Kenya.   Jomo Kenyatta. Prime Minister, 1963–1964. President, 1964–.
Liberia.   William V. S. Tubman. President, 1944–.
Malawi.   Hastings Banda. Prime Minister, 1962–.

Malgache Republic. Philibert Tsiranana. Prime Minister, 1958–1959; President, 1959–.

Mali. Modibo Keita. Prime Minister, Soudan, 1958–1959; President, Federation of Mali, 1959–1960; President, Mali, 1960–.

Morocco. Mohammed V. Sultan, 1927–1961.
Hassan II, Sultan, 1961–.

Nigeria. Nnamdi Azikiwe. Prime Minister, Eastern Region, 1953–1960; Governor General, 1960–1963; President, 1963–1966.

Rhodesia. Godfrey Huggins (Lord Malvern from 1955). Prime Minister, Southern Rhodesia, 1933–1953; Prime Minister, Federation of Rhodesia and Nyasaland, 1953–1956.
Roy Welensky. Prime Minister, Federation of Rhodesia and Nyasaland, 1956–1963.

Senegal. Léopold Senghor. Prime Minister, Senegal, 1958–1959; President of Assembly, Federation of Mali, 1959–1960; President, Senegal, 1960–.

South Africa. Jan Christiaan Smuts. Prime Minister, 1919–1924, 1939–1948.
James B. Hertzog. Prime Minister, 1924–1939.
Daniel Malan. Prime Minister, 1948–1954.
Hendrik Verwoerd. Prime Minister, 1958–1966.

Tanganyika. Julius Nyerere. Prime Minister, 1961–1962; President, 1962–1964; President, Tanzania, 1964–.

Togo. Sylvanus Olympio. Prime Minister, 1956–1963 (also President, 1960–1963).

Tunisia. Habib Bourguiba. Prime Minister, 1956–1957; President, 1957–.

Uganda. Milton Obote. Prime Minister, 1962–.

WESTERN HEMISPHERE

Argentina. Juan Domingo Perón. President, 1946–1955.

Bolivia. Victor Paz Estenssoro. President, 1952–1964.

Brazil. Getulio Vargas. Dictator, 1930–1945; President, 1950–1954.

Canada. William Lyon Mackenzie King. Prime Minister, 1921–1930, 1935–1948.

Costa Rica. José Figueres. President, 1953–1958.

Cuba. Fulgencio Batista. Dictator (nominally under other presidents), 1933–1940; President, 1940–1944, 1952–1958.
Fidel Castro. Prime Minister, 1959–.

Dominican Republic. Rafael Leónidas Trujillo. President, 1930–1936; Dictator (under various presidents), 1938–1961.

Jamaica. Alexander Bustamante. Majority Leader, Jamaican Legislature, 1944–1953; Prime Minister (after independence), 1962–.

Mexico. Venustiano Carranza. President, 1914–1920.
Lázaro Cárdenas. President, 1934–1940.
Miguel Alemán. President, 1946–1952.
Adolfo Lopez Mateos. President, 1958–1964.

Puerto Rico. Luis Muñoz Marín. Governor of Commonwealth, 1948–1964.

Trinidad. Eric Williams. Chief Minister, 1956–1962; Prime Minister (after independence), 1962–.

United States.   Woodrow Wilson. President, 1913–1921.
            Franklin D. Roosevelt. President, 1933–1945.
            Harry S. Truman. President, 1945–1953.
            Dwight D. Eisenhower. President, 1953–1961.
            John F. Kennedy. President, 1961–1963.
            Lyndon B. Johnson. President, 1963–.
Venezuela.   Juan Vicente Gomez. Dictator–President, 1908–1935.
            Rómulo Betancourt. President, 1945–1947; 1959–1964.

AUSTRALIA
William M. Hughes. Prime Minister, 1915–1923.
Robert Gordon Menzies. Prime Minister, 1949–1966.

UNITED NATIONS
Trygvie Lie. Secretary-General, 1946–1952.
Dag Hammarskjöld. Secretary-General, 1953–1961.
U Thant. Secretary-General, 1961–.

BIBLIOGRAPHY

The titles in this bibliography are divided into two sections, paperback and clothbound books. Paperback books are listed with the name of the series or publisher only. The clothbound books are listed with the name of the publisher and the date of the most recent edition. Preference is given in this bibliography to paperback books, since these are cheaper and more easily obtainable, though most college libraries should have at least some edition of all clothbound books recommended here.

Some of the books deal with the periods covered in more than one chapter. The student is therefore advised to look also under other chapters which deal with the same subject.

CHAPTER 1: THE MAKING OF PEACE

PAPERBACK BOOKS:

Bailey, T. A. *Woodrow Wilson and the Great Betrayal.* Quadrangle.
———. *Woodrow Wilson and the Lost Peace.* Quadrangle.
Czernin, F. *Versailles, 1919: The Forces, Events and Personalities That Shaped the Treaty.* Capricorn.
Esposito, V. J., ed. *A Concise History of World War I.* Praeger.
Farmer, Frances, ed. *The Wilson Reader.* Oceana.
Lederer, I. *The Versailles Settlement: Was it Foredoomed to Failure?* Heath.
Link, A. S. *Wilson the Diplomatist.* Quadrangle.
Mantoux, E. *The Carthaginian Peace—or the Economic Consequences of Mr. Keynes.* University of Pittsburgh.
Meyer, A. J. *Wilson* v. *Lenin: Political Origins of the New Diplomacy.* Meridian.
Wheeler-Bennett, J. W. *Brest-Litovsk: the Forgotten Peace.* St. Martin's.

CLOTHBOUND BOOKS:

Gathorne-Hardy, G. *The Fourteen Points and the Treaty of Versailles.* Oxford, 1940.
Keynes, J. M. *The Economic Consequences of the Peace.* Harcourt, Brace, 1920.
Nicolson, H. *Peacemaking, 1919.* Harcourt, Brace, 1939.

CHAPTER 2: THE AFTERMATH OF WAR—INTERNATIONAL RELATIONS TO THE RISE OF THE THIRD REICH

PAPERBACK BOOKS:
Aron, R. *A Century of Total War.* Beacon.
Carr, E. H. *Twenty Years Crisis, 1919–1939.* Harper.
Jaszi, O. *The Dissolution of the Habsburg Monarchy.* Phoenix.
Schumpeter, J. A. *Capitalism, Socialism and Democracy.* Harper.

CLOTHBOUND BOOKS:
Angress, W. T. *Stillborn Revolution: The Communist Bid for Power in Germany, 1921–1923.* Princeton, 1964.
Carr, E. H. *International Relations between the Two World Wars.* Macmillan, 1947.
Coper, R. *Failure of a Revolution: Germany in 1918 and 1919.* Cambridge, 1955.
Footman, D. *Civil War in Russia.* Praeger, 1962.
Kennan, G. F. *Russia Leaves the War.* Princeton, 1956.
Walters, F. P. *A History of the League of Nations.* 2 vols. Oxford, 1952.
White, E. G. L. *Vanguard of Nazism: The Free Corps Movement in Postwar Germany.* Harvard, 1952.
Wolfers, A. *Britain and France Between Two Wars.* Harcourt, Brace, 1940.

CHAPTER 3: SOVIET RUSSIA BETWEEN TWO WARS

PAPERBACK BOOKS:
Campbell, R. W. *Soviet Economic Power: Its Organization, Growth, and Challenge.* Houghton Mifflin.
Deutscher, I. *Stalin: A Political Biography.* Vintage.
———. *Trotsky.* 3 vols. Vintage.
Fischer, L. *The Life of Lenin.* Harper.
Kennan, G. F. *Russia and the West under Lenin and Stalin.* Mentor.
Rauch, Georg von. *A History of Soviet Russia.* 3rd ed., rev. Praeger.
Schapiro, L. *The Communist Party of the Soviet Union.* Vintage.
Seton-Watson, R. W. *From Lenin to Khrushchev: A History of World Communism.* Praeger.
Shub, D. *Lenin* (abridged). Mentor.
Trotsky, L. *My Life.* Universal.
Vernadsky, G. *A History of Russia.* Yale.
Wolfe, B. *Three Who Made a Revolution.* Delta-Dell.

CLOTHBOUND BOOKS:
Carr, E. H. *The Soviet Impact on the Western World.* Macmillan, 1954.
Fainsod, M. *How Russia is Ruled.* Rev. ed. Harvard, 1963.
Randall, F. B. *Stalin's Russia: A Historical Reconsideration.* Free Press, 1965.

CHAPTER 4: DEMOCRACY AND TOTALITARIANISM IN
GERMANY AND ITALY

PAPERBACK BOOKS:
Arendt, H. *Origins of Totalitarianism*. Meridian.
Bullock, A. *Hitler: A Study in Tyranny*. Bantam. (Also rev. ed. Harper.)
Finer, H. *Mussolini's Italy*. Universal.
Fromm, E. *Escape from Freedom*. Avon.
Halperin, S. W. *Germany Tried Democracy*. Norton.
Hitler, A. *Mein Kampf*. Sentry.
Leuwy, G. *The Catholic Church in Nazi Germany*. McGraw-Hill.
Schaefer, L. F., ed. *The Ethiopian Crisis: Touchstone of Appeasement*.
Heath.
Shirer, W. L. *Berlin Diary*. Popular Library.
————. *Rise and Fall of the Third Reich*. Crest.
Stern, F. *The Politics of Cultural Despair*. Anchor.
Turner, H. A., Jr. *Stresemann and the Politics of the Weimar Republic*.
Princeton.

CLOTHBOUND BOOKS:
Fermi, L. *Mussolini*. Chicago, 1961.
Kirkpatrick, I. *Mussolini: A Study in Power*. Hawthorn, 1964.
Neumann, F. L. *Behemoth: The Structure and Practice of National Social-
ism*. Oxford, 1942.
Nolte, E. *Three Faces of Fascism*. Holt, Rinehart & Winston, 1966.
Salvemini, G. *Under the Axe of Fascism*. Viking, 1936.

CHAPTER 5: THE IBERIAN PENINSULA

PAPERBACK BOOKS:
Atkinson, W. C. *A History of Spain and Portugal*. Penguin.
Brenan, G. *The Spanish Labyrinth*. Cambridge.
Orwell, G. *Homage to Catalonia*. Beacon.
Thomas, H. *The Spanish Civil War*. Harper.

CLOTHBOUND BOOKS:
Bowers, C. *My Mission to Spain*. Simon and Schuster, 1954.
Manuel, F. E. *The Politics of Modern Spain*. McGraw-Hill, 1938.
Sanchez, J. M. *Reform and Reaction: The Politico-Religious Background
of the Spanish Civil War*. North Carolina, 1966.

CHAPTER 6: THE SUCCESSOR STATES OF THE TSARIST AND
HABSBURG EMPIRES

PAPERBACK BOOKS:
Pounds, N. J. G. *Poland between East and West: Soviet and German
Diplomacy toward Poland*. Searchlight.

CLOTHBOUND BOOKS:
Buell, R. L. *Poland, Key to Europe.* Knopf, 1939.
Gehl, J. *Austria, Germany and the Anschluss, 1931–1938.* Oxford, 1963.
Gulick, C. A. *Austria from Habsburg to Hitler.* 2 vols. California, 1948.
Macartney, C. A. *October Fifteenth: A History of Hungary, 1929–1945.* 2nd ed. Aldine, 1961.
———, and Palmer, A. W. *Independent Eastern Europe.* St. Martin's, 1962. Martin's, 1962.
Seton-Watson, H. *Eastern Europe between the Wars, 1918–1941.* Cambridge, 1946.
Shepherd, G. *The Rape of Austria.* Macmillan, 1963.
Wuorinen, J. H. *A History of Finland.* Columbia, 1965.

CHAPTER 7: THE BALKAN PENINSULA AND TURKEY

PAPERBACK BOOKS:
Armstrong, H. C. *Grey Wolf: The Life of Kemal Atatürk.* Capricorn.
West, R. *Black Lamb and Grey Falcon.* 2 vols. Compass.

CLOTHBOUND BOOKS:
Howard, H. N. *The Partition of Turkey: A Diplomatic History, 1913–1923.* Oklahoma, 1931.
Kinross, Lord. *Atatürk: A Biography of Mustafa Kemal.* Morrow, 1965.
Lewis, B. *The Emergence of Modern Turkey.* Oxford, 1961.
Roberts, H. L. *Rumania: Political Problems of an Agrarian State.* Yale, 1951.
Stavrianos, L. *The Balkans since 1453.* Holt, Rinehart & Winston, 1958.
Wolff, R. L. *The Balkans in Our Time.* Harvard, 1946.

CHAPTER 8: THE OLDER DEMOCRACIES OF EUROPE AND THE BRITISH DOMINIONS

PAPERBACK BOOKS:
Brogan, D. *The Development of Modern France,* Vol. II. Harper.
Cameron, W. J. *New Zealand.* Spectrum.
Childs, M. *Sweden: The Middle Way.* Yale.
Crawford, R. M. *Australian Perspective.* Wisconsin.
Eyck, F. G. *The Benelux Countries: An Historical Survey.* Anvil.
Graves, R., and Hodge, A. *The Long Week-end: A Social History of Great Britain, 1918–1939.* Norton.
Masters, D. C. *A Short History of Canada.* Anvil.
Thomson, D. *Democracy in France since 1870.* Oxford.
———. *England in the Twentieth Century.* Penguin.
Ward, R. *Australia.* Spectrum.

CLOTHBOUND BOOKS:
Cobban, A. *France of the Republics* (Vol. III of *A History of Modern France*). Cape, 1965. (Also in abridged version, 1800–1940, Penguin.)
Giraud, A ("Pertinax"). *The Grave-Diggers of France*. Doubleday, 1944.
Mowat, C. L. *Britain between the Wars, 1918–1940*. Chicago, 1955.
Taylor, A. J. P. *English History, 1914–1945*. Oxford, 1965.
Weber, E. *Action Française*. Stanford, 1962.
Werth, A. *The Twilight of France, 1933–1940*. Harper, 1942.

CHAPTER 9: THE WESTERN HEMISPHERE BETWEEN THE WARS

PAPERBACK BOOKS:
Adams, S. H. *The Incredible Era: The Life and Times of Warren Gamaliel Harding*. Capricorn.
Allen, F. W. *Only Yesterday*. Harper.
Burns, J. McG. *Roosevelt: The Lion and the Fox*. Harvest.
Feis, H. *Diplomacy and the Dollar: First Era, 1919–1932*. Norton.
Galbraith, K. *The Great Crash*. Sentry.
Hicks, J. D. *Republican Ascendancy, 1921–1933*. Harper.
Kline, H. *Mexico*. Oxford.
Leuchtenberg, W. E. *Franklin D. Roosevelt and the New Deal*. Harper.
———. *The Perils of Prosperity, 1914–1932*. Chicago.
Malone, D., and Rauch, B. *War and Troubled Peace, 1917–1939*. Appleton.
Perkins, D. *The New Age of Franklin Roosevelt, 1932–1945*. Chicago.
Roosevelt, F. D. *Nothing to Fear* (ed. B. D. Zevin). Popular.
Schlesinger, A. M., Jr. *The Age of Roosevelt*. 2 vols. Sentry.
Scott, R. E. *Mexican Government in Transition*. Illinois.
Shannon, D. A., ed. *The Great Depression*. Spectrum.
Simpson, L. B. *Many Mexicos*. California.

CLOTHBOUND BOOKS:
Adler, S. *The Uncertain Giant, 1921–1941: American Foreign Policy between the Wars*. Macmillan, 1966.
Soule, G. *Prosperity Decade: From War to Depression, 1917–1929*. Holt, Rinehart & Winston, 1947.

CHAPTER 10: ASIA AND THE MIDDLE EAST BETWEEN THE WARS

PAPERBACK BOOKS:
Antonius, G. *The Arab Awakening*. Capricorn.
Brecher, M. *Nehru: A Political Biography* (abridged). Beacon.
Clubb, O. *Twentieth Century China*. Columbia.
Fischer, L. *The Life of Mahatma Gandhi*. Collier.
Griswold, A. W. *Far Eastern Policy of the United States*. Yale.
Snow, E. *Red Star Over China*. Black Cat.

CLOTHBOUND BOOKS:

Brown, D. M. *Nationalism in Japan.* California, 1955.

Fisher, S. N. *The Middle East: A History.* Knopf, 1959.

Furnivall, J. S. *Colonial Policy and Practice: A Comparative Study of Burma and Netherlands East Indies.* Cambridge, 1948.

Hayden, J. R. *The Philippines: A Study in National Development.* Macmillan, 1942.

Jones, F. C. *Japan's New Order in Asia: Its Rise and Fall.* Oxford, 1954.

Longrigg, S. H. *Iraq, 1900–1950.* Oxford, 1953.

———. *Syria and Lebanon under French Mandate.* Oxford, 1958.

Monroe, E. *Britain's Moment in the Middle East.* Johns Hopkins, 1963.

Romein, J. *The Asian Century: A History of Modern Nationalism in Asia.* California, 1962.

Young, A. N. *China and the Helping Hand, 1937–1945.* Harvard, 1963.

CHAPTER 11: THE COMING OF WORLD WAR II

PAPERBACK BOOKS:

Rowse, A. L. *Appeasement.* Norton.

Snell, J. N. ed. *The Outbreak of the Second World War: Design or Blunder?* Heath.

Taylor, A. J. P. *Origins of the Second World War.* Premier.

Wheeler-Bennett, J. W. *Munich: Prologue to Tragedy.* Compass.

CLOTHBOUND BOOKS:

Deakins, F. W. *Brutal Friendship: Mussolini, Hitler, and the Fall of Italian Fascism.* Harper, 1962.

Gedye, G. E. R. *Betrayal in Central Europe.* Harper, 1939.

Langer, W. L., and Gleason, J. E. *Challenge to Isolation: The World Crisis of 1937–1940.* 2 vols. Harper.

Namier, L. B. *Diplomatic Prelude, 1938–1939.* Macmillan (London), 1948.

Neumann, S. *The Future in Perspective.* Putnam, 1946.

Schuman, F. L. *Europe on the Eve: The Crisis of Diplomacy.* Knopf, 1939.

CHAPTER 12: WORLD WAR II

PAPERBACK BOOKS:

Borsody, S. *The Tragedy of Central Europe.* Collier.

Churchill, W. *The Second World War.* 6 vols. Bantam.

Eisenhower, D. D. *Crusade in Europe.* Dolphin.

Esposito, V. J., ed. *A Concise History of World War II.* Praeger.

Feis, H. *The Road to Pearl Harbor.* Atheneum.

Frank, Anne. *Diary of a Young Girl.* Pocket Books.

Montgomery, B. L. *Memoirs.* Signet.

Sherwood, R. *Roosevelt and Hopkins.* Universal.

Snell, J. L. *Illusion and Necessity: The Diplomacy of Global War.* Houghton Mifflin.

Snyder, L. L. *The War.* Dell.

Werth, A. *Russia at War*. Avon.
Wilmot, C. *The Struggle for Europe*. Harper.

CLOTHBOUND BOOKS:
Aron, Robert. *History of Vichy*. Macmillan, 1958.
De Gaulle, Charles. *Memoirs*. 3 vols. Simon and Schuster, 1958–1960.
Farmer, P. *Vichy Political Dilemma*. Columbia, 1955.
Feis, H. *Churchill, Roosevelt, Stalin*. Princeton, 1957.
Harris, W. R. *Tyranny on Trial: The Evidence at Nuremberg*. Southern Methodist, 1954.
Taylor, T. *The March of Conquest*. Simon and Schuster, 1958.

CHAPTER 13: THE AFTERMATH OF WAR—POSTWAR DISAGREEMENTS AND THE FOUNDATION OF THE UNITED NATIONS

PAPERBACK BOOKS:
Bailey, S. D. *The United Nations: A Short Political Guide*. Praeger.
Boyd, A. *The United Nations: Piety, Myth, and Truth*. Penguin.
Coyle, D. C. *The United Nations and How it Works*. Mentor.
Jones, J. M. *The United Nations at Work*. Pergamon.
Seton-Watson, H. *Neither War Nor Peace: The Struggle for Power in the Postwar World*. Praeger.
Truman, H. S. *Memoirs*. 2 vols. Signet.

CLOTHBOUND BOOKS:
Alperowitz, G. *Atomic Diplomacy: Hiroshima and Potsdam*. Simon and Schuster, 1965.
Davidson, E. *The Death and Life of Germany: An Account of the American Occupation*. Knopf, 1959.
Feis, H. *Between War and Peace: The Potsdam Conference*. Princeton, 1960.
Moore, B. T. *NATO and the Future of Europe*. Harper, 1958.
Murray, J. N. *The United Nations Trusteeship System*. University of Illinois, 1957.
Price, H. B. *The Marshall Plan and its Meaning*. Cornell.

CHAPTER 14: THE RECONSTRUCTION OF EUROPE—MOVEMENTS TOWARD INTEGRATION

PAPERBACK BOOKS:
Boyd, F. *British Politics in Transition, 1945–1963*. Praeger.
Freymond, J. *Western Europe since the War: A Short Political History*. Praeger.
Grosser, A. *The Federal Republic of Germany: A Concise History*. Praeger.
Kitzinger, U. W. *Politics and Economics of European Integration*. Praeger.
Lichtheim, W. *The New Europe*. Praeger.
Luethy, H. *France against Herself*. Meridian.
Pickles, D. *The Fifth French Republic*. Praeger.
Sampson, A. *Anatomy of Britain*. Harper.
Shanks, M., and Lambert, J. *The Common Market Today and Tomorrow*. Praeger.

CLOTHBOUND BOOKS:
Cole, G. D. H. *The Postwar Condition of Britain.* 1957.
Fleischer, W. *Sweden: The Welfare State.* Day, 1956.
Horne, A. *Return to Power.* Praeger, 1956.

CHAPTER 15: THE SOVIET UNION AND EASTERN EUROPE

PAPERBACK BOOKS:
Brzezenski, Z. K. *The Soviet Bloc: Unity and Conflict.* Praeger.
Djilas, A. *The New Class.* Praeger.
Fischer-Galati, S., ed. *Eastern Europe in the 60's.* Praeger.
Hoffman, G. W. *The Balkans in Transition.* Searchlight.
Ionescu, G. *The Breakup of the Soviet Empire in Eastern Europe.* Penguin.
Moore, Barrington, Jr. *Soviet Politics: The Dilemma of Power.* Harper.
Moseley, P. E., *The Kremlin and World Politics.* Vintage.
Palmer, A. W. *Yugoslavia.* Oxford.
Schwartz, H. *The Red Phoenix: Russia since World War II.* Praeger.
Werth, A. *Russia under Khrushchev.* Crest.

CLOTHBOUND BOOKS:
Hiscocks, R. *Poland: Bridge for the Abyss.* Oxford, 1963.
Hoffman, G. W., and Neal, F. W. *Yugoslavia and the New Communism.* Twentieth Century Fund, 1962.
Neal, F. W. *Titoism in Action: The Reforms in Yugoslavia after 1948.* University of California, 1958.
Wolff, R. L. *The Balkans in Our Time.* Harvard, 1956.

CHAPTER 16: THE WESTERN HEMISPHERE SINCE WORLD WAR II

PAPERBACK BOOKS:
Bernstein, H. *Venezuela and Colombia.* Spectrum.
Draper, T. *Castro's Revolution: Myths and Realities.* Praeger.
Eisenhower, D. D. *White House Years: Mandate for Change.* Signet.
Friedman, J. *Venezuela: From Doctrine to Dialogue.* Syracuse.
Goldman, E. *The Crucial Decade.* Vintage.
Hamill, H. M., Jr., ed. *Dictatorship in Spanish America.* Knopf.
Hughes, E. C. *French Canada in Transition.* Phoenix.
Hughes, E. J. *Ordeal of Power,* Dell.
Latham, E. *The Meaning of McCarthyism.* Heath.
Lieuwen, E. *Arms and Politics in Latin America.* Praeger.
―――. *Generals v. Presidents: Neocolonialism in Latin America.* Praeger.
Niebuhr, R. *The Irony of American History.* Scribner's.
Pearcy, G. E. *West Indian Scene.* Spectrum.
Rodriguez, M. *Central America.* Spectrum.
Ross, S. R., ed. *Is the Mexican Revolution Dead?* Knopf.
Rovere, R. H. *Senator Joe McCarthy.* Meridian.

Szulc, T. *Winds of Revolution: Latin America Today and Tomorrow.* Praeger.
Zallin, M., and Scheer, R. *Tragedy in Our Hemisphere.* Black Cat.

CLOTHBOUND BOOKS:
Eisenhower, M. *The Wine Is Bitter.* Doubleday, 1963.
Gerassi, J. *The Great Fear.* Macmillan, 1963.
Pflamm, P. *Arenas of Decision: Latin America in Crisis.* Prentice-Hall, 1964.
Schlesinger, A. M., Jr. *A Thousand Days.* Houghton Mifflin, 1965.
Stone, I. F. *The Haunted Fifties.* Random House, 1963.

CHAPTER 17: DECOLONIZATION OF EAST ASIA—THE RISE OF COMMUNIST CHINA

PAPERBACK BOOKS:
Barnett, A. D. *Communist China and Asia.* Vintage.
Butwell, R. *South East Asia Today—and Tomorrow.* Praeger.
Crankshaw, E. *The New Cold War—Moscow v. Peking.* Penguin.
Crozier, B. *Southeast Asia in Turmoil.* Penguin.
Feis, H. *The China Tangle.* Atheneum.
Hale, R. B., Jr. *Japan: Industrial Power of Asia.* Searchlight.
Higgins, B. and J. *Indonesia: The Crisis of the Millstones.* Searchlight.
Lamb, B. P. *India: A World in Transition.* Praeger.
Walker, R. L. *China under Communism.* Yale.
Warner, D. *The Last Confucian.* Penguin.
Zagoria, D. S. *Sino-Soviet Conflict, 1956–1961.* Atheneum.

CLOTHBOUND BOOKS:
Cady, J. F. *A History of Modern Burma.* Cornell, 1958.
Fall, B. *The Two Vietnams.* Praeger, 1963.
———, and Raskin, M. G., eds. *The Vietnam Reader.* Random House, 1965.
Friend, I. *Between Two Empires: The Ordeal of the Philippines.* Yale, 1965.
Harrison, S. S. *India: The Most Dangerous Decades.* Princeton, 1960.
Kahin, G. McT. *Nationalism and Revolution in Indonesia.* Cornell, 1952.
Lacouture, J. *Vietnam between Two Truces.* Random House, 1966.
Lancaster, D. *The Emancipation of French Indochina.* Oxford, 1961.
Mills, Lennox. *Malaya: A Political and Economic Appraisal.* University of Minnesota, 1958.
Rees, D. *Korea—The Limited War.* St. Martin's, 1964.
Snow, E. *The Other Side of the River.* Random House, 1963.

CHAPTER 18: WESTERN ASIA, EGYPT, AND THE EASTERN MEDITERRANEAN

PAPERBACK BOOKS:
Ben-Gurion, David. *Israel: Years of Challenge.* Holt, Rinehart & Winston.
Berger, M. *The Arab World Today.* Anchor.

Harari, M. *Government and Politics of the Middle East*. Praeger.
Kirk, G. E. *A Short History of the Middle East*. Praeger.
Mansfield, P. *Nasser's Egypt*. Penguin.
Nasser, G. A. *The Philosophy of the Revolution*. Economica.

CLOTHBOUND BOOKS:
Lorch, N. *The Edge of the Sword: Israel's War of Independence, 1947–1949*. Putnam, 1961.
Polk, W. R. *The United States and the Arab World*. Harvard, 1965.
Upton, J. M. *The History of Modern Iran: An Interpretation*. Harvard, 1960.

CHAPTER 19: THE END OF COLONIALISM IN AFRICA

PAPERBACK BOOKS:
Adam, T. R. *Government and Politics in Africa South of the Sahara*. Random House.
Brace, R. M. *Morocco, Algeria and Tunisia*. Spectrum.
Carter, G. *Independence for Africa*. Praeger.
Clark, M. S. *Algeria in Turmoil*. Universal.
Duffy, J. *Portugal in Africa*. Penguin.
Easton, S. C. *The Rise and Fall of Western Colonialism*. Praeger.
Emerson, R. *From Empire to Nation*. Beacon.
Harris, R. *Independence and After: Revolution in Undeveloped Countries*. Oxford.
Hodgkin, T. *Nationalism in Colonial Africa*. New York University.
Keatley, P. *The Politics of Partnership*. Penguin.
Strachey, J. *The End of Empire*. Praeger.

CLOTHBOUND BOOKS:
Brace, R. and J. *Ordeal in Algeria*. Van Nostrand, 1960.
Cohen, A. *British Policy in Changing Africa*. Northwestern, 1959.
Foster, G. M. *Traditional Cultures and the Impact of Technological Change*. Harper, 1963.
McKay, V. *Africa in World Politics*. Harper, 1963.
Moore, C. H. *Tunisia Since Independence: The Dynamics of One Party Government*. University of California, 1965.
Perham, M. *The Colonial Reckoning*. Knopf, 1962.
Thompson, V., and Adloff, R. *The Emerging States of French Equatorial Africa*. Stanford, 1960.
———. *French West Africa*. Stanford, 1958.
———. *The Malagasy Republic: Madagascar Today*. Stanford, 1965.

CHAPTER 20: INTERNATIONAL RELATIONS AND THE COLD WAR

PAPERBACK BOOKS:
Gatzke, H. W. *The Present in Perspective*. Rand McNally.
Graebner, N. *Cold War Diplomacy: American Foreign Policy*. Anvil.

Kissinger, H. A. *The Necessity for Choice: Prospects of American Foreign Policy*. Anchor.

Luard, E., ed. *The Cold War*. Praeger.

Lukacs, J. *History of the Cold War*. Anchor.

Malone, D., and Rauch, B. *America and World Leadership, 1940–1965*. Appleton.

Pachter, H. M. *Collision Course: The Cuban Missile Crisis and Co-Existence*. Praeger.

Seton-Watson, H. *Neither War Nor Peace: The Struggle for Power in the Postwar World*. Praeger.

Spanier, J. W. *The Truman-MacArthur Controversy and the Korean War*. Norton.

Stillman, E., and Pfaff, W. *The Politics of Hysteria: The Sources of Twentieth Century Conflict*. Harper.

Wint, G. *Communist China's Crusade*. Praeger.

CLOTHBOUND BOOKS:

Donnelly, D. *Struggle for the World: The Cold War, 1917–1965*. St. Martin's, 1965.

Fleming, D. F. *The Cold War and Its Origins*. 2 vols. Doubleday, 1961.

Schuman, F. L. *The Cold War: Retrospect and Prospect*. University of Louisiana, 1962.

CHAPTER 21: SCIENTIFIC AND CULTURAL DEVELOPMENTS SINCE WORLD WAR I

PAPERBACK BOOKS:

Beauvoir, S. *The Mandarins*. Meridian.

Boulding, K. *The Meaning of the Twentieth Century: The Great Transition*. Harper.

Brown, H. *The Challenge of Man's Future*. Compass.

Clarke, A. C. *Profiles of the Future*. Bantam.

Frankel, C. *The Case for Modern Man*. Beacon.

Heilbroner, L. *The Future as History*. Evergreen.

Myrdal, G. *Challenge to Affluence*. Vintage.

Ortega y Gasset, J. *The Revolt of the Masses*. Norton.

Reichenbach, H. *The Rise of Scientific Philosophy*. University of California.

Trilling, L. *The Liberal Imagination*. Anchor.

White, M., ed. *The Age of Analysis: Twentieth Century Philosophers*. Mentor.

Wilson, E. *To the Finland Station*. Anchor.

CLOTHBOUND BOOKS:

Asimov, I. *The Intelligent Man's Guide to Science*. 2 vols. Basic Books, 1960.

Henry, J. *Culture and Man*. Random House, 1964.

Levi, A. W. *Philosophy and the Modern World*. Indiana, 1959.

KEY EVENTS

1917 (April)	United States declaration of war with Germany
1917 (November)	**Bolshevik Revolution in Russia**
1918 (March)	Treaty of Brest-Litovsk
1918 (November)	Armistice between Allies and Central Powers
1919 (June)	**Treaty of Versailles**
1920 (January)	Beginning of League of Nations
1920 (March)	Final rejection of Versailles Treaty by United States Senate
1921–1927	New Economic Policy in Russia
1922 (October)	**Mussolini's "March on Rome"**
1923 (January)	Franco-Belgian invasion of Ruhr
1923 (November)	Hitler "Beer-Hall Putsch"
1925	Treaties of Locarno
1928	First Five-Year Plan in Russia
1929	Stock-market crash in United States
1930–1935	**Great Depression**
1931	Statute of Westminster (complete independence of British dominions)
1931 (September)	Japanese invasion of Manchuria
1933 (January)	**Hitler becomes chancellor of Germany**
1933 (January)	Franklin Roosevelt becomes United States President
1935 (October)	Italian invasion of Ethiopia
1936 (July)	Beginning of Spanish Civil War
1936 (October)	Rome-Berlin Axis
1938 (March)	German annexation of Austria
1938 (September)	Pact of Munich
1939 (March)	German occupation of Czechoslovakia
1939 (August)	**Nonaggression agreement between Russia and Germany**
1939 (September)	German invasion of Poland
1939 (November)–1940 (March)	Russo-Finnish War
1940 (April)	German invasion of Norway

1940 (May)	German invasion of Holland and Belgium
1940 (June)	German occupation of Paris
1941 (June)	German invasion of Russia
1941 (December)	Japanese attack on Pearl Harbor
1942 (August)	Beginning of siege of Stalingrad by Germans
1942 (November)	Landing of United States forces in North Africa
1943 (September)	Surrender of Italy
1944 (June)	**Allied invasion of Normandy**
1944 (July)	Expulsion of Germans from Russia
1944 (August)	Liberation of Paris
1944 (October)	Decisive naval victory by United States over Japan
1945 (February)	Conference of Yalta
1945 (May)	**Unconditional surrender of Germany**
1945 (August 6)	**Atomic bomb dropped on Hiroshima**
1945 (August 14)	**Unconditional surrender of Japan**
1945 (October)	Establishment of the United Nations
1946 (May)	Withdrawal of Soviet troops from Iran
1947 (March)	Announcement of Truman Doctrine
1947 (June)	Announcement of Marshall Plan
1948 (February)	Communist coup in Czechoslovakia
1948 (April)	Formation of Organization of American States at Bogotá
1948 (May)– 1949 (July)	Arab-Israeli War
1948 (June)	Expulsion of Tito from Cominform
1949 (April)	**Signing of North Atlantic Treaty (NATO)**
1949 (May)	Proclamation of basic law for Federal Republic of Germany
1949 (October)	Proclamation of People's Republic of China
1950 (June)	**Beginning of Korean War**
1950 (November)	Uniting for Peace Resolution passed by United Nations General Assembly
1953 (March)	Death of Stalin
1954 (July)	Geneva Agreements on Vietnam
1954 (September)	Formation of Southeast Asia Treaty Organization (SEATO)
1954 (October)	Signing of Western European Union treaty
1954 (November)	Nasser becomes president of Egypt
1955 (October)	Completion of Bagdad Pact (later CENTO)
1956 (February)	Khrushchev denounces Stalinism at Twentieth Soviet Party Congress
1956 (October)	Invasion of Sinai peninsula by Israelis
1956 (November)	Hungarian revolt crushed by Russians
1957 (January)	Proclamation of Eisenhower Doctrine
1957 (October)	Launching of "sputnik" by Russians
1958 (January)	Beginning of European Common Market
1958 (May)	French army coup in Algeria—government of de Gaulle
1958 (July)	Intervention in Lebanon by United States

1958 (September)	Referendum on French constitution—beginning of Fifth Republic
1959 (January)	Castro takes over Cuban government
1960 (July)	United States institutes economic sanctions against Cuba
1960 (November)	**Election of John F. Kennedy as United States president**
1961 (April)	Abortive invasion of Cuba by Cuban exiles
1961 (August)	Erection of wall between East and West Berlin
1962 (July)	Independence of Algeria
1962 (July)	Geneva Agreements on Laos
1962 (October)	Confrontation of United States and Soviet Union over missiles in Cuba
1962 (October)– (November)	Frontier war in Himalayas between India and China
1963 (January)	French veto of Britain's entry into European Common Market
1963 (April)	Encyclical *Pacem in Terris* issued by Pope John XXIII
1963 (May)	Formation of Organization of African Unity (OAU)
1963 (August)	**Limited test-ban treaty signed**
1963 (September)	Establishment of Malaysia—beginning of Indonesian-Malaysian confrontation
1963 (November)	Murder of Ngo Dinh Diem
1963 (November)	**Assassination of President Kennedy—succession of Lyndon B. Johnson as United States president**
1964 (October)	First atomic device exploded by Communist China
1965 (February)	Beginning of bombing of North Vietnam by United States
1965 (April)	Intervention by United States in Dominican Republic
1965 (August)	Secession of Singapore from Malaysia
1965 (August)– (October)	Clash between India and Pakistan in Kashmir
1966 (January)	Limited agreement between India and Pakistan at Tashkent
1966 (February)	De Gaulle announces intention of withdrawing French troops from NATO command
1966 (February)	Nkrumah ousted from Ghanaian presidency
1966 (July)	Sukarno reduced to figurehead in Indonesia—recognition of Malaysia by Suharto government

INDEX

Aaland Islands, 17
Abdul Hamid II, sultan of Turkey, 128
Abdul Rahman, Tunku, 320
Abdullah, king of Jordan, 199–200, 339
Abyssinia; *see* Ethiopia
Acción Democrática, 300
Acheson, Dean, 250, 366–367
Action Française, 150
Addis Ababa, 211
Aden, 198, 340
Adenauer, Konrad, 266
Afghanistan, 178, 197–198
Africa, 178, 225, 228–229, 234, 263, 345–362; *see also under separate countries*
Agricultural Adjustment Act, 167
Aguiyi-Ironsi, J. T. U., 351
Ahidjo, Ahmadou, 354
Albania: before World War II, 17–18, 113, 117–119, 128, 218; in World War II, 128, 227, 229; since World War II, 242, 247, 286, 333
Albert I, king of the Belgians, 224
Alessandri, Jorge, 303
Alexander I, king of Greece, 126
Alexander I, king of Yugoslavia, 18, 114–117
Alexandria, 221, 229
Algeria, 254, 262–264, 337, 346, 348–349
Allende, Salvador, 303
Alliance for Progress, 297–298, 311
Allied Control Council (Austria), 268
Allied Control Council (Germany), 236
All-India Muslim League, 189–191
All-Russian Congress of Soviets, 38, 147
Almazán, Juan Andreau, 177
Alphonso XII, king of Spain, 83

Alphonso XIII, king of Spain, 85–87
Alsace-Lorraine, 2, 11, 149
Alvarado, Modesto Rodas, 307
Amanullah, emir and king of Afghanistan, 198
Ambassadors, Conference of, 17, 108
Anatolia, 13–14, 126, 129
Andalusia, 88–89, 93
Anglo-Egyptian Sudan, 335
Anglo-German Naval Agreement (1935), 209
Anglo-Iranian Oil Company, 197, 341
Angola, 269
Añido, Martinez, 84
Ankara, 14, 126, 130
Annam, 196, 324; *see also* Vietnam
Anschluss, 214–215; *see also* Austria
Anti-Comintern Pact, 117, 121, 183, 213, 218
Antonescu, Ion, 125, 244
Anual, Battle of, 85
ANZUS, 148
Apartheid, 148
Arab Legion, 200, 339
Arab Revolt (World War I), 131, 199–200
Arabian-American Oil Company, 199
Arabs: in Palestine, 256, 339–340; in Zanzibar, 359
Arbenz Guzmán, Jacobo, 307, 374
Archangel, 42
Arcos, 55, 141
Aref, Abdul Salam, 339
Arévalo, Juan, 307–308
Argentina, 159, 302–303
Armenia, 13–14, 43, 45, 130–131
Arosemena, Carlos Julio, 306
Aruba, 314
Asia, 178–196, 366–371; *see also under separate countries*